Branding and Advertising

EDITED BY
FLEMMING HANSEN & LARS BECH CHRISTENSEN

Branding and Advertising

© *Copenhagen Business School Press*
Printed in Denmark by Narayana Press
1. edition 2003

ISBN 87-630-0118-7

Distribution:

Scandinavia
Djoef/DBK, Mimersvej 4
DK-4600 Køge, Denmark
Phone: +45 3269 7788, fax: +45 3269 7789

North America
Copenhagen Business School Press
Books International Inc.
P.O. Box 605
Herndon, VA 20172-0605, USA
Phone: +1 703 661 1500, fax: +1 703 661 1501

Rest of the World
Marston Book Services, P.O. Box 269
Abingdon, Oxfordshire, OX14 4YN, UK
Phone: +44 (0) 1235 465500, fax: +44 (0) 1235 465555
E-mail Direct Customers: direct.order@marston.co.uk
E-mail Booksellers: trade.order@marston.co.uk

Table of contents

Table of contents

Table of contents

Table of contents

Introduction:

Branding & Advertising

In 2002, at the Copenhagen Business School, the Center for Marketing Communication organized the First International Conference on Research in Advertising. The purpose of the conference was to create a forum, where people concerned with advertising research in the academic world could meet and exchange views, and where they could meet with practitioners experienced with advertising research in the commercial world.

Up until then, advertising researchers had had to rely upon general consumer behaviour, marketing, communication, economic psychology, and similar conferences for presenting their research and having professional feed-back on their work. This rarely created interesting discussion on research topics with colleagues working in similar lines. There may have been many reasons for this state of affairs. One being the low esteem associated with advertising research by other researchers in communication and related areas. Another being the almost unbreakable wall that existed between what went on in commercial studies of media, advertising effects, advertising budgeting, etc. on the one hand, and academicians' attempts to gain insight to how advertising works, how it should be characterised, and how its role in society should be appreciated.

The Copenhagen event and the present publication demonstrates an obvious need for a forum of the kind where people in different locations can get together, and exchange views on important advertising related issues.

The material in the present publication represents chapters that have been developed from presentations at the Copenhagen meeting, together with a few other, relevant contributions from researchers in the area. The title of the book, "Branding and Advertising", was not decided upon prior to the planning of the conference, but as the material came in and was organized it became evident that this would be the proper denominator for the material presented here.

In general, advertising and advertising research may be viewed as covering problems relating to

- Determination of the advertising budget
- Choice of media group
- Development of advertising message
- Timing of the campaign.

There are contributions in the present book, relating to practically all of these issues, but almost all the contributions are concerned with branding issues, or at least have an undertone of this. Advertising may work in many other contexts than for specific branding purposes. Future conferences on the topic may bring more of those into light. Research on public advertising, and on advertising in social aid organisations, and very specific advertising topics, such as advertising for recruiting and for real estate, may be just a few such examples.

The material in the present book is organized in four sections. The first section is titled "Branding and Communication". Here, the issues on brand equity, brand personality, corporate brand character, and brand architecture, are central topics. Some of these are seen in the light of consumer behaviour brands, others relating to the mutual funds industry, e-commerce, branding in Eastern Europe, and studies of the content of corporate brand advertising.

The second major section is concerned with advertising effects. Here, papers are presenting different models applied to single-source data, with the purpose of demonstrating advertising effects, studies of recall and attention in different kinds of contexts, advertising effects, and effects of political advertising.

In the third section focus is changed to media and target groups. Here, concern is with new forms of advertising, advertising to children, and structuring the content of particularly television advertising.

Finally, in the fourth section an important issue is brought up, which we think will become a major topic in future research. Emotional processes, low-involvement effects, central and peripheral advertising, and different kinds of memory for advertising are looked upon.

Introduction: Branding and Advertising

Throughout the book, the contributions demonstrate a concern for a number of very varied topics, relating to the functioning of advertising. They also demonstrate the lack of a total, integrated theory in the area. The traditional effect hierarchy thinking is reduced to one out of several possible advertising effect models. The need for workable tools for classifying different kinds of advertising is demonstrated, and the need for seeing how advertising may function very differently, depending upon such things as involvement, fast moving consumer goods versus durables and services, new introductions versus ongoing competitive advertising, developing new media and the changing nature of existing ones, etc.

An undertone present in most of the presentations reflects the need for understanding also the role of advertising in a more societal context. In resent years, advertising has undergone dramatic changes. Some talk about the "end of advertising as we know it". Other concerns themselves with emergence of still more and different media in which advertising appear. We are living in a world where the role of advertising is changing dramatically. The need for a forum where this can come up for debate is evident, and the need for a forum for people to meet who are concerned with these issues is obvious. At the time of writing these introductory remarks to "Branding and Advertising" the Second International Conference on Research in Advertising has already been held in Amsterdam in June 2003. The variety of contributions presented here, the number of researchers attending, and the variety of issues taken up, confirm the relevance of the present, introductory remarks.

The book "Branding and Advertising" is a product of contributions from a number of people. The editors only represent the final organizers of the publication. Many thanks should be given to research assistants Jens Halling, Lotte Yssing Hansen, Jeanette Rasmussen, Pernille Christiansen, and Morten Hallum Hansen, for their invaluable contributions in organizing and finalising the programme and the material for the book. Also thanks to our colleagues at the Marketing department at the Copenhagen Business School: Jens Carsten Nielsen, Lars Grønholdt, and many others.

Much appreciation should be given also to our colleagues at ASCoR, the Amsterdam School of Communications Research at the University of Amsterdam for their interest in the programme, and for their willingness to carry on the idea of organizing advertising research conferences. Our thanks goes to all our Dutch colleagues, but a special, warm appreciation should be expressed towards Peter Neijens for his contribution to the present book and his future related work.

Finally, we should thank "Dansk Erhvervslivs Pris for Afsætningsøkonomisk Forskning", "Foreningen til Unge Handelsmænds Uddannelse" and special funds at the Copenhagen Business School, making the organisation of the conference and particularly the publication of this book possible.

Copenhagen, August 2003

Flemming Hansen
Professor, ekon.dr.

Lars Bech Christensen
Research Assistant, M.Sc.

1

Advertising and Brand Equity

LARRY PERCY

Advertising and Brand Equity

To understand the relationships between advertising and brand equity, it pays to first understand just what we mean by a 'brand.' The original meaning of the word 'brand' seems to derive from an Old Norse word *brandr*, which meant 'to burn' (Interbrand Group, 1992). Yet in the etymology of the word, this idea of branding as a "permanent mark deliberately made with hot iron" now takes second place to "goods of particular name or trade mark" (Oxford English Dictionary, 1990). But does this really describe what we understand as a brand? The American Marketing Association describes a brand as a "name, term, sign, symbol, or design, or a combination of them intended to identify the goods and services of one seller or group of sellers and differentiate them from those of competitors." The AMA definition reminds us of the *reason* for a brand: to enable a person to identify one alternative from a competitor. All of this is true, but a brand must be a *label* in the true sense of that word: something "attached to an object to give information about it" (Oxford English Dictionary, 1990). But how is that information communicated?

The Nature of Brands

When we think of brands, we usually think of products we buy: Coke, Cadbury, Ford, Hoover, Persil, and Mars. But just about anything can be 'branded.' Products, services, corporations, retail stores, cities, organizations, even individuals can be seen as 'brands.' Remember, a brand name is meant to embody information about something, information that represents an added value, differentiating it in a marked way from alternatives. A brand name is meant to trigger in memory positive associations with that brand. Politicians, hospitals, entertainers, football clubs, corporations, all want their name, their *brand*, to mean something very specific to their market. It is how they wish to be seen, and how they wish to be distinguished from competitive alternatives.

Brand Attitude

A brand does provide *information*. But what kind of information does a brand provide, and where does it come from? Think about some brands you know. What comes to mind when you think about them? No doubt a great deal more than the fact that it is a particular product. Perhaps you were thinking about how much you like it, that it is well known, or that it is 'one of the best.' All of these thoughts reflect what we call *brand attitude*. A brand name represents everything a person knows about a particular product and what it means to them. It provides a convenient summary of their feelings, knowledge and experience with the brand. It means they do not need to spend a great deal of time 'researching' a product each time they are considering a purchase. A person's evaluation of a product is immediately reconstructed from memory, cued by the brand name. But again, where does that brand attitude come from?

Brand Equity

The effect of a positive brand attitude leads to something marketers call *brand equity*. What exactly is brand equity? Most marketers would agree that it is that 'something' attached to a brand that adds value over and above the objective characteristics of the product or service. Whatever that 'something' is, it is embodied in people's attitudes towards that brand. It is dynamic, and subject to change over time. It attaches itself to the brand name, providing a current summary of people's feelings, knowledge and experience with that product or service.

Think about chocolate for a minute. Basically, chocolate is chocolate. Or is it? Are some *brands* better than others? Why? What about washing-up powder? They all get the job done, and use the same basic ingredients. Or do you think some do a better job than others? What about toothpaste, or vodka, or underwear? Where do the differences among brands in these product categories come from? How much of the difference is 'real' versus perceived? Why do you prefer one brand over another, especially if when looked at with a coldly objective eye, there is very little, if any, actual difference in the products?

Measuring Brand Equity

Brand equity is a result of brand attitude, and this is what provides the key to its understanding. In many ways, building and ensuring a continuing positive brand attitude is what strategic brand management is all about, because it does lead to strong brand equity.

The most important thing to understand when you are trying to measure brand equity is that what is needed is a measure of *understanding,* not a measure of the results or consequences of a brand's equity. Too often, when people 'measure' brand equity, they are really only tracking summary measures of what is going on in the market as a result of the brand's equity. What is needed is a measure of the *components* that lead to brand equity, and this means measures of how the market forms current attitudes towards the brand. If we are to really understand a brand's equity, we must understand how it is constructed. It is this understanding that ensures an effective positioning in our marketing communications, and the ability to adjust that positioning over time as needed to continue building and sustaining positive brand equity.

We measure brand attitude using an Expectancy-Value model (considered by most researchers in consumer behaviour to be the best model of attitude). Basically, this model states that a person's attitude towards something, a brand or product in our case, is the sum of everything they know about it weighted by how important those beliefs are to them. Obviously, we are not able to study 'everything' about a brand or product, but we can and should consider everything critical to the *benefit positioning* of the brand. If we are to understand the current equity of a brand, it is necessary to 'deconstruct' its positioning in order to access the strengths and weaknesses of the belief structure that sustains people's attitudes towards it.

It should now be clear that to a large extent a brand is not a tangible thing at all, but rather the sum of what someone knows, thinks, and feels about a particular product. In a very real sense, brands only exist in the minds of consumers, but that does not make them any less real. And to a very real extent, brands and the equity attached to them exist as a result of marketing communication, and especially *advertising*. It is advertising (when successful) that positions a brand in the consumer's mind, nurtures salience, and builds positive brand attitude that leads to a strong brand equity.

Brand Positioning

At its most general, a brand position is a 'supercommunication' effect that tells the consumer what the brand is, who it is for, and what it offers. This reflects the relationship between brand positioning and the two core communication effects of brand awareness and brand attitude. It's easy to understand that one must have strong awareness if a brand is to be considered when the 'need' for that type of product (however the *consumer* defines it) occurs. Strong brand awareness (for almost any brand) must be generated and sustained with marketing communication. It is marketing communication, and advertising in particular, that builds and maintains *brand salience*. It is not enough for a brand to be recognized if it is to be successful. A brand must occupy a 'salient' position within the consumer's consideration set. In fact, the strength of a brand's salience is one indicator of the brand's equity. (A useful measure of this is the ratio of top-of-mind recall to total recall among competitive brands in a category.)

Brand attitude, however, is not quite so easy to deal with. Who exactly *is* the target audience? Is everyone looking for the same thing; or the same things all the time? What is important, and to whom? How are brands seen to deliver on the things important to the target audience? Answers to these questions are critical if we are to positively effect brand attitude.

15

The role of benefits in effective positioning in communication is of course essential. But benefits must be considered in relationship to brand attitude, which in its turn is the link to purchase motive. Consumers hold what we might think of as an overall summary judgement about a brand, following the Expectancy-Value notion of attitude: 'Hush Puppies makes great shoes' is an *attitude* about Hush Puppies that connects the brand in the consumer's mind with what is the likely purchase motive, sensory gratification (i.e. they buy Hush Puppies to *enjoy* them). This brand attitude, however, which we might think of as a 'superbelief,' doesn't just spring from nowhere, but is the result of one or more beliefs about the *specific benefits* the brand is thought by the consumer to offer in support of that overall attitude. Effective communication strategy requires an understanding of what that belief structure is, and how it builds brand attitude.

Within the overall positioning that results from this understanding, one we must determine what the benefit emphasis and focus should be (cf. Percy, Rossiter, and Elliott, 2001). To begin with, it is important to remember that purchase motive is really the *underlying* basis of benefit. Purchase motives are, after all, the fundamental 'energizers' of buyer behavior. These same motives also energize the usage of products. Motive-based positioning requires a *correct* answer to the question of why consumers in the category are *really* buying particular *brands*. Unfortunately, most benefits tend to be motivationally ambiguous.

One must also be careful to distinguish between motives that drive product category decisions rather than brand decisions. People may buy (say) active casual footwear because they are comfortable (a negative motive), but buy particular brands for more 'style' related reasons (a positive motive). This is an absolutely critical distinction. Benefits like comfort or low price relate to negative motives, and are unlikely to drive *specific brand* purchases. Yet, someone may be looking for a good price in the category, but *not* at the expense of 'style.' The reason this is such an important point is that positive motives suggest marketing communication where the execution itself actually becomes the product benefit. Here more than ever a truly unique execution is required where the brand owns the 'feeling' created by the advertisers for the brand. You can't 'prove' you have a more 'stylish' or popular shoe, but you can make people *believe* you do.

I-D-U Benefit Emphasis

The benefits a brand emphasizes in marketing communication should be selected according to three major considerations: Importance, Delivery, and Uniqueness (cf. Rossiter and Percy, 1997). *Importance* refers to the relevance of the benefit to the underlying motivation. A benefit assumes importance *only if* it is instrumental in helping meet the consumer's purchase motivation. *Delivery* refers to a brand's perceived ability to provide the benefit. *Uniqueness* refers to a brand's perceived ability to deliver on the benefit relatively better than other brands. What we are looking for are one or two benefits, relevant to the underlying motive, that can produce a perceived difference between alternative brands. These benefits should then be emphasized in the brand's marketing communication.

A note in passing. We are talking about *perceived* delivery and uniqueness. Just because a brand may not now be perceived to provide benefits that could optimize purchase against important motives does not mean this perception cannot be created (unless, of course, it stretches the consumer's understanding of the brand, which is one reason we need to fully understand current brand equity).

Benefit Focus

The overall positioning of a brand basically chooses a location for the brand in the consumer's mind. The I-D-U analysis helps one decide which benefit(s) to emphasize. After that, one must decide what aspect of the benefit to concentrate on in the execution of marketing communications.

Up to now we have used the term 'benefit' in a rather general way. We have considered a benefit as any potential positive or negative reinforcer for a brand, in line with our definition of brand attitude as representing the overall delivery on the underlying motivation. Since a 'reinforcer' is anything that tends to increase a response, benefits as we have been talking about them underlie and help increase brand attitude. Now we will distinguish more sharply between attributes, benefits, and emotions, as discussed by Rossiter and Percy (2001).

If we think about the underlying motive as 'why the consumer wants the brand,' we may consider that

- *Attributes* are 'what the product has'
- *Benefits* are 'what the consumer wants,' and
- *Emotions* are 'what the consumer feels.'

A brand, for example may offer attributes that the consumer may or may not think of as a benefit. Benefits, in their turn may have various emotional consequences or antecedents, depending upon the underlying motive.

All marketing communication presents or implies a 'benefit' as either an attribute, benefit, or emotion as defined above. The key to *effective* communication is using the appropriate benefit *focus*. At this point it must seem we are overly complicating things, but this really is a powerful way of 'fine-tuning' a positioning, and not nearly as confusing as it may appear.

When the benefit focus is not consistent with the underlying purchase motivation, the logic of the message breaks down, and the effectiveness of the communication breaks down. To effectively position a brand, it is necessary to understand what brand attitudes link the brand to the purchase motivation in the consumer's mind, the proper benefit to emphasize, and how to focus the consumer's attention on that benefit. Approaching positioning in this way will have a significantly positive effect on building and sustaining brand equity, and in its turn on the success of the brand.

Brand Attitude Strategy

Proper positioning encourages a strong link between category need and the brand and it builds positive brand attitude. And as we have seen, it is this positive brand attitude that builds and sustains brand equity. As Rossiter and Percy (1997) define it, effective brand attitude strategy is a function of the level of involvement in the purchase decision (as defined by the level of risk, either psychological or fiscal) and the underlying motivation driving behaviour in the category (negative vs. positive). These two dimensions define the four quadrants of the brand attitude strategy components of their planning grid: low involvement/informational, low involvement/transformational, high involvement/informational, and high involvement/transformational (where informational strategies reflect negative motives and transformational strategies reflect positive motives). Picking the correct brand attitude strategy, as defined by the Rossiter-Percy Grid, is essential for effective marketing communication (Rossiter, Percy and Donovan, 1991).

This is especially true for advertising built upon transformational strategies. When dealing with positive motives (such as sensory gratification or social approval) the key to an effective execution is *emotional authenticity*. It must 'ring true' to the receiver. While brand equity is more likely to be a function of attributes or benefits when dealing with informational strategies, with transformational strategies brand equity will be strongly influenced by the emotional component of the brand benefit structure.

One of the best examples we can offer of this idea of the importance of emotional authenticity in the execution of transformational advertising to effectively build a strong positive brand attitude is advertising for beer in the U.S. market. In the US. market, not only is beer brand equity *directly* related to the advertising execution, so is the taste of beer! In a fascinating study conducted by the author (along with John Rossiter), beer drinkers were asked to taste and evaluate a number of beers ranging from lower-calorie Miller Lite to premium beers like Budweiser, all the way through malt liquors and Guinness Stout. Represented were beers marketed as 'regular beers' (Pabst) vs. premium beers (Budweiser), and 'lighter' beers (Miller Lite, Coors) vs. 'stronger' beers (Colt 45 Malt Liquor, Guinness Stout). These two dimensions represented the dominant marketing dimensions in the U.S. beer market.

In a tightly controlled experiment, subjects tasted the beers presented randomly in clear glass containers, and rinsed their mouths with distilled water and unleavened wafers between tastings. When the results of these taste tests were evaluated and analyzed, the 'lighter' beers were separated from the 'stronger' beers, and the 'regular' beer from the 'premium' beer (as we see in Figure 1:1). The tastes of these beers were positioned exactly as their advertising presented them.

Figure 1:1   Perceptual Mapping of Beer Taste Evaluations When Brands are Known

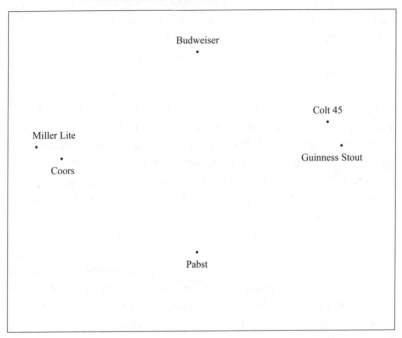

However, a matched set of beer drinkers went through the same exercise, but they tasted the beers blind, not knowing what beers they were tasting. When taste evaluations were analyzed, with the exception of Guinness Stout (which is clearly in Figure 1:2). The brand equity and taste of these beers was wholly defined by their advertising.

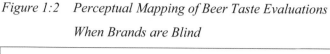

Figure 1:2   Perceptual Mapping of Beer Taste Evaluations
When Brands are Blind

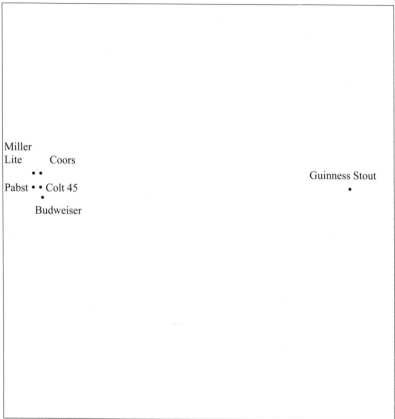

Summary

Advertising and brand equity are related in the strongest possible way, as we have shown. Without marketing communication in general, and advertising in particular, there would be little likelihood of any brand awareness, and less of brand salience; the managed development of brand attitude almost impossible. And without both brand awareness and brand attitude there would be no brand equity. It is advertising, effectively positioned to build and nurture a positive brand attitude that leads to the building and maintaining of brand equity.

2

Brands are just like real people!

The development of SWOCC's Brand Personality Scale

EDITH G. SMIT, EMILIE VAN DEN BERGE & GIEP FRANZEN

Introduction

When Kodak is sincere, then IBM can be competent, Marlboro cool and Revlon a little sophisticated. Just like humans, brands can be plain and closed or show their faces and have opinions of their own. Examples are Diesel, Absolut, but also ABN AMRO and Ben. What these brands "say" and "do" have a distinctive style and signature that can be described in terms of personality traits. Brands as human beings: an attractive metaphor. Sometimes they are even positioned as a person, for instance Ben and Ilse. The expectation is that the stronger and more powerful the personality is, the more bonding there can be between brands and consumers. Compare it with the people you know: those with outspoken opinions are interesting. Dull people –in your own perception, of course- are less interesting.

Brand personality is not new, and sometimes confused with related brand concepts: brand identity, brand image, brand values, brand loyalty, and user image. Another complicating factor is the measurement of brand personality. In the Netherlands a lot of different approaches and scales are used by practitioners to measure brand personality. A lot of different views and ditto measurement approaches are proposed in the literature.

SWOCC started a brand personality project in 2000, in which the concept was explored theoretically and empirically. The theoretical part resulted in a SWOCC-publication by Marieke van den Berg (2001). The empirical part was published in 2002 by Emilie van den Berge. In this conference paper, we will focus on the development of our measurement scale for brand personality. First, we will briefly introduce the concept. Then we sketch the research program as well as the results. Finally, we will give some examples of results for individual brands.

Brand personality in theory

The term brand personality has been borrowed from theories on human personality. Humans are unique and have their own unique personality. Since Aristotle, personality has been studied in many different ways: from a psychoanalytic viewpoint, within behaviorism, from an existential point of view, using the psycho lexical approach and within cognitive psychology (to name only a few different approaches). Exempting differences, the basic view is that personality has something to do with the way people –or better *persons*- differ from each other. Personality is 'the thing' that makes someone a person; it's the part of an individual that most of the time is consistent and durable. Most of the time, because we interact constantly with persons and objects and differ in different situations (Lippa, 1994).

Several attempts have been made to categorize people on the basis of their personalities. Within personality psychology this resulted in the famous "Big Five" (Caprara, Barbaranelli & Guido, 2001; Digman, 1990; Goldberg, 1990; Lippa, 1994; McCrae & John, 1992): Extraversion, Agreeability, Consciousness, Emotional Stability and Openness/Culturedness (see Figure 2:1).

A person scoring high on Extraversion could be described as someone who likes to talk (a lot), is active and assertive, energetic and outgoing – instead of quite, shy and silent. Someone scoring low on Agreeableness is described as cold, unfriendly, quarrelsome, while a conscious person is thought to be organized, thorough, efficient and responsible.

Not only persons (consumers) are categorized, brands are as well. Brand managers do so in terms of brand and product strategies or brand identities. Consumers do so too, in terms of images they have from brands, experiences and feelings.

Figure 2:1 The 'Big Five' dimensions of human personality

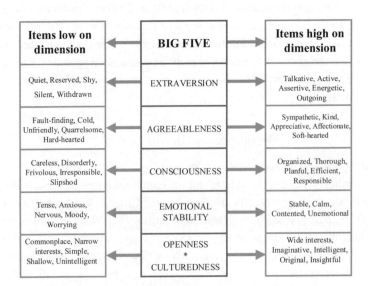

One of many ways to categorize certain brand attributes is brand personality. Brand personality characteristics are derived directly from people associated with the brand or persons' own characteristics, and more indirectly via product-related attributes, brand name, logo, communication style, prices and distribution. All resulting in brand personality (Bauer, Mäder & Keller, 2001; Fournier, 1998; Timmerman, 2001).

Brand personality, however, has been poorly conceptualized (e.g. Caprara et al., 2001; Patterson, 1999; Van den Berg, 2001). In his literature reviews on brand research until the nineties, Patterson (1999) concluded "Our understanding of brand image has been hampered by poor conceptual development. Although it has been the focus of branding research since 1950s, there continues to be a large degree of confusion about what brand image actually means. In particular, most authors have failed to highlight the distinction between the concepts of brand image, brand personality and user image and, as a consequence, these three concepts have tended to be used interchangeably". A few examples of brand personality definitions:

- "An attitude of mind and tone of voice and set of values" (King, 1973, in Lippa, 1994);

- "The extent to which consumers perceive a brand to possess various human characteristics or traits" (Alt & Griggs, 1988, p.9);
- "The way in which a consumer perceives the brand on dimensions that typically capture a person's personality" (Batra, Lehman & Singh, 1993);
- "The personality consists of a unique combination of functional attributes and symbolic values" (Hankinson & Cowking, 1995);
- "Brand personality displays the brand's core characteristics, embodied, described and experienced in human terms" (Restall & Gordon, 1994);
- "A brand's personality … embodies all of the qualities it has to offer over and above its primary characteristics and its functional purpose" (Tennant, 1994, in Patterson, 1999);
- "Brand personality reflects customers' emotional response to a company and its product" (Triplett, 1994);
- "The outward 'face' of a brand; its tonal characteristics most closely associated with human traits" (Upshaw, 1995);
- "The set of human characteristics associated with a brand, which makes it unique, compared to other brands" (Aaker, 1996, p.1);
- "The consumer's emotional response to a brand through which brand attributes are personified and are used to differentiate between alternative offerings" (Patterson, 1999).

One of the differences in these definitions is the difference in perspectives: an advertiser versus a consumer view. In an advertiser view, brand personality is an important driver for brand identity (Kapferer, 1996), which is shown by the definitions of Restall and Gordon ('brand's core characteristics') and Tennant ('the qualities it has to offer'). From a consumer's perspective, brand personality is seen as one of the components of brand image (Batra, Myers & Aaker, 1996), for instance in the first three definitions: 'attitude of mind', 'consumers perceive a brand to have …'.

Although the definitions are different, they are similar in that brand personality is about perception (in the consumer's view), about personality characteristics attributed to brands, about associations and symbolic values and about emotional responses on the brand or emotional relationships with brands. In our research project, we defined brand personality as the set of personality characteristics associated with a brand in comparison with other brands (based on Aaker, 1996).

Brand personality measurement

To measure brand personality a lot of different methods are used, in academic as well as commercial research, simply because 'the' method does not exist. A widely used (qualitative) method is to ask respondents to imagine a brand as a person (Is it a boy or a girl? Is it young or old?) or an animal (Aaker, 1996; Alt & Griggs, 1988; Fournier, 1998). Also photo-sort techniques are used (Floor & Van Raaij, 1998). In fact, association methods are mostly used, varying from free associations to aided associations (qualitative or quantitative, unstructured or structured).

Here, we focus on the Brand Personality Scale of Jennifer Aaker, which is a structured quantitative measurement technique (scaling). The main reason for choosing this kind of technique is that it is standardized and that results for different brands are thus comparable. Aaker's scale is the most recent fundamentally tested scale found in the literature and not only based on the "Big Five," but also on other well-defined brand personality scales (e.g. Malhotra's semantic differential of 1981, Alt and Griggs' Brand Personality Rating Scale of 1988, Batra et al.'s semantic differential of 1993). Aaker's procedure – which she described in several articles- can be summarized into six steps:

First, Aaker (1996, 1997) collected personality characteristics from psychology ("Big Five" based personality scales; 204 unique traits), from brand practitioners (advertising agencies, scholars and research agencies; 133 unique traits), and from a small-scale qualitative study in which respondents (n=16) were asked to write down characteristics that came to mind when naming six different brands (295 traits). This procedure resulted in 309 non-redundant candidate personality traits.

Second, the 309 items were reduced by asking respondents (n=25) to judge the items on a 7-point scale, ranging from (1) not at all descriptive to (7) extremely descriptive. Respondents were asked to think of as many different types of brands as possible. Items with an average score of 6 and more (very descriptive) were selected, leaving 114 personality traits for the subsequent study.

Third, an US representative non-student sample (n=631 respondents from a national mail panel) was asked to rate 37 brands that serve symbolic and utilitarian functions or both on 114 items[1] (scale: 1 = not at all descriptive, 5 = extremely descriptive). Factor analysis (Varimax rotation) for the aggregate database (with average scores on the 114 items per brand) showed five dimensions (total explained variance of 92%): Sincerity, Excitement, Competence, Sophistication and Ruggedness. Factor analyses for sub samples (men versus women, younger versus older respondents) also showed these five dimensions, resulting in a stable and robust five-factor-solution. Yet, only three of these brand personality factors were those appearing in the Big Five model for human personality (Caprara et al., 2001).

Fourth, for every factor a new factor analysis was done (Aaker, 1997) to identify the traits that most reliably, accurately, and comprehensively represent the five dimensions. This resulted in 15 so called 'facets' (see underlined items in Figure 2:2).

Each facet was then split into three clusters to select the item with the highest item-to-total correlation (> 0.60). Test-retest correlations (test sample of n=81; r > 0.70) and reliability analyses (Cronbach's alphas > 0.85) were also used. Based on these steps, the resulting list consisted of 42 items.

Fifth, the scale of 42 items was tested again by using a new sample (n=180 respondents of a national mail panel) and a different set of 20 brands. This study confirmed the other results (Confirmatory Factor Analysis with GLS; AGFI = 0.86).

Sixth, Aaker repeated her approach in other countries. Based on four studies (Aaker, 1999b; Aaker, Benet-Martinez & Garolera, 2001), a set of brand personality dimensions was revealed that was the same for Japan, Spain and the US: Sincerity, Excitement, Competence and Sophistication (although Competence not as clear in Spain). She also found culture-specific dimensions: an American Ruggedness dimension; a Japanese Peacefulness dimension; and a Spanish Passion dimension. In both non-American countries, the original 42 brand personality items were complemented with culture-specific brand-

---

[1] Aaker (1996) used primarily positively valenced traits, which were rotated completely.

Figure 2:2 Brand Personality dimensions (based on Aaker, 1997; 2001)

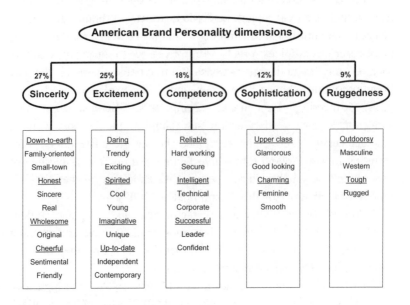

related attributes, based on personality scales used in that country as well as association tasks by participants from Japan and Spain. Aaker's approach was also used by other researchers, for instance by researchers from the Mannheim University in Germany (Bauer et al., 2001), who used the 42 item-scale of Aaker (1997) for measuring brand personality for seven brands in Germany and Spain. This study, however, did not find the five factor solution of Aaker, maybe because they used convenient samples (i.e. students) and did not –as Aaker did– complement their set of personality items with culture-specific items.

Overview research project

The aim of our research project was not to replicate Aaker's studies. Our aim was to have a clear understanding of brand personality, to sketch the usefulness of the concept for brand strategy, and especially to develop a standard method (i.e. scale) for measuring brand personality. Within the scope of SWOCC, we aimed to develop a scale –in a fundamental way– that is useful for practitioners.

The empirical part of our project consisted of two phases. In the first phase, we developed and measured our scale for 20 brands in four product categories. Based on these results, we found seven dimensions of brand personality. In the second phase, we used the same procedure and questionnaire for 73 extra brands in eight product categories. The aim of this second phase was to validate our seven dimensions and to have a more solid base (in terms of number of brands) for the reduction of items.

Selection of Personality items

First, we translated Aaker's Brand Personality Scale of 42 items into Dutch. However, the problem with our language is that most American terms have more than one equivalent in Dutch. Therefore, seven persons, who spoke English as well as Dutch fluently were asked to translate the Aaker list into Dutch. We selected the items which were most agreed upon.

Second, we added a list of Dutch personality items because research by Aaker (1999b), Aaker et al. (2001) and Bauer et al. (2001) showed that not all of Aaker's American dimensions were found in other cultures (Japan, Spain and Germany). We used items from the Dutch Personality Scale by Brokken (1978), who based his list on the standard Dutch dictionary and a study in which 200 couples were asked to judge one another or themselves. These judgments eventually resulted in 1203 items and six factors. Like the "Big Five", Brokken found dimensions expressing a sympathetic factor (agreeableness), emotional factors (stability and extraversion) and 'organized' factors (consciousness or orderliness/preciseness).

As a third step, we reduced the Brokken list by removing 'old-fashioned' words (his dissertation was published in 1978) and removed items with factor loadings lesser than |0,35|. We then asked four experts in the field of brand research and six non-experts (consumers) to go through the remaining list and select those items that can be descriptive for a brand. They were asked to think of as many different brands as possible, not one specific brand. Finally, we based the selection on the items that were mostly agreed upon (no differences were found between experts and others). This resulted in 60 Brokken and 42 Aaker items. Appendix A shows our list of 102 personality items.

Selection of Brands

We started with 20 different brands in four product categories (see Table 2:1). We selected salient well-known brands from different categories: cars, beer, shampoo and tele services. After this phase, several organizations were willing to finance the measurement of their brand(s) according to our procedure (with the 102 items). This gave us the opportunity to enlarge our sample of brands to a total of 93 brands in 11 product categories. The only 'disadvantage' of these extra measurements was that some brands were –on request- measured more than once (see * in Table 2:1).

Table 2:1 Measured brands

Product category	Brands
	Phase I
Cars	BMW, Volvo, Mazda
Beer	Heineken, Grolsch, Amstel, Bavaria, Palm, Dommelsch
Shampoo	Andrélon, Nivea, Head & Shoulders, Pantène Pro-V, Sanex, Organics
Tele Services	KPN, Libertel, Telfort, Dutchtone, Ben
	Phase II
Beverages	Douwe Egberts *, Nescafé, Max Havelaar, Coca Cola *, Spa *, Cup a Soup, Pickwick, Lipton Ice Tea, Appelsientje
Cigarettes	Gauloises Blondes, Caballero, Barclay, Lucky Strike, Marlboro *, Philip Morris *, Chesterfield *, Camel *, Mild Seven *
Rolling tobacco	Drum, Van Nelle, Samson, Brandaris, Javaanse Jongens, Jacobs
Financial banks	ING Bank, Postbank, ABN AMRO, Rabobank
Mail carriers	PTT Post, Deutsche Post, Royal Mail, UPS, TNT
Insurances	Delta Lloyd *, Nationale Nederlanden *, Aegon *, Centraal Beheer *, Amev *, Ohra, Interpolis
Tele Services	Libertel, Dutchtone, KPN, Ben (* all in phase I as well)
Shops	Albert Heijn, Konmar, C1000, Aldi, Bijenkorf, Hema

Note: * = measured more than once

Method

Because we had two phases of data gathering, our measurements were done in two online panels. By email the respondents were asked to complete the questionnaire for one product category with a maximum of six brands per questionnaire (i.e. respondent). In the first phase (summer 2001), we used the CentERpanel of the University of Tilburg (the Netherlands), which is a so-called 'real' household panel with a firm number of panel members. To avoid the possibility that someone would answer the questionnaire again, we used another online panel in the second phase (February 2002), namely the online Internet panel of Interview/NSS. This second panel differed from the first one, because it was a so-called 'occasional' panel with thousands of respondents known to possess certain characteristics and willing to complete questionnaires on a regular basis. The advantage was the possibility to 'select' a lot of sub samples for the different product categories while, at the same time, exerting some control over the composition of the sub samples (in terms of sex, age and education).

Questionnaire

Brand personality was measured with ten matrices. Each matrix showed the brands and the option "none of these brands" in the columns (between three and six brands per matrix) and the characteristics in the rows (about 10 items per matrix).

The rating was done by means of ASSPAT, which stands for ASSociation PATtern method. In ASSPAT, respondents were asked to compare objects (brands in this study) for different items. The respondent was asked to mark one or more brands when he or she finds an item descriptive for the brand(s). It was also possible to mark "none of these brands". In other words, brands were scored (per item) on a dichotomous scale (0 = not descriptive, 1 = descriptive). Although the richness of data is less than would be the case for an interval or ordinal scale (like Aaker used), the great advantage of this method is that 102 items and several brands can be measured in one questionnaire without exhausting the respondent. This is especially important in online measurement. The items were offered randomly, in other words: there was no fixed sequence in matrices or items within a matrix.

Besides brand personality, we measured experience with products or services, most used brands in the category and likeability of the brands (school mark, rating from 1 tot 10). The demographics were already

Edith G. Smit • Emilie van den Berge • Giep Franzen

known since we worked with online panels. In the first phase, we combined the scores with scores of the respondents on themselves (which were already known per panel member). In the second phase, we added questions about the ideal brand in the measured product category (see Discussion).

Response and Sample

In the first phase, we worked with a total net sample of 1009 respondents (1294 members were asked to complete a questionnaire of which 78% responded). In the second phase, 3524 of the 9650 panel members completed the questionnaire (response of 37%). When comparing sample characteristics (sex, age and education), the second sample was more representative for the Dutch population than the first one. This was due to the selection process in the second panel (quota sampling). The first panel consisted of more men, higher educated respondents and more respondents in the age of 31-55. Although not representative for the Dutch population, the sample reflected the Internet population (mean age sample I = 46.5, mean age sample II = 40).

Table 2:2 Characteristics, two samples (column %)

	Sample I (n=1009)	Sample II (n=3524)	Population
Men	55.4	49.8	48.9
Women	44.6	50.2	51.1
Low education	14.3	9.7	38.1
Medium education	30.0	46.2	33.9
High education	55.7	44.1	28.0
Age: 13-19	0.8	9.4	9.4
Age: 20-30	12.0	17.8	17.7
Age: 31-40	25.9	20.2	20.0
Age: 41-55	35.7	26.4	26.5
Age: 56+	25.5	26.2	26.4

Source population: Intomart/GfK 2002, January

Results

Dimensions

First, we factor analyzed the 42 Aaker-items (see * in appendix A), at the respondent as well as the aggregate or brand level. As Aaker, we used Principal Components Analysis with Varimax rotation based on the correlation matrix. Based on data of the first phase (20 brands), the exploratory factor analysis (EV>1) resulted in six factors (with cumulative R^2 of 92%). Only two of these six factors corresponded with Aaker's dimensions, namely 'Sincerity' and 'Excitement'. Although the factor analysis did not show the Aaker-dimensions in our study, the reliability of the proposed items per Aaker-dimension was high (Cronbach's alpha per Aaker dimension was between 0.81 and 0.98). We repeated the analyses for all 102 items (the Aaker items plus the extra Dutch items). Factor analyses resulted in seven factors (explained variance of 93%, EV>1), again with the two factors 'Sincerity' and 'Excitement'.

Second, we repeated our analyses on the complete dataset of two waves (93 brands), after we checked for panel differences[2]. The exploratory factor analysis (Principal Components with Varimax rotation, based on correlation matrix, EV > 1) resulted in 10 factors of which the last three did not have distinctive factor loadings (also shown in the screen plot). The factor analysis for seven factors resulted in the dimensions listed in Table 2:3, which were more clear and distinctive than it was the case for 20 brands (although the cumulative R^2 is a little less, namely 87%). In Table 2:3, the results of the factor analysis are listed. Items that scored relatively high on the factor (factor loadings ≥ 0.60)[3] and relatively low on the other dimensions

---

[2] T-tests with average scores on the items as dependent variables and panel, as group variables showed no significant differences (p > 0.05), except for the three items 'decent' (t(df=91)=2.15, p=0.03), 'exciting' (t(df=91)=2.33, p=0.02), and 'unfriendly' (t(df=91)=-2.39, p=0.02).

[3] The items 'vital', 'western', 'rebellious', 'good looking' (factor 2), 'vulnerable' (factor 3), 'radical', 'outdoorsy' (factor 4) and 'uncomplicated' (factor 7) are excluded because of their factor loadings (<0.60) and their item-to-total correlations (alpha improves by removing them from the scales). We also excluded 20 items with a skewedness of more than 2: tough, self-important, small-town, impulsive, dominant, individualistic, loud, upper class, different, bold, sunny, cool, juvenile, technical, exuberant, fierce, exciting, provoking, and glamorous.

(based on Nunnally, 1978; Aaker, 1997) are listed. We also tested the reliability by means of Cronbach's alpha (first column).

Because many of the dimensions are broad, focusing on the different 'facets' should provide more breadth and depth in the personality dimensions (according to Chuch & Burke, 1994; McCrae & Costa, 1989). We followed the procedures of Aaker by performing factor analyses per dimension, which resulted in nine so-called 'facets' for the dimensions 'Competence+', 'Excitement+' and 'Annoying'. The other dimensions resulted in one-factor solutions. Also in line with Aaker, we used reliability analyses and item-to-total correlations to select items that would describe the sub dimensions best, but also differ enough from each other.

Table 2:3 shows that factor 7 ('Sophistication') is a rather weak factor with only one item left (based on factor loading as well as reliability analyses). The first dimension, 'Competence-plus', shows some resemblance with Aaker's Competence-dimension plus the facets 'down-to-earth' and 'honest' from Aaker's Sincerity-dimension. Aaker's Excitement- and Ruggedness-dimensions are found as well. This is also true for the Sophistication-dimension, although this is a rather weak factor in our analysis.

Differences are found in the three smaller dimensions: the negatively valenced dimension 'Annoying' and the two dimensions 'Gentle' and 'Distinguishing'. The Gentle factor was also found in personality studies, such as the one by Brokken (1978), and shows resemblance with 'Agreeableness' in the "Big Five".

Further description

Based on Table 2:3 as well as average brand scores per dimension (see Appendix B), we are able to describe our dimensions in more detail. Brands scoring relatively high or relatively low on a dimension are used as examples.

1. Competence+

The first dimension 'Competence' is described in breadth (that is by the facets) as confident (with other items such as successful, resolute, strong-minded and sure), sympathetic (items: nice, honest and decent), accurate (items: precisely, secure, careful and efficient) and steady

Table 2:3 The Brand Personality Dimensions with Facets (93 brands, total n=4533)

Dimension	Facet 1	Facet 2	Facet 3	Facet 4
Competence+ EV=26.8, R^2=33% α=0.99	Confident* Successful* Enterprising Resolute Strong-minded Leader* Powerful Vigorous Independent* Sure Hard-working* (α=0.97)	Sympathetic Friendly* Open-hearted Nice Honest* Sincere* Real* Decent (α=0.97)	Accurate Corporate* Precisely Neat Secure* Careful Efficient Intelligent* Wholesome * Down-to-earth* (α=0.97)	Respectable Conventional Family-oriented* Firm Stabile Steady Reliable* (α=0.98)
Excitement+ EV=18.1, R^2=22% α=0.98	Cheerful* Happy Jolly Good-humored Spontaneous Pleasant Sprightly (α=0.97)	Spirited* Active Modern* Contemporary* Easy (-mannered) Enthusiastic Lively (α=0.97)	Imaginative * Creative Original* Trendy* (α=0.96)	
Gentle EV=8.5, R^2=10% α=0.93	(no facets) Soft-hearted, Soft, Kind, Feminine, Amiable, Sentimental, Charming			
Ruggedness EV=5.9, R^2=7% α=0.87	(no facets) Rugged, Masculine, Firm			
Annoying EV=4.9, R^2=6% α=0.85	Unkind Whimsical Annoying (α=0.83)	Childish Silly Whiney (α=0.77)		
Distinguishing EV=4.1, R^2=5% α=0.83	(no facets) Unique, Non-conformist, Daring			
Sophistication EV=3.3, R^2=4%	Smooth			

Note: only items with factor loadings high on the dimension (>0.60) and low on the other dimensions are shown; bold = factor name; underlined = facet name (based on highest item-to-total correlation per facet); * = Aaker-items

(items: firm and stabile). This dimension is actually a combination of Aaker's Competence and Sincerity dimensions – that is why we labeled it 'Competence *plus*'. Our dimension consisted of 16 Aaker items, of which 12 Competence-items (combining our facets confident, accurate and respectable) and 4 Sincerity-items (especially our facet sympathetic). With 33% explained variance, Competence-plus is our strongest dimension.

Examples of brands that score relatively high on Competence+ are: some car brands (Volvo, BMW), and some financial institutions (ABN AMRO, Postbank and Rabobank). Examples of brands scoring very low on the Competence+ dimension (in other words are not found to be described by items belonging to this factor) are different cigarette and rolling tobacco brands, and some shampoo brands (Pantene Pro-V and Organics).

2. Excitement+

The Excitement-dimension with 22% explained variance is more or less the same as Aaker's dimension (5 of her Excitement items were grouped here), although broader. Our dimension combines items such as Cheerful (Jolly, Happy, Spontaneous and Enthusiastic), Spirited (Active) and Imaginative (Creative and Original). Also in this dimension, we found a small part of Aaker's Sincerity dimension (her Cheerful facet).

Relatively high scoring brands are: beverages (Coca Cola, Lipton Ice Tea, Grolsch), but also for instance the two tele service brands Libertel and Ben. 'Low' scoring brands are cigarette and rolling tobacco brands as well as the insurance brands Amev, Ohra and Delta Lloyd.

3. Gentle

With 10% explained variance, Gentle is our third one-facet-dimension with no resemblance to one of Aaker's dimensions. It does, however, show some resemblance with the "Big Five" dimension Agreeableness. The dimension is best described by the items softhearted, kind, feminine and amiable.

Beverages is a product category that scores relatively high on Gentle. Examples of Gentle-brands are: Pickwick, Appelsientje and Spa. Also Nivea and Mazda are seen as 'gentle'. On the low side, we found some not Gentle brands such as Coca Cola and Head & Shoulders.

Our last four factors are not very strong (<10% explained variance), but may form reliable scales.

4. Ruggedness

Ruggedness resembles Aaker's American Ruggedness; a small factor in her analyses as well. This is a remarkable finding, because she did not find this dimension before in other cultures (that is: Spain or Japan). Our Ruggedness is best described by rugged, masculine and firm.

Examples of ruggedness are: BMW, Volvo, Coca Cola, Grolsch and Marlboro; only one of which is a real Dutch brand (Grolsch). The following brands were not described as rugged: Mazda, some shampoo brands (Nivea, Pantene Pro-V, Andrelon) and some beverages (Appelsientje, Pickwick, Spa).

5. Annoying

Another small dimension is a typically Dutch one, which we have labeled Annoying. This dimension is made up of two facets: unkind and childish.

Examples of brands that scored relatively high on this dimension are two supermarkets (Aldi and Konmar) and some tele services brands (Ben, KPN and Dutchtone). Examples of brands that scored low on the dimension Annoying are shampoo brands (Sanex, Organics, Pantene Pro-V, Andrelon) and some beer brands (Grolsch and Palm).

6. Distinguishing

A distinguished brand is described using words such as unique, non-conformist and daring. Examples of distinguished brands are (scoring relatively high on this dimension): Ben, Palm, Grolsch and BMW. Examples of brands that scored low on this dimension are shampoo brands (Nivea, Andrelon, Sanex, Head & Shoulders) and some cigarettes or rolling tobacco brands (Philip Morris, Mild Seven, Chesterfield, Samson, Jacobs).

Item reduction

In order to limit the number of items to be used in other Brand Personality studies, we followed several steps after completing the previously described factor and scale analyses. Following Aaker (1997), we selected the items loading high on the facets in terms of item-to-total correlations. For the one-facet dimensions, we selected the items loading high and avoided too much redundancy in terms. This resulted in 38 items. As previously explained, we excluded Sophistication. The factor analysis for the 38 items resulted in six dimensions, a total explained variance of 89%. As expected, these were the same six factors as before. A reliability analysis per dimension showed a Cronbach's alpha of more than 0.65. The final scale and sub-scales are summarized in the next table.

Table 2:4 Reduced SWOCC Brand Personality Scale (38 items)

Dimension	R^2	EV	α	Items
Competence+	32	13.1	0.98	Confident, Successful, Resolute, Determined, Sure, Sympathetic, Nice, Honest, Accurate, Precise, Secure, Careful, Efficient, Respectable, Firm (stout)
Excitement+	24	9.9	0.96	Jolly, Happy, Cheerful, Enthusiastic, Lively, Spirited, Active, Imaginative, Creative, Original
Gentle	11	4.5	0.82	Soft-hearted, Feminine, Amiable
Distinguishing	9	3.7	0.83	Unique, Non-conformist, Daring
Ruggedness	8	3.2	0.87	Rugged, Masculine, Firm (single-minded)
Annoying	6	2.5	0.81	Unkind, Annoying, Silly, Childish

(All 38 items: α=0.95)

Discussion

Although our aim was not to replicate Aaker, we compared our findings. Our Brand Personality dimensions are not quite the same, but also not too different. Shared dimensions are Competence and Excitement. We also found the dimension Sophistication, but it is a rather small factor. The dimensions Gentle, Annoying and Distinguishing could be culture-specific as a result of our addition of

Dutch personality items. If we think of culture-specific stereotypes, it is not surprising that Dutch brands are described as Annoying.

The aim of SWOCC was to develop a Brand Personality Scale for practitioners. Therefore, we reduced the items to a more practical number of 38 with six personality dimensions. Several analyses showed that the dimensions can be used as a reliable scale or reliable sub-scales. The personality scale consisting of six dimensions was also found in different sub-samples: comparing men and women, and comparing younger and older respondents (Van den Berge, 2002). Finally, it was shown that different types of brands score differently on the different dimensions.

Besides describing dimensions and reducing the number of items, we also analyzed to what extent brand personality related to consumer choices. We could only test this for brand attitude, which we measured as a school mark. Significant correlations were found, for some brands about 0.40, for other brands less, but overall 0.35.

In the first phase, we combined our data with data that was already known from the panel, namely the way respondents see themselves. Although we expected a relation, we did not find one. We also checked this for measurements about the 'ideal self', but also with no result, that is: no significant relations.

In the second phase of the data gathering, we asked respondents not only to score specific brands on personality items, but also to do this for their "ideal brand" in that product category. First analyses showed that a fit between a personality score for a specific brand and that for the ideal brand results in a higher brand attitude (in other words: the less difference between the two, the more positive the brand attitude).

Since functional differences between brands are often difficult to see, marketers try to differentiate their brands on the emotional level. Brand personality can be a useful tool for positioning a brand in a consumer's head (i.e. brand positioning). Moreover, the comparison of a brand's personality with that of competitive brands, or the identification of differences in consumers' perceptions of a brand's personality, is valuable.

The expectation concerning brand personality is that it is enduring. But the question is to what extent? How enduring is brand personality and what developments would cause changes in brand personality?

Edith G. Smit • Emilie van den Berge • Giep Franzen

Another interesting question is to what extent brand personality is predictive of several emotional responses towards brands, and other consumer choices. This, together with more research in origins of brand personality, is what we would like to investigate next.

Appendix A – SWOCC list of 102 personality items

Dutch	English	Min	Max	Mean	SD
Accuraat**	Accurate	0,02	0,55	0,14	0,11
Actief**	Active	0,01	0,46	0,19	0,11
Goedig**	Amiable	0,01	0,31	0,11	0,07
Vervelend**	Annoying*	0,03	0,27	0,11	0,05
Brutaal	Bold	0,01	0,54	0,11	0,09
Zorgvuldig**	Careful	0,04	0,61	0,17	0,12
Charmant	Charming*	0,01	0,42	0,10	0,06
Opgewekt**	Cheerful*	0,02	0,39	0,14	0,08
Kinderachtig**	Childish	0,01	0,26	0,06	0,04
Zelfverzekerd**	Confident*	0,02	0,59	0,20	0,12
Hedendaags	Contemporary*	0,04	0,52	0,23	0,12
Conventioneel	Conventional	0,03	0,54	0,14	0,10
Cool	Cool*	0,01	0,55	0,10	0,09
Zakelijk	Corporate*	0,01	0,70	0,20	0,15
Creatief**	Creative	0,02	0,51	0,13	0,09
Gedurfd**	Daring*	0,01	0,40	0,10	0,07
Geschikt	Decent	0,03	0,54	0,20	0,12
Doelbewust**	Determined	0,02	0,53	0,20	0,11
Apart	Different	0,01	0,49	0,11	0,09
Dominant	Dominant	0,01	0,64	0,12	0,11
Nuchter	Down-to-earth*	0,03	0,51	0,16	0,10
Vlot	Easy (-mannered)	0,02	0,53	0,15	0,10
Efficiënt**	Efficient	0,02	0,55	0,16	0,11
Ondernemend	Enterprising	0,01	0,54	0,17	0,10
Enthousiast**	Enthusiastic	0,01	0,45	0,14	0,09
Opwindend	Exciting*	0,00	0,45	0,07	0,06
Uitbundig	Exuberant	0,01	0,51	0,09	0,08
Familiemens	Family-oriented*	0,01	0,64	0,15	0,12
Vrouwelijk**	Feminine*	0,01	0,35	0,11	0,09
Heftig	Fierce	0,01	0,50	0,08	0,07
Standvastig**	Firm (Single-minded)	0,02	0,60	0,18	0,11
Ferm**	Firm (stout)	0,01	0,44	0,11	0,07
Vriendelijk	Friendly*	0,02	0,50	0,19	0,11
Glamoureus	Glamorous*	0,01	0,58	0,09	0,08
Knap	Good looking*	0,00	0,31	0,08	0,05
Goedgehumeurd	Good-humored	0,03	0,35	0,16	0,09
Blij**	Happy	0,02	0,40	0,11	0,07
IJverig	Hard working*	0,02	0,34	0,13	0,08

Eerlijk**	Honest*	0,02	0,53	0,18	0,11
Fantasierijk**	Imaginative*	0,01	0,45	0,11	0,08
Impulsief	Impulsive	0,00	0,34	0,09	0,06
Onafhankelijk	Independent*	0,03	0,34	0,17	0,08
Individualistisch	Individualistic	0,03	0,46	0,12	0,06
Intelligent	Intelligent*	0,02	0,43	0,13	0,09
Vrolijk**	Jolly	0,01	0,43	0,13	0,09
Puberaal	Juvenile	0,01	0,46	0,08	0,08
Zachtaardig	Kind	0,01	0,37	0,10	0,07
Leider	Leader*	0,00	0,61	0,13	0,13
Levendig**	Lively	0,02	0,43	0,15	0,09
Lawaaierig	Loud	0,01	0,46	0,09	0,08
Mannelijk**	Masculine*	0,00	0,64	0,14	0,10
Net	Neat	0,03	0,59	0,17	0,12
Prettig**	Nice	0,04	0,46	0,19	0,11
Non-conformistisch**	Non-conformist	0,01	0,20	0,06	0,03
Hartelijk	Open-hearted	0,01	0,39	0,13	0,09
Origineel**	Original*	0,02	0,48	0,13	0,09
Buitenmens	Outdoorsy*	0,01	0,31	0,11	0,08
Plezierig	Pleasant	0,02	0,46	0,17	0,11
Krachtig	Powerful	0,01	0,59	0,17	0,11
Precies**	Precise	0,03	0,50	0,15	0,10
Provocerend	Provoking	0,00	0,47	0,08	0,06
Radicaal	Radical	0,01	0,28	0,08	0,05
Echt	Real*	0,02	0,45	0,18	0,10
Rebels	Rebellious	0,01	0,37	0,09	0,08
Betrouwbaar	Reliable*	0,02	0,75	0,25	0,16
Resoluut**	Resolute	0,01	0,41	0,14	0,08
Degelijk**	Respectable	0,03	0,81	0,21	0,14
Ruig**	Rugged*	0,00	0,40	0,08	0,08
Veilig**	Secure*	0,01	0,83	0,18	0,15
Zelfingenomen	Self-important	0,02	0,59	0,13	0,09
Sentimenteel	Sentimental*	0,01	0,23	0,07	0,04
Onbenullig**	Silly	0,01	0,20	0,08	0,04
Oprecht	Sincere*	0,02	0,46	0,15	0,09
Provinciaals	Small-town*	0,02	0,46	0,10	0,07
Glad(jes)	Smooth*	0,02	0,39	0,11	0,06
Zacht	Soft	0,01	0,40	0,10	0,08
Zachtmoedig**	Soft-hearted	0,01	0,32	0,09	0,07
Energiek**	Spirited*	0,01	0,54	0,15	0,09
Spontaan	Spontaneous	0,02	0,38	0,12	0,07
Levenslustig	Sprightly	0,02	0,44	0,15	0,09
Stabiel	Stabile	0,03	0,75	0,22	0,14
Evenwichtig	Steady	0,03	0,61	0,17	0,11
Succesvol**	Successful*	0,01	0,67	0,22	0,14
Zonnig	Sunny	0,01	0,66	0,12	0,09

Zeker**	Sure	0,01	0,68	0,19	0,12
Sympathiek**	Sympathetic	0,03	0,45	0,17	0,09
Technisch	Technical*	0,01	0,54	0,10	0,09
Stoer	Tough*	0,00	0,62	0,12	0,10
Trendy	Trendy*	0,01	0,57	0,14	0,10
Ongecompliceerd	Uncomplicated	0,02	0,49	0,14	0,09
Uniek**	Unique*	0,03	0,32	0,09	0,06
Onvriendelijk**	Unkind	0,00	0,28	0,08	0,05
Elitair	Upper class*	0,01	0,57	0,10	0,10
Modern	Up-to-date*	0,02	0,49	0,18	0,12
Levenskrachtig	Vigorous	0,01	0,44	0,16	0,09
Vitaal	Vital	0,01	0,48	0,14	0,09
Kwetsbaar	Vulnerable	0,02	0,33	0,08	0,06
Avontuurlijk	Western*	0,01	0,36	0,13	0,09
Grillig	Whimsical	0,01	0,23	0,08	0,05
Zeurderig	Whiney	0,02	0,19	0,08	0,04
Gezond	Wholesome*	0,00	0,66	0,14	0,14
Jeugdig/jong	Young*	0,00	0,58	0,11	0,11

Note: ** = 38 SWOCC items (reduced scale) (1st column), * = 41 Aaker items (2nd column

Appendix B – Brands scoring high or low on the brand personality dimensions

Dimension	Brands scoring high	Brands scoring low
Competence M=17, SD=10	Volvo, BMW, PTT Post, KPN, Libertel, Douwe Egberts, ABN AMRO, Postbank, Rabobank, Hema, Albert Heijn (all >30%)	Mild Seven ,Lucky Strike, Gauloises Blondes, Philip Morris, Chesterfield, Caballero, Barclay, Javaanse Jongens, Jacobs, Brandaris, Samson, Royal Mail, Telfort, Dutchtone, Ben, Pantene Pro-V, Organics (all < 10%)
Excitement M=14, SD=7	Ben, Libertel, Coca Cola, Lipton Ice Tea, Cup a Soup, Grolsch, Albert Heijn, Bijenkorf, Hema, BMW, Mazda, Centraal Beheer, Postbank, PTT Post (all > 20%)	Jacobs, Brandaris, Samson, Van Nelle, Mild Seven, Chesterfield, Barclay, Philip Morris, Gauloises Blondes, Caballero, Lucky Strike, Royal Mail, Deutsche Post, Head & Shoulders, Nivea, Amev, Ohra, Delta Lloyd, Max Havelaar (all < 10%)

Gentle M=10, SD=6	Pickwick, Appelsientje, Spa, Nivea, Mazda, Mild Seven (all > 20%)	Deutsche Post, UPS, Royal Mail, TNT, Head & Shoulders, Caballero, Lucky Strike, Marlboro, Philip Morris, Brandaris Coca Cola, Telfort, Delta Lloyd, Aegon (all < 5%)
Ruggedness M=11, SD=7	BMW, Volvo, Coca Cola, Grolsch, Marlboro (all > 20%)	Mild Seven, Barclay, Chesterfield, Jacobs, Appelsientje, Pickwick, Spa, Royal Mail, Nivea, Pantene Pro-V, Andrelon, Organics, Mazda (all < 5%)
Annoying M=8, SD=3	Aldi, Konmar, Ben, KPN, Dutchtone, Rabobank, Postbank, ABN AMRO, BMW, Mild Seven, Jacobs, Head & Shoulders, PTT Post (all > 11%)	Sanex, Organics, Pantene, Nivea Pro-V, Andrelon, Royal Mail, UPS, TNT, Deutsche Post, Douwe Egberts, Spa, Palm, Grolsch, Volvo, Bijenkorf (all < 5%)
Distinguishing M=8, SD=5	Ben, Max Havelaar, Palm, Grolsch, Bijenkorf, Lipton Ice Tea, BMW, Aldi, Centraal Beheer (all > 15%)	Nivea, Andrelon, Sanex, Head & Shoulders, Deutsche Post, Royal Mail, Philip Morris, Mild Seven, Chesterfield, Aegon, Samson, Jacobs, Telfort (all < 5%)

Note: M=mean (%), SD=standard deviation, average brand score means that x % of the respondents thought that dimension to be descriptive for that specific brand

3

Behavioural Finance-based advertising research in the mutual fund industry

KLAUS PETER KAAS & JENNY JORDAN

Advertising in the Mutual Fund Industry

In the last years, advertising expenditure within the mutual fund industry has increased significantly. In Germany, it rose to 145.61 million Euro in 2001, which is more than twice as high as three years earlier (66.75 million Euro, AC Nielsen 2002). This development was caused by a promising market potential and fierce competition in the investment industry, which in turn was the result of the internationalisation of financial markets, technological changes, and fundamental changes in the investment behaviour of private households. Obviously, advertising has become an important marketing instrument in the financial services industry (Meidan, 1996; McKechnie & Leather, 1998). But what do we know about its effectiveness? Until now, advertising research has neglected industry-specific product characteristics in the investment market and their relevance for advertising effectiveness. There is no doubt that many theoretical and empirical findings of behavioural advertising research also apply to investment products, among these the creation of awareness or emotional experiences through advertising. There are, however, special features of investment products which advertising research should take explicitly into account. Like all investment products, mutual funds are intangible, complex and very homogenous products, the customer benefit of which originates in abstract monetary values (Meidan, 1996; McKechnie, 1997; Sirri/Tufano, 1993).

Moreover, investment decisions are characterised by high exogenous uncertainty, as future product performance must be estimated on the basis of a set of noisy and vague variables. Consequently, investors' expectations to uncertain future events play a crucial role in investment decision-making (Wärneryd, 1999). Most importantly, purchase decisions in investment markets follow two dominant criteria: perceived investment risk and expected return (Ganzach, 2000; Olsen, 1997), constructs which apply exclusively to the financial services industry. Risk and return are crucial variables in financial decision-making, as indicated in the fundamental normative model of investment behaviour, the mean-variance portfolio analysis (Markowitz, 1952; Tobin, 1958; Sharpe 1994). Marketing research should detect how investors' perception of these product-specific decision criteria is influenced by marketing instruments, e.g. advertising stimuli. This paper describes a new theoretical approach to advertising in the mutual fund industry and presents empirical insights regarding the influence of advertising on private investors' risk-return perceptions. Hypotheses are tested by means of an extensive experimental study, and practical implications are described in the last section of the paper.

Behavioural Finance-Based Advertising Research: Risk-Return-Perceptions as Variables of Advertising Effects

Behavioural Finance, a field of research that interfaces with economics, finance and psychology, is a relatively young paradigm, which was developed in the US in the late 80's because of increasing empirical evidence that existing financial theories were deficient in a real market setting (Shefrin, 2000; De Bondt, 1998; Kahneman & Riepe, 1998). Contrary to the normative approach of classical portfolio theory, Behavioural Finance deals with the descriptive analysis of actual behaviour of individuals in financial markets and analyses psychological influences on information processing and financial decision-making. Risk perception and return estimations are considered to be crucial constructs in the context of financial decision-making (Ganzach, 2000; MacGregor et al., 1999; Olsen, 1997; Antonides & van der Sar, 1990). However, traditional behavioural advertising research focuses on rather general categories of advertising effects, like awareness, recall or attitude change (Meyers-Levy & Malaviya, 1999; Vakratsas & Ambler, 1999). In this paper, private investors' risk-return perceptions are considered special variables of advertising effectiveness in the mutual fund industry. How does advertising influence private investors' perceived risk and expected return? Answering this question leads to a product-specific and selective analysis of the persuasive impact of advertising in the investment industry.

The notion of risk refers to the uncertainty of future returns. In classical finance theory, risk is interpreted in terms of variations of returns and measured as variance or betas (Olsen & Cox, 2001; Spremann, 2000). Investment risk is considered a precise, abstract and purely technical statistical concept. This risk concept, however, does not reflect private investors' understanding of risk. In particular, private investors have a more intuitive, less quantitative, rather emotionally driven risk perception (Olsen & Cox, 2001). Empirical studies that deal with investors' risk perceptions (Olsen & Cox, 2001; MacGregor et al., 1999; Olsen, 1997; Holtgrave & Weber, 1993) detect four different dimensions of perceived risk:

- *Downside Risk*: The risk of suffering financial losses due to negative deviations of returns, starting from an individual reference point.
- *Upside Risk*: The chance of realising higher-than-average returns, starting from an individual reference point.
- *Volatility*: The fluctuations of returns over time.
- *Ambiguity*: The subjective feeling of uncertainty due to lack of information and lack of competence.

All these different aspects have to be taken into account, as single item-measures lead to an incomplete and simplified measurement of the perceived risk construct (Farrelly & Reichenstein, 1984). Expected return, on the other hand, is a simpler, one-dimensional numerical construct, which can be measured in absolute or relative terms or in intuitively quantitative evaluations (MacGregor et al., 1999). Private investors' risk-return perceptions are always subjective in nature and marked by situational influences. Cognitive aspects as well as emotional states determine their formation (Olsen & Cox, 2001; Ganzach, 2000; Geist, 1999). Therefore, informative and emotional stimuli in the ad will influence risk-return perceptions. Depending on the way information and emotions are communicated in the ad, investors will form different risk-return perceptions with regard to the advertised mutual fund.

Relevance of Private Investors' Judgmental Heuristics for Risk-Return Perceptions and Advertising Content

Judgmental heuristics used by investors during information perception and information processing are a field of special interest in Behavioural Finance theory (Kahneman & Riepe, 1998; Tversky & Kahneman, 1974). Behavioural Finance looks at the investor as a 'homo heuristicus', using judgmental heuristics instead of formal statistical analysis in information processing and decision-making. Judgmental heuristics are abridged, often sub-optimal information processing strategies, so-called 'mental shortcuts' or 'rules of thumb', which are used systematically but often unconsciously to simplify decision-making (Kahneman & Tversky, 1996). Heuristics are of special relevance in situations with uncertain or incomplete information and whenever quantitative forecasts, predictions or evaluations of uncertain future events have to be made (Tversky & Kahneman, 1974). As a result of this decision context, cognitive and emotional heuristics produce systematic bias in risk-return perceptions (Raghubir & Das, 1999; Kahneman & Riepe, 1998; Evensky, 1997). These heuristics have to be taken into account when assessing advertising effectiveness.

In the next sections, we will give a brief description of two fundamental cognitive heuristics and one affect-based heuristic and develop hypotheses for advertising content and advertising effectiveness.

Anchoring Heuristic

When making forecasts, predictions or probability assessments, people tend to rely on a numerical anchor value that is explicitly or implicitly presented to them (Chapman & Johnson, 1999, 1994; Kahneman & Tversky, 1974). Anchoring effects are not restricted to numerical values that are logically coherent with the subsequent numeric estimate. According to the so-called "Basic Anchoring Effect" (Wilson et al., 1996), any random and uninformative starting point might represent an initial anchor value which leads to bias in forecasts and estimates towards the value of that initial starting point. Anchoring effects have been identified in many empirical studies and in various decision fields (Mussweiler & Strack, 2001). This robust judgmental heuristic is of particular relevance in financial markets, where it applies to financial forecasts (e.g., stock market prices), leading to severe bias (Stephan, 1999).

In practice, numerical data play an important role for the informative content of mutual fund ads. Almost every print ad and many TV-spots highlight figures like past performance data, assets under management, distribution of dividends etc. In addition to direct anchor values (e.g., "10 %", "10 billion Euro"), indirect and uninformative anchor values with dimensions other than return or monetary units (e.g., "15,000 research specialists worldwide", "1,000 dreams come true") can also exert an influence on estimates. In accordance with the anchoring heuristic, these figures will distort return perceptions towards the anchor value.

H 1: A low anchor value in an ad will lead to a lower return estimation, compared to a high anchor value.

Representativeness Heuristic

People tend to rely on stereotypes. They judge the likelihood of an event according to how it fits into a previously established schema or mental model. They consistently judge the event appearing to be the more representative to be the more likely, without considering the prior probability, or base-rate frequency of the outcomes (Kahneman & Tversky, 1973; 1972). Representativeness is a commonly used and very problematic heuristic in financial markets, as it leads to misinterpretation of empirical or causal coherence (Fisher & Statman, 2000; De Bondt & Thaler, 1993). Illusory correlation and bias in the use of judgment criteria are typical consequences. For instance, past performance data and trend patterns of mutual funds' performance charts are extrapolated into the future without considering the exogenous uncertainty and randomness of financial markets (Hilton,

2001; Raghubir & Das, 1999; Moore & Kurtzberg, 1999; Hulbert, 1999).

In terms of practice, mutual fund ads suggestively promote stereotype thinking by communicating positive past performance data, rankings and awards, and by pointing out specific brand values like trustworthiness, competence and experience. Due to stereotype thinking (brand associations, brand schemata), private investors' risk-return perceptions will depend heavily on the investment company behind the investment product.

H 2: A well-known investment company with a clearly positive brand image will evoke better risk-return perceptions at the product level than an unknown investment company without a clear and positive brand image profile, even though both companies advertise identical products and provide identical product information.

Affect Heuristic

Modern financial theory increasingly recognises the fact that financial decision-making is also determined by affective states (Shefrin, 2000; MacGregor et al., 2000). Negative emotions such as fear, worry, anger or shame, and positively experienced emotions like hope, greed, pleasure and joy may influence risk-return perceptions and investment behaviour (Shefrin, 2000; Geist, 1999; Young & O'Neill, 1992).

A direct influence of emotions on risk perception and expected returns can be deduced from the affect heuristic (Slovic, 2001; Finucane, Alhakami, Slovic & Johnson, 2000), which assumes that perceptions of risks and benefits related to an alternative are derived from global affective evaluations and associations. If a stimulus arouses a positive affective impression, the decision-maker will judge the risks related to this alternative to be lower and the benefits to be higher, compared to neutral emotional states. If a stimulus is associated with negative affective impressions, the opposite effect will occur: risks are judged to be higher; whereas the benefits are judged to be lower. In practice, mutual fund ads most often contain emotional pictures and emotional slogans in addition to product information. In terms of the affect heuristic, these emotional elements exert a direct influence on investors' risk-return perceptions.

H 3: If the emotional content in the ad (pictures, slogans, tonality) succeeds in evoking positive affective impressions towards the advertised mutual fund, the investor will judge the investment risk to be lower and the return to be higher, compared to a purely informative ad.

The Moderating Impact of Private Investors' Expertise

It is important to discuss possible moderating factors in the use of heuristics. Do only inexperienced, unmotivated and relatively incompetent investors use these heuristics, or are they applied by novice and expert investors as well? The question whether or not knowledge influences heuristic information processing has been a topic of discussion. Some researchers propose the unconsciousness and automatism of judgmental heuristics, implying that both lay and expert investors make systematic use of them (Tversky & Kahneman, 1974). Indeed, some empirical findings reveal that investors' expertise has no influence on the use of judgmental heuristics (Northcraft & Neale, 1987; Joyce & Biddle, 1981; Stephan, 1999). Others, however, demonstrate the moderating role of individuals' knowledge, stating that knowledgeable persons do not, or only to a moderate extent, apply judgmental heuristics (Mussweiler & Strack, 2000; Wilson et al., 1996).

H 4: Less knowledgeable investors make use of the judgmental heuristics to a larger extent than more knowledgeable and experienced investors.

Experimental Study

Method

Design

The hypotheses were explored with a large-scale laboratory experiment between subjects and a 2 (anchor height: low vs. high) x 2 (emotional content: emotional vs. non-emotional ad) x 2 (brand logo: "Fidelity" vs. "DWS") x 2 (investors' expertise: competent vs. incompetent investors) factorial design (see Table 3:1). The different graphical elements of the ad represented the experimental factors and were systematically varied to test for possible interaction effects. Investors' expertise as a separate experimental factor was controlled by ex post-blocking of the experimental groups. In accordance with their subjective self-assessment of their knowledge and experience in mutual funds and investment products, participants were divided into groups of incompetent and competent investors after the experiment.

Table 3:1 Experimental Design

	brand: „Fidelity"				brand: „DWS"			
	high anchor		*lLow anchor*		*high anchor*		*low anchor*	
emotional ad	*competent investors*	incompetent investors	competent investors	incompetent investors	competent investors	incompetent investors	competent investors	incompetent investors
	n=28	n=35	n=37	n=36	n=35	n=30	n=38	n=21
non-emotional ad	*high anchor*		*low anchor*		*high anchor*		*low anchor*	
	competent investors	incompetent investors	competent investors	incompetent investors	competent investors	incompetent investors	competent investors	incompetent investors
	n=27	n=27	n=28	n=34	n=31	n=36	n=25	n=31

n=499

Stimuli

The advertising stimulus was a print ad promoting a European large and mid-cap mutual fund. Each experimental group was presented with a different version of the print ad representing the systematically varied experimental factors, in accordance with the experimental design. Apart from those experimentally manipulated factors, all ads were identical, containing the same product information and communicating the same risk-return profile of the mutual fund.

The anchor value in the ad was an uninformative, irrelevant numerical value, according to the "basic anchoring effect" (Wilson et al., 1996), and was included in the ad as an integral part of the mutual fund's name (low anchor: "Euro Star 100 Fund^{TM}", high anchor: "Euro Star 500 Fund^{TM}"). The mutual fund's name was a prominent element of the ad. Besides product information, the emotional ad included an emotional image and an emotional claim. The non-emotional ad, on the other hand, did not contain any emotional elements, only emotionally neutral visual background elements and claims. To test for representativeness effects, one half of the ads contained the brand logo of a large, well-known German investment company ("DWS") and the

other half the brand logo of a large, but in Germany widely unknown American investment company ("Fidelity Investments").

Participants and Procedure

The experimental study was carried out with business students at Frankfurt University, Germany, during December 2001. 526 students of various levels and courses participated in the study (27 incomplete questionnaires had to be excluded from the analysis). After watching the print ad, they were asked to fill in a questionnaire containing the following dependent variables:

Measures

- *Perceived risk*: four items measuring the different aspects of the construct (downside risk, upside risk, volatility, ambiguity)
- *Expected return*: participants had to estimate the average rate of return per year in the following years

Additionally, participants' subjective *knowledge and experience* with regard to investment decisions (four items) were measured via self-assessment. Questions capturing brand image, brand awareness and emotional evaluation of the mutual fund completed the questionnaire in order to comprehend and reconstruct relevant heuristic influences. The most important scales are shown in the appendix.

Results

The impact of the anchoring heuristic

In case of the low anchor value ("Euro Star 100 Fund[TM]") mean *expected return* estimation was 11.8 %, in case of the high anchor value ("Euro Star 500 Fund[TM]") 22.6 %. As these results indicate, return evaluations are significantly distorted by anchor size. An analysis of variance revealed a significant main effect ($F(1, 483)= 122,371, p < 0.01$) with strong effect size[1] ($eta^2 = 0.202$). These results demonstrate the "basic anchoring effect" (Wilson et al., 1996): Uninformative and implicitly presented anchor values without logical

---

1 In accordance with Cohen's (1988) classification of effect sizes, we assessed effect sizes of $eta^2 = 0.01$ as small, 0.06 as mean and 0.14 as strong effect sizes.

coherence to the estimate are able to bias return perceptions significantly.

The impact of the representativeness heuristic

The use of different brand logos („Fidelity" vs. „DWS") in the print ad and, correspondingly, the evocation of varying brand associations, have no significant influence on *expected return*. The direct numeric estimate is obviously not affected by variations in associated brand image. However, there was a significant ($F(1, 483)=530,956$, $p < 0.01$) and large ($eta^2= 0.524$) main effect of brand logo *on perceived investment risk*: Integration of the brand logo "Fidelity" leads to a mean factor score of perceived risk of 0.63, the logo "DWS" leads to a mean factor score of -0.634. This means that the participants perceived investment risk as lower when the mutual fund was offered by the brand "DWS", although the same product information and risk-return-profile was communicated. Apparently, thinking in stereotypes and brand schemata leads to bias in risk perception. Further analyses clarify the functionality of representativeness: The image[2] of the brand „DWS" was judged better (mean: 26.8) than the brand image of „Fidelity"(mean: 18.7), $t=-16.291$, $p < 0.01$. Similarly, the brand awareness of "DWS" is higher (mean: 4.3) than that of „Fidelity" (mean: 2.4), $t=-18.038$, $p< 0.01$. To sum up, thinking in stereotypes, combined with a higher awareness of the corporate brand, affects perceived investment risk at the product level: A good brand image and high brand awareness result in a lower perception of investment risk.

The impact of affect heuristic

The emotional content of the print ad had no significant influence on *expected return*. Apparently, direct numeric estimates are not distorted by emotional elements in the ad. But again, analysis of variance revealed a significant ($F(1, 483)=274,107$, $p < 0.01$) and strong ($eta^2= 0.362$) main effect of emotional content on *risk perception*: The emotional ads resulted in a mean factor score of perceived risk of – 0.456, the non-emotional ads, on the other hand, led to a mean factor

---

2 Brand image was measured by means of seven items. As Cronbach's alpha was high (.92), items were summed up to form a brand image score.

score of 0.452. Thus emotional elements in the ad evoke a decrease in investment risk perception. Further analyses illustrate these emotional effects: Participants' affective evaluation of the advertised mutual fund ("I have a good feeling with regard to this mutual fund") is better if emotional elements are present in the ad (mean: 3.3, five point scale) compared to a purely informative ad (mean: 2.1), t=16.046, p < 0.01. In conclusion, positive emotional associations caused by emotional advertising decrease perceived investment risk

The moderating impact of participants' expertise

An analysis of variance revealed a significant (F(1, 483)=10,288, p < 0.01) but small (eta^2= 0.021) main effect of participants' expertise[3] on *expected return*: On average, participants with low knowledge and experience had an estimated return of 18.8 %, while competent participants had a higher estimated return of 15.6 %. Furthermore, there was a significant (F (1, 483)=22,567, p < 0.01) but small (eta^2= 0.045) main effect of participants' competence on *perceived risk*. Competent participants show lower risk perceptions than incompetent participants (mean factor score of incompetent participants: 0.128, of knowledgeable participants: -0.132). This result is probably due to the perceived ambiguity in the evaluation of risky alternatives. This special aspect of risk perception (perceived risk item no. 2) is directly related to participants' subjective knowledge and available information. The degree of perceived ambiguity differs clearly between incompetent and competent participants, as separate analyses of variance on each aspect of perceived risk reveal: Competent participants experience lower ambiguity (mean: 2.5) in the decision context than their incompetent colleagues (mean: 3.3); F (1, 483)=88,327, p < 0.01, eta^2= 0.155 (large effect).

Table 3:2 shows the interaction effects between participants' expertise and the use of heuristics.

---

3 The four items which measured knowledge and experience related to one factor labelled „competence". Factor scores were calculated and competence ranks were constructed (2 percentiles): One group was formed for incompetent participants, one for competent participants. Participants' competence was treated as a separate experimental factor in the factorial design.

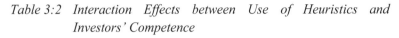

Table 3:2   Interaction   Effects   between   Use   of   Heuristics   and
Investors' Competence

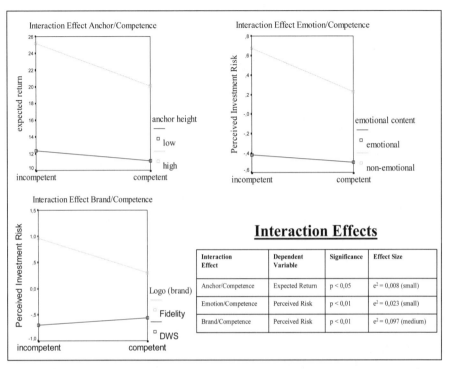

As an analysis of variance reveals, the biasing effect of the anchoring heuristic is larger for incompetent participants than for more knowledgeable participants. This result is very informative, as it reveals that both competent and incompetent investors use heuristics, but incompetent investors show a bias which is larger in magnitude. This magnitude effect also applies to the affect heuristic. The biasing effect of emotional content on risk perception is larger for incompetent participants than for competent participants. Furthermore, thinking in stereotypes and brand schemata leads to more severe effects on risk perception in the case of incompetent investors. The difference in risk perception due to integration of various brand logos is larger for incompetent participants. Further analyses reveal that competent participants perceive differences in brand image between „Fidelity" (mean: 21.5) and „DWS" (mean: 27.0), t=-7.736, p < 0.01, as lower than incompetent participants (mean "Fidelity": 16.2, mean "DWS":

26.5), t=-16.857, p < 0.01). Similar effects can be found for differences in brand awareness: Brand awareness differences between "Fidelity" and "DWS" are smaller for competent participants (mean "Fidelity": 3.1, mean "DWS": 4.6, t=-9.854, p < 0.01) than for incompetent participants (mean "Fidelity": 1.8, mean "DWS": 4.0, t=-18.565, p < 0.01) As a consequence, these differences in brand associations and brand awareness lead to varying effects on risk perception. These results support our findings that although both competent and incompetent participants make use of heuristics, the bias is larger for incompetent participants.

Apart from these interaction effects between participants' expertise and the use of heuristics, no other interaction effects were found.

Conclusion

- Anchoring, representativeness and affect heuristic are used by private investors in an advertising context and lead to bias in risk return judgments, with the following restrictions:
- Anchoring effects only occur in case of expected return, i.e. direct numeric estimates.
- Affect and representativeness heuristic only affect perceived investment risk.
- The referred judgmental heuristics are found in both groups of competent and incompetent investors, but the latter show larger bias than competent investors.

Discussion

Advertising in the mutual fund industry may become more effective if advertising firms are aware of and apply the fundamental insights of Behavioural Finance theory.

Besides more general variables of advertising effectiveness, private investors' risk-return perceptions should be considered as special variables of advertising effects in the mutual fund industry, as such decision-relevant perceptions can be influenced by advertising stimuli.

Private investors make use of judgmental heuristics during the processing of advertising stimuli, regardless of their expertise in investment decisions. Incompetent investors, however, make use of heuristics to a larger extent, resulting in larger bias in the perception of risks and returns. These findings highlight the necessity of target group or market segment-specific advertising strategies in the investment industry, as differences in knowledge and experiences lead to different risk-return perceptions.

Numerical values in print ads serve as anchor values and bias expected returns, even when there is no logical connection between anchor value and return estimation. Therefore, prominent numbers and figures in mutual fund ads have to be integrated very carefully, taking their potential biasing influence fully into account.

Brand awareness and brand image play a central role in the processing of ads, as they are able to distort private investors' risk perception at the product level. Investment risk is judged to be lower if the advertised mutual fund is offered by a highly reputable and well-known investment company. As a consequence, investing in brand equity is important.

Emotional states influence private investors' risk perceptions. As emotional stimuli in the ad can lead to a more favourable, positive affective evaluation of the advertised mutual fund, emotional ads lead to a lower perception of investment risk compared to a merely informative advertising style. This indicates that emotional advertising is an effective tool, even in the abstract, rational, risk-return orientated investment industry.

Appendix

Risk perception was measured by means of four items with regard to the different aspects of the construct, using five-point scales labelled "strongly disagree" to "strongly agree":

- "This mutual fund bears a high risk of losing money or of missing personal investment objectives" (downside risk)
- „I feel uncertain about investing in this mutual fund, as I feel uninformed and incompetent about it." (ambiguity)
- „Investing in this fund also entails high chances to realise higher, above-average returns." (upside risk)
- „Regarding this mutual fund, I reckon with high performance variations over time." (volatility)

As all items related to one factor which we called "risk perception", factor scores were calculated and used to form an aggregate perceived risk measure.

Expected return as a direct numeric estimate was captured by the following question:

"Please estimate the mutual fund's average rate of return per year (time horizon: the next few years)": on average _____ % per year."

Investors' expertise in investment decisions and mutual funds, consisting of subjective knowledge and experiences (Alba & Hutchinson, 1987; MacInnis, Moorman & Jaworski, 1991), was measured by means of four items:

1. „How do you assess your knowledge about mutual funds?"
   (five-point scale, labelled „I have a lot of knowledge" to „I have very small knowledge"

2. „Please evaluate to what extent you have already gained experiences with mutual fund investments."
   (five-point scale, labelled "I am very experienced" to "I am very inexperienced")

3. „I know a lot about investing money."
   (five-point scale, labelled „strongly agree" to „strongly disagree")

4. „I am very experienced in investing money"
   (five-point scale, labelled „strongly agree" to „strongly disagree")

An Evaluation of Corporate Brand Character

PERNILLE SCHNOOR

"Corporate branding is one of those things that everyone believes is important, yet there is very little consensus as to what it means. Words such as 'values', 'image' and 'communication' swirl around. It is undoubtedly related to all these things." *(Ind, 1997)*

Abstract

This article is concerned with the role of credibility in relation to corporate brands. By adapting the method of evaluating a person's credibility, the article will present evidence in favour of developing a more comprehensive evaluation method. This method will show how corporate brands are perceived differently along five evaluative dimensions: success, credibility, exuberance, forcefulness and sincerity.

Background

In recent years, a great deal of literature has focused on the effects and advantages of using a corporate branding strategy. Increasingly, companies seek to present themselves as corporate brands, following a corporate branding communication and management strategy. However, there is little empirical evidence of a corporate branding strategy's positive impact on a company brand image. Focus is primarily on internal perspectives and how to manage corporate brands (Bengtsson, 2002). A key object in the brand management literature is how to evaluate *brand equity*. Brand equity can be seen as the set of assets linked to a brand's name and symbol; assets that can add to the value provided by a product and/or a service (Aaker, 1996). Brand management literature is primarily concerned with product brands, and even though differences in product and corporate brands are pointed out, evaluation tools most often mix brands on a product and corporate level. Examples of this are Young & Rubicam's Brand Asset Valuator (BAV) and Jennifer Aaker's Brand Personality Scale (see, for instance, Keller, 2003).

Corporate brand equity occurs when relevant constituents hold strong, favourable and unique associations about the corporate brand in memory (Keller; in Schultz et al., 2000). Hence, understanding how consumers and other stakeholders perceive corporate brands is an important research task.

The literature provides no general definition of a corporate brand, but when looking at the term 'corporate brand' it might be useful to divide it into two parts, as done by Ind (1997): 'Corporate' implies organizations in their totality and '*the idea of people coming together and working towards a common goal.* 'Brand' implies something that is *(...)*

"distinct from the simple idea of a product, in that there is a suggestion in the notion of a brand of values that go beyond mere functional performance" (Ind, 1997).

A corporate brand can encompass a wider range of associations in the minds of consumers, and therefore it is distinct from a product brand (Keller, 2003). The literature reveals two overall understandings of corporate brands. One sees the company brand as the corporate brand and is typically called a company-as-brand-strategy or a monolithic corporate brand strategy. In this perspective, only one brand is communicated and the focus is very much on internal aspects, such as employees, corporate values, identity, etc (Chernatony, 2001; Ind, 1997). Examples would be *The Body Shop* and financial corporate brands such as mortgage-credit institutions. The other perspective sees the company brand as having an endorsement function behind other main brands and as the top-of-brand-hierarchy (Aaker &

Joachimsthaler, 2000; Keller, 2003). There are numerous examples of this strategy, such as *Microsoft, Nestlé* and *Scandinavian Airlines (SAS)*. This latter understanding focuses very much on the market with the consumer as the key player. The two strategies are not mutually exclusive but have different focuses, which are relevant when dealing with different contexts, such as the specific product category and/or industry.

Many researchers agree that rather than focusing on communicating individual product brands, corporations can benefit from focusing their efforts to communicate values embedded in the corporation as such (Ind, 1997; Thomson et al., 1999; Chernatony, 2001). This strategy is not only more economical – because communicating one brand is less expensive than communicating subbrands, brand extensions, etc. individually, but also a focus on the company values as such, rather than on the individual product benefits, can strengthen the perception and *credibility* of the company's brands. The use of the company name reduces consumer insecurity and transfers *credibility* from the company to its products (Franzen & Bouwman, 2001; Aaker 1996). On the other hand, lack of corporate credibility can lead consumers to question the validity of claims by the company as such, and as a consequence consumers are less likely to buy its products (Franzen & Bouwman, 2001; Goldsmith, Lafferty & Newell, 2000). Thus, lack of corporate credibility can be crucial for a company and therefore credibility is a key notion in relation to discussing corporate branding.

Corporate brands and credibility

According to Aaker (1996), credibility plays an important role in relation to defining and/or creating a brand identity. He mentions credibility as one of three elements in his brand identity system, the two others being core/extended identity and the value proposition. These are elements which will lead to a brand-customer relationship. Aaker also states that the credibility of a firm contributes to building brand equity for its products, both tangible goods and intangible services (Aaker, 1991).

Whereas credibility of a product brand is based on more tangible features, such as product quality and technology, which are easier to evaluate for consumers – i.e. most products can be tasted, smelled or touched - credibility in corporate brands, such as service brands, is more complex, because it is based on intangible variables, such as people and systems (Clutterbuch et al. 1993; de Chernatony & Segal-Horn, 2001).

Corporate credibility relates to the reputation that a firm has achieved in the marketplace. In a marketing context, it refers to the extent to which consumers believe that a company is able to deliver products and services that satisfy customer needs and wants (Keller in Schultz, 2000). Newell and Goldsmith define it more broadly as the *'extent to which consumers feel that the firm has the knowledge or ability to fulfil its claims and whether the firm can be trusted to tell the truth or not'* (Newell & Goldsmith, 2001).

Unfortunately, the brand management literature does not provide much conceptual discussion of the credibility construct. Most research on the topic of credibility has been done in the field of communication and rhetoric.

Credibility and rhetoric

As previously argued, consumers choose brands by corporations they trust. Credibility and trust are closely linked. According to Garver (1994), 'when *ethos* disappears, so does trust.' The discussion of *ethos,* or more popularly *source credibility,* dates back to Aristotle, who found that ethos is the most crucial factor in successful communication (McCroskey & Young, 1981).

In Aristotle's view, persuasion is created through the character (*ethos*) of the communicator, when s/he communicates in a way that establishes credibility (*The Rhetoric of Aristotle, II-15*). Aristotle found three important dimensions of ethos: intelligence or sound sense, moral character, and good will or benevolence (McCroskey & Young, 1981; Corbett, 1965). In a rhetorical perspective, the aim is therefore to create the impression by a discourse that one is a person of sound sense, high moral character and benevolence. According to Larson (1983), ethos consists of two elements, namely the persuader's reputation and delivery:

> *'Whether the persuaders are politicians, corporations, or organizations, they can all have an image or ethos, and it is based on their reputation as well as the delivery of the message.'*

Based on Aristotle's thoughts on the importance of ethos, a massive scholarly interest has been shown in the topic of source credibility, which can be defined as *'the attitude towards a source of communication held at a given time by a receiver'* (McCroskey & Young, 1981).

For the last 50 years or so, communication scholars have studied the components of source credibility intensively. However, this research has mostly concentrated on persons. This research was initiated by Hovland et al. (1953) , summarized by, for instance, Andersen and Clevenger (1963), and followed up by many others, such as McCroskey (1966), Whitehead (1968), Tuppen (1974) and Hansen & Kock (2001). The number and type of credibility dimensions vary in the studies. Typically, two or three dimensions are identified for persons: for instance, competence and character (McCroskey & Young, 1981) or competence and trustworthiness (Bowers & Phillips, 1967).

The study

The purpose of this study is to conceptualize and operationalize credibility in relation to the stakeholder perception of corporate brands. We hypothesize that the public image of spokespersons and of corporate brands can be evaluated by using the same method. Moreover, credibility may depend on different characteristics for different categories of corporate brands (Cronkhite & Liska, 1976). Hence, in trying to conceptualize a "corporate brand character", we may expect a complex, multidimensional picture to emerge. Whereas studies of credibility, or other qualitative character dimensions of communicators, tend to produce factor analysis solutions with three or, at most, four dimensions, it is natural to expect an even larger number of factors when looking at "corporate character." This is because corporations are not only communicators, however important that aspect might be, but also makers of physical products as well as sales organizations consisting of people. Thus, we hypothesize, the character of corporations is evaluated by the public along a broader range of dimensions.

Research questions

To sum up: In the present study, we want to test the following:

- Along which dimensions are corporate brands evaluated?
- How is credibility perceived when evaluating corporate brands?
- Are corporate brands perceived as more complex than persons are – so that more dimensions will appear?
- Does it make sense to evaluate corporate brand credibility by using the same method as for persons?

Method

In testing this, a large number of corporate brands should ideally be evaluated along a large number of scales. To do so would result in a questionnaire so extensive that it was feared it would probably influence the response rate and the quality of the responses. For this reason, a decision was taken to limit the study to 10 different corporate brands presented in pairs, which are related in their line of business but expected to have very different profiles.

Following the tradition of source credibility research, a battery of relevant adjectives was constructed. The adjectives were adopted from previous studies on public spokespersons primarily done by Berlo, Lemert and Mertz (1969) and Hansen & Koch (2001). Berlo, Lemert and Mertz identified 128 pairs of polar adjectives that were frequently used to describe highly acceptable or unacceptable sources. This selection was done on the basis of interviews and literature reviews. The number of adjectives was reduced to 83 by asking faculty judges to group the scales on the basis of similarity in meaning. Berlo, Lemert and Mertz identified four factors, which they named: Safety, Qualification, Dynamism and Sociability. These factors relate to the credibility of persons.

In order to adapt their study, which was concerned with the credibility of spokespersons, to this study of corporate brands, it was necessary to exclude adjectives that did not make sense. Adjectives such as stubborn, biased and intimate were therefore excluded from this study. In order to avoid too extensive a questionnaire, 38 adjectives were included in this study.

Data analysis

The study was carried out with the use of a questionnaire mailed to all new undergraduate students at Copenhagen Business School in the spring of 2001, and a total number of 169 useful responses were received (response rate 35%).

Self-rating of the respondents' awareness of the 10 corporate brands was also included in the questionnaire.

Factor analysis was conducted for each of the 10 corporate brands. Factor analysis was chosen as the data analysis method because of its function of being able to identify underlying constructs in the data. In the factor model, there is a small set of independent variables, termed factors, which is hypothesized to explain or cause the dependant variable (here: source credibility). The aim is not so much to reduce the variables but to understand the interdependent variables in relation to the perception of corporate brands and credibility. Factor analysis also identifies variables that are redundant – measuring the same construct (Aaker, Kumer, Day, 2001). The factor analysis procedure employed in this study is principal component analysis.

It appears that the solutions emerging here have significant similarity across individuals. With five factors, 30% of the total variance in the data is accounted for. The essence of this solution is shown in Table 4:1.

Why five factors? There is no clear answer as to when to stop including factors. A rule of thumb is that all included factors (prior to rotation) must explain at least as much variance as an 'average variable'. If a factor is meaningful and capable of representing one or more of the variables, it should absorb at least as much variance as an average original input variable. In this case, with as much as 38 variables, each of the five factors accounts for more than the average, i.e. here more than 3 %. In addition, Table 4:2 shows that after the fifth factor there is a 'corner' or a distinct break of the scree plot. Experimental evidence indicates that this point where the scree begins denotes the true number of factors. At the same time, the factor analysis shows that the content of the factors does not make sense when going beyond five factors.

Table 4:1 – A five-dimensional solution

	1	2	3	4	5
successful	0.70	0.02	0.02	0.05	0.00
intelligent	0.60	0.06	0.03	-0.03	0.05
strong	0.59	0.06	-0.04	0.15	0.03
powerful	0.57	0.05	-0.13	0.34	-0.04
admirable	0.57	-0.03	0.12	-0.02	-0.04
visionary	0.54	-0.03	0.22	0.01	0.15
Self-confident	0.52	0.11	-0.02	0.34	0.07
purposeful	0.47	0.21	0.27	0.03	-0.19
ambitious	0.44	-0.04	0.38	-0.02	-0.10
knowledgeable	0.42	0.17	-0.04	0.07	0.13
professional	0.42	0.41	0.00	0.08	0.08
efficient	0.37	0.23	0.16	-0.03	0.04
decisive	0.34	0.29	0.06	0.03	-0.01
serious	0.24	0.52	0.04	0.00	-0.10
organized	0.16	0.50	0.15	0.09	-0.01
responsible	0.07	0.47	-0.02	0.01	0.14
competent	0.29	0.43	0.11	-0.07	-0.07
trustworthy	0.03	0.39	-0.07	-0.08	0.17
correct	0.17	0.38	-0.01	-0.10	0.23
sensible	-0.09	0.32	0.03	-0.01	0.04
just	-0.01	0.31	-0.01	-0.07	0.15
active	0.00	0.21	0.61	0.03	0.01
energetic	0.10	0.06	0.60	0.01	0.00
colourful	0.14	-0.10	0.55	-0.12	0.18
extrovert	-0.01	0.13	0.50	0.14	0.21
cheerful	0.07	-0.19	0.49	0.03	0.26
boastful	0.17	-0.10	0.07	0.64	-0.04
arrogant	0.18	-0.14	-0.06	0.62	-0.03
aggressive	0.12	0.07	0.19	0.44	-0.24
superficial	-0.10	-0.15	0.03	0.43	0.09
authoritative	0.10	0.24	-0.06	0.42	0.04
original	0.05	0.11	0.15	0.03	0.54
capable of admitting mistakes	0.05	-0.05	0.04	0.04	0.51
warm	-0.03	0.12	0.10	0.01	0.43
honest	-0.02	0.15	-0.03	-0.06	0.42
sympathetic	0.14	0.23	0.13	-0.20	0.34
thoughtful	-0.01	0.24	0.05	0.07	0.34
open-minded	0.06	-0.17	0.10	-0.12	0.24

Extraction Method: Principal Component Analysis.

Rotation Method: Varimax with Kaiser Normalization.

One way to investigate how the 10 corporate brands are differently evaluated among these five dimensions is to calculate factor scores for the respondents on each brand, which is done in Table 4:3. This table shows how the different corporate brands are perceived in relation to the five factors. Whereas the insurance company *Tryg* is perceived as somewhat credible, this seems not to be the case for the insurance company *Top Danmark*.

Table 4:2 – Scree Plot

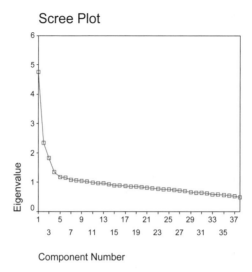

Scree Plot

Component Number

Microsoft scores very high on success and forcefulness, but very low on credibility, which is very different from the IT company *Jubii*, which is perceived as highly exuberant but not very credible.

Results

A five-dimensional solution accounts for 30% of the total variance in the data. The variance might seem low, but it can be explained by the relatively high number of initial variables (38). The solution has significant similarity across individual corporate brands. We have labelled the five dimensions *credible, successful, sincere, forceful* and *exuberant*. This set, which is shown in Table 4:5, we suggest reflects how corporations are perceived as actors in a drama where many mutually independent aspects together shape the profile of any given character. Closer inspection reveals striking instances where two corporations, even in the same industry, have markedly different strengths and weaknesses (see Table 4:4). This means that if we want a useful representation of how corporations are perceived by the public, we need an analysis of corporate character along several

Pernille Schnoor

Table 4:3 – Factor scores on the five dimensions for the 10 corporate brands

Cumulative factor scores	Factor 1 (success)	Factor 2 (credibility)	Factor 3 (exuberance)	Factor 4 (forcefulness)	Factor 5 (sincerity)
DSB, railways	-46.9289	-7.96426	-1.5123	57.24812	84.15601
SAS, airlines	50.77089	138.50256	-6.3688	-5.30379	-12.50966
TRYG, insurance	-57.1398	50.30896	-35.70028	8.41077	10.34194
SILVAN, DIY centre	-54.8908	-16.36889	11.78852	-34.51207	17.82281
GO, airlines	-40.4618	-47.68128	72.66616	-19.2098	-50.52329
TOP DANMARK, insurance	-36.2668	18.74747	-48.30261	-20.31004	-41.41174
JUBII, IT	36.90343	-114.75805	153.56481	-34.04615	30.51399
MICROSOFT, IT	254.3846	-41.11393	-64.24009	118.3205	-65.51323
POST DANMARK, postal service	-41.7527	49.78966	-45.0751	-33.00442	35.43083
BYGGEKRAM, DIY centre	-64.618	-29.46193	-36.81959	-37.59227	-8.30785

mutually independent dimensions. One or two dimensions will not suffice. Credibility, for example, may be equally high in two corporations, but for very different reasons.

Conclusion and implications

Factor scores show that the 10 corporate brands are evaluated very differently along the five dimensions, indicating that this is a powerful and distinct instrument and that managers could learn much from using it.

The study implies that this evaluation method can be used to describe a company's character (- or image) *relative* to the other companies in the analysis. The method does not provide tools to describe a corporate brand character in relation to an *ideal* corporate brand character situation. Thus, it would be interesting to evaluate brands from the same industry in order to be able to compare the individual corporate brands to the perception of the industry as a whole.

The present study has a number of limitations. Since we used existing items to measure credibility, it can be concluded that the quantitative analysis established the reliability and validity of the concepts. However, it cannot be assured that we really discovered the existence of the concepts. The next step would be to apply the questionnaire to a second sample other than students.

Table 4:4 – An example of the perception of three different corporate brands along the five dimensions

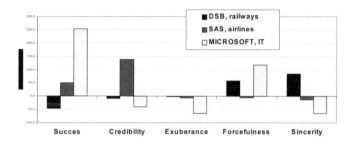

Factor scores on the five dimensions for three different brands

Table 4:5 – The five dimensions of perceived corporate brand character

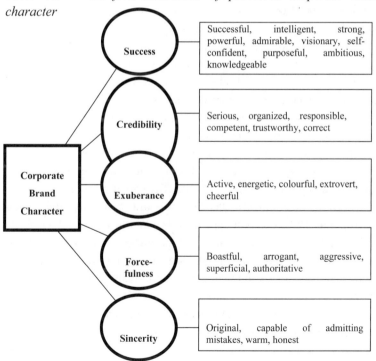

5

Barriers to e-Commerce

GORM KUNØE

The barriers to e-commerce that have an impact on young people's buying behavior on the World Wide Web (WWW) are investigated in an exploratory research design. A factor analysis is carried out to examine propositions on five barriers to e-commerce. The analysis placed the factors in the following range of importance to buyers on the WWW: (1) patience, a new term to marketing research, (2) trust, (3) motivation, (4) Internet maturity and (5) the effect of traditional shopping experience. The findings allow for a theoretical explanation on how these barriers are formed and how theories of relationship management and one-to-one communications can be used to reduce these barriers. The results indicate that companies should focus on the barriers of e-commerce as fundamental preconditions for their e-commerce strategy. The managerial implications from the barriers are extensive, serious and affect any e-commerce vendor.

E-commerce has already changed the world of buying and selling (Negroponte, 1995; McKenney, 1995). The World Wide Web (WWW) and @mail open radically new opportunities for consumers and marketers to communicate in dialogue and to buy and sell via the screen. Yet users of the Internet do not shop indiscriminately or leave private information to the vendors at will. There are profound barriers to e-commerce of significant importance to the vendors and to governments who have a keen interest in promoting e-commerce.

The e-commerce web site tries to make the virtual shop look like the shop with which we are familiar. The buyer fills a "basket", the tone of voice is polite and much is done to strengthen familiarity on the web site, with the traditional shopping environment as a model. Visible attempts are made to build relations on the WWW by collecting lifestyle and other kinds of personal information not directly connected to the purchase, in order to get closer to the customer.

As a concept the web store seems to be a flawless place to shop. Recent research has been devoted to studying how the optimal pages should look and function (Nielsen, 2000), and the web site visitor's clicking behaviour (Murphy, 1999) is engaging Web analysts all over the world. However, the users are not as frantic as the vendors, and e-commerce companies go broke every week.

Research shows (MMI, 2001) that 74% of the Norwegian respondents were deeply concerned over the possibilities of handing over their credit card number to any vendor on the Internet. As the chance of having one's credit card misused is fractional, there might be a more complex resentment or uncertainty towards e-commerce, which has passed unnoticed by the vendors. Consequently, we set out to explore the perceived barriers or barrier system to e-commerce.

We felt that a series of barriers might be inherent in the mind of the shopper, who has the good old physical shop in mind when shopping on the WWW. By revealing the barriers to e-commerce, we also gain a new perspective on our relationship building and the handling of data in a traditional shopping environment. All over the world, considerable data analysis is systematically carried out to track where and when potential shoppers leave an e-commerce web site. In an example from ACNIELSEN NetRatings[1] (March 2001), characterised as being a typical example, an American pet food store on the Internet experienced that 6% of the visitors on its web site finalised the purchase. 80% left the site before putting anything in the "basket". Of the remaining 20% who placed something in the "basket", 10% subsequently left the site. At this stage, 10% of the users still remained on the web site, who should thus be a good prospect for a purchase. This group proceeded to the payment site, of whom 4% left without paying. The remaining 6 % are buyers. The example illustrates the

---

[1] We are thankful to ACNielsen NetRating, Norway for sharing this information with us.

problem: Is this the best result the pet shop could expect? Or is it a poor outcome compared to what is happening when people visit the real store? Dog lovers seldom take a stroll through the pet food store just to have a look. They either stay outside or go inside to buy something.

Literature Review

A well-functioning relationship between seller and buyer is acknowledged as a cornerstone of marketing, and something most marketers of today want to achieve. The development of the WWW has accelerated the possibilities of being able to approach individuals by the million and still be personal and relevant. It is possible to copy the best of relationship building from real shops onto the web shop. The roots of what is sought for on the WWW and on print as One-to-One Marketing (Peppers and Rogers, 1993) are far-reaching, and should be understood by e-commerce vendors. With the paradigm shift from a transactional orientation to a relations orientation (McKenna, 1991; Gummesson, 1995), another way of influencing the customers through dialogue was presented as One-to-One communication by (Peppers and Rogers, 1993) and Dialogue Marketing by (Kunøe, 1989) using traditional methods from communication in industrial marketing in the business-to-consumer market. One of the common features of these theories is the more or less explicit "revolt" against mass communication in any media, including the WWW, and its lack of ability to establish and effectively maintain relations. Examples of different contributions on more or less the same issue include: issues on relationship selling by (Evans, 1963); relationship marketing by (Håkonsson, Johanson and Wootz, 1976), (Christopher, Payne and Ballantyne, 1991) and (Gummesson, 1995); direct marketing by (Nash, 1986), (Stone, 1988), and (Roberts and Berger, 1989); interactive marketing by (Blattberg and Deighton, 1991) in "Cyperspace", as well by Roehm and Haugtvedt; and database marketing by (Shaw and Stone, 1988). The area of dialogue marketing is represented by (Kunøe, 1989; 1998) and by (Pine, 1993). Advocates of individualised marketing and marketing communication are (Schultz, Tannenbaum and Lauterborn, 1993) and (Hutton, 1996), being examples of closely related ideas. Our research into barriers to e-commerce set out to reveal what antecedents this relationship building will have to take into account. (Van den Poel and Leunis, 1999) have studied the WWW as a channel of distribution and show that heavy users of the Internet evaluate the Internet more favourably than light users do. They also researched the risk perception and found that users have a clear notion of the risks involved in e-commerce.

We present and discuss the antecedents to the attitudes towards e-commerce by frequent and less frequent users of e-commerce. In addition, we discuss the individual barriers, present the results, and explore the implications of the results for further research and managerial practice.

The Research Agenda

In the context of this study, a barrier is defined as a relatively well-considered negative reaction of complex nature to an e-commerce offer. Using this definition, the barriers we have researched are more than temporary negative reactions to a single purchase offer. Consequently, our findings have to be taken more seriously if they are to be used as input for an e-commerce strategy than if our aim was to research minor adjustments to those web sites which cause irritation and defection. One of our research issues is the degree of the uniqueness of the WWW and e-commerce pages as commercial tools. Does the WWW constitute a new media with characteristics that make the use of traditional communication theory and models impossible? Are we in need of a particularly new approach to theories and methodologies if the WWW itself is a paradigm shift? Or is in fact e-commerce just another ordinary marketing tool, subject to the same kind of profound understanding of how to treat consumers? Our main findings fall within five barriers and are identified as *patience, trust, motivation, Internet maturity and the effect of the shopping experience.* In Table 5:1, we present the questions and the results of the factor analysis.

Patience

The term "patience" is a seldom discussed and rarely used variable in marketing research. It is a term focused on in the social cognition literature (.e.g Augoustinos and Walker, 1995) in connection with understanding the attitude-behaviour link. "Patience" as a research term should be more focused as an explanatory variable, because Internet users have their patience tried by marketers on the WWW as often as the users log on to the marketer's web site. A negative experience with a web site does not build a positive attitude towards the brand. The feelings connected to time spent in front of a computer screen can be divided into two main areas of interest to our research. One area is the positive or negative feelings connected to waiting time spent in interaction with the application. The other area is the duration of forced idleness, where one waits for something to happen on the screen. Some of this idleness is self-inflicted by the user or forced upon the user by the application. Whoever is the cause of the wasting of the user's time, the feeling of wasting one's time is a barrier to e-commerce. The term "patience" in our research is connected to the subjective reflections and reactions made by the potential buyer on the following variables:

- *Experience*: How much *time* does the individual expect to use on this kind of operation?
- *Functionality* seen from the buyer: The individual understanding of the potential buyer on how to navigate the web site should meet the competence of the individual. If it does not, the individual does not always blame him/herself for the lack of skills. Whether or not "functionality" can be seen as a barrier to e-commerce is a judgement by the potential buyer on the WWW.
- *Necessity*: The importance of the purchase has an impact on the amount of patience the potential buyer feels can be set aside for the operation. The urgency can in a "patience context" lead to an extension of patience or to the opposite, namely impatience.

In our questionnaire, "experience" and "functionality" were phrased as examples of scaling of "time spent" in the opening of an e-commerce page and the navigation. We asked how *impatient* users felt and how this affectedtheir behaviour and attitude towards e-commerce. There is a significant correlation between these two questionnaire items: *"How often are you on the Internet?"* and *"If the web site is difficult to navigate, I get easily annoyed."* The more often the respondents are on the Internet, the easier they become irritated when they have difficulty navigating the site. One could assume that frequent use would make the customer more indulgent. However, that does not seem to be the case.

The wording of our questions for the factor analysis can be found in Table 5:1.

P_1: The factor "patience" is related to the psychological state into which the user of a web site is moving when the user has spent time waiting for a web page to open and when navigating the web site. This mood raises a barrier to e-commerce.

Trust

Trust is considered a major variable in the understanding (Morgan and Hunt, 1994) of how to establish, develop and maintain successful relational exchanges in Business-to-Business. Within marketing research, trust has been subject to some research from various focus points. (Dwyer, Schurr and Oh, 1987) focused on commitment, as did (Morgan and Hunt, 1994). In our e-commerce context, trust should be viewed from the supplier's as well as from the Internet user's point of view, an interesting area of research which we have as yet had no possibility of pursuing. Our trust variable solely rests on the opinion of the user of e-commerce. (Doney and Cannon, 1997), researchers in social psychology, define trust as the perceived *credibility* and *benevolence* of a target of trust. The objective credibility is the expectance within the mind of the buyer that the other partner's word or written statement can be relied upon. The benevolence element in the definition stands for the extent to which a partner is genuinely interested in the other partner's welfare and joint business prosperity. Trust is thus a matter of not being misused either in economic matters or in other matters where one has placed oneself open to distrust. The user's perception of the seller's attitude to the possible misuse of information given in confidence, such as credit card numbers and personal information, was tested in the questionnaire. Trust consists of the reciprocity in the dyad, where the buyer delivers economic and personal data which enables the seller to withdraw money from the buyer's bank account and continue a marketing process. An intriguing difference between the trust antecedents discussed by (Doney and Cannon, 1997) is the intuitive form trust has with the buyers on the

WWW. Especially newcomers to e-commerce do not have an established relationship with their e-commerce supplier, except with their bank, and therefore are reluctant to trust what goes on in e-commerce as such. The lack of a common relational history in the buyer-seller dyad darkens the potential buyer's attitude towards e-commerce as a trustworthy way of buying products.

> P_2: Trust is a relationship building variable in a fair and reciprocal context of e-commerce trade, where valuable information and money is given in return for goods and services. Lack of trust contributes to the building of barriers towards e-commerce in the mind of the buyer .

Motivation

Motivation in an e-commerce context is the inclination of acting according to one's attitude towards the seller. In our context, to "act" means to buy something on the Internet or to register information or not. In such a concrete setting, it is possible to pose questions which are relevant to the respondent. We asked three questions: To what extent was their buying behaviour influenced by (1) the lack of visual experience with the product, (2) the intensity of the wish to try the product, and to what extent (3) did a general uneasiness towards the quality of the product influence their behaviour on the screen.

> P_3: The motivational factor consists of the extent of the perceived lack of visual experience with a product. The intensity of the wish to try the product, and the extent a general uneasiness towards the quality of the product influenced the potential buyer's behaviour on the screen, contributes to raising a barriertowards e-commerce.

Internet Maturity

The use of the Internet as a buying tool is new to many people. Norwegian research (SIFO 1999) shows that the three most preferred products purchased on the WWW were CDs, technology and data equipment. All products can be described as being of relatively inferior value, so if one was cheated, it would not matter much. The research shows that the interest in e-commerce is keen. However, the respondents distrust the vendor for having motives one would encounter among persons one did not know. (Van den Poel and Leunis, 1999) show that use itself of the Internet will relieve some of the perceived risk over time. Consequently, a variable of major importance to the use of e-commerce could be *practice* and the fact that one becomes more and more accustomed to the WWW through use. The outcome of trial and error over time construct the individual's learning curve, a curve over which the vendors on the WWW have possibilities to gain some control. This is what we refer to as "Internet maturity".

The maturity parameter has a dynamic effect on the learning curve, which constantly receives input from various sources of marketing and the use of the Internet. In order to cope with the challenge of identifying a rather intangible parameter, we asked our respondents about their feelings related to the use of e-commerce web sites. Three questions were asked about the buyer's feelings and experiences from e-commerce. The first question (1) asks how irritated the respondent becomes if the site is difficult to navigate. The second question (2) asks to what degree one defects from the site when the site seems difficult to navigate. Finally (3), we inquired about the consequence of bad experience with a web site difficult to navigate. We asked to what extent they hesitated when the experience was negative.

> P_4: Three terms can contain the phrase "Internet maturity." It can be expressed at the level of irritation when web sites are difficult to navigate. Furthermore, the extent to how quickly one leaves the site when it is found to be difficult to navigate and the extent the bad experience with a certain web site influences the inclination to log on to the vendor's web site contributes to the building of barriers to e-commerce in the mind of the buyer.

Traditional Shopping Experience

The shopping experience from real shops is one of the foremost comparisons buyers make when clicking onto a web site. We have sought to gather all the impressions from real shopping by forcing the respondent into a relational mode by recalling the shopping experience. The seller, being aware of that, tries to build a shopping environment similar to the one encountered in real shops to help the recollection of a positive, safe shopping environment. As a screen shop experience is rather different from the experience of a real shop, there could well be a barrier towards this new buying media. Other relevant comparisons on behalf of the potential buyer are experiences with other e-commerce web sites, a point we shall leave to further research.

We constructed five variables to cover some of the contents in the phrase *shopping experience*. The first question asked fathoms the respondent's attitude towards Internet shopping as such. The second and third question, respectively, concerned to what degree the wish for shopping in a real shop discouraged Internet shopping, and to what degree abstention from e-commerce is caused by general negativity towards mail order, which is a close comparison to e-commerce. We asked if the respondent did not buy on the Internet because of general uncertainty of how e-commerce functions. Finally, we asked about the importance of the security regarding personal information delivered. The following proposition was formed:

> P_5: The positive relational feeling from shopping in ordinary shops is a barrier to e-commerce and can be explained by five variables. The barrier can be identified by an expression that includes a person's general attitude towards e-commerce. The extent of preference towards ordinary shops, the degree of a positive attitude towards mail order as such, the degree of uncertainty towards how e-commerce functions, and the extent to which the respondent wishes to be free of unwanted mail after having used e-commerce, contribute to the building of barriers to e-commerce in the mind of the buyer.

Method

The research method is an exploratory, quantitative research design based on five propositions. Data were collected by a questionnaire distributed to 199 students aged 19-27 years. All studied at The Norwegian School of Marketing in Oslo. Three classes were selected for the questionnaire: One part-time class with older students all having full-time jobs, a standard class of full-time students specialising in economics, and one class from the School of Marketing. The two latter classes were approx. five years younger than the part-time class. We anticipated that there would be interesting variations between the classes, but no variations were found.

The questionnaire contained 45 questions which measured on a Likert scale from 1-7. Included in the number are six questions regarding the user's Internet access, their frequency on the Internet, as well as their gender, age and income. What we present here is the factor analysis being the quintessence of the research. Various other results of minor interest to our research are omitted.

Results

Table 5:1 shows the results of the factor analysis from questions 3, 5 and 6 of the questionnaire. The eigenvalue should be larger or similar to 1 (Kaisers' rule). When we set this as a precondition, we obtain these results in our five-factor structure.

We conducted a factor analysis on the five parameters: *patience, trust, motivation, Internet maturity* and the *effect of shopping experience*. These barriers are thought to be crucial to the way people react to e-commerce as such.

The results are presented in two ways: Statistics and cross tabulations in the text and the factor analysis in the form of Table 5:1.

The structure we obtain is statistically significant, which should meet a demand of significance >0,05. A general rule is that the larger the significance, the larger the probability that the structure is correct. The five-factor structure explains 58% of the total variance. The factor structure is based on a Maximum Likelihood Extraction.

Goodness-of-fit Test

Chi-Square	df	Sig.
79.944	73	.270

Patience is the highest ranked factor. 84% (valid percentage) of the respondents who are on the Internet daily do not want to wait for a web site to open. This is 10% more than those respondents who are on the Internet once a week. 78% of the daily Internet users and 72% of the

Table 5:1 The results of the factor analysis

	Factor 1 Patience	Factor 2 Trust	Factor 3 Motiva- tion	Factor 4 Internet maturity	Factor 5 Shopping experience
3.1) I think it is positive that one can purchase goods and services on the Internet					-.420
3.2) I think that the seller on e-commerce web sites uses my information for other purposes than I expect		.356			
3.3) It is safe to use one's credit card when buying on the Internet		-.615			
5.1) I have not been buying on the Internet because I distrust the security		.858			
5.2) I have not bought anything on the Internet because there is a risk of my credit card being misused		.927			
5.3) I have not traded on the Internet because I will not give away my credit card number		.907			
5.4) I have not traded on the Internet because I want to see the products before I buy			.770		
5.5) I have not traded on the Internet because I want to try the products before I buy			.817		
5.6) I have not traded on the Internet because I am not sure about the quality of the products			.634		
5.7) I have not traded on the Internet because I prefer to buy in a real shop					.525
5.8) I have not traded on the Internet because I do not like to buy goods on mail order					.361
5.9) I have not traded on the Internet because I am insecure about how the Internet functions					.385
6.1) If the web site is difficult to navigate when I am going to buy, I get easily irritated				.796	
6.2) If the web site is difficult to navigate when I am buying on the Internet, I easily defect and leave the site				.681	
6.3) If my experience with the navigation of a special web site is negative, I hesitate to log on again				.575	
6.4) I think it is o.k. that it takes some time to open the site when I am going to buy something on the Web	.760				
6.5) I think it is o.k. that it takes some time to find my way into the set up when I am trading on the Internet	.999				
6.6) It is important to me that the seller guarantees that I do not get any unwanted mail					-.241

weekly users disliked having to spend time navigating their way through some set-up on the page. The large majority of Internet users do not want to wait. As the patience factor is as important as it seems, the functionality of the web site should be examined very closely in order to meet customers' demand for easy and logical access. The proposition of "patience" is verified.

Trust is the second factor and has five variables connected, which is three more factors than the two contained in the factor "patience". The cross tabulation between the frequency of use (daily, weekly, more seldom) and the belief to what degree the buyer expects the vendor to misuse information from e-commerce is interesting. There are no significant differences depending on how often one buys on the web. 53% of the three highest grades on the Likert scale state that they think information is misused. One would think that frequent use of the Internet would reduce our proposition, but this is not the case. This could mean that the distrust is relatively profound and must be seriously addressed by the vendors. There is no significant correlation between the feeling of how safe it is to use one's credit card in an e-commerce transaction and how frequent the respondents trade on the Internet. Measured on the three lowest ranks on the Likert scale, 53% do not feel safe when using their credit cards in an e-commerce transaction. An interesting observation is that there is a gender difference in the attitude towards the use of credit cards for Internet purchases. 45% of those who felt that using credit cards is safe are men, while 24% of the same sample are women.

The proposition is valid. There is a relatively huge barrier of distrust towards e-commerce which blocks a normalisation of trade on the Internet. Vendors should concentrate on actions and communication about security and seek to further legislation that can punish abuse.

The third ranking of our factor analysis is the *motivation* to buy on the Internet. Our findings show that there are at least three motivators to e-commerce. The buyers want to see the products, they want to test and try, and they are not sure about the quality they get. 34% of the respondents did not answer questions related to the motivation factor. We are here at a crucial point in relation to e-commerce: the difference between selling a virtual product and the "real thing" you can test and try. We asked how important it was for the respondents that the web site was marked with a security guarantee and a money-back guarantee. 90% answered that they were interested in these guarantees. However obvious this question is, such guarantees must be taken into account, as they are keys to one of the barriers.

Gorm Kunøe

Great expectations were connected to results connected to the "*Internet maturity*" factor. Especially in times where e-commerce is taking its first staggering steps, it is interesting to research into the variables that constitute "maturity" on the Internet. The three variables analysed show that our proposition is valid.

Irritation caused by low perceived functionality on a web site will grow when the maturity variable increases. What we today excuse as teething problems to e-commerce web sites will not be tolerated in the future. And functionality will hopefully be improved on a one-to-one basis.

Discussion
Summary of Results

Overall, the results provide strong support for our five propositions and help clarify the roles of patience, trust, motivation, Internet maturity and the effect of traditional shopping experience on e-commerce. Our exploratory study indicates that (1) there are perceived barriers to e-commerce among a group of people who are in the main segment for the vendors on the WWW. These barriers are psychological and hinder the development of e-commerce. In addition, they are not connected to any special brand or organisation selling on the WWW. Our results show that the relationship between the user and the vendor on the WWW can be compared to the absence of a one-to-one relation or what one experiences in a mass marketing context. The hybrid of intimacy many e-commerce vendors of today are exposed to has little to do with one-to-one communication, dialogue marketing or relevant interactive marketing. Our findings show: (1) that instead of a strong inclination to buy on the WWW, young people feel very uneasy and refrain from buying; (2) that the "tallest" barrier found in our study is *patience,* a new term to marketing research. The users of the Internet are reluctant to try and retry a web site - as long as they think it does not meet with their expectations of navigational effectiveness and efficiency. (3), that when we view the four remaining barriers: *trust, motivation, Internet maturity* and *the effect of traditional shopping experience,* they are part of relationship management in a direct marketing context; and(4) that shopping on the WWW is new to the world, but e-commerce does not overrule important fundamentals of ordinary trade.

82

Managerial Implications

To the vendors on the Internet, the barriers explored in our study are lethal threats to their business. Patience is the most important barrier found in our study. Potential Internet buyers react when the vendor wastes their time, and now we know that they punish him by not logging on again. This must be dealt with by the vendors, and should be relatively easy to target. Increased effectiveness and better functionality, based on customer orientation and not on technical limitation, must be the goal. When a marketing organisation has a profound trust problem, as revealed in our study, the organisation must take action to remedy this situation. If the vendor wants to motivate its users to shop, the vendor must present the product to the potential buyer in a traditional way. This could be seen as a shortcoming of the virtual community where the consumer still wants to try the shoes or the shirt before making a purchase.

The motivational factor is connected to the factor that had the lowest ranking in the factor analysis, *traditional shopping experience.* Together, the two results show that potential shoppers on the Internet want to test before buying. It is then up to the vendor on the Internet to arrange for this possibility, which among others Amazon.com has planned to do by purchasing a building for a traditional bookstore.

Limitations and Further Research

The relationship marketing and dialogue marketing literature deal with the five factors analysed in our study. At the start of the second millennium, e-commerce vendors and e-commerce research seems much occupied with the right way of measuring user behaviour on web sites; a stronger focus on why people do not buy in the first place, and if they buy why they restrict their purchases to low-cost items, such as books and CDs. Further research on how the five factors interact is planned. We still do not know what happens when one factor is fulfilled, and we do not know if the five factors are interlocked, although the respondents have ranked their answers. The result of this study form part of our research programme, "Dialogue on the Internet".

6

Advertising research: a case study of Lithuanian breweries

LAIMONA SLIBURYTE & REGINA VIRVILAITE

Introduction

To act in the market successfully one has to know what motivates a consumer to buy. A number of questions have to be answered: what needs of the consumer the product or service will satisfy? How to meet his needs in a differential way and better than the competitors do? How to reach the customers? Various research - of product, market, customer, promotion strategy and effectiveness - help to find answers to these and many other questions. The latter ones can help to evaluate the effectiveness of advertising before using the means of media, during the advertising campaign or after it.

Is it necessary to analyse the effectiveness of advertising? Usually, certain goals are set for the employees to achieve. Evaluation of their work is based on employees' ability to achieve the goals. Advertising is not an exception. It is important to estimate whether the communication programme functions well and to assess its effectiveness by research. Advertising is a connective link between producer and consumer. It is an especially effective means of advertising retaining existing consumers and attracting new ones. At the same time, advertising becomes one of the most effective means of competition.

There is a constant search for ways to measure the effectiveness of advertising. By the application of various methods, both clients and agencies try to find out whether their messages are presented effectively. Some companies have chosen a research methodology most appropriate to them and also useful to the companies conducting the research.

Research conducted before advertising and after it allows for estimating its effectiveness in perspective and avoiding "costly" mistakes in the future: wrong advertising can do much harm for the image of a company and reduce demand for its production.

During the last decade, fundamental changes have taken place in the Lithuanian beer market. In order to acquire or maintain a competitive advantage, more and more often, local breweries use foreign investments. Such well-known Scandinavian breweries as Carlsberg, BBH, Olvi, Orkla, Danish Brewery Group A/S and others became the investors. The Lithuanian beer market is rather special, as it developed much more rapidly than other branches of the economy. Foreign investors not only invested in new technologies, but also generated very active competition. Today with intense competition in the Lithuanian beer market, advertising becomes one of the most important means to inform, present and generate interest, as well as convince the customer. Advertising helps the customer to choose a product, encourages the purchasing of it and acts purposefully.

Background

Lithuanian beer market analysis

The Lithuanian beer market has grown significantly within the last few years and today's per capita consumption is 59 litres. The increased beer consumption is mainly due to the economic growth in Lithuania and generally improved quality of production. Lithuania is still a growing market and an annual 5-7% increase in beer consumption is expected during the next five years.

Growth of the sector was mainly due to large foreign investment, which facilitated the renewal of the technological equipment in the breweries, improved the quality of the beer and increased sales. Foreign investment in food and beverage is the largest in Lithuania. In 2001, Baltic Beverages Holding (a Pripps-Hartwall company) invested USD56.3m in the Kalnapilis and Utenos breweries. Another world-famous brewery, Carlsberg, invested USD47.1m in Svyturys brewery.

In 1998 alone, general foreign investment in the country reached LTL764.8 million or 36.31%.

Today there are about 80 beer production licensees in Lithuania. 5% of the market belongs to the small-size breweries. Ten breweries dominate the Lithuanian beer market; their production capacity is over 20 million dekalitres. According to data from the Department of Statistics, 18.343 million dekalitres (dal) of beer was produced in 1999, which is 17.7% more than in 1998. According to data from the Lithuanian Association of Brewers, the ten largest Lithuanian breweries produced 17.681million dekalitres of beer in 1999, which is 20.3% more that in 1998.

Companies working in the Lithuanian beer market can be divided into two large groups: producers and importers (see Table 6:1).

Table 6:1 Producer companies and importer companies in the Lithuanian beer market.

Producers of beer		Importers
Main brewers	Beer brewers in rural areas	
AB Kalnapilis	Rinkuškiai	Amstel Bierbrouwerij Zoeterwoude
AB Svyturys	Senas Malūnas	Anheuser-Busch
AB Utenos alus	Panoras	Faxe bryggeri A.S.
AB Ragutis	Vilkmergė	Mast-Jagermeister
AB Vilniaus Tauras	Dalitas	Sinebrychoff
AB Gubernija	Jūsų geradarys	Holsten
AB Žalsvytis	IĮ Mintis	Ceres Breweries Ltd. Aarhus
AB Mažeikių Lokys	Stumbras	Zipfer
UAB Biržų alus	Žaldokas	Aldaris
UAB Daiga	Gesevičiaus IĮ	Tuborg
		Calsberg

Our research shows that three large breweries, major competitors, produce the largest amount of beer in the Lithuanian beer market, i.e. Utenos alus (until 1998 called Utenos gėrimai), Kalnapilis and Svyturys. Several middle-scale breweries are active in the market as well. These also compete among themselves and plan to get a bigger market share in the future. They are Vilniaus Tauras, Ragutis, Gubernija, and small-scale breweries, who mainly sell their production locally. The above-mentioned three largest breweries have the best technological and production potential. Beer brands produced at these companies are being sold in the whole of Lithuania and, as research shows, are popular among beer consumers.

Such a distribution of breweries acting in the market necessitates a further analysis. Analysis of the Lithuanian beer production market focuses on the activity of major companies (large and middle-size group breweries) in the market. We can make an assumption that small-scale companies and import, at the time of analysis, cannot make a significant impact on the competitive environment in the beer market.

The following represents the structure of the Lithuanian beer market from 1997-2001.

Figure 6:1 Structure of the Lithuanian beer market in 1997

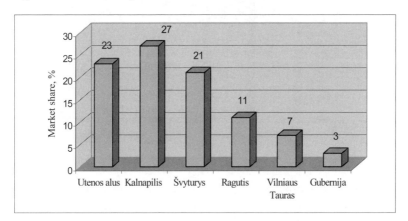

In 1997, the ten largest Lithuanian breweries produced 136.1mion litres of beer. That was 20.5% more than in 1996. Kalnapilis became the market leader by producing and selling 36.4 million litres of beer and took 27% of the market share. The Panevezys region competed with their largest brewery Utenos alus. This was due to the decreased production and sales of the latter to 31.78 million litres of beer. In 1997, the difference between the largest breweries and other breweries was quite significant. In 1997, the market share of Klaipeda's Svyturys, compared with 1996, increased from 15.5% to 21%. In the same year, Kalnapilis, Utenos alus, Svyturys and Ragutis produced 110.85 million litres of beer and all these companies together had 82% of the market. The structure of the Lithuanian beer market was a tight oligopoly with one dominant company Kalnapilis. In 1997, the company Utenos alus lost its leading position in the beer market; its market share compared to 1996, decreased from 35.1% to 23%.

The same year, most companies, not only the largest, but also smaller ones, such as Vilniaus Tauras and Ragutis redesigned their production and thus improved the quality of their beer. The modernization of production significantly affected the marketing strategies applied by the breweries.

Figure 6:2 Structure of the Lithuanian beer market in 1998.

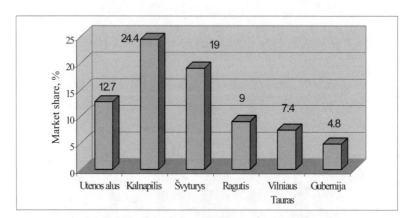

Analysis of the structure of the Lithuanian beer market in 1998 (see Figure 6:2) supports the conclusion that the structure remained the same: a tight oligopoly with strong domination of one company. Although the Kalnapilis market share in 1998, compared to 1997, decreased from 27% to 24.4%, the company remained in a leading position in the beer market.

Market shares of other large breweries decreased as well. Svyturys market share in 1997, compared with 1998, decreased from 21% to 19%, and the Utenos alus market share was only 12.7%. Such a significant decline of the market share of the brewery was influenced by the reconstruction of the company, which was aiming at increasing its production capacity. The company experienced difficulties working to full capacity.

The market shares of middle-size breweries Ragutis, Vilniaus Tauras and Gubernija increased slightly.

Figure 6:3 Structure of the Lithuanian beer market in 1999.

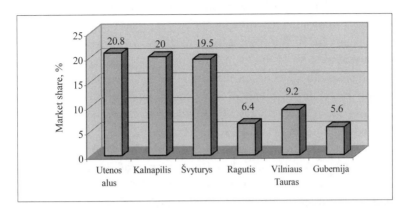

Analysis of the Lithuanian beer market structure for 1999 shows (see Figure 6:3) its change compared to the situation in the market in 1997 and 1998.

Figure 6:4 Structure of the Lithuanian beer market in 2000.

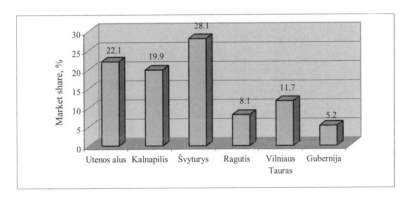

There was no one dominating company, as the market shares of the largest breweries were very similar: Utenos alus had 20.8%, Kalnapilis – 20.0%, Svyturys – 19.5%. Analysis of market shares reveals that the Utenos alus market share had significantly increased, as did the Svyturys share, while the Kalnapilis market share had decreased. We can conclude that the changes mentioned were influenced by the altered competitive behaviour of Utenos alus, namely by increased production capacity after the reconstruction and the successfully implemented strategy of market differentiation. Small-scale breweries Vilniaus Tauras and Gubernija increased their market shares, while the market share for Ragutis decreased to 6.4%.

Analysis of sales of the main Lithuanian beer producers in the year 2000 supports the conclusion that Svyturys became the market leader moving from third position in 1999 to the first in 2000 and taking 28.1% of the market. Shares of the other two largest beer producers changed insignificantly: Utenos alus reached 22.1% in 2000, and the Kalnapilis share dropped to 19.9%. Although Kalnapilis changed its marketing strategy and introduced new brands of beer, nevertheless strong competition in 2000 and weak efforts to establish the Kalnapilis image in the market influenced the decrease of its market share. The structure of the market can be described as a tight oligopoly with one dominant company: Svyturys.

Figure 6:5 Structure of the Lithuanian beer market in 2001

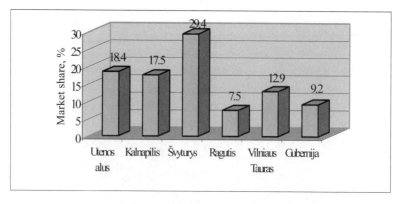

In 2000, there were no significant changes within the group of middle-size beer producers: Ragutis and Vilniaus Tauras increased their market shares up to 8.1% and 11.7% respectively, while the share of "Gubernija dropped to 5.2%.

In 2001, Svyturys remained the market leader with a slightly increased market share of 29.4%. The market structure remained unchanged – an oligopoly with one dominant company. The market share of Utenos alus dropped to 18.4%; the Kalnapilis share dropped to 17.5%. Within the group of middle-size breweries, the market share of Gubernija changed by increasing to 9.2%. The shares of the other two companies increased insignificantly: The Ragutis share dropped down to 7.5%, and the Vilniaus Tauras share increased to 12.9%.

Our analysis shows that competition between Lithuanian beer producers is very high. The main strategic investors in the Lithuanian breweries are Baltic Beverages Holding, Carlsberg, Olvi, Faxe Bryg Holding and others. The joint Finnish-Swedish company, Baltic Beverages Holding, invested in the Kalnapilis and Utenos alus breweries. In June 1999, the Danish Company, Carlsberg A/S, which owns the Estonian brewery, Koff, acquired Svyturys of Klaipeda. In September 1999, the third largest Finnish brewery Olvi acquired 49.98% of Ragutis shares. Olvi owns Estonian and Latvian breweries Tartu and Cesus. In October 1999, the strategic investor of Vilniaus Tauras became the Danish Brewery Group A/S, and at present owns 95.19% of company shares.

In May 2000, the Norwegian company Orkla announced the merge of its brewery Prips Ringnes with Danish Carlsberg, which created the largest brewery in the world Carlsberg Breweries. Orkla group owns 50% of Baltic Beverage Holding shares, which manages the Lithuanian breweries Kalnapilis and Utenos alus. Carlsberg own Klaipeda's brewery Svyturys. After the merge, Carlsberg Breweries and its companies Svyturys, Utenos alus and Kalnapilis gained the dominant position in the Lithuanian beer market.

On 14 September 2001, the Utenos alus, Jungtinis alaus centras and Svyturys companies were reorganised into one joint-stock company Švyturio-Utenos alus. This decision was made during the meeting of shareholders of the companies: Švyturio shareholders own 55.9% of Švyturio-Utenos alus shares, and shareholders of Utenos alus own 44.1%. Baltic Beverages Holding AB sold its 86.6% share of Kalnapilis brewery to Bryggerigruppen A/S (The Danish Brewery Group A/S) at a price of LTL135.1mm. Minority shareholders of whom several are employees, own the remaining share capital. "Kalnapilis was sold due to Lithuanian competition authorities insisting that in order for them to approve the merge of the activities of BBH and Carlsberg in Lithuania, the parties had to sell one of their three breweries. The ownership of BBH is divided 50/50 between Carlsberg Breweries A/S and Oyj Hartwall Abp.

On October 6, 2001 Danish brewery The Danish Brewery Group and the then owner of Kalnapilis, - the BBH company, signed the contract for the Kalnapilis shares purchase. The competition authorities permitted the Danish Brewery Group to purchase up to 100% of the Kalnapilis' shares. The Danish Brewery Group currently owns 97.72% of the shares of another Lithuanian brewery Vilniaus Tauras.

One may expect even stronger competition within Lithuanian beer companies as further investment in new technologies will take place and new products will be introduced. Also, marketing expenditure will increase. The decision by Scandinavian-owned Baltic Beverages Holding (BBH) to sell part of its assets in Lithuania will change the composition of the beer market in the country. The sale of the Panevezys-based brewery Kalnapilis will surely mean more competition that is likely to drive prices down. The main competitors in the market without any doubt will be Svyturys-Utenos alus and Vilniaus Tauras-Kalnapilis.

Trends in the Lithuanian advertising market

In 2002 the real (net) Lithuanian advertising market increased by 5.7% or LTL107m: from LTL187m to LTL197.7m, including mass media and other discount rates.

Table 6:2 Analysis of the revenues of media channels for the Lithuanian advertising market in 2000-2001, LTL m.

Channel	2000	2001	2001 %	Variation 2000/2001
Television	68	75	38	10.29
Newspapers	66	69	35	4.55
Magazines	23	26	13	13.04
Radio	17	17.7	9	4.12
Outdoor advertising	13	10	5	-23.08
Total	187	197.7	100	5.72

By comparing the Baltic advertising markets, it was calculated that Lithuania lies behind Estonia and Latvia with respect to the amount of money allocated for advertising for one inhabitant. In Lithuania

(3.491million inhabitants) one inhabitant receives Euros 16.3, in Latvia (2.375 million inhabitants) around Euros 26.1, in Estonia (1.372 million inhabitants) Euros 35 are received per inhabitant.

The company leaders in advertising in 2001 were: Colgate Palmolive, Procter&Gamble, Coca-cola, Kraft Foods, Bitė, Omnitel, Unilever, Tele 2 and Švyturys. The earnings of these companies made up an even 40% of the total revenues for TV, press, radio and outdoor advertising, calculated in gross prices (without consideration of volume and other discounts, based on official price lists in the mass media).

Figure 6:6 Distribution of Lithuanian advertising net revenue according to media channels in 2001

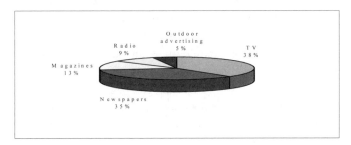

Calculation based on media channels shows that most of NET revenue last year was received from advertising on TV (38% or LTL75m), newspapers (35% - LTL 69m) and magazines (13% - LTL 26m). Radio and outdoor advertising generated 9% - LTL 17.7m and 5% - LTL 10m of revenue. The TV advertising market increased by 10.29%; magazine advertising increased by 13.04%, though outdoor advertising decreased by 23.08%. Advertising in catalogues, on the Internet and in cinemas was not considered.

Purpose of research

As our analysis shows, after remarkable changes in the beer market one might expect an even higher competition. Companies find it extremely important to learn about the main factors of competition in the market; whether advertising can play the main role in the competition for consumers; and how the customer perceives advertising.

Laimona Sliburyte • Regina Virvilaite

This research was designed to answer the following questions:

- During the process of differentiation in the Lithuanian beer market, does an interrelationship exist between the company's expenditure for advertising and its market share?
- If the relationship does exist, then how strong is it?
- How do consumers perceive advertising of beer? What brands do consumers like most and what is the basis for their choice?

Methodology

Quantitative and qualitative research methods were used for the research. To conduct correlation and estimate whether relationship exists between expenditure for advertising and owned market share, Pearson, Kendall's tau_b, Speraman's rho correlation coefficients were calculated using SPSS (Statistical Package for Social Sciences, 8; Package of analysis of numbering characteristics) statistical programme. In order to conduct a qualitative research, to research the concept, and branding of advertising, 682 consumers were interviewed. The main requirement for the sample was their actual consumption of beer. A special questionnaire consisting of open-ended and closed questions was prepared.

Findings

As our preceding analysis shows, intense competition takes place in the Lithuanian beer market. One of the methods used by competitors in an oligopoly market is the differentiation of products by the use of means of advertising. The following will analyse resources allocated for advertising in the Lithuanian beer industry in 1998-2001, as illustrated in Figure 6:7.

Our analysis shows that the Lithuanian beer market expenditure for advertising in 1998 (LTL6.7m) constituted 1.76% of total expenditure (LTL 384m) in Lithuania, and in 1999, about 2.05% (Lithuanian beer industry was LTL10.1m, total expenditure for advertising in Lithuania was LTL 496m). Comparing data for 1998 with data for 1999, it is evident that expenditure for beer advertising increased by a factor of 1.5. In 2000, expenditure continued to increase and reached LTL16.9m, which represented 9.1% of the total expenditure for adver-

Figure 6:7 Resources allocated for advertising in the Lithuanian beer market in 1998 –2001, LTL million.

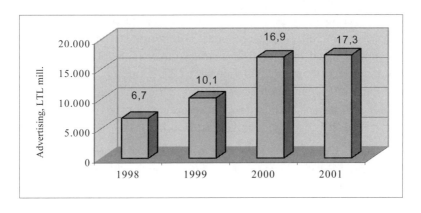

tising in Lithuania. Expenditure for advertising of the companies analysed came to LTL14.2m, which represents an even 84% of the total expenditure for beer advertising in Lithuania. In 2001, a small but still growing increase of expenditure of LTL361.200 was observed for advertising and reached LTL17.3m. Comparing data for the year 2001 with data for the year 2000, there was an increase of 8.8% of Lithuanian expenditure for advertising. The amount allocated by the major Lithuanian beer producers for advertising is illustrated in Figure 6:8.

Figure 6:8 Expenditure of the major Lithuanian beer producers for advertising in 1998-2001, LTL Million.

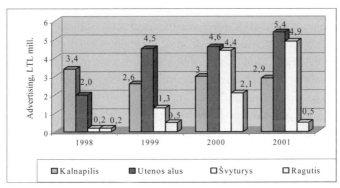

Laimona Sliburyte • Regina Virvilaite

According to the data presented in Figure 6:8, financial allocations for advertising tended to grow. In 1999-2001, Utenos alus allocated the largest amount for advertising. In the same period, Kalnapilis allocated about LTL3m. Švyturys has significantly increased expenditure for advertising in 2001, compared with 1999, from LTL1.3m to LTL4.9m. Ragutis changed its advertising strategy as well: allocations in 1999 were only LTL0.5m, in 2000 they were LTL 2.1m.

Figure 6:9 illustrates the comparative weight of expenditure of the main Lithuanian beer producers allocated for advertising within general advertising expenditure of the beer industry.

Figure 6:9 Comparative weight of expenditure of the main Lithuanian beer producers allocated for advertising within general beer advertising expenditures in 1998-2001 in percent

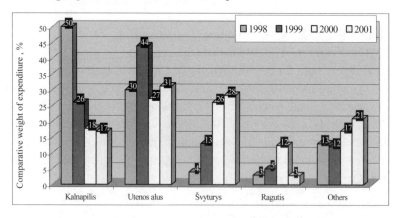

According to the data analysis, three major companies - Utenos alus, Kalnapilis and Švyturys - allocate the largest amount for advertising, which represents respectively from 28% to 50% of the comparative size. Nevertheless, it is evident that allocations are made following the chosen strategy, i.e. they can be smaller and larger if one compares different periods.

As our research shows, expenditure for advertising is one of the key actions of competitors in the oligopoly market, therefore we think that it is expedient to conduct a correlative analysis between two variables: expenditure for advertising and owned market share.

Analysis of Quantitative Data: Correlation Analysis of Expenditure for Advertising and Owned Market Share

Data from monthly periods between 1998 and 2001 of the four main Lithuanian companies in the beer market - Kalnapilis, Utenos alus, Švyturys, and Ragutis – were used for the analysis. By marking the market share with RISA98 and further marking every month, the data selection was created; expenditure for advertising was marked as SA98 and further marked every month. By applying the data in calculations, the selection was transferred to the statistics programme SPSS (Statistical Package for Social Sciences, 8; Package of Analysis of Numbering Characteristics).

The first thing undertaken was running the Kolmogorov-Smirnov test. Thus the hypothesis H(0), that distribution is normal was tested. Test results showed that this hypothesis cannot be rejected, as the level of significance α was higher than 0.05. As distribution is normal, the Pearson coefficient of correlation was applied for calculations.

Pearson's, Spearman's and Kendall's ranks correlation were used to calculate the correlation coefficients. As the results of the calculations take up sixty-three pages, only the cumulative tables are presented in the appendix in order to avoid overloading this chapter.

During the correlation analysis, numbering characteristics of the market shares and expenditure for advertising by Utenos alus, Kalnapilis, Švyturys, and Ragutis from 1998 to 2001 were calculated. The market share was marked as RIDAL, and expenditure for advertising was marked as ISL.

The results of the analysis on number characteristics of the data shows that in 1998 mean expenditure for advertising totalled LTL1,481,154.90 in 1999, LTL2,248,855.80 in 2000, LTL3,560,610.00 and in 2001, LTL3,422,376.00, and the market share was accordingly 16.275%, 16.675%, 17.55% and 18.2%. The calculated median for number characteristics shows that 50% of all companies in the market do not allocate more resources for advertising (or owned market share) than the suggested median. Calculation of mode allowed definition of the most frequent value of advertising expenditure (owned market share). By calculating the standard deviation, the value of advertising expenditure (owned market share) furthest from the average was defined. During the correlation analysis, both minimum and maximum values of analysed data were calculated. The calculation of percentiles has indicated the amount of expenditure for advertising (owned market share), namely 25%, 50%, and 75% of the companies analysed in the beer market.

Table 6:3 Pearson, Kendall's tau_b, Spearman's rho Correlation Coefficients, 1998 – 2001.

Correlation Coefficient	1998	1999	2000	2001
Pearson	0.626	0.661	0.885	0.812
Kendall's tau_b	0.667	1.000	0.667	0.667
Spearman's rho	0.800	1.000	0.800	0.800

Results of our research calculations showed that a correlation relationship of medium strong exists between advertising expenditures and market share in 1998 and 1999. As calculated, Pearson's correlation coefficients fall between ranges of 0.5-0.7. Strong correlation relationship was determined in 2000 and 2001, as the coefficients are higher than 0.7. Also, the correlation coefficients of Spearman and Kendall were calculated. The results of the correlation analysis conducted supports the conclusion that according to the Spearman coefficient, in 1998, 2000, and 2001 a strong correlation relationship existed, and in 1999, the relationship was very strong – perfect positive correlation, as the correlation coefficient was equal to 1. According to the Kendall correlation coefficient, in 1998, 2000 and 2001 the correlation relationship was medium strong, and in 1999, the correlation relationship between expenditure for advertising and owned market share was very strong.

This correlation analysis shows that there is a correlation relationship between advertising expenditure and owned market share. As the expenditure for advertising increases, the market share increases as well and vice versa. This provides a basis for the statement that the breweries who are competing in the oligopoly in the Lithuanian beer market and who are allocating more resources for advertising than their competitors can increase the owned market share. The results of the research once again confirm that in an oligopoly, market dominates a non-price competition.

Analysis of Qualitative Data: The Concept and Branding Exploration

The next question the research deals with is how the consumer perceives beer advertising. It is also very important to estimate what brands consumers prefer most and what the reason for their choice is.

When analysing the consumers' perception of beer advertising, it is important to pay attention to one of the aspects of beer consumption habits, i.e. the place or venue where the consumers like to drink beer. Only after assessment of this factor, can reasoned conclusions be made about the formation of specific product concentration towards consumer. In this respect, we are not only interested in the general analysis of the respondents' answers, but also in analysis according to age and income of the consumers. Figure 6:10 clearly illustrates the differentiation of habits of consumers of different ages.

Figure 6:10 Venues for beer consumption according to respondents' ages.

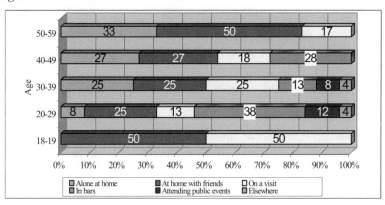

The graph analysis reflects the tendency that as the age of the group decreases, the venue for beer consumption changes as well. People of fifty most often drink beer at home or when on a visit, whereas among people of forty a tendency to drink beer in bars appears. Venues for beer consumption for people in their thirties includes attending public events and other places, though this group still represents only 20% of the total of beer consumption by this group. In the group of people of 20 to 29 years, consumption of beer in "outdoor" and "indoor"

environment (bars, public events) changes rather significantly: in consumption of beer by these respondents "outdoors" exceeds 50%.

Data for the youngest group is not objective, as the number of respondents for this group is not sufficient. Now we can return to the statement that beer consumed in an "outdoor" environment is draught, while in an "indoor" environment is bottled. This brings us to the conclusion that by targeting consumers of 20-40 years of age, it is essential to develop and implement promotion of beer sold in both shops and bars. Nevertheless, based on sales statistics, the absolute sales of draught beer are still smaller than of the bottled variety; therefore, promotion of bottled beer should remain a priority.

Figure 6:11 Distribution of beer consumption according to income

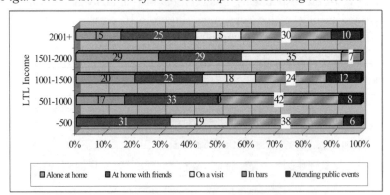

Analysis of beer consumption venue according to income of consumers also indicated certain tendencies. As income decreases, consumption of draught beer (beer consumption in bars and at public events) decreases. Nevertheless, this tendency, which was clearly observed in the lower income group, changes substantially within the highest income group: here again almost a half of the total beer consumed is draught beer. This supports the conclusion that highest-income consumers visit bars more often than public events, as they have the wherewithal to do so. However, as the largest group of consumers consists of middle-income persons (LTL1001-1500 monthly income), the habits of this group strongly affect the results of the survey. It reflects the main tendency to consume about 65% of bottled beer in an "indoor" environment.

In the case of targeting consumers with a middle income (this group of consumers is quite large and their purchasing power is rather strong), attention to promotion of bottled beer becomes very important.

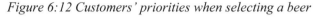

Figure 6:12 Customers' priorities when selecting a beer

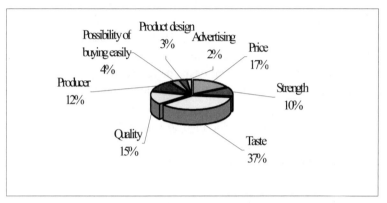

Among the criteria of analysis which helps to define the reasons for choice of beer, one of the main criteria is the taste of beer. Respondents indicated 37% to importance for this criterion. Price and quality of beer were significantly less important for consumers. It means that when choosing a beer, reputation and the good name of the producer is not that important; the consumption qualities of the product has a greater importance. This supports the conclusion that the producer has to pay a lot of attention to the improvement of taste and the qualitative factors of the beer. The second stage of these efforts (only if the qualitative parameters of the beer are sufficient) should focus on the emphasis of these qualities in advertising. The subconscious of the consumer should contain a positive image of a beer, the qualities of which are associated with a good, reliable taste and high quality. And if these characteristics transferred by advertisement prove themselves when the buyer consumes the beer, then the consumer becomes a permanent buyer of this product.

In order to understand the psychology of consumers better, analysis based on respondents' sex was conducted. The results of this analysis show that men give greater importance to the taste of beer, while women give far less importance to that. The priorities of the women interviewed have a more even distribution than men's priorities, and compared with men, the quality of beer has a critical preponderance (women give an even 20% of importance to quality). For women the price is not as important, although this can be due to the fact that women consume far less beer than men. Here again the different psychologies of the two sexes could be identified: women are more inclined to analyse factors, therefore they understand the taste of beer as a secondary expression of quality and pay more attention to the primary factor – the quality. On the other hand, men are more inclined to make decisions on a practical basis, therefore they perceive the taste of beer as its main characteristic. The fact that the producer of the beer has a greater importance for women than for men, can also serve as a proof that women are more inclined to trust the company image and advertising efforts.

An analysis to determine how consumers perceive the matching of a brand of beer with a certain slogan was conducted.

Table 6:4 Most suitable slogan to describe a beer.

Slogan	Brands of beer							
	Carlsberg	Faxe Premium	Gubernija	Kalnapilis	Ragutis	Švyturys	Utenos alus	Vilniaus Tauras
Seeking for the best	5	0.4	2.7	30.1	1.6	32.5	25.4	2.2
When did you last time…?	1.8	0.7	2.0	10.9	2.7	13.3	66.6	2.1
How are you doing?	5.8	2.7	8.4	19.7	8.3	24.9	25.7	4.6
Probably the best beer in the world?	19.4	1.4	2.2	12.2	1.9	40.2	19.9	2.7
Basketball country's beer	0.3	0	1.9	13.1	1.9	68.3	13.5	1.0
Legendary men's beer	1.1	0.6	7.2	7.6	3.1	19.7	12.9	47.8
So natural to be together	1.4	1.0	3.7	14.7	4.1	48.4	23.7	3.0
Let beer talks	2.9	1.7	10.5	13.8	25.8	17.8	18.7	8.7
Always feel certain	5.5	3.9	10.0	17.7	9.3	24.7	23.3	5.5
Danish quality	35.3	45.3	1.0	3.8	1.6	5.4	6.1	1.5

We can state that beer advertising slogans used by Utenos, Švyturys, "Vilniaus Tauras, and Ragutis were remembered best by consumers. Nevertheless, some of the slogans used for beer advertising earlier were confused: "Seeking for the best" was used in Kalnapilis advertising, while consumers attribute it to Švyturys – 32.5%.

"Probably the best beer in the world" consumers attribute to Švyturys (40.2%) although Carlsberg used it (19.4%). "Always feel certain" was used in advertising Utenos alus beer, but many consumers (24.7%) attributed the slogan to Švyturys.

This analysis shows that a clear leader is Švyturys while other beer brands, even if a little behind, are perceived by consumers differently than stressed in advertising, and this is a rather dangerous situation as some of these consumers can be lost.

As the main tool for advertising, beer producers use TV advertising, allocating for it from 60% to 80% of all expenditure for advertising. Respondents were asked what commercials they saw. The data obtained is presented in Table 6:5.

Table 6:5 Recollection of beer commercials on TV

Advertisement	Have seen the advertisement	
	Yes	No
Carlsberg fountain	17.2	82.8
Carlsberg (The beer is tipping into the mug, jottings are changing on the screen)	23.5	76.5
Švyturys ŠNARas	41.5	58.5
Švyturys – the basketball country's beer	63.2	36.8
Utena When did you last time..?	58.6	41.4

Most consumers saw the Švyturys beer commercial, and the least number of consumers saw the Carlsberg commercial. Though taking into consideration the fact that the Carlsberg commercial was not run as often as of the Švyturys one, we can make an assumption that this implies less notice being taken of the advertising ffor this brand of beer.

An analysis to estimate how the consumers liked beer commercials seen on TV was conducted.

Most respondents (57.6%) liked the commercial "When did you last time..?" by Utenos alus where well-known and popular Lithuanians were participating. Although Švyturys was mentioned as the leader in the beer market, in the category of most disliked commercials its commercial "Švyturys ŠNARas" was mentioned most often (19.7%). The latest commercial "Pure water" by Utenos alus unfortunately did not account for much popularity among consumers. The Carlsberg commercial where "beer is being poured into glass, messages change on the screen" was difficult for consumers to evaluate (49.6%). This

Table 6:6 Evaluation of beer advertising on TV.

Advertisement	How did you like the advertisement		
	I didn't like it	Neither/ nor	I liked it very much
Carlsberg fountain	17.6	44.5	37.9
Carlsberg (The beer is tipping into the mug, jottings are changing on the screen)	17.0	49.6	33.4
Švyturys ŠNARas	19.7	42.9	37.4
Švyturys – the basketball country's beer	10.4	35.4	54.2
Utena When did you last time..?	10.3	32.1	57.6

analysis shows that advertising ideas were not always successfully applied in the market. In the future, it is important to avoid similar mistakes, as consumers, who are more strongly affected by the competitors' advertising, can turn to the competitiors' product.

Our analysis of beer brands shows that there are three dominant brands in the beer market at the moment: Švyturys, Utenos and Kalnapilis. They have a similar number of consumers; only Švyturys stands out as having a larger number of loyal consumers. The strong attraction of these brands and loyalty for them shows that consumers are satisfied with the beer these companies offer. Products and images are strong, but there is a threat of reaching a stage where consumption of these brands starts to drop. Although these three brands are in a favourable market situation, their growth potential is not high. It is very important for these three brands to maintain their current consumers and put a lot of effort into paying attention to the needs of the consumers not yet attached to one particular brand.

Carlsberg is another brand in the Lithuanian beer market which has similar attractiveness and holds the loyalty of its consumers, although it has a smaller number of consumers. Insufficient possibilities of buying it and not enough familiarity among potential consumers impede the potential growth of Carlsberg. In the future it will be necessary to increase the familiarity of Carlsberg if it wishes to increase its consumers.

An analysis of unattached Švyturys consumers allows us to identify a number of their main motives: the best beer produced in Lithuania, tasty beer and highest-quality beer – all these criteria are met by

Švyturys, as are many other criteria. Utenos alus and Kalnapilis are major competitors of Švyturys. Loyal consumers of Švyturys do not consider it as an international beer, while Carlsberg takes a leading role in this respect. They also do not consider Švyturys as being suitable in a situation where there is no better beer; then they drink Ragutis beer.

Based on the results of the analysis, the most important reasons for being unattached consumers of Švyturys are: my company beer, tasty and the best Lithuanian beer. Image, campaign priorities and brand position in the market are not important for this group. Švyturys fails within such qualities as: gives peace of mind, produced from the best water, international beer. The main competitor within this segment is Utenos beer.

Situations suitable for drinking beer: in the evening, while watching TV, after stress, after work, to have a peaceful rest, to relax and as a tasty drink, to enjoy. Loyal consumers of Švyturys consider this beer as a perfect match to all these situations.

In understanding the unattached consumers, the survey reveals that the Švyturys brand fails against other brands on the following qualities: "suitable to suppress thirst" and "suitable for youth". It has a weak match with "suitable for drinking with friends"; therefore this perception has to be altered, as it is a very important part of image. Consumers associate Švyturys beer with "the basketball country's beer statement.

Research results show that Švyturys risks losing about 3.6% of the market to Carlsberg, while they can attract only about 0.25% consumers from Carlsberg. Currently Švyturys has threats from Kalnapilis and Utenos. Carlsberg and Faxe Premium can cause the main threat in the future.

According to the data from our research, the Utenos brand risks losing some of its consumers to the Carlsberg, "Faxe Premium, Kalnapilis, and Švyturys brands. The main reasons for being loyal consumers are: my company beer, tasty beer, beer I would recommend to my friend. Loyal consumers perceive Utenos beer as a perfect match with these criteria. Rather unusually Utenos beer is considered as "having international recognition" or "international beer". A clear competitor is Švyturys beer, which is closest to Utenos according to most of the qualities analysed. The main reasons for unattached Utenos consumers are: tasty beer, my company beer, light to drink, and this beer is not perceived as a good match to these criteria.

Both loyal and unattached Utenos consumers identify three main beer consumption situations: a) to relax after stress and work; b) while communicating with friends; c) to suppress thirst. Loyal consumers perceive Utenos beer as most suitable "when one wants to relax". Utenos beer is not perceived as "beer suitable to drink while watching a basketball match" and "to offer to business partners". Utenos beer is most often associated with the slogan "When did you last time...?", and most rarely with basketball.

Based on results acquired, Kalnapilis risks losing some of its consumers, who are ready to start consuming Carlsberg and Faxe Premium. Kalnapilis can attract most consumers from Utenos, also from Švyturys. Kalnapilis beer is being perceived as complying with qualities most important for loyal consumers: my company beer, tasty, giving pride. Kalnapilis is not considered an international beer or beer produced from the best water. Kalnapilis is strongly associated with the slogan "In a search for the best!" Its main competitors are the Utenos and Švyturys brands.

Analysis supports the conclusion that Carlsberg has the potential to attract a part of the market share from other brands, mostly from Kalnapilis, Švyturys, and Utenos. In this brand, consumers are looking for quality. Loyal Carlsberg consumers like both the Švyturys and the Faxe Premium brands. Unattached consumers of Carlsberg note that this beer is of high quality, tasty and international, although this is not what they want. Carlsberg is considered as a beer for special occasions. Consumers of this brand most often associate it with the slogan "Probably the best beer in the world". In the future advertising of this brand should lay stress upon requirements for taste, pride and quality.

Conclusions

Our research and the results acquired support the following conclusions.

We can state that the Lithuanian beer market, after experiencing a growth in 1999, will continue to grow this year as well, only at a slower pace. In the unanimous opinion of the market participants, this branch of industry – one of a few sectors of industry –will remain as one of the most viable branches of industry in 2002. We can forecast that the branch will continue to grow with tens of millions of Litas investment.

The Lithuanian beer market leaders should remain the same, unless Švyturys gets ahead of its competitors Utenos and/or Kalnapilis. Brewery Švyturys has a very strong position in the western part of Lithuania, and if it starts to expand more successfully to other regions, it will acquire a really large growth potential. Change of shareholders of Vilniaus Tauras and Ragutis should positively affect beer quality, marketing strategy and management of these breweries; these companies should maintain similar proportions within the beer market as they do at the moment. Šiauliai Gubernija will maintain the same market share (about 6-9%), although it has implemented large investment projects. Smaller breweries, such as Ragutis and Vilniaus Tauras, will grow at the expense of smaller breweries, only if they succeed in advertising and decreased prices. Hard times are ahead for small Lithuanian breweries – these companies will remain if at all only by having their own niche in provincial areas.

Based on our analysis we can state that the Lithuanian beer market has a tight oligopoly structure with its specific characteristics: the three largest breweries own more than 60% of the market.

Correlation analysis of the relationship between market share and advertising expenditure in 1998-2001 of Utenos alus, Kalnapilis, Švyturys, and Ragutis was determined. The results generated support the statement that a correlation relationship between advertising expenditure and market share does exist. As the Lithuanian beer market's structure is a tight oligopoly, the results of correlation analysis obtained prove that non-price means of competition prevail in the oligopoly market. One of such means is differentiation by advertising, which in fact dominates in the Lithuanian beer market.

The analysis conducted supports the conclusion that by targeting consumers of the age group between 20-40, it is important to largely develop and implement the promotion of beer sold in shops and bars. Nevertheless, sales statistics show that absolute sales of draught beer are lower than those of bottled varieties; therefore advertising priority should be given to the promotion of the consumption of bottled beer.

When targeting middle-income consumers (this group is rather large and its purchasing power is strong), we find it important to pay more attention to bottled beer advertising.

Beer which is associated with the words: good, reliable taste and high quality, must form a positive image in the consumers' subconscious. And if these characteristics, stated in the advertising, prove themselves to be true while the buyer consumes the beer, then that person becomes a loyal consumer of this product.

Analysis of beer brands shows that in the beer market currently three brands dominate: Švyturys, Utenos and Kalnapilis. They have similar numbers of consumers; only Švyturys stands out as having a larger number of loyal consumers. The high attractiveness of these brands and the attachment to them shows consumers' satisfaction with the beer. Brands and imagines are strong, yet there is a risk of reaching a stage where consumption of these brands starts to drop. Although these three brands are in a favourable market situation, yet potential of growth is not high. It is important for these brands to maintain current consumers and pay more attention to the needs of not yet attached consumers.

Analysis of attractiveness and loyalty to beer brands shows the strong market positions of Švyturys, Kalnapilis, Utenos and Carlsberg. It is evident that in this respect Švyturys is in the strongest position. Yet, all these brands, except Carlsberg do not have much potential for growth. Other beer brands - Ragutis, Gubernija and Vilniaus Tauras - have lower than medium loyalty and this is caused by problems of the product. This should receive the primary and the greatest attention.

Three market leaders – Utenos, Švyturys and Kalnapilis – share the largest market share. In order to avoid loss of market shares, these brands should focus more on current consumers instead of non-consumers. These brands have a large segment of loyal consumers, their products are strong and therefore it is recommended that they increase mass advertising. Such strengths of brands as quality, taste, patriotism (pride), and socialisation should be emphasised and presented in advertising for target groups.

Carlsberg beer is related with a different market segment. This beer is associated with quality, taste, internationalisation, and elitism. This brand still has a considerably small number of consumers; therefore, it is important to increase the familiarity of the brand by increasing advertising and by stressing its positive qualities.

Appendix

Correlations

		RIDAL98	RIDAL99	RIDAL00	RIDAL01	ISL98	ISL99	ISL00	ISL01
RIDAL98	Pearson Correlat	1,000	,675	,586	,557	,626	-,009	,190	,311
	Sig. (2-tailed)	,	,325	,414	,443	,374	,991	,810	,689
	N	4	4	4	4	4	4	4	4
RIDAL99	Pearson Correlat	,675	1,000	,888	,759	,583	,661	,804	,886
	Sig. (2-tailed)	,325	,	,112	,241	,417	,339	,196	,114
	N	4	4	4	4	4	4	4	4
RIDAL00	Pearson Correlat	,586	,888	1,000	,971*	,169	,403	,885	,910
	Sig. (2-tailed)	,414	,112	,	,029	,831	,597	,115	,090
	N	4	4	4	4	4	4	4	4
RIDAL01	Pearson Correlat	,557	,759	,971*	1,000	-,023	,188	,810	,812
	Sig. (2-tailed)	,443	,241	,029	,	,977	,812	,190	,188
	N	4	4	4	4	4	4	4	4
ISL98	Pearson Correlat	,626	,583	,169	-,023	1,000	,511	,054	,206
	Sig. (2-tailed)	,374	,417	,831	,977	,	,489	,946	,794
	N	4	4	4	4	4	4	4	4
ISL99	Pearson Correlat	-,009	,661	,403	,188	,511	1,000	,676	,718
	Sig. (2-tailed)	,991	,339	,597	,812	,489	,	,324	,282
	N	4	4	4	4	4	4	4	4
ISL00	Pearson Correlat	,190	,804	,885	,810	,054	,676	1,000	,987*
	Sig. (2-tailed)	,810	,196	,115	,190	,946	,324	,	,013
	N	4	4	4	4	4	4	4	4
ISL01	Pearson Correlat	,311	,886	,910	,812	,206	,718	,987*	1,000
	Sig. (2-tailed)	,689	,114	,090	,188	,794	,282	,013	,
	N	4	4	4	4	4	4	4	4

*·Correlation is significant at the 0.05 level (2-tailed).

Correlations

			RIDAL98	RIDAL99	RIDAL00	RIDAL01	ISL98	ISL99	ISL00	ISL01
Kendall's tau_	RIDAL98	Correlation Coeffic	1,000	,333	,333	,333	,667	,333	,000	,000
		Sig. (2-tailed)	,	,497	,497	,497	,174	,497	1,000	1,000
		N	4	4	4	4	4	4	4	4
	RIDAL99	Correlation Coeffic	,333	1,000	,333	,333	,667	1,000*	,667	,667
		Sig. (2-tailed)	,497	,	,497	,497	,174	,042	,174	,174
		N	4	4	4	4	4	4	4	4
	RIDAL00	Correlation Coeffic	,333	,333	1,000	1,000*	,000	,333	,667	,667
		Sig. (2-tailed)	,497	,497	,	,042	1,000	,497	,174	,174
		N	4	4	4	4	4	4	4	4
	RIDAL01	Correlation Coeffic	,333	,333	1,000*	1,000	,000	,333	,667	,667
		Sig. (2-tailed)	,497	,497	,042	,	1,000	,497	,174	,174
		N	4	4	4	4	4	4	4	4
	ISL98	Correlation Coeffic	,667	,667	,000	,000	1,000	,667	,333	,333
		Sig. (2-tailed)	,174	,174	1,000	1,000	,	,174	,497	,497
		N	4	4	4	4	4	4	4	4
	ISL99	Correlation Coeffic	,333	1,000*	,333	,333	,667	1,000	,667	,667
		Sig. (2-tailed)	,497	,042	,497	,497	,174	,	,174	,174
		N	4	4	4	4	4	4	4	4
	ISL00	Correlation Coeffic	,000	,667	,667	,667	,333	,667	1,000	1,000*
		Sig. (2-tailed)	1,000	,174	,174	,174	,497	,174	,	,042
		N	4	4	4	4	4	4	4	4
	ISL01	Correlation Coeffic	,000	,667	,667	,667	,333	,667	1,000*	1,000
		Sig. (2-tailed)	1,000	,174	,174	,174	,497	,174	,042	,
		N	4	4	4	4	4	4	4	4
Spearman's rh	RIDAL98	Correlation Coeffic	1,000	,400	,400	,400	,800	,400	,200	,200
		Sig. (2-tailed)	,	,600	,600	,600	,200	,600	,800	,800
		N	4	4	4	4	4	4	4	4
	RIDAL99	Correlation Coeffic	,400	1,000	,400	,400	,800	1,000**	,800	,800
		Sig. (2-tailed)	,600	,	,600	,600	,200	,	,200	,200
		N	4	4	4	4	4	4	4	4
	RIDAL00	Correlation Coeffic	,400	,400	1,000	1,000**	,200	,400	,800	,800
		Sig. (2-tailed)	,600	,600	,	,	,800	,600	,200	,200
		N	4	4	4	4	4	4	4	4
	RIDAL01	Correlation Coeffic	,400	,400	1,000**	1,000	,200	,400	,800	,800
		Sig. (2-tailed)	,600	,600	,	,	,800	,600	,200	,200
		N	4	4	4	4	4	4	4	4
	ISL98	Correlation Coeffic	,800	,800	,200	,200	1,000	,800	,400	,400
		Sig. (2-tailed)	,200	,200	,800	,800	,	,200	,600	,600
		N	4	4	4	4	4	4	4	4
	ISL99	Correlation Coeffic	,400	1,000**	,400	,400	,800	1,000	,800	,800
		Sig. (2-tailed)	,600	,	,600	,600	,200	,	,200	,200
		N	4	4	4	4	4	4	4	4
	ISL00	Correlation Coeffic	,200	,800	,800	,800	,400	,800	1,000	1,000*
		Sig. (2-tailed)	,800	,200	,200	,200	,600	,200	,	,
		N	4	4	4	4	4	4	4	4
	ISL01	Correlation Coeffic	,200	,800	,800	,800	,400	,800	1,000**	1,000
		Sig. (2-tailed)	,800	,200	,200	,200	,600	,200	,	,
		N	4	4	4	4	4	4	4	4

*.Correlation is significant at the .05 level (2-tailed).

**.Correlation is significant at the .01 level (2-tailed).

7

Advertising and the Prominence of the Corporate Brand

Identifying Brand Architecture Use through Content Analysis

KIM CRAMER, PETER C. NEIJENS & EDITH G. SMIT

The corporate brand has become increasingly important in today's markets and society. Not only do corporate brands provide companies with competitive advantages, they also represent the way in which companies behave towards society. Products and brands have been fulfilling consumers' needs for quite some time, but now, as markets are full of interchangeable products and brands, consumers increasingly look for distinguishing companies. Companies use a corporate branding strategy - that is, a strategy in which the corporate brand plays a central role - to radiate reliability, innovativeness, or social responsibility, for example. Consumers use such company associations to evaluate the company. This evaluation is often referred to as the corporate image. Consumers' evaluations of the company's products and services are generally considered to be moderated by this corporate image and vice versa; the product evaluations influence the image of the corporate brand. This process is called brand value transfer or association transfer (e.g., Brown & Dacin 1997; Keller & Aaker, 1992; Wansink, 1989; Yoon, Guffey & Kijewski, 1993). The influence of the corporate image on the evaluation of a company's products or services partly depends on the degree with which the corporate brand is visible in the communication of products or services, e.g. advertising. A prominently visible corporate brand increases the brand value transfer effect, because it provides easier access to the corporate associations that are present in consumers'

Kim Cramer • Peter C. Neijens • Edith G. Smit

minds (Berens & Van Riel, 2001). This indicates that if companies want consumers to transfer corporate associations to the company's products or services, they should show their corporate brand name in product advertising. However, as Herbig and Milewicz (1995, p. 9) say, using the corporate brand "may be counterproductive if buyers see no meaningful relationship between the old and new business and brand reputation transference is not successful." The effect that a negative product evaluation has on the corporate brand has been studied under the name *dilution* (e.g., Ahluwalia & Gürhan-Canli, 2000; Milberg, Whan Park, & McCarthy, 1997; Roedder John, Loken, & Joiner, 1998). To reduce the risk of dilution, companies should try to prevent the transfer of associations by not using the corporate brand in product advertising.

In spite of the growing importance of corporate branding, there is not much research explaining the determinants and effects of corporate branding. However, for managers to understand how corporate branding can benefit their companies, it is important to have insight into both the determinants and effects of corporate branding, and in the actual prominence of the corporate brand in the company's communication.

In this study, we have used content analysis to investigate the prominence of corporate brands in the advertisements of companies operating in two service markets: the temporary labor market and the financial services market (banks and insurance companies). By looking at the brand architecture used in each advertisement - that is, the combination of brands representing a product or service -, we learned whether or not the corporate brand was used, and if so, how prominent it was. We also investigated the factors that influence the use of certain brand architectures. To the best of our knowledge, no previous studies have analyzed advertising contents from the perspective of brand architecture. With this study, we aim to contribute to the existing branding literature by investigating corporate brand prominence and discovering determinants of corporate branding. Our central research question is: Which factors determine the prominence of the corporate brand in advertising?

Three questions further develop the central research question:

RQa: Which brand architectures are used in advertising?
RQb: To what degree is the corporate brand visible in advertising?
RQc: Which factors are connected with corporate brand prominence?

First, we will present a short overview of the relevant literature in the field of corporate branding and its determinants. Second, we will present our content analysis of brand architectures in advertising. Third, we will look at previous studies in which we used desk research and interviews to uncover the factors that influence the brand portfolio strategies of the selected companies in the temporary labor market and the financial services market (Blom & Cramer, 2002; Cramer, 2001). We will be linking the data of these studies with the data of the content analysis to find determinants that are connected with corporate brand prominence in advertising. Finally, we will discuss our findings.

Corporate Branding

There are two viewpoints when looking at corporate branding: the viewpoint of corporate image (e.g., Brown, 1998; Maathuis, 1999; Van Riel, 1994) and the viewpoint of brand portfolio management (e.g., Laforet & Saunders, 1999). In this section, we will first look at the corporate brand from the viewpoint of corporate image, and then the viewpoint of brand portfolio management.

The Role of the Corporate Brand in Corporate Image

The first builders of - what we now call - corporate image were architects and designers. By integrating the design of indoor and outdoor furniture, equipment, and trademarks of shops in the late 1800's, they attempted "to influence people's perceptions of a company through consistent presentation of the company to its various publics" (Brown, 1998, p. 216). Since the late 1950's, the notion of the existence of corporate identity and personality has existed in the industry; however, there has been some debate in the marketing literature about the definition of the corporate image concept. Related concepts like corporate reputation, corporate identity, corporate personality, and brand image, make it hard to define corporate image, because it is not clear what the differences and similarities between the concepts are (see Brown (1998) and Patterson (1999) for an overview of related concepts and definitions). Brown (1998) observes three key characteristics of corporate image: first, it exists in the minds of individuals and may differ from individual to individual; second, there are different audiences for any company, such as consumers, financial analysts, and shareholders; third, various psychological phenomena are believed to form a corporate image. For example, some authors think of corporate image as a person's perception of a company (e.g., Carlson, 1963; Gronroos, 1984), or a mental picture (e.g., Britt, 1971; Hardy, 1970). Others include feelings, attitudes, or evaluations of a company in their definition of the concept (Barich & Kotler, 1991; Keller, 1993). To circumvent the definitional confusion, Brown and Dacin (1997) refer to corporate associations as a collective label for all the information individuals have about a company, be it cognitive, affective, or evaluative.

The services marketing literature has paid little attention to the concept of corporate image (De Ruyter & Wetzels, 2000). This is surprising because the intangibility of services leads to a greater dependency on company reputation than tangible products that can be evaluated on the basis of look, feel, taste, and smell. According to De Chernatony and Dall'Olmo Riley (1999), consumers use the company's size and reputation as criteria for service quality.

The lack of attention for corporate image and service branding as concepts in the service literature can be explained by the fact that, traditionally, the service industries have not been very brand-oriented (Camp, 1995). For example, consumers do not often regard the names of financial companies as (corporate) brand names (Kapferer, 1995). This is illustrated by the fact that no financial company is listed in the top ten, or even twenty, of the world's most valuable brands (Day, 1997).

A good reputation is important for companies, especially service companies, to have consumers evaluate the company and its products and services positively. One strategy for reputation building is the use of corporate branding: "the process of creating and maintaining a favorable reputation of the company and its constituent elements, by sending signals to stakeholders using the corporate brand" (Maathuis

1999, p. 5). 'Constituent elements' can e.g. be business units, subsidiaries, products and services of the company. Stakeholders are people or groups that have a relationship with the company, such as consumers, shareholders, suppliers, retailers, trade organizations, journalists, regulators, and organizational members. Harris and De Chernatony (2001) add that, to create this favorable reputation, the messages about the brand identity should be consistent and the delivery uniform across all stakeholder groups.

Figure 7:1 Relationship between brand portfolio strategy and corporate brand prominence.

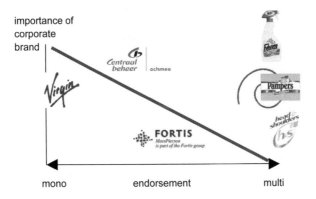

The Role of the Corporate Brand in Brand Portfolio Management

If we look at corporate branding from the second viewpoint, brand portfolio management, we find that the role of the corporate brand varies across different brand portfolio strategies. A brand portfolio consists of a company's brands, products, and services. To manage a brand portfolio effectively, managers must make, implement, and monitor choices regarding the number of and relationships between brands, products, and services (Den Engelsen & Hurts, 2001). In general, three brand portfolio strategies are distinguished in the literature (Douglas, Graig, & Nijssen, 1997; Kapferer, 1992; Olins, 1989; Van Riel, 1994). In a mono brand strategy, the corporate brand name is used for all products and services of the company. In a multi brand strategy, every product or service has its own individual brand name. In an endorsement strategy, a product or service combines its own individual brand name with the corporate brand name. Some authors distinguish several forms of endorsement branding, for example dual branding (Franzen, 2000; Laforet & Saunders, 1999), or weak versus strong endorsement (Berens & Van Riel, 2001). With dual branding, the individual brand and the corporate brand are combined with equal emphasis on both brands. A weak endorsement is characterized by less emphasis on the corporate brand, while a strong endorsement is characterized by more emphasis on the corporate brand. The mono endorsement and multi brand strategies thus form a continuum, with the corporate brand being less important towards the direction of multi branding. Figure 7:1 shows the relationship between brand portfolio strategy and corporate brand prominence.

Virgin is a classic example of a company that uses a mono brand strategy. All Virgin products or services, be it airline companies, wedding dresses, or holidays, wear the Virgin brand name, sometimes accompanied by a label (e.g., Virgin Atlantic, Virgin Brides, or Virgin Holidays). Sometimes it is accompanied by a label, like Virgin Brides, but it is always Virgin. To the right side of the continuum, an example of dual branding is Centraal Beheer Achmea (Centraal Beheer is an insurance brand of the Achmea company). An example of endorsement branding is the way the individual Fortis brand MeesPierson is connected to Fortis, by mentioning that MeesPierson is part of the Fortis group. An example of a company that uses a multi brand strategy is Procter & Gamble. Most of their products have their own individual brand name. The corporate Procter & Gamble brand is not prominently visible.

Determinants of Corporate Brand Prominence

Several authors have investigated the factors that influence marketing, advertising and branding strategies (Aaker, 1996; Cramer, 2000, 2001; Kapferer, 1992; Keller, 1998; Kotler & Armstrong, 1993; Laforet & Saunders, 1999; Maathuis & Van Riel, 1996; Van Riel & Berens, 2000). Kotler and Armstrong (1994, p. 69) define the marketing surroundings of a firm as "the actors and forces that are not part of marketing itself, but which have an influence on the success of the transactions between the company and its target groups". Figure 7:2

presents an overview of the factors mentioned in the literature, categorized into three groups: characteristics of the company, objectives of the company, and environment of the company. The objectives of the company can sometimes be determinants and effects at the same time, as indicated by the dashed arrow. For example, a company's wish to increase employee involvement may be a determinant leading to a mono brand strategy (strong corporate brand prominence), but employee involvement may also be an effect, evolving from a mono brand strategy.

In our study, it was not possible or feasible to test all expectations about the factors that determine the corporate brand prominence, as presented in Figure 7:2. For example, we could not test the expectation that companies in homogeneous markets use their corporate brand more prominently than companies in heterogeneous markets, since both the temporary labor market and the financial services market are homogeneous. In this paper, we investigated three factors on the basis of which the companies could be distinguished and which managers of the companies regard as highly important: available budget, degree of fit between products and core business, and globalization. Available budget and degree of fit between products and core business belong to the category 'characteristics of the company'. Globalization belongs to the category 'objectives of the company'. Our previous studies (Blom & Cramer, 2002; Cramer, 2001) gave us insight into these independent variables belonging to the selected companies. The three factors will be briefly introduced.

Advertising Budget

One of the factors influencing brand portfolio strategy is the available budget for brand development and communication. Building and supporting a brand is extremely expensive; building and supporting more than one brand is even more expensive. Cost efficiency often leads to mono branding, because this brand portfolio strategy reduces the costs of supporting the brand. The investments in production, design, packing, and advertising need to be done for only one brand, allowing the company to promote all of its products, while advertising only one (Murphy, 1987). Therefore, we expect that companies with small advertising budgets make more use of corporate branding than companies with large advertising budgets (H1).

Figure 7:2. Determinants of corporate brand prominence.

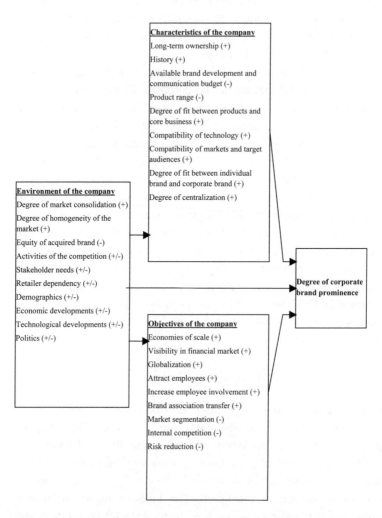

(+) Positive relationship. For example: the higher the degree of centralization, the higher the degree of corporate brand prominence.
(-) Negative relationship. For example: the wider the product range, the lower the degree of corporate brand prominence.
(+/-) Neutral relationship. For example: if the competition moves towards mono branding, the company can either follow or not; there is no clue about the direction of the influence.

Degree of Fit between Products and Core Business

Fit is one of the most discussed concepts in the literature on brand portfolio management. The concept of fit is defined in many different ways by different authors (e.g., Aaker & Keller, 1990; Franzen & Van den Berg, 2002; Loken & Roeder John, 1993, Sheinin, 1998). In general, it means similarity between two phenomena. Aaker and Keller (1990) distinguish three components of fit: Complement (the extent to which consumers view two product classes as complements), Substitute (the extent to which consumers view two product classes as substitutes) and Transfer (the perceived ability of a firm operating in a product class to make a product in another product class). In contrast to Aaker and Keller, Loken and Roedder John (1993) do not explicitly define fit, but use the concept of typicality of brand extensions to relate to the same concept. When a new product is introduced under an existing brand name (brand extension), consumers may perceive this product as either typical or atypical for the family brand. This interpretation mostly resembles the Transfer component of fit: does the new product or service logically match the company's core business? For financial services, Blom and Cramer (2002) suggest a continuum that ranges from banking services, via *all finance* services (both banking and insurance services), to insurance services. Companies can be placed on this continuum according to their core business; they are originally banks or insurance companies. Some companies diverge from their original core business and move towards the all finance position in the middle of the continuum, which reduces fit.

When a new product is introduced under its own individual brand name, it may still be desirable to link it to the company by means of endorsement branding. Additionally, a different kind of fit is in question here: the fit between the individual brand and the corporate brand. If the values of both brands do not match, endorsement branding is less used. An example that illustrates the importance of matching brand values is Nutricia, a firm that sells children's nutrition, medical food supplements, and natural foods. The natural foods have the brand name Zonnatura. Nutricia does not endorse them, because the brand values of Zonnatura – 'as natural as possible, no additives' – do not match with those of Nutricia: 'added vitamins' (Hoogeweegen, 2000).

Kim Cramer • Peter C. Neijens • Edith G. Smit

In our study, we focus on the meaning of fit as the degree in which the services provided by the company match its core business. We expect that companies with a range of different kinds of services (low degree of fit between product and core business) make less use of corporate branding than companies with similar services (large degree of fit between products and core business) (H2).

Globalization

Due to political and economic integration, a growing global market infrastructure and the growing mobility of consumers and other stakeholders, geographic boundaries are fading (Douglas, Craig, & Nijssen, 2001). This has led companies to increase global activities. If globalization is an objective, companies generally use one brand name to be strongly represented all over the world. Therefore, we expect that companies with global activities make more use of corporate branding than companies that are not globally active (H3).

Study

To answer the central research question, which factors determine the prominence of the corporate brand in advertising, we conducted a quantitative content analysis. Here our aim was to answer the first two questions: RQa) which brand architectures are used in advertising? and RQb) to what degree is the corporate brand visible in advertising? In the content analysis, we used companies' advertising messages as the units of analysis. Second, we connected the data of the content analysis with information about the companies' budget, degree of fit between products and core business and global activity, which we obtained through desk research and interviews with managers in previous studies (Blom & Cramer, 2002; Cramer, 2001), to answer the third question: RQc) which factors are connected with corporate brand prominence?

Corporate Brand Prominence: Content Analysis
Sample

Advertisements from eighteen companies that appeared in various media during a one-year period (from July 2000 to August 2001) were analyzed. The companies were selected within two Dutch markets: the temporary labor market (7 companies) and the financial services market (11 companies). The selection of markets and firms had already been carried out in our previous related studies concerning the determinants of brand portfolio strategies (Blom & Cramer, 2002; Cramer, 2001). We selected service markets because branding research has principally focused on physical goods, leaving the possible problems and challenges of service branding unexplored. Both the temporary labor and the financial services market have easily identifiable leading firms. Recent brand changes in these markets made it relatively easy to identify underlying considerations while interviewing the managers. Only firms that operate and advertise on a national scale were selected; most companies operate worldwide or mainly in Europe. The selected period for the content analysis corresponds with the period during which managers were interviewed about the determinants of their company's brand portfolio strategy (Blom & Cramer, 2002; Cramer, 2001).

The advertisements were gathered with the help of an advertising agency (PPGH/JWT), using a national advertising database and an archive of print ads. The media in which the advertisements appeared were television, radio, newspapers, consumer magazines, trade magazines, and outdoor media. Almost every company advertised more than one brand. The sample we took contained one advertisement per brand per medium. We decided to select the most expensive advertisement that had appeared most frequently, assuming that both costs and frequency indicate the importance of the ad. The sampling procedure led to a sample of 368 ads.

Codebook

A codebook containing 33 variables was used to analyze the advertisements (see Appendix A). To determine the brand architectures used (RQa), we looked at the number of brands, the nature of the brands, and the combinations of brands. To specify the number of brands within an advertisement, we simply counted and listed the brands (variable no. 17 in the code book). To define the brands' nature, the brands were included in one of the categories 'corporate brand', 'individual brand', 'sub brand', or 'label'[1] (variable no. 20). To determine how brands were combined, we listed the (parts of) sentences in which two or more brands were mentioned (nos. 29 and 30). Also, coders included the advertisement in one of fifteen brand architecture categories, as identified in Box 1 (no. 33). Kok (1997) presents four categories: 1) corporate brand; 2) corporate brand with support from product brand; 3) product brand with support from corporate brand; 4) product brand. Several other authors also suggest such a typology of possible brand combinations, most of them being quite comparable (Bath, Kelley, and O'Donnell, 1998; Saunders & Guoqun, 1996; Van Riel & Berens, 2000). Franzen (2000) distinguishes seven variants of brand combinations, featuring main brands, endorsement brands, sub brands, and labels. To be able to analyze the advertisements as precisely as possible, we combined and adapted the various categories, resulting in the brand architecture typology presented in Box 1.

In the first category, an individual brand is used as a stand-alone brand. This type of brand does not necessarily need or want support from the company behind it. Consequently, with individual branding the corporate brand is not present in the advertisement. An example is 'Visa Cards'[2]. A sub brand or a label, or both, may accompany the individual brand. A sub brand is a subordinate brand that is added to a main brand (corporate or individual). It adds meaning to the brand combination (Franzen, 2000), but it is never used alone. An example is 'Visa Cards FlexInvest', in which FlexInvest is a sub brand representing a flexible form of investing money. The difference between sub brands and labels is that a label is not a brand. A brand is the property of the company, while a label is 'everyday language', which cannot be claimed (Franzen, 2000). It is a generic description that helps to identify a product, e.g. 'Visa Cards Business' (category 1c) or 'Visa Cards FlexInvest Business' (category 1d). In this case, the addition 'Business' is not a brand, but it explains that this product is especially meant for the business user. In the second category, the individual brand is visibly supported (endorsed) by the corporate brand, e.g. 'Visa Cards is a member of Fortis' or 'Visa Cards by Fortis'. The emphasis is on the individual brand. Sub brands and labels may be used to further identify the products or services. In the third category, dual branding, the emphasis is on both the individual and the corporate brand, as is the case with 'Visa Cards Fortis' or 'Fortis Visa

Cards'. It is obvious that in this case a choice must be made as to which brand should be mentioned first and which last.

Box 7:1. Brand Architecture Typology

1) Individual branding
    a) Only individual brand
    b) Individual brand + sub brand
    c) Individual brand + label
    d) Individual brand + sub brand + label
2) Endorsement branding (emphasis on individual brand)
    e) Corporate brand + individual brand
    f) Corporate brand + individual brand + sub brand
    g) Corporate brand + individual brand + label
    h) Corporate brand + individual brand + sub brand + label
3) Dual branding (emphasis on both brands)
    i) Corporate brand + individual brand
    j) Individual brand + corporate brand
4) Corporate branding
    k) Corporate brand + sub brand
    l) Corporate brand + label
    m) Corporate brand + sub brand + label
    n) Only corporate brand

The emphasis on each brand is thus not exactly the same (the first brand being more emphasized than the last). In the last category, the corporate brand is used, with or without additions. An example of category 4n would simply be: Fortis.

The four main brand architecture categories correspond with the three brand portfolio strategies (mono, endorsement, and multi brand strategy). If a company uses a mono brand strategy, we expect that only the corporate brand is used in the company's advertisements. So, the advertisements are expected to be included in category 4. In case of a multi brand strategy, we expect that the advertisements contain only individual brands (category 1). In case of an endorsement strategy, we expect that a combination of the corporate brand and the individual brand is used. This is the case in both category 2 (endorsement branding) and 3 (dual branding).

Kim Cramer • Peter C. Neijens • Edith G. Smit

The prominence of the brands, with special attention on the corporate brand (RQb), was measured in two ways: objectively and subjectively. The objective variables were: the frequencies with which the brand(s) were verbally and visually used, the duration of the use (in seconds)[3], whether or not a logo was shown, the relative size of the brand(s), the physical position of the brand, and the colors used (no. 21 to 27). If a brand is most often mentioned orshown, and if it is shown the longest, the biggest, in a prominent position, and intensely colored, it can be considered the most important brand of that ad. In addition, in a more direct but also more subjective way, the coders were asked to identify the most prominent brand (no. 31) and to classify the degree of prominence of the corporate brand on a 5-point scale (from 'not at all prominent' to 'very prominent', no. 32).

Other variables in the codebook were, among others, market, company, advertising medium, appearance frequency, and the mentioning of a specific product or service in the ad.

Three coders were instructed. After testing the validity and usability of the codebook, each of the coders encoded a part of the sample. To determine inter-coder reliability, 60 ads (16 % of the total number of ads) were encoded by all coders.

Company Information: Desk Research and Interviews

It was not possible or feasible to test all expectations about the factors that determine the corporate brand prominence, as presented in Figure 7:2. For example, we could not test the expectation that companies in homogeneous markets use their corporate brand more prominently than companies in heterogeneous markets, since both the temporary labor market and the financial services market are homogeneous. We chose to use three factors based on which the companies could be distinguished and which the company managers regard as highly important: advertising budget, degree of fit between products and core business, and globalization. Previous studies, in which we interviewed the managers of the eighteen companies after extensive desk research (Blom & Cramer, 2002; Cramer, 2001), gave us insight into these variables of the selected companies. First, to test the assumption that globally active companies make more use of corporate branding than companies that are not globally active, we categorized the companies according to whether they were globally active or not. Companies were categorized as globally active if (most of) their brands, and their corporate brand as a minimum, were represented around the world. Second, we expected companies with large budgets to make more use of individual branding than companies with small budgets. Therefore, we categorized the companies as having either a large advertising budget or a small advertising budget, based on the total advertising expenditures in guilders, in the selected one-year period. Third, we expected that companies with a range of different kinds of services (low degree of fit between product and core business) would make more use of individual branding and less use of corporate branding than companies with comparable services (large degree of fit between products and core business). To categorize the companies, we used the continuum for financial services suggested by Blom and Cramer (2002), which ranges from banking services, via *all finance* services (both banking and insurance services), to insurance services. Companies providing only banking services or only insurance services were both categorized as offering comparable services (fit). Companies providing both banking and insurance services (all finanz services) were categorized as offering different kinds of services (no fit). In the temporary labor market, only a few companies provide other services than temporary labor, for example education, childcare, and cleaning services. These companies were categorized as having a low degree of fit between products and core business.

Results

Inter-coder reliability was established using Cohen's Kappa[4]. When Kappa values were low, the coders reconsidered their coding performance together and decided which was the best value for the variables in specific cases. However, after that, some variables still had very low Kappa values (<.65) and were therefore excluded from further analysis. Kappa values then ranged from .69 to 1.00 with an average of .90, which is sufficient.

More than 200 different brands were used 741 times in total within the 368 ads. Individual brands were the most used type of brands (43%), followed by corporate brands (27%), and then labels (21%). Sub brands were the least used (9%).

Kim Cramer • Peter C. Neijens • Edith G. Smit

Brand Architectures in Advertising

In 78 ads (21%), the corporate brand was used alone, or with a sub brand or label. These ads were categorized as having a corporate branding architecture. In 117 ads (32%), the corporate brand was combined with an individual brand (with or without sub brands or labels). In 88 of these ads (24%), the brand architecture was categorized as endorsement branding, and in 29 ads (8%) as dual branding. In 159 ads (43%), the corporate brand was not used at all; individual brands were used, with or without sub brands or labels. These ads were categorized as having an individual branding architecture. The codebook also left room for 'other' brand architectures. In 14 ads (4%), other brand architectures were found; for example, an individual brand that seemed to endorse another individual brand. Surprisingly, in some cases no brands were mentioned in the ad. Table 7:1 represents the distribution of brand architectures in general, and across the two markets.

Table 7:1 Brand Architecture per Market

Brand architecture	Temporary labor	Financial services	Total
Corporate branding	40%	20%	21%
Dual branding		8%	24%
Endorsement branding	25%	24%	8%
Individual branding	30%	44%	43%
Other	5%	4%	4%
Total (N=368)	100%	100%	100%

If we divide the brand architectures between the two markets, we see that corporate branding is used more by temporary labor companies than by financial service providers (40% versus 20%). Dual branding is only used in the financial market (8%). Endorsement branding is distributed evenly (25% versus 24%) and individual branding is used somewhat more in the finance market (30% versus 44%). These differences are, however, not significant.

Corporate Brand Prominence in Advertising

Mostly, the corporate brand is not the most prominent brand in the ad, as can be seen in Table 7:2, which shows the figures of the objective brand prominence measures.

Table 7:2 Objective Brand Prominence Measures

Prominence measure	Corporate	Individual	Sub brand	Label	Total
Verbalized	1.7	2.0	3.4	.9	1.8
Visualized	3.4	4.3	4.0	2.0	3.5
Duration (s)	4.7	4.6	11.3	6.3	5.3
Logo	58%	86%	28%	18%	59%
Size (biggest)	45%	77%	37%	9%	50%

Note. The values for the variables verbalized and visualized represent frequencies (mean). The values for the variable duration represent duration in seconds (mean).

On average, the corporate brand was verbalized 1.7 times and visualized 3.4 times for 4.7 seconds. In 58% of the cases when a corporate brand was used in the ad, its logo was shown. In 45% of the cases when a corporate brand was used in the ad, it was the biggest brand of that ad. Sub brands were the most verbalized (3.4 times) brands. Individual brands were the most visualized (4.3 times) brands. In television ads, sub brands were on screen for the longest stretch of time (11.3 seconds). Individual brand's logos were the most often shown (in 86% of the cases in which an individual brand was used). Individual brands were most often the biggest brands in the ads as well (77%).

According to the subjective opinions of the coders, the corporate brand was not very prominent: its mean was 1.8 on a 5-point scale, from 'not at all prominent' to 'very prominent'. As could be expected, the corporate brand prominence was more prominent in the brand architecture categories 'corporate branding' (4.3), 'dual branding' (4.1), and 'endorsement branding' (2.1), than in the category 'individual branding' (0.1). This correspondence indicates that the coders chose between the brand architecture categories in consistence with their opinions about brand prominence.

Kim Cramer • Peter C. Neijens • Edith G. Smit

Determinants of Corporate Brand Prominence

Advertising budget.

Table 7:3 shows the distribution of brand architecture categories with regard to advertising budget. Companies with small budgets make more use of the corporate brand architecture (46%) than companies with large advertising budgets (17%). Conversely, companies with large advertising budgets make more use of the individual brand architecture (44%) than companies with small advertising budgets (40%); however; this difference is smaller. These results are significant ($\chi^2(4, N=368) = 48.41, p = .00$) and confirm our expectation (H1).

Table 7:3 Distribution of Brand Architectures across Companies with Large and Small Budgets

Brand architecture	Large budget	Small budget
Corporate branding	17%	46%
Dual branding	9%	
Endorsement branding	26%	11%
Individual branding	44%	40%
Other	3%	4%
Total (N=368)	100%	100%

Degree of fit between products and core business

Table 7:4 shows the distribution of brand architecture categories with regard to the degree of fit between products and core business. As we expected (H2), companies with a higher degree of fit between their products and their core business make more use of the corporate brand architecture (27%) than companies with a lower degree of fit (16%). However, the data show that companies with a lower degree of fit do not make more use of the individual brand architecture (42%) than companies with a higher degree of fit (45%). The results are significant ($\chi^2(4, N=368) = 30.92, p = .00$), but do not completely confirm our expectation.

Table 7:4 Distribution of Brand Architecture across Companies with High and Low Degree of Fit

Brand architecture	High degree of fit	Low degree of fit
Corporate branding	27%	16%
Dual branding	1%	14%
Endorsement branding	22%	26%
Individual branding	45%	42%
Other	5%	2%
Total (N=368)	100%	100%

Globalization

Table 7:5 shows the distribution of brand architecture categories with regard to global activity of the company. Companies that are globally active make more use of the corporate brand architecture (25%) than companies that are not globally active (12%). Conversely, companies that are not globally active make more use of the individual brand architecture (47%) than companies that are globally active (41%). The results are significant ($\chi^2(4, N=368) = 86.70, p = .00$) and confirm our expectation (H3).

Table 7:5 Distribution of Brand Architecture across Globally Active versus Not Globally Active Companies

Brand architecture	Globally active	Not globally active
Corporate branding	25%	12%
Dual branding		28%
Endorsement branding	29%	11%
Individual branding	41%	47%
Other	5%	2%
Total (N=368)	100%	100%

Kim Cramer • Peter C. Neijens • Edith G. Smit

Other Results

Our data show that brand architectures are not always used consistently. Only six of the eighteen companies use the same brand architecture category every time. Four companies always use corporate branding and two companies always use individual branding. The other companies use several brand architectures in different advertisements. For example, Achmea uses corporate branding (Achmea), endorsement branding (Eduard de Graaf & Co., Member Achmea Group), dual branding (Centraal Beheer Achmea), and individual branding (Eurocross International).

Even if we look at the brand level, we see that companies sometimes use the same brand with and without a corporate endorsement. This is, for example, the case with the brand Hedson. This brand is sometimes endorsed by the corporate brand Randstad (endorsement brand architecture), and is sometimes used alone (individual brand architecture). The media in which the advertisement is placed seems to be a reason for this - radio commercials usually mention only one brand, while this same brand is combined with the corporate brand in, for example, a magazine ad - however, these results are not significant. Another interesting finding is that the objective measures of brand prominence do not always correspond with the subjective opinion of the coders. Although a brand is objectively the biggest and most often mentioned, this is not necessarily the most prominent brand according to the coders.

When we compare the results of the content analysis with our previous studies concerning determinants of brand portfolio strategies (Blom & Cramer, 2002; Cramer, 2001) we can conclude that, in most cases, companies' advertising is 'on strategy'; that is, the brand architectures used in the advertisements mainly correspond to the strategies as revealed by the managers. Exceptions are, for example, companies that describe their brand portfolio strategy as endorsement branding (always use the corporate brand as endorsement), but that also use the individual brand architecture (without the corporate brand as endorsement) in advertising. It is worth noticing that, in some cases, the brand portfolio strategy seems to be 'off strategy', because some brands are not advertised during the selected one-year period.
Discussion

The main aim of this study was to investigate the prominence of the corporate brand in advertising and the factors connected to this corporate brand prominence. We conducted a quantitative content analysis of advertisements for leading companies in the temporary labor market and the financial services market in the Netherlands. The results show that the corporate brands of these companies were used in almost half of the ads. The corporate brand architecture (in which a corporate brand is used either alone, or with a sub brand or label) was the most often used, followed by the dual brand architecture and the individual brand architecture. Although the corporate brand was much used, it was generally not the most prominent brand in the ad.

Our results confirm the expectation that companies with small advertising budgets make more use of corporate branding than companies with large advertising budgets (H1). This is also the case with the expectation that companies with global activities make more use of corporate branding than companies that are not globally active (H3). Our expectation that companies with a range of different kinds of services (low degree of fit between product and core business) make less use of corporate branding than companies with comparable services (large degree of fit between products and core business) was not confirmed (H2). This result is surprising, because it does not correspond with the managers' opinions about the importance of fit when establishing their brand portfolio strategies. One explanation may be that the companies do not differ enough across the fit variable to find an effect of degree of fit on corporate brand prominence. In further research, it would be valuable to include companies with a larger range of different products or services.

Another important finding of this study is that the typology of brand architectures seems to be incomplete. We found brand architectures in advertisements that could not be included in any of the categories in Box 1. For example, we did not foresee the possibility that companies use no brands in their ads at all. Also, in some cases, an individual brand endorsed another individual brand. These results contribute to the existing branding literature in which such brand architectures are not distinguished.

We observed that the objective measures of brand prominence do not always correspond with the subjective opinion of the coders. This suggests that consumers may not perceive the brand that, objectively

Kim Cramer • Peter C. Neijens • Edith G. Smit

measured, is expected to attract the most attention, as the most important brand in the ad. This has implications for producing the advertisement, as well as establishing the effect of the ad. Further research investigating consumer responses is needed to draw conclusions concerning the effect of using certain brand architectures in advertising.

Notes:
1. Although we state that a label is not a brand, it was treated as a brand during the coding in order to be as specific as possible.
2. The authors note that for the sake of illustration, most examples are fictional.
3. In case of a television commercial.
4. For some variables, the inter-coder reliability could not be computed, as the coders used different values in some cases, and exactly the same value in other cases. Kappa can only be computed if the rows and columns of the interjudge contingency table are symmetric. If, for example, coder A uses 4 different values, while coder B uses only 3, Kappa cannot be computed. If coders use only 1 (and the same) value, this is considered a constant and Kappa is not computed either. 'Problem variables' were taken into account by looking at individual cases.

8

Analyzing Effects of Advertising Using Conditional Logistic Regression

KRISTINA BIRCH

Abstract

In this paper, a statistical model is proposed of how to analyze effects of advertising in cases where observations consist of single-source data. The conditional logistic regression can profitably be used as a supplement to the conventional logistic regression. Unlike the latter, the conditional logistic regression model takes into account the fact that the same respondent is observed several times. Here, the model is presented along with its properties, and it is used to analyze the exposure and loyalty effects for various brands from the British AdLab data. It is demonstrated that the embedded adstock based on the comparative opportunity to see (OTS) is generally insignificant. Furthermore, it is demonstrated that the choice of brand is closely related to the consumer's five most recent purchases in the particular category. This means that consumers tend to buy the same product as last time or that the choice of brand is constant over long periods of time.

Introduction

Measuring the effectiveness of market activities is crucial when it comes to media planning. Fortunately, pure single-source data as they are defined in (Jones, 1995) have now become available. This gives rise to a broader class of analyses. Single-source data allow us to analyze individual consumer behavior. It is possible for each individual consumer to relate the exposure of a particular brand to the actual purchase, see for example (McDonald, 1997). We may learn about the exposure effects on consumers for the brands involved, the brand purchased earlier, and the promotion activities of the brand along with demographic data for the consumer. Conventional aggregated data do not contain all this information and hence new quantitative models and methods need to be introduced.

In the case of conventional data, where a respondent is asked about exposure and brand purchase on one single occasion, the response is a simple binary variable, yes or no. Data will then consist of one observation for each respondent, possibly along with other information about the brand, activities promoting the brand and/or information about the consumer. The logistic regression is a natural choice to model effects of advertising based on such data.

However, logistic regression based on pure single-source data of the kind described above cannot immediately be used.

This chapter is divided into four sections. The following section introduces the logistic regression, its properties and its assumptions and explains why this method generally cannot be used on pure single-source data. Section three presents the conditional logistic regression (see Breslow and Day, 1980), along with its assumptions and properties, and in section four some results are presented using the AdLab data (note that this model is not identical to the conditional model, presented by Nordmoe and Jain, 2000). Section four also discusses why results from the conditional and conventional logistic model may differ, and how this affects the perceived performance of an advertising campaign and hence the media planning process. For an overview on media planning, see (Broadbent, 1999).

Logistic Regression

Let us assume that we want to analyze the effects of an advertising campaign for brand B in a specific fmcg category. Data are collected in such a way that immediately after the campaign, 50 consumers are asked which brand they purchased the last time they bought a product in the category. Furthermore, consumers are asked whether or not they have seen an advertisement for brand B before making the purchase.

Analyzing Advertising Effects Using Conditional Logistic Regression

Let y_p be a binary variable, either 1 or 0, where 1 means that brand B was purchased and 0 means that another brand than B was purchased. The subscript p means person number p, where $p = 1,...,P$. Note that the y_p's are mutually independent. Let x_p be the exposure to person p. Then x_p can be either 1 or 0; 1 if person p has seen an advertisement for brand B and 0 if this is not the case. Let π_p represent the probability that person p purchased brand B.

In this case, it is natural to use the simple logistic model, according to which

$$\pi_p = P(y_p = 1) = \frac{\exp(\alpha + \beta x_p)}{1 + \exp(\alpha + \beta x_p)} \tag{1}$$

or equivalent

$$\eta_p = \text{logit}(\pi_p) = \alpha + \beta x_p \tag{2}$$

The term α is a constant which indicates the willingness to purchase brand B if no advertisements have been seen, i.e. when x_p is zero. The likelihood function is

$$L(\alpha, \beta; \underline{y}) = \prod_{i=1}^{P} \left(\frac{\exp(\alpha + \beta x_p)^{y_p}}{1 + \exp(\alpha + \beta x_p)} \right) \tag{3}$$

It should be kept in mind that we want to analyze the effects of exposure. Let us now look at the hypothesis

$$H_0 : \beta = 0 \tag{4}$$

versus

$$H_1 : \beta \neq 0 \tag{5}$$

which is equivalent to comparing the two models

$$\text{Model 0: } \eta_p = \alpha \tag{6}$$

$$\text{Model 1: } \eta_p = \alpha + \beta x_p \tag{7}$$

Note that acceptance of model 0 means that the analyzed data do not provide evidence for any effect of the advertising campaign. Let us assume that the consumers answered according to the following 2-by-2 table.

Table 8:1: Answers for a population of 50

	See	Not see
Buy	16	10
Not Buy	13	11

Testing for independence in the above table, i.e. testing for no effects of advertising (model 0), gives us a p-value of 0.60, which means that these data do not indicate any effects of advertising. Similarly, if the logistic regression model is used, we achieve the same results. Hence, by asking 50 people and getting the results above, we arrive at a rather sad conclusion regarding the effects of the advertising campaign. There is no statistical evidence that the campaign has had any effects at all. (For more about 2-by-2 tables and tests, see Broadbent and Smith, 1999)

The above analysis was based on 50 consumers who were asked once about their purchase. Let us then assume that we want to construct single-source data and we have the same 50 consumers in our panel. Once a month, these consumers are asked the same questions as before: Did you buy a product in this category? If so, what brand was it? Furthermore, have you seen any advertisements for the brand (within a specific period)?

Let us then assume that we keep asking each person in the panel until 50 purchases have been recorded. It should be kept in mind that the product under analysis is an fmcg. Assume now, that the consumers in our panel have almost the same habits over time. This is not an unrealistic assumption, and it implies that consumers tend to buy the same brand that they bought last time and that they watch the same kind of TV-shows and programs. Since advertisements are often related to programs, it is possible that the consumer watches advertisements for the same brand again and again. In the extreme case, the consumers in our panel will behave in almost the same way every month. They will buy the same products and watch the same advertisements.

Mathematically, we label the number of purchases made by person p in the category of interest as y_{pi}, $i = 1,...,n_p$. First we assume that x_p is constant over time, i.e. x_p is independent of the purchase. The probability that consumer p will buy brand B at the ith purchase is

$$\pi_{pi} = P(y_{pi} = 1) = \frac{\exp(\alpha + \beta x_p)}{1 + \exp(\alpha + \beta x_p)} \qquad (8)$$

In the extreme case, the 2-by-2 table consisting of observations of the above scenario will then look like this after 50 months

Table 8:2: Answers, single-source data with population of 50

	See	Not see
Buy	800	500
Not Buy	650	550

In this case, a test for independence, which is equivalent to the test for $\beta = 0$ in the logistic regression, gives $p = 0.0002$, which is markedly different from the earlier result. Here the means of exposure cannot be ignored, as the p-value is quite less than 0.05. If this form of analysis is used, the advertising campaign appears to be very successful.

Keep in mind the difference between the two setups: First, 50 people were asked once about their habits. In the second analysis we asked the same people on repeated occasions. The problem with the second analysis is that the observations are mutually dependent because we use the same people. Hence, an analysis of single-source data is not an analysis of independent observations. The above example shows that due to the same habits over time, loyalty towards a product and individual taste, the conventional logistic model cannot be used. This method does not overcome the problem with dependent data, even if several demographic explanatory variables are introduced.

Conditional Logistic Regression

One way to overcome the dependency problem is to introduce personal parameters, i.e. parameters that reflect the fact that each observation relates to a certain consumer. Next, we want to ignore the variations caused by personal characteristics and focus on consumers' brand choice over time with loyalty and exposure (OTS) as explanatory

Kristina Birch

variables. This is done by conditioning on the total number of purchases made of the brand under review.

As was the case in section two, the purchases of consumer p in the category are labeled $i = 1,\ldots, n_p$ and we put down:

$$\pi_{pi} = P(y_{pi} = 1) = \frac{\exp(\alpha + \beta x_p)}{1 + \exp(\alpha + \beta x_p)}, \qquad (9)$$

where $p=1,\ldots,P$ and $i=1,\ldots,n_p$.

At this point we introduce personal parameters. Let α_p be the effect of a factor on P levels, one for each person. This will enable us to formulate the probability that consumer p buys brand B at the ith purchase as follows:

$$\pi_{pi} = \frac{\exp(\alpha_p + \beta x_p)}{1 + \exp(\alpha_p + \beta x_p)} \qquad (10)$$

The above model is not, however, an appropriate model since the exposure is constant over purchases. All variations of brand choice will be explained by the personal parameters.

The effects of the personal characteristics held in the parameter α_p are indeed of interest to the advertiser, but in this case we only analyze the effects of the purchase-dependent variables. By analyzing only the influences of the consumers' demographic characteristics, we are able to keep the explanatory variables constant. Hence, we can use the sum of purchases of brand B for consumer p as a dependent variable, and the P observations may probably be properly analyzed by means of a logistic model. It should be noted that the goodness-of-fit test for the logistic model is likely to be rejected, but in that case an overdispersion model may be used successfully. However, this goes beyond the limits of this paper and will not be further discussed here.

Now we relax the assumption that x_p is constant over time. Before every purchase i, person p has been exposed to brand B to some degree, which we now label x_{pi} and

$$\pi_{pi} = \frac{\exp(\alpha_p + \beta x_{pi})}{1 + \exp(\alpha_p + \beta x_{pi})} \qquad (11)$$

The term $\alpha_p + \beta x_{pi}$ can easily be extended in the way that is shown in the examples. Here we concentrate on the simple case, where x_{pi} is the only explanatory variable of interest.

It should be noted that x_{pi} can be any positive value, $x_{pi} \geq 0$ depending on the definition of the exposure. This modification allows us to analyze the brand choice of consumer p for different levels of exposure; but the dependency problem still has not been solved.

In order to explore the ad effects, we want to modify our model in such a way that the personal parameters cancel out. As a consequence, the only explanatory variables will be the purchase-dependent parameters, which could for example be relative exposure or time-dependent loyalty based on the most recent purchases made. The solution is here presented using one explanatory variable, and we condition on the sum of purchases for each consumer p.

Proposition 1: For the conditional distribution of y_{pi}, given the sums $y_{p.}$, the likelihood function is

$$L(\beta; \underline{y}) = \prod_{p=1}^{P} \left(\frac{\exp\left(\sum_{i: y_{pi}=1} (\beta x_{pi}) \right)}{\sum_{M} \exp\left(\sum_{i \in M} (\beta x_{pi}) \right)} \right) \qquad (12)$$

where the sum in the denominator is the sum of all subsets M of $\{1,\ldots, n_p\}$, which consists of exactly $y_{p.}$ elements.

Brief proof: Assume that we look at consumer p, and label the purchases $i = 1,\ldots,n_p$. Assume that consumer p out of the total of n_p purchases made purchased the brand of interest in j out of n_p cases. The conditional likelihood function for the consumer can be put down as

$$\frac{\prod_{i: y_{pi}=1} \pi_{pi} \cdot \prod_{i: y_{pi}=0} (1 - \pi_{pi})}{\sum_{M} \left(\prod_{i \in M} \pi_{pi} \cdot \prod_{i \notin M} (1 - \pi_{pi}) \right)} \qquad (13)$$

Kristina Birch

where $M = \{\{1, 2\}, \{1, 3\}, \{2,3\}\}$ if $j = 2$ and $n_p = 3$, for example. Now the above can be written as

$$\frac{\prod\limits_{i:y_{pi}=1}\left(\frac{\exp(\alpha_p + \beta x_{pi})}{1 + \exp(\alpha_p + \beta x_{pi})}\right) \cdot \prod\limits_{i:y_{pi}=0}\left(\frac{1}{1 + \exp(\alpha_p + \beta x_{pi})}\right)}{\sum\limits_{M}\left(\prod\limits_{i \in M}\left(\frac{\exp(\alpha_p + \beta x_{pi})}{1 + \exp(\alpha_p + \beta x_{pi})}\right) \cdot \prod\limits_{i \notin M}\left(\frac{1}{1 + \exp(\alpha_p + \beta x_{pi})}\right)\right)} \tag{14}$$

from which follows that the denominators cancel out and we get

$$\frac{\prod\limits_{i:y_{pi}=1}\left(\exp(\alpha_p + \beta x_{pi})\right)}{\sum\limits_{M}\left(\prod\limits_{i \in M}\left(\exp(\alpha_p + \beta x_{pi})\right)\right)} \tag{15}$$

Since the number of α_p in the nominator and in all terms of the denominator is exactly y_p, the α_p cancel too, and we end up with

$$\frac{\exp\left(\sum\limits_{i:y_{pi}=1}(\beta x_{pi})\right)}{\sum\limits_{M}\left(\exp\left(\sum\limits_{i \in M}(\beta x_{pi})\right)\right)} \tag{16}$$

Then, for all the consumers involved

$$L(\beta; \underline{y}) = \prod\limits_{p=1}^{P}\left(\frac{\exp\left(\sum\limits_{i:y_{pi}=1}(\beta x_{pi})\right)}{\sum\limits_{M}\exp\left(\sum\limits_{i \in M}(\beta x_{pi})\right)}\right) \tag{17}$$

which finishes the proof.

Note that the demographic parameters and personal parameters that are constant for the individual consumers are now excluded from the model. We are now ready to analyze the data.

AdLab Results

In the following, data from AdLab are used to show the results produced by the estimation of a conditional logistic model. The AdLab data consist of several product categories, but here we limit the analysis to consist of two categories (For more information of AdLab, see Moseley and Parfitt, 1987). As explanatory variables we use "exposure" and "loyalty". The first is a fractional exposure, which means that the relative OTS for the brand being analyzed is a fraction of the total OTS in the particular category. The fractional OTS used in the analysis is then a weighted average of the last 28 days of fractional exposure, where a retention rate of $r = \dfrac{1}{1.05} \approx 0.95$ is used for all brands in both categories. Note that we can regard the parameter "exposure" as a brand's empirical "share of voice" (also known as share of mind) for the particular consumer at the day of purchase. Since we look only at exposure for the last 28 days, we are only able to analyze the short-term and probably medium-term effects. The data used in this analysis do not allow any conclusion about long-term effects of the exposure.

Note that the fractional OTS will compensate for different viewing habits. Theoretically, the heavy viewer will watch more advertisements than a medium viewer, who in turn will watch more ads than a light viewer. One ad for a particular brand shown to the three different kinds of consumer will give different fractional OTS, simply because the total OTS is different. The heavy viewer, who watches a lot of TV, will see a lot of ads during the day, and it will only be natural if s/he cannot distinguish one ad from another. The fractional OTS captures the differences in the viewing pattern over time.

The second explanatory variable is "loyalty", which is defined as a weighted average of the five latest purchases. Hence, loyalty is high if more of the five latest purchases were of the particular brand. We use the five latest purchases to incorporate a measure for loyalty or taste parameter that is allowed to vary over time. Note that loyalty here cannot be used as an overall measure of the individual consumer's loyalty, as we condition on the total number of purchases in the model. Loyalty is an indication of consumers' inclination to purchase the brand in question in the recent past. Thus, a significant effect of loyalty means that the consumer tends to buy a brand in bursts, i.e. the purchases of a specific brand tend to cluster in time.

The results for the chocolate bar category is shown in Table 8:3. The parenthesized figures are the numbers of total purchases for the specific brand.

Table 8:3: Results for the chocolate bars category.

Brand	Parameter	Estimate	Std.dev.	U	P
6801 Mars	exposure	0.00618	0.005884	1.050	0.293650
(no=2078)	loyalty	0.729	0.1757	4.152	0.000033
6802 Milky Way	exposure	0.0058	0.01351	0.432	0.666039
(no=524)	loyalty	0.819	0.2850	2.873	0.004067
6803 Bounty	exposure	0.0174	0.01331	1.310	0.190182
(no=435)	loyalty	1.601	0.2805	5.707	0.000000
6805 Marathon	exposure	-0.00130	0.008900	-0.146	0.883736
(no=537)	loyalty	0.653	0.2736	2.387	0.016988
6807 Crunchie	exposure	-0.0090	0.01245	-0.721	0.471148
(no=424)	loyalty	1.490	03593	4.148	0.000034
6811 Double Decker	exposure	0.0556	0.01342	4.143	0.000034
(no=392)	loyalty	-0.379	0.3813	-0.993	0.320776
6813 Wispa	exposure	0.00473	0.009164	0.516	0.605842
(no=761)	loyalty	0.217	0.2730	0.797	0.425702
6816 Aero	exposure	0.0067	0.009098	0.733	0.463636
(no=645)	loyalty	-0.165	0.3580	-3.253	0.001140

At first, the results are rather discouraging. Unlike the results found by (Hansen and Hansen, 2001), the exposure does not seem to have any influence on the brand chosen. The fractional OTS is generally insignificant, which means that we cannot relate exposure or opportunity-to-see to a specific purchase. In fact, there is no statistical evidence to support the hypothesis that watching an advertisement for a specific brand several times during the week before the purchase may change the choice of brand.

On the contrary, the loyalty parameter is significant for almost all brands. It should be noted here that loyalty cannot be viewed as an overall loyalty parameter or taste parameter. This is due to the fact that loyalty values are based on the five most recent purchases and that we condition on the number of purchases. Hence, the significance of the loyalty parameter is found in the fact that consumers apparently tend to buy the same product as they did the last time. The purchases of a specific brand are closely related to each other in time.

Furthermore, one of the estimates (for the brand "Aero") of loyalty parameters is significantly negative. This is discouraging because it might mean that the average consumer dislikes the product. Negative loyalty is a sign that a consumer who bought the product last time has a higher probability of purchasing another brand the next time.

Note the results for the "Double Decker" which are quite different from the others. Here, the estimate of loyalty effect is negative but insignificant, which indicates that the latest purchases are irrelevant to the purchase of a "Double Decker". Surprisingly, the estimate of exposure effect is significant. This means that the advertising for this product does have a short-term effect. Due to the negative (but still insignificant) estimate of the loyalty effect, the advertising effect is not permanent. Consumers change brand quickly after the first purchase.

A few of the exposure estimates are negative. This may be due to poor advertising or a successful competitor advertising campaign.

In the breakfast cereal category (see Table 8:4), the general pattern is the same as for the chocolate bar category. In most cases loyalty is significant, and exposure is insignificant. But for the brand "Other Kellogg's" this is different. This brand is not really a brand but rather a sum of different brands, i.e. other Kellogg's brands than those already mentioned in the table. Here the significance might be due to the difference between brands. A new product may have been introduced on the market along with a very successful advertising campaign. Hence, the consumers see the ad and buy the product. Note that loyalty here is also significant, which in turn means that purchases made of the specific brand are related in time.

Alternatively, let us assume that one of the brands above is advertised regularly during a period. Sales of the brand are low but almost constant. The manufacturer decides to remove the brand from the market and immediately stops advertising it.

In this situation, there is a positive exposure for some consumers at the time when the brand was on the market, and zero exposure for all consumers shortly after the brand was removed from the market. Obviously, but perhaps somewhat puzzling, this means that the estimated exposure effect for this particular brand will be strictly positive. It is very likely that the exposure effect will be significant as sales were concentrated in the advertising period. This is a possible reason for the significant exposure effect for "Other Kellogg's". The brand "Kellogg's Frosties" has in fact a significant exposure at $\alpha = 0.05$ level. This is rather surprising since a negative estimate means that consumers do not buy "Kellogg's Frosties" if they have a positive exposure to the brand. This is not crucial, as significance will appear in one of out twenty cases, at least on an average.

Table 8:4: Results for the breakfast cereals category.

Brand	Parameter	Estimate	Std.dev.	U	P
0418 K Cornflakes	exposure	0.00272	0.002215	1.228	0.219398
(no=12414)	loyalty	1.4695	0.05819	25.253	0.000000
0421 K Rice	exposure	0.00241	0.006120	0.393	0.694295
Krispies	loyalty	1.776	0.1009	17.599	0.000000
(no=3633)					
0422 K Bran Flakes	exposure	0.00924	0.005203	1.776	0.075751
(no=2952)	loyalty	1.759	0.1187	14.814	0.000000
0427 K All Bran	exposure	0.00976	0.006307	1.547	0.121838
(no=2330)	loyalty	0.987	0.1466	6.731	0.000000
0428 K Special K	exposure	0.01309	0.006410	2.042	0.041187
(no=2527)	loyalty	1.953	0.1523	12.823	0.000000
0429 K Frosties	exposure	-0.01459	0.007136	-2.045	0.040848
(no=2910)	loyalty	2.038	0.1092	18.661	0.000000
0433 Other K	exposure	0.01609	0.002283	7.046	0.000000
(no=5729)	loyalty	2.3646	0.07447	31.751	0.000000
0434 Nabisco S. W.	exposure	0.01871	0.006006	3.115	0.001841
(no=3379)	loyalty	1.834	0.1155	15.884	0.000000
0436 Nabisco S.	exposure	0.0119	0.01135	1.052	0.292625
(no=1451)	loyalty	2.315	0.1580	14.649	0.000000
0440 Quaker S. P.	exposure	0.0058	0.01165	0.502	0.615829
(no=2146)	loyalty	2.465	0.1267	19.459	0.000000
0442 Weetabix	exposure	0.00528	0.003298	1.601	0.109277
(no=8622)	loyalty	1.4385	0.06786	21.199	0.000000

In order to compare the logistic regression and the conditional logistic regression, loyalty and exposure effects are estimated using both methods. Table 8:5 shows the results for the chocolate bar category.

We see the same pattern for all brands in this category. For all brands, the loyalty parameter is extremely significant. The estimate is about five times higher than before. Note in the cases of the "Double Decker" and the "Wispa" that loyalty parameters were insignificant when the conditional logistic model was used. Here, a poor choice of model gives the opposite conclusion.

Surprisingly, it seems like all advertising is wasted when this method is used. Personal differences are not taken into account, and at least a few significant exposure parameters are expected. This is, however, not the case, perhaps for the following reason: The constant

Table 8:5: Results for the chocolate bars category using the logistic model.

Brand	Parameter	Estimate	Std.dev.	U	P
6801 Mars	exposure	0.00567	0.004684	1.211	0.225894
(no=2078)	loyalty	4.438	0.1053	42.132	0.000000
	constant	-2.5088	0.06407	-39.18	0.000000
6802 Milky Way	exposure	0.0062	0.01127	0.547	0.584586
(no=524)	loyalty	5.209	0.1955	26.650	0.000000
	constant	-3.397	0.07572	-44.11	0.000000
6803 Bounty	exposure	0.0089	0.01130	0.786	0.431737
(no=435)	loyalty	5.778	0.2158	26.769	0.000000
	constant	-3.6460	0.0976	-40.17	0.000000
6805 Marathon	exposure	-0.00860	0.007913	-1.087	0.277041
(no=537)	loyalty	4.804	0.1958	24.531	0.000000
	constant	-3.1446	0.07640	-41.16	0.000000
6807 Crunchie	exposure	-0.0022	0.01156	-0.193	0.847322
(no=424)	loyalty	5.856	0.2247	26.063	0.000000
	constant	-3.5951	0.08261	-43.52	0.000000
6811 Double Decker	exposure	0.0164	0.01111	1.474	0.140520
(no=392)	loyalty	5.970	0.2505	23.833	0.000000
	constant	-3.6154	0.08239	-43.88	0.000000
6813 Wispa	exposure	0.00335	0.008463	0.395	0.692485
(no=761)	loyalty	5.128	0.1657	30.945	0.000000
	constant	-3.1422	0.06655	-47.22	0.000000
6816 Aero	exposure	0.00553	0.008036	0.688	0.491706
(no=645)	loyalty	5.268	0.1950	27.013	0.000000
	constant	-3.1730	0.06865	-46.22	0.000000

determines the probability that brand B was purchased, and it remains the same for all consumers and irrespective of time. All variations between observations must be explained by the five latest purchases or by exposure. Loyalty may be regarded as some sort of personal parameter because it is linked to the individual consumer's latest purchases. Hence, it becomes a measure of taste and preference. The use of loyalty as an explanatory variable will naturally explain most of the variation in the data, because it is directly related to the consumers in the panel. This leads to the conclusion that personal parameters are indeed important, but the aim was to extract personal differences and analyze the remaining variation. The results for the breakfast cereal category are shown in Table 8:6.

Not surprisingly, the same pattern emerges as in the case of the chocolate bar category; the loyalty term is extremely significant. Only in one case, namely with respect to the "Other Kelloggs" brand, a significant exposure parameter is estimated. It should be noted that this was also the case for this brand when the conditional model was used.

It is not surprising that the U-statistics are large. Because the model is inappropriate for single-source data, the variables connected to pseudo-personal parameters will be extremely significant. The choice of model is vital, and a poor choice may result in a wrong decision. Single-source data allow us to relate purchase to exposure, and it is possible to analyze advertising effects in more detail if we choose appropriate models.

Conclusion

It has been demonstrated that the conditional logistic regression model can be used to good advantage when modeling ad effects based on single-source data. Two categories of the AdLab database were analyzed by means of a model of two explanatory variables, loyalty and exposure. Only in a few cases did the data exhibit significant exposure. Furthermore, in one of these cases, exposure had a negative estimate. Hence the data generally provide little or no evidence for fractional OTS being related to brand choice, at least in the short term. The important parameter here is the loyalty, which is extremely significant.

Table 8:6: Results for the breakfast cereal category using the logistic regression

Brand	Parameter	Estimate	Std.dev.	U	P
0418 K Cornflakes (no=12414)	exposure	0.00157	0.001915	0.817	0.413650
	loyalty	4.8475	0.04144	116.980	0.000000
	constant	-2.8754	0.02343	-122.70	0.000000
0421 K Rice Krispies (no=3633)	exposure	-0.00347	0.005347	-0.723	0.459758
	loyalty	5.9322	0.08036	73.834	0.000000
	constant	-0.3785	0.02781	-132.29	0.000000
0422 K Bran Flakes (no=2952)	exposure	0.00941	0.004926	1.910	0.056146
	loyalty	7.1403	0.08591	83.115	0.000000
	constant	-4.2576	0.03767	-113.02	0.000000
0427 K All Bran (no=2330)	exposure	0.01211	0.006050	2.003	0.045225
	loyalty	7.594	0.1009	75.253	0.000000
	constant	-4.4919	0.04101	-109.53	0.000000
0428 K Special K (no=2527)	exposure	0.00792	0.005263	1.505	0.132269
	loyalty	8.0609	0.09968	80.864	0.000000
	constant	-4.6995	0.04099	-114.65	0.000000
0429 K Frosties (no=2910)	exposure	-0.00283	0.006301	-0.449	0.653089
	loyalty	6.8074	0.08878	76.679	0.000000
	constant	-4.0431	0.03232	-125.10	0.000000
0433 Other K (no=5729)	exposure	0.01248	0.00200	6.238	0.000000
	loyalty	5.3718	0.05959	90.139	0.000000
	constant	-3.4748	0.02559	-135.80	0.000000
0434 Nabisco S. W. (no=3379)	exposure	0.00675	0.005811	1.161	0.245683
	loyalty	6.7556	0.08450	79.948	0.000000
	constant	-3.9896	0.02893	-137.90	0.000000
0436 Nabisco S. (no=1451)	exposure	-0.0075	0.01107	-0.679	0.497154
	loyalty	7.397	0.1337	55.332	0.000000
	constant	-4.4638	0.03603	-123.90	0.000000
0440 Quaker S. P. (no=2146)	exposure	0.00722	0.008837	0.817	0.414013
	loyalty	6.920	0.1070	64.689	0.000000
	constant	-4.1942	0.03116	-134.58	0.000000
0442 Weetabix (no=8622)	exposure	0.00120	0.0022839	0.424	0.671542
	loyalty	4.9753	0.04960	100.304	0.000000
	constant	-3.0406	0.02196	-138.45	0.000000

9

Modelling Purchases as a Function of Advertising and Promotion

FLEMMING HANSEN, LOTTE YSSING HANSEN
& LARS GRØNHOLDT

Abstract

This chapter describes the preliminary studies of the effect of advertising and promotion on purchases. The British single-source database Adlab has been the basis for this study of advertising and promotion effectiveness. The STAS measure and logit modelling have been used to estimate the effect of advertising. The results from the two measures have been compared to determine the extent to which, the two measures give occasion for the same conclusions. To indicate the accuracy of the two measures, their respective level of significance have been studied. Two logit models have been estimated; one model only includes the effect of TV exposure, while the other also includes the effect of promotions. The results from the two logit models are compared to determine which model give the most accurate estimate of the effect of advertising. When comparing the results from the STAS measure with the parameter estimates from the second logit model, it is found that these two different measures largely give occasion for similar conclusions. Suggestions for further research and developments of the models are given.

Introduction

Since the 1960'ies (Grønholdt, 1990) there has been great interest in using different models to describe and explain the effects of advertisements on purchases. The interest is seen from both the advertisers and the ad-agencies point of view. The ad-agencies have an interest in giving their customers greater assurance of the strategies used, while the advertisers may want to see documentation that shows them that their "investment" in the different media give a revenue. Many researchers (See Little 1979 for an overview) have been involved with such models. (Little, 1979) divides the models into two classes, one class of models that mainly draw upon intuition and one class of models where the main focus lies in econometrics and/or statistics. However, it is crucial that the models either give the same result or at least give reason to assume that identical conclusions are drawn. In the worst case scenario it could be imagined that models give occasion for different conclusions, and this could very well be misused in the sense that the result wanted, determines which method to use.

Until the 1990'ies most analyses have been based on aggregated data, but now, with the availability of single-source data, new methods have emerged. Single-source data allow consumer purchases and advertising exposures to be directly linked, and have given rise to the Short-Term Advertising Strength measure, STAS measure, (Jones, 1995a; 1995b).

The STAS measure has showed the analyses potential of single-source data to give a better understanding of the effect of advertising on purchase. However, a theoretically more attractive method of analysis is logit modelling. The STAS measure is a relatively simple measure, while the logit model is a more complex approach.

The purpose of this chapter is to examine the results from the simple measure and the complex model and learn whether they give occasion for the same conclusions.

The data material

Single-source data means that the data coming from one source, i.e. a person or household, is recorded in such a way that it is possible to identify the actions of the individual sources in a unique way. Particularly purchases and ad exposures are measured for the same individuals. Therefore, data collected and stored as single-source data, makes it possible to analyse relationships at the individual level. This allows for much more detailed analysis, compared to analyses at an aggregated level based on market data. In this work, the Adlab database, a large British single-source database, has been used.

Adlab was a diary-based single-source panel, which was set up by Central Independent Television in September 1985 and ran through March 1990. The panel was set up with the intent to study in-depth the relationship between advertising and purchase (Moseley et al., 1987). The panel had about 1000 respondents reporting in a diary their radio usage, TV viewing, reading of newspapers and magazines and daily purchases in 48 product categories with numerous brands in each category (McDonald, 1997). In addition to the media-usage files, there exists a file with information of where and when advertisements for the various brands did occur. Finally, there is an extensive file describing each individual respondent by 40 demographic variables.

By combining the above-mentioned files, it is possible to determine whether or not the individual respondents have been in Opportunity-To-See (OTS) positions for advertisements for the brand studied. In the files, it is also possible to see information about whether or not the purchase was made in connection with a promotion activity. However, this promotion activity is recorded only at the time of purchase. There is no information regarding promotion activities during the week.

Data-collection method

The data has been recorded in a media- and a purchase diary on a daily basis. This means that the individual respondents have completed a diary on a daily basis recording their media-usage and their purchases. The diary itself is very extensive, and the amount of data collected is almost overwhelming. The validity of such data can of course be debated since all recording relies totally on the respondent and it is understandable how a respondent can "choose" to forget, especially when they have purchased many products or when they are sitting watching television and have left their media-usage diary somewhere else. In the analysis are only included data that have passed a critical data control.

Today, it is common to use different automatic measures connected directly to the television set called meters. The respondent presses a button on the remote control to register as a viewer. The meter then automatically registers which program is being watched. When the respondent is done watching the television he again presses a button to let the meter know that he is no longer watching. However, radio and print media still needs the respondents' own recording.

Opportunity-To-See

The number of Opportunity-To-See (OTS) positions for ads have been used to indicate the media pressure. This number has been determined by combining the media-usage file with the advertisement records file. In the present reporting we look only at the effects of television advertising. Here, there is some uncertainty as to whether or not the respondent actually was exposed for the ad, since the placement of the advertisement is indicated with an exact time and the respondent's media usage has been recorded in intervals of 15 minutes each. Another uncertainty regarding the accuracy of the OTS number is whether or not people actually were in an opportunity to see during the commercial breaks, whether they engaged themselves in other activities than watching television in the room, or if they for instance were making coffee in the kitchen (Collett, 1986).

Age of the data

Data were collected in the period September 1985 to March 1990, so they are quite old. There have been changes in the purchase behaviour of the respondents and the way/philosophy of advertising since the late 1980'ties, but the data can still be used to establish connections and these can with some modifications be transformed so they apply to today. If the data is studied on a per year basis this reveals how the ad effects have changed over the years, and even though it is likely that the strategy of advertising today have also changed since the mid-80'ies, the basic effects of advertising may still be the same. It is, however, rare to have access to a single-source database such as the Adlab database with observations over a continuous 5-year period, and the opportunity to analyse these effects have been welcomed.

Flemming Hansen • Lotte Yssing Hansen • Lars Grønholdt

Purchase-Viewing bias

(Broadbent, 1999) and (McDonald, 1997) have worked with the idea that there is a relationship between media usage and purchase behaviour, a so-called Purchase-Viewing bias, P-V bias:

> "A Purchase-Viewing bias occurs if a brand is bought more (or less) heavily by heavy television viewers than by light television viewers, so that occasions preceded by advertising come from one group more than they do from the other group" (McDonald, 1997)

The P-V index is computed as the share of purchases with prior advertising among the heavy media users, divided by the share of purchases with prior advertising among the low media users.

If the P-V index is greater than 100 the brand's share of purchase occasions among the heavy media users is larger than that of the low media users. However, if the index is smaller than 100 this indicates that the brand-share purchase is larger among the low media users. (Broadbent, 1999) has illustrated these scenarios by an example:

> "Take Bird's Mild Coffee, and compare this with Nestlé's Gold Blend, a rather bitter 'coffee-lovers' brand. Because of the demographics of buyers of these brands – and of television viewers – it happens that the Purchase/Viewing index for Mild coffee is above one, or *positive*. People who prefer Nestlé's Gold Blend are older, downgrade and watch more commercial television than average. But the index for Gold Blend is below one *(negative)*. That is, people who prefer the bitter coffee are younger, more upgrade and watch less commercial TV." (Broadbent, 1999)

It is interesting to learn that a P-V index smaller than 100 can be explained by studying the demographics of the purchasers of the two coffee brands. This example therefore suggests that simply to monitor the media-usage is not enough, it is necessary either to include other variables in the analysis to get a more detailed description of the situation at the time of purchase, or to seek explanations for unexpected results.

(Broadbent et al., 1997) has also studied the P-V bias situation and found that in every case they had looked at, an explanation for the bias could be found in the demographics of the respondents. From their study, they conclude that the weight of viewing should not be neglected as a factor that has influence on the result of the STAS calculations. The researchers furthermore suggest a multivariate analysis, rather than the relatively simple contingency tables.

Some preliminary studies of a P-V bias with the datasets from the Adlab database have been done (Hansen, 2000). Here we find that the P-V bias plays a minor role in influencing the effect scores. More important are the models for explaining the effect, and other analyses of the data show that the occurrence of deals, offers and other promotion activities plays an important role.

Loyalty

When studying the purchase data per respondent, it is in most cases obvious that the respondents have their preferred brands. I.e., they have a degree of loyalty towards a set of 3-4 brands depending on the category. Since this is probably the case for all respondents; some questions emerge: Does advertising for the brands that make up the loyalty-set have the same effect on the purchase decision as the advertising for brands not included in the loyalty-set? How can the data be corrected for this, and is it necessary?

To the first question can be argued that whether advertising was seen or not, the respondent would have purchased the brand from the loyalty-set anyway. Whereas no matter how much advertising seen for a non-loyalty brand may not generate sales, simply because the respondent is not at all interested in this particular brand. Whether this is necessary to correct for is yet to be decided. A possible way to correct the data for this inequality is to quantify degrees of loyalty towards the different brands and include such a measure in the analysis. This, however, is not done in this first initial public reporting.

Another interesting issue would be to study the degree to which consumers buy a brand they have not purchased previously. What is it that makes the consumer interested in buying a new brand? Is it advertising alone, or is it in combination with for example a promotion activity?

Flemming Hansen • Lotte Yssing Hansen • Lars Grønholdt

The methodology

Two methods have been studied in this work: the STAS-measure and a logit model. The comparison between the two methods has not been on the results per se, but rather on the tendency in the results. I.e., whether or not there seems to be a positive or negative connection between advertising exposures and the purchases made. The two methods will be described in greater detail in the following sections. Here, we will just note that there is great difference in the two methods, one is simplistic, whereas the other is more complex with a stronger theoretical foundation.

The datasets we are working with have been created from the Adlab database by using the TV media usage files, the purchase information file, and the file containing information about the occurrence of advertisements. These files have been compared in order to determine the OTS per respondent for each purchase made. The datasets have information about the current purchase, which brand was bought, was there a promotion activity, and how many pence was spend. There is also information about when the last purchase within that specific category took place, and which brand was purchased on this last occasion. Finally, there is information about the number of ads the respondent have seen for the brand studied, in a 28 day period prior to each purchase. All in all, each dataset has 64 columns containing the above-mentioned information. Thus, we have 73 datasets for brands selected as those brands, for which most advertising and purchases were seen. The datasets represents 15 product categories.

The STAS measure

STAS, an acronym for Short-Term Advertising Strength, introduced by (John Philip Jones, 1995a), is a measure that directly relates the OTS to the purchase data. The STAS index is calculated as the ratio between the brand's share of purchase occasions among those respondents who have been exposed to advertising during a seven-day period prior to purchase, p_1, and the brand's share of purchase occasions among those respondents who have not been exposed to advertising during a seven-day period prior to purchase, p_2. The STAS score is calculated as $\frac{p_1}{p_2}$, where $p_1 = \frac{Y_1}{n_1}$ and $p_2 = \frac{Y_2}{n_2}$. Y_1, Y_2, n_1 and n_2 are given from Table 9:1.

Table 9:1: General structure for calculating STAS scores (Hansen et al., 1999)

	Purchase of the brand	Not purchased the brand	Total
Has seen the ad	Y_1	$n_1 - Y_1$	n_1
Has not seen the ad	Y_2	$n_2 - Y_2$	n_2
Total	$Y.$	$n - Y.$	N

The interpretation of STAS is rather intuitive; if the STAS index is greater than 100 for a specific brand, it means that the brand's share of purchase occasions is greater among those previously exposed to advertising, thereby indicating that advertising has had an effect. If the STAS index is smaller than 100, it means that the brand's share of purchase occasions is smaller among those previously exposed to advertising, indicating that advertising has not had an effect on the brand decision or perhaps has had a negative effect.

However, there has been some debate (Lodish, 1997; Lodish, 1998) as to whether or not the STAS measure is a realistic way of describing the effects of advertising. It can be argued that STAS is too simple in its current form, and takes too few variables into consideration, i.e., it does not for example consider promotion, pricing, competitor activities or prior advertising. (Lodish, 1997) argues the importance of correcting the data for inequalities due to, i.e., promotion activity being different in different shops, pricing, and competitor activities. Another point of argument which (Lodish, 1997) states, is that one can question the fairness of giving all of one weeks advertising similar weight in estimating the effect of advertising and disregarding all previous advertising. A third point (Lodish, 1997) brings up is the loyalty-question. If a household is loyal to a particular brand, how much effect will advertising for this brand really have – the household would most likely have purchased the brand anyway.

One way of validating the STAS measure is to determine it's significance. If the STAS table (see Table 9:1), is thought of as two independent binomial distribution, it is possible to calculate whether or not the two proportions $p_1 = \dfrac{Y_1}{n_1}$ and $p_2 = \dfrac{Y_2}{n_2}$ are significantly different from each other. The significance is determined by a z-test. If the z-test value is greater than 1.96, it is significant on level 0.05. If this is not the case, p_1 and p_2 cannot be said to be significantly different from each other, meaning the proportion who have purchased with prior advertising cannot be separated from the group of people that purchased without prior advertising.

The logistic regression model

As the other measure of the effects of advertising, we have chosen a logistic regression model, logit model. The logit models used, estimates the probability that a household purchases a particular brand, given the explanatory variables. The dependent variable is perceived as being binary, i.e. it takes on two values "0" if the brand is not purchased and "1" if the brand is purchased. Using a linear regression model when the dependent variable is binary gives problems with the error function. A logit model has the advantage that it takes account for these issues, and furthermore it also assures that the response function is curvilinear with asymptotes at both zero and one which naturally meets the original constraints when the dependent variable is binary, (Neter et al., 1989). Another advantage of working with a logit model is the possibility of including numerous explanatory variables, so that it is possible to make a more varied analysis taking account for i.e. a P-V bias, promotion activities, and so forth. The general logit model formulation is given by Equation 1:

$$E\{Y\} = \frac{\exp(\beta_0 + \beta_1 X_1 + \ldots + \beta_n X_n)}{1 + \exp(\beta_0 + \beta_1 X_1 + \ldots + \beta_n X_n)} \qquad \text{(Eq. 1)}$$

where
$E\{Y\}$ is the expected outcome, i.e., the probability of purchase.

$X_1 \ldots X_n$ are the various explanatory variables, β_0 is the base level of sales and $\beta_1 \ldots \beta_n$ are the parameter estimates for the various explanatory variables. The sign of these parameter estimates indicates whether an increase in the explanatory variable will have a positive or a negative influence on the purchase probability. The β's indicates the increase/decrease of a unit increase in the respective explanatory variables. However, since the model has undergone a logistic transformation, it is necessary to calculate $\exp(\beta)$ to find the sensitivity value of the respective explanatory variables.

For this work, two logit-models have been estimated. In the first model, advertising information was included as the only explanatory variable, while in the second logit model, both the advertising and promotion information at time of purchase were included as explanatory variables. The ad-effect was quantified, by use of adstock calculations. The adstock values have been calculated on the basis of advertising information in a 28-day period prior to each individual purchase.

Adstock weighs advertising in previous periods by a retention rate, such that advertising seen ten days ago does not influence the consumer today with the same effect as advertising seen one day ago. The formula for calculating adstock in this work is presented by (Broadbent, 1979) and given by Equation 2:

$$Adstock_t = (1-r)\cdot(OTS_t + r\cdot OTS_{t-1} + r^2\cdot OTS_{t-2} + \ldots + r^n\cdot OTS_{t-n}) \quad \text{(Eq. 2)}$$

$Adstock_t$ denotes the value of the current ad-pressure as a function of prior advertising. OTS are the Opportunities-To-See in the different time periods – here per day, and "r" denotes the retention rate. The crucial issue in the adstock calculation is the determination of the retention rate. In order to choose the retention rate we have tried different values ranging from 0.5, 0.6,..., 0.9, 0.95, 0.96,..., 0.99. The value that had the "best fit" to the data was chosen. In this work we chose to work with a retention rate of 0.97. It is important to remember that we are working with daily data, and a daily retention rate of 0.97 is equivalent to a weekly retention rate of 0.80. These rates are equivalent to a half-life of 22.8 days or 3.1 week respectively. The half-life has been calculated using equation 3 (Broadbent, 1979).

$$\text{half}-\text{life in periods} = \frac{\log \frac{1}{2}}{\log (r)} \quad \text{(Eq. 3)}$$

Flemming Hansen • Lotte Yssing Hansen • Lars Grønholdt

For some of the brands we found that the optimum retention rate was either higher or lower than the chosen 0.97, but we decided to use the retention rate 0.97 overall.

Presentation of results

The following results are based on calculations on 73 fmcg distributed upon 15 product categories. The media-pressure has been determined by studying the number of OTS positions for each respondent. The STAS calculations have been done on the basis of the OTS 7 days prior to each purchase, whereas the adstock calculation, as explained, have been done using a retention rate of 0.97, to describe advertising pressure today as a function of advertising 28 days prior to each purchase.

The results from the STAS measure and both logit models for the 73 brands are shown in Appendix I. The first column indicates the product category, while the second column specifies the brand name within the categories. Column 3 shows the STAS indices and the calculated significance of the indices is shown in column 4. In column 5 are shown the results from logit model 1, where "b1" is the parameter estimate for the adstock value. Significance of the b1 values are given in Column 6. Results from the second logit model with two explanatory variables are given in Columns 7 through 10. Again "b1" is the parameter estimate for the adstock value, which is given in Column 7 and the significance of these values are given in Column 8. "b2" is the parameter estimate for the promotion variable, which is shown in Column 9, and the corresponding significance is shown in Column10.

The "b's" indicate the percentage change in the purchase probability of a one unit change in the respective explanatory variable. However, because of the logarithmic transformation it is necessary to calculate exp(b) to get the percentage value. The "b's" can be said to indicate the sensitivity of the respective explanatory variable.

STAS results

The STAS-index has been calculated for all the brands. Furthermore the significance (Hansen et al., 1999) of this index has been calculated to decide its accuracy.

63 percent of the 73 brands had a positive STAS index, meaning that there is a positive effect from advertising while the remaining 37 percent proved to be negative. A total of 51 percent of the indices were found to be significant. The range of the STAS indices is from 73.4 till 140.0. See Appendix 1, Columns 3-4.

(McDonald, 1996) shows how his Adlab STAS indices are distributed in quintiles, quite similar to the results from the study reported by (John Philip Jones, 1995a). This is interesting in many aspects, mostly since the two studies were done with two different datasets, one from the US and the other the Adlab database from the UK. If the STAS indices calculated in this study are divided into quintiles, it is seen that the results are somewhat similar to both the Jones and the McDonald study, see Table 9:2.

Table 9:2. STAS indices divided into quintiles

	Number of brands			STAS range			Average STAS		
	Jones	McDonald	This study	Jones	McDonald	This study	Jones	McDonald	This study
1st quintile	15	12	13	44-94	38-94	73-97	82	81	91
2nd quintile	16	13	16	95-106	94-104	97-102	100	99	99
3rd quintile	16	14	14	106-119	104-110	102-106	112	107	104
4th quintile	16	14	13	120-149	110-120	106-111	130	115	108
5th quintile	15	14	17	150-300	121-315	111-140	198	151	120

Logit model results

In the first logit model, an adstock calculation of the OTS in a 28-day period prior to purchase is the only explanatory variable. As mentioned, we use a daily retention rate of 0.97 in our adstock calculation. In this model, we do not correct for any promotion activity at the time of purchase.

Equation 1 gives the general logit model formulation. For logit model 1, we can take the estimated b-values for a specific brand, for instance Kelloggs Cornflakes. This gives us the following expression:

$$E\{Y\} = \frac{\exp(0.1539 + 0.0377 \cdot X_1)}{1 + \exp(0.1539 + 0.0377 \cdot X_1)}$$

X_1 is the explanatory variable, the adstock calculation, and for any given value the purchase probability of this specific product can be calculated. The b1 value is in this case 0.0377, and the corresponding sensitivity value is $\exp(0.0337) = 0.034$, meaning that a one unit

Flemming Hansen • Lotte Yssing Hansen • Lars Grønholdt

increase in the adstock calculation gives a 3.4 percent increase in the purchase probability of Kelloggs Cornflakes.

To summarise the results from logit model 1, we found that 63 percent of the adstock parameter estimates were positive and the remaining 37 percent were negative. In total, 67 percent of the parameter estimates were significant. See Appendix 1. An explanation for these negative parameter estimates could very well be that there is something in the data that this logit model does not account for. However, it is worth considering the possibility that the brands, for which we have found negative adstock parameter estimates, have decided to use another media-strategy, which for some reason has failed. Yet another possibility is that the brand exists in a market that is a highly competitive, and it is therefore easy to "drown" in the crowd if the brand or the advertisements for the brand are not unique.

In the second of the two logit models, we include promotion as an explanatory variable beside the adstock calculation of the OTS. This is done to see whether or not promotion can be a helpful factor in explaining some of the negative adstock parameter estimates from the first logit model, or simply if it contributes to generating a better level of overall explanation. The promotion activity information is included as a binary variable, i.e. either there was a promotion activity associated with the purchase or not. From the 73 brands, we find that 64 percent of the adstock parameters were positive, while the remaining 36 percent were negative, and a total of 67 percent of the adstock parameter estimates were significant. Studying the parameter estimates "b2", we see that they are distributed quite evenly with 52 percent being positive and 48 percent being negative. A total of 89 percent of the promotion estimates are significant, see Appendix 1.

In this case, the purchase probability for Kelloggs Cornflakes will be:

$$E\{Y\} = \frac{\exp(0.1528 + 0.0383 \cdot X_1 + 0.0124 \cdot X_2)}{1 + \exp(0.1528 + 0.0383 \cdot X_1 + 0.0124 \cdot X_2)}$$

X_1 is the adstock variable and X_2 is the promotion variable. For any given values of these two explanatory variables, the purchase probability of this specific product can be calculated. The b1 value is in this case 0.0383 with the corresponding sensitivity $\exp(0.0383) =$ 0.039, meaning that a one unit increase in the explanatory variable will give a 3.9 percent increase in the purchase probability of the brand, all other things being equal.

When promotion was introduced in the model as the second explanatory variable, we could see that the variance of the residuals decreased. For some of the brands, the significance of the b1 parameter estimate also became larger. It was also seen that very many of the promotion parameter estimates were significant in the second model. Therefore we decided to continue with the second logit model, i.e. the model with two explanatory variables.

To understand why some of the brands exhibit negative adstock parameter estimates, we have formulated three hypotheses:

H1: The brands with negative adstock parameter estimates have positive promotion parameter estimates. In other words, the purchases of these brands are made more on the basis of promotion than advertisements and since promotion and advertising are correlated, promotion may pick up on the effect of advertising as well, and thus overrule the effect of advertising.

H2: The brands with negative adstock parameter estimates can be explained on the basis of studies of the share-of-voice/share-of-market situation.

H3: Failing ad-campaigns.

Re H1: Half of the brands that had negative adstock parameter estimates had, a significant positive promotion parameter estimate. On average 13.6 percent of all purchases made for these brands were made in connection with a promotion activity. On average 11.7 percent of all purchases have been made in connection with a promotion activity. The other half of the brands that have negative adstock estimates the promotion parameter estimates were found to be negative and significant. For these brands, only 5.5 percent of the purchases were made in connection with a promotion activity.

Re H2: One of the characteristics of the brands that are not explained by H1 is that they do not belong to the same product category, but represent 8 different product categories. This is a strong indication of a connection between the share-of-voice/share-of-market situation.

Within each product category there will be a category leader, and since we are studying the brands in each category with the highest number of purchases and most advertising, we study a situation that roughly could be compared to a zero-sum game. There will be brands losing market share on account of other brands winning market share. However, at the moment we do not have the data available to completely support this hypothesis, but investigations on this subject are in the process of being carried out.

Re H3: We do not have access to the actual advertisements themselves, nor do we have any other material indicating whether the different ads or campaigns were good or bad. A satisfying test of this hypothesis is therefore not possible, but this hypothesis is rather meant as a reminder that bad ads and poorly planned campaigns do occur. The 9 cases not explained are:

- A gravy maker: Brooke Bond Oxo
- A chocolate covered biscuit or wafer: Twix
- A cat food: Kit-e-Kat
- A toilet roll: Andrex
- An instant soup: Batchelors Slim a Soup
- An instant coffee: Nescafe
- An instant coffee: Nescafe Gold Blend
- A washing powder: Ariel
- A shampoo: Head & Shoulders

Maybe somebody in the UK may remember reasons for the failure of these campaigns and/or brands.

When we compare the logit parameter estimate for adstock found in model 2 with the STAS indices, another interesting result appears. The summary of the results is shown in Table 9:3.

Table 9:3. Comparison of STAS and logit adstock parameter estimates

	Positive adstock parameter estimate	Negative adstock parameter estimate
Positive STAS	40	6
Negative STAS	7	20

From Table 9:3, it is interesting to see that in the cases where a positive adstock parameter estimate was found, a corresponding positive STAS index was also found and vice versa for the negative estimates. Only a total of 13 cases had opposite STAS indices and logit

162

parameter estimates. This means that in spite of the fact that only few significant STAS indices were found, they still give a good indication of whether the group exposed to ads in a 7-day period prior to purchase is more likely to purchase the brand or not. We do not say that the two methods give the same result, we simply suggest that the general trend in the results from the two methods is the same.

Summary

In this work we have studied 73 fmcg brands from different product categories. We have calculated their STAS indices and further determined the significance of these indices. We have also estimated two logistic regression models, to determine if this would give a more varied and specific picture of what affects the consumers in their purchase decision. We can conclude that working with the STAS index, a relatively simple method, gives fewer significant results than the logit model, however when the results from the two methods were compared, it was clear that the STAS method and the logit method gave indication for the same trend of the effect of advertising. This is interesting in the sense that it seems to be possible that the simple measure describes the complex purchase decision process almost as good as the complex model.

It is also important to observe that even though in the majority of cases advertising and promotions have positive effects it is not always so. In some instances the effect of promotion overrule the effect of advertising. In other instances, competitive activities, other changes in the market (introductions, withdrawals, "fashion changes", etc.) may result in negative ad and/or promotion effect. In some cases poorly done advertising or poor promotion may provide the negative results.

It was thus interesting to note that half of the cases where we found negative adstock parameters in the logit model could be explained by a large share of promotion activity. The STAS calculations do not take into account other factors than the advertising exposures 7 days prior to purchase. However, we believe, based on the results from the logit analysis, that promotion is a crucial factor in the purchase decision, and it is therefore necessary to consider this in the analysis, even though in many cases the introductions of promotional activities into the model does not change the estimates of the advertising effect per se dramatically.

On the basis of our results, we will continue working with the logit model, simply because of its possibilities of including more explanatory variables, and because we find more significant results. The STAS measure cannot be changed to account for more variables, but in itself it does provide results in line with the logit results.

Future research will concentrate on the logit model and the explanatory variables rather than the STAS measure. If it is possible to improve on the STAS measure what factors would be the ones to consider? The answer to this question depends on how one believes a brand decision is made. The whole brand decision process is a very complex process that involve for example factors such as in-store promotion, price deductions, competitor actions and so forth. However, the process also includes factors that are not easily measurable, such as customers' loyalty, not only toward the brand, but also toward the store. A factor that is important to remember is the advertisement itself, how is it made – is it a good advertisement or not? What is a good advertisement? These last two issues are important to be aware of, but extremely difficult if not impossible to measure in practice.

For the adstock calculation, future research involves a more varied study of the retention rate, to determine if it perhaps should be either brand specific or category specific. In this study, promotion was included as a binary variable. However, it could be very interesting to study how the different types of promotion affects the purchase decision. Another issue would be to include the weight of viewing in the model to correct for a possible P-V bias.

Since we have noticed that the ad-pressure changes for some brands dramatically over the years, it may be valuable to divide the data into the different years and study the results. Some preliminary studies on this topic have been done, and this change in ad-pressure was seen reflected in the parameter estimates of the logit models.

Finally, it should be considered if more explanatory variables should be included in the logit model to give an even more varied and realistic picture of the purchase decision process.

Appendix I – Results from the STAS and logit model analyses

Product category	Brand	STAS-Index	Sig. of STAS-index (critical value: 1.96)	Advertising parameter estimate (b1) from logit model 1	Significance of b1 from logit model 1, the Chi-square value (critical value: 3.84)	Advertising parameter estimate (b1) from logit model 2	Sig. of b1 from logit model 2, the Chi-square value (critical value: 3.84)	Promotion parameter estimate (b2) from logit model 2	Significance of b2 from logit model 2, the Chi-square value (critical value: 3.84)
Breakfast Cereal	418 - Kelloggs Cornflakes	105.6	3.89	b1: 0.0377	99.50	b1: 0.0383	102.66	b2: 0.0124	9.69
	421 - Kelloggs Rice Krispies	105.5	2.17	b1: 0.0193	23.42	b1: 0.0206	26.60	bb2: 0.0216	80.50
	422 - Kelloggs Bran Flakes	111.7	3.82	b1: 0.0162	39.70	b1: 0.0173	45.44	b2: 0.0201	98.45
	427 - Kelloggs All Bran	109.8	2.81	b1: 0.0178	54.63	b1: 0.0181	55.83	b2: 0.0037	4.15
	428 - Kelloggs Special K	117.3	4.46	b1: 0.0197	58.76	b1: 0.0195	57.89	b2: -0.0084	19.73
	429 - Kelloggs Frosties	84.2	6.13	b1: -0.0232	42.34	b1: -0.0227	40.60	b2: 0.0088	15.78
	433 - Other Kelloggs	136.1	15.60	b1: 0.0204	118.26	b1: 0.0208	121.74	b2: 0.0105	12.78
	434 - Nabisco Shredded Wheat	105.5	1.78	b1: 0.0098	2.70	b1: 0.0091	2.31	b2: -0.0092	16.59
	436 - Nabisco Shreddies	91.6	1.59	b1: -0.0131	8.42	b1: -0.0118	6.90	b2: 0.0229	214.20
	440 - Quaker Sugar Puffs	108.6	2.08	b1: 0.0176	18.35	b1: 0.0177	18.75	b2: 0.0057	9.49
	442 - Weetabix	102.8	1.83	b1: 0.0198	12.95	b1: 0.0177	10.30	b2: -0.0314	77.43
Cat food	6070 - Whiskas Supermeat	96.0	5.27	b1: -0.0887	523.80	b1: -0.0896	535.77	b2: 0.0945	526.16
	6071 - Kit-e-Kat	87.4	7.63	b1: -0.0312	49.28	b1: -0.0301	45.80	b2: -0.0221	77.23
	6073 - Katkins	108.3	2.18	b1: 0.0126	7.33	b1: 0.0112	5.78	b2: -0.0314	269.53
	6074 - Kattomeat	119.9	12.15	b1: 0.1323	534.03	b1: 0.1320	534.30	b2: 0.0707	613.57
Dog food	6130 - Pedigree Chum	97.9	1.34	b1: 0.0065	2.15	b1: 0.0074	2.81	b2: 0.0718	158.57
	6132 - Pal	103.9	1.70	b1: 0.0218	23.89	b1: 0.0218	23.89	b2: -0.0182	24.78
	6133 - Bounce	107.8	1.12	b1: 0.0092	0.66	b1: 0.0091	0.64	b2: -0.0177	41.90
	6135 - Cesar	98.2	0.72	b1: 0.0308	35.90	b1: 0.0301	34.30	b2: 0.0348	88.36
	6138 - Winalot Prime	93.3	3.04	b1: -0.0418	84.61	b1: -0.0414	83.06	b2: 0.0097	7.25
	6198 - Other Dog Foods	130.9	8.29	b1: 0.0682	96.12	b1: 0.0657	89.36	b2: -0.0281	72.14
Chocolate Bars	6801 - Mars Bar	111.2	3.58	b1: 0.1283	22.11	b1: 0.1247	21.15	b2: 0.1197	138.02
	6802 - Milky Way	98.2	0.27	b1: 0.0108	0.17	b1: 0.0111	0.18	b2: 0.0134	4.76
	6803 - Bounty	107.3	0.99	b1: 0.0239	2.46	b1: 0.0255	2.82	b2: -0.0377	47.48

165

	6805 - Marathon	99.9	0.01	b1: -0.0235	2.30	b1: -0.0223	2.09	b2: -0.0287	25.49
	6807 - Crunchie	104.6	0.53	b1: -0.0110	0.57	b1: -0.0097	0.44	b2: -0.0245	22.27
	6811 - Double Decker	105.3	0.51	b1: 0.0070	0.21	b1: 0.0072	0.22	b2: -0.0184	13.05
	6813 - Wispa	99.6	0.05	b1: -0.0020	0.01	b1: -0.0012	0.00	b2: -0.0149	5.05
	6816 - Aero	126.5	3.29	b1: 0.0599	11.78	b1: 0.0612	12.34	b2: 0.0318	28.06
Automatic Washing Powder	9002 - Ariel Automatic	99.7	0.14	b1: -0.0071	3.97	b1: -0.0075	4.42	b2: -0.0290	41.15
	9003 - Bold 3	140.0	15.37	b1: 0.1058	311.89	b1: 0.1049	306.76	b2: -0.0149	14.84
	9005 - Daz Automatic	109.5	3.98	b1: 0.0243	14.36	b1: 0.0236	13.60	b2: -0.0124	11.09
	9011 - Levers Wisk Liquid Detergent	110.9	2.84	b1: 0.0164	10.95	b1: 0.0156	9.91	b2: -0.0105	18.90
	9013 - Persil Automatic	97.9	1.64	b1: -0.0345	14.54	b1: -0.0306	11.53	b2: 0.1134	456.87
	9015 - Surf	105.9	1.93	b1: 0.0116	2.94	b1: 0.0131	3.76	b2: 0.0261	69.44
Toilet Rolls	6501 - Andrex	96.6	3.21	b1: -0.0441	53.70	b1: -0.0442	53.77	b2: -0.0149	4.24
	6513 - Kleenix	94.0	2.04	b1: -0.0158	10.46	b1: -0.0156	10.11	b2: 0.0231	45.52
	6523 - Dixcel	101.6	0.84	b1: -0.0072	1.70	b1: -0.0071	1.65	b2: 0.0526	107.73
Biscuits and Wafers	5501 - Penguin	99.4	0.21	b1: -0.0083	0.23	b1: 0.0060	0.12	b2: 0.0941	591.87
	5508 - Jacobs Club	112.2	4.19	b1: 0.0134	0.91	b1: 0.0141	0.99	b2: -0.0061	2.16
	5509 - Jacobs Trio	102.9	0.28	b1: -0.0212	0.59	b1: -0.0256	0.86	b2: -0.0293	151.82
	5512 - Kit Kat	108.3	4.87	b1: 0.1762	128.20	b1: 0.1938	156.39	b2: 0.1104	486.11
	5515 - Twix	89.6	3.54	b1: -0.0663	50.49	b1: -0.0656	49.24	b2: -0.0044	1.89
Gravy makers - cubes	3633 - Knorr	116.9	1.08	b1: -0.0150	0.67	b1: -0.0156	0.72	b2: -0.0377	11.32
	3634 - Brooke Bond Oxo	97.7	2.27	b1: -0.0550	7.78	b1: -0.0491	6.26	b2: -0.2513	136.68
	3638 - Bovril	101.2	0.26	b1: 0.0561	5.94	b1: 0.0547	5.75	b2: 0.3148	286.69
Instant Coffee	8520 - Maxwell House High Blend	94.43	1.90	b1: -0.0296	60.01	b1: -0.0298	61.57	b2: 0.1609	893.12
	8529 - Brooke Bond Red Mountain	120.7	6.60	b1: 0.0318	79.10	b1: 0.0317	78.76	b2: 0.0096	3.95
	8530 - Birds Mellow	118.3	3.86	b1: 0.0166	8.83	b1: 0.0163	8.49	b2: 0.0419	125.44
	8562 - Nescafe Gold Blend	102.6	0.58	b1: -0.0117	12.08	b1: -0.0120	12.61	b2: -0.0215	50.87
	8526 - Nescafe	97.1	2.13	b1: -0.0502	64.62	b1: -0.0509	66.64	b2: -0.1310	235.14
Shampoo	9776 - Head and Shoulders	90.5	2.19	b1: -0.0242	9.60	b1: -0.0264	11.45	b2: -0.0162	16.62
	9778 - Vosene	112.6	2.93	b1: 0.0623	17.95	b1: 0.0607	17.02	b2: -0.0172	11.41

	9780 - Alberto VO5	96.2	0.34	b1: -0.0083	0.27	b1: -0.0037	0.05	b2: 0.0739	463.89
	9782 - Palmolive	106.2	0.63	b1: 0.0082	0.19	b1: 0.0070	0.14	b2: -0.0051	2.61
	9785 - Silvikrin	125.2	1.85	b1: 0.0082	0.79	b1: 0.0099	1.16	b2: 0.0442	166.15
	9786 - Sunsilk	97.4	0.22	b1: 0.0077	0.25	b1: 0.0109	0.50	b2: 0.0246	62.78
	9788 - Timotei	99.4	0.11	b1: 0.0217	4.12	b1: 0.0215	4.06	b2: -0.0024	0.34
	9798 - Other Branded	110.7	4.37	b1: 0.0485	25.87	b1: 0.0464	41.93	b2: -0.0425	39.85
Toothpaste	9605 - Crest Standard-Plus	112.3	3.31	b1: 0.0074	0.76	b1: 0.0045	0.38	b2: -0.0186	24.71
	9617 - Aquafresh 3	115.8	2.95	b1: 0.0620	17.27	b1: 0.0630	17.77	b2: 0.0052	1.69
	9619 - Signal	89.6	1.34	b1: -0.0346	5.05	b1: -0.0306	3.94	b2: 0.0190	34.21
	9631 - Macleans Freshmint	114.4	3.28	b1: 0.0531	15.52	b1: 0.0587	19.11	b2: 0.0630	275.90
Deodorants	6460 - Sure	107.1	2.01	b1: 0.0802	14.55	b1: 0.0802	14.54	b2: 0.0007	0.01
	6461 - Soft & Gentle	103.9	0.57	b1: 0.0186	0.36	b1: 0.0143	0.21	b2: 0.0276	24.90
	6462 - Body Mist 2	98.1	0.20	b1: -0.0214	1.13	b1: -0.0215	1.14	b2: 0.0038	0.49
	6465 - Right Guard	106.9	1.09	b1: -0.0190	1.10	b1: -0.0190	1.11	b2: 0.0008	0.02
	6467 - Amplex	98.0	0.34	b1: 0.0243	1.47	b1: 0.0199	0.99	b2: 0.0453	71.73
	6498 - Other branded	103.5	0.77	b1: 0.0666	14.58	b1: 0.0688	14.67	b2: -0.0165	5.85
Instant Soup	8142 - Any Batchelors Cup a Soup	103.4	1.44	b1: 0.1278	27.79	b1: 0.1276	27.76	b2: -0.1029	30.94
	8143 - Batchelors Slim a Soup	73.4	5.35	b1: -0.1071	38.09	b1: -0.1066	37.74	b2: -0.0660	27.23
Tub Margarine	9408 - Stork SB	107.2	2.91	b1: 0.0590	46.77	b1: 0.0568	43.38	b2: 0.0492	160.66
Tea Bags	9907 - Typhoo One Cup	104.4	0.80	b1: 0.0150	24.06	b1: 0.0149	23.81	b2: -0.0043	3.91

10

What do Art Directors think the Effects of Advertising are?

KJELL GRØNHAUG

Abstract

This paper reports on a study conducted to gain insights into art directors' thinking. It is concerned with the questions of how to create effective advertising, to what extent the thought processes of the art directors affect this procedure, and, resultantly, how the advertisements are produced. Our findings clearly demonstrate that the art directors studied advocate individual theories that are predominantly based on already established insights.

Introduction

Advertisements are costly, highly directed activities, whereby advertisers aim to inform and influence target groups. This is achieved by making them aware of, and/or creating changes in attitudes towards, preferences for and a propensity to purchase their product/service offerings. In applying advertising as a means of market communication, the advertiser faces a multitude of decisions. She (the advertiser) must define the target group(s), select the advertising medium (media), and make decisions regarding message, content and format. Advertisements are assumed to be effective, i.e. to fulfil the advertisers' intended goals both for their advertising and business.

Extensive research shows that the advertising message plays an important role in the effectiveness of the advertising. Two driving questions underlie the choice of advertising message. Firstly, "What to say?" and secondly, "How to say it?". Research findings also show, that choice of advertising content and presentation of that content can dramatically influence the result of the advertising (for an overview, see, for example, Rossiter & Percey 1997).

Effective advertising messages are the outcome of creative and thoughtful processes. The "creative" people, i.e. art directors and their staff, have over the years played a key role in the creation of advertising messages. For this reason, some of these people have obtaine the status of "advertising gurus".

Over the years, the question of "how advertising works" has been intensively discussed, and has also been subject to considerable research (for recent overview, see Vakratsas & Ambler 1999). However, the "truths", beliefs, and theories of how advertising work are still multiple. Beliefs and theories of how to make effective advertising are reflected in various "creative philosophies" among advertising agencies and their art directors (see e.g. Bagozzi 1986, pp. 381-388).

Art directors, as do other human beings, think and following this, they adhere to implicit theories. Their thought processes, as reflected in their private theories, influence their actions and thus the advertisements that they create. Only modest research has addressed the question of how art directors, think about how to make effective advertising (for exceptions, see e.g. Kover 1995; and Kover et al 1997). The present paper r attempts to gain some insight into this question.

The remaining part of the paper is organized as follows: In the next section we address the importance of knowledge and thinking, and factors that influence this process. Here we also develop a tentative perspective (model) to guide, but not dictate, our empirical investigation. Following this, we report on the research methodology underlying the empirical part of our study. After this we report the findings, followed by our concluding remarks.

Thinking, Knowledge and Doing

Thinking often, but not necessarily, precedes doing. However, when trying to exhibit goal-directed behaviour, e.g. to create effective advertising, this will often be the case. Because advertisers are embedded in hostile, ever-changing environments, and because they must be effective in order to survive and prosper, conscious and thought-based doing are believed to be prevalent.

"Thinking" is a rather broad term and has been defined in multiple ways. Most definitions emphasize that thinking subsumes multiple mental activities, such as problem finding, interpretations, problem solving, and decision making (see e.g. Galotti 1994).

Thinking relates to learning and knowledge. Systematic thinking, i.e. the ability to think related thoughts, may also create new insights, leading to knowledge and learning (Holyvak & Spellman 1993, s. 269). Over time, individuals, including directors, develop knowledge structures. The development of such knowledge structures is facilitated by a variety of factors, e.g. the tasks that the individuals are involved in, experience and education.

When individuals are exposed to new data, this data must be interpreted in order to become information (knowledge). A process which requires conscious thinking. Newly interpreted data only becomes new knowledge when it produces changes in memory and thinking (Brucks 1985, p. 2). When stimuli (data) are interpreted, they tend to be categorized into existing knowledge structures or schemes (cf. Rosch 1979). Existing knowledge structures - often termed "mental models" - influence what is captured and how it is understood (cf. Johnson - Laird 1983). Such mental models can also be seen as the reality constructions of individuals (cf. Berger & Luckman 1969). Elaborate knowledge structures ease absorption of new information, in particular when this information is congruent with existing knowledge structures. Due to the fact that established knowledge structures tend to be rather rigid (Sanford 1986), new information does not necessarily lead to changes in memory (learning) and doing. This latter point is demonstrated in Argyris' fascinating article, "Teaching smart people how to learn" (Argyris 1991).

Art directors

Art directors hold important positions in advertising agencies. Due to the emphasis on creativity in the advertising business, art directors often influence the philosophy and actions of their organization. The emphasis on creativity is reflected in several ways. In Norway, for example (where the study was undertaken), a variety of awards to enhance creativity (and advertising effectiveness) have been established, such as the "Stella"-award and "Gullblyanten". Also, the "creative heroes" are embraced e.g. in their outlet campaign. Ratings among the advertising agencies are conducted regularly, ranking the agencies according to the "most creative".

Art directors vary in educational background, both with regard to substance and level. They also vary with regard to types of products/services they work with and work environment. Some agencies favour creativity more than others. Organization of work also varies across advertising agencies. Such factors are important, as they may influence the art directors' thinking and doing. This is illustrated in Figure 10:1.

Figure 10:1 represents our tentative perspective. The Figure is to be understood as follows: Box 1 indicates that the art directors' educational background, training, experiences and expectations may influence his or her thinking and doing - and therefore their solutions in advertising work.

Most art directors are employed by advertising agencies that vary individually with regard to advertising philosophy and organization of work. The art directors' relative position and influence within the agency may also vary (Box 2a). Advertising agencies and art directors work with clients. Clients differ with regard to products/services and requirements. The contract between agency and clients ranges between discrete meetings to continuous interactions. The traditional "briefing", i.e. meetings between the traditional agency and the client to get the needed information and to clarify requirements and expectations, reflects agency-client relationships characterized by "arm-length", discrete meetings. Such factors may, of course, influence art directors' expectations, thinking and doing.

New ideas and trends continuously emerge. Such ideas are spread in various ways, e.g. through educational programmes, magazine articles, presentations and informal discussion. Art directors may, to a varying degree, become aware of and thus take such new ideas and trends into account.

Kjell Grønhaug

Figure 10:1 Perspective

3. New ideas/trends

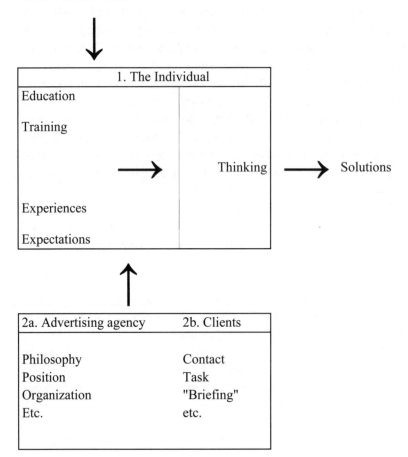

Research methodology

As stated above, the prime purpose of this paper, is to gain insights into how art directors think when creating effective advertising. Due to modest, 'a priori insights', an explanatory, discovery-oriented approach was chosen. The study was conducted among art directors in Norwegian advertising agencies.

To be able to include all the varying factors assumed to influence art directors thinking (cf. Figure 10:1), subjects with a variety of experience and educational background, coming from advertising agencies that varied in size, organizational structure and philosophy, were chosen. A key requirement underlying the present study is to capture art directors' thinking. Multiple methods or approaches to capture thinking exist (cf. Huff, 1990). In this paper, methods both based on secondary and primary research were employed.

Our approach included content analysis of interviews and arguments expressed in advertising magazines, as well as advertisements and brochures made by the agencies. In this context, it is interesting to note that Chapman & Schwenk (1991) claim that published statements are a superior source for the capturing of cognitive aspects of managers.

Furthermore, to collect information for the study, we conducted semi-structural interviews with art directors. An interview-guide based on analysis of the secondary material was developed. Prior to the interviews appointments were made by phone. The interviews were conducted in the art directors' agencies.

The interviews were related to the advertising campaigns that the agencies most recently had been involved in. When contacted, the art directors were asked to bring material from these projects to the interview meeting. The interviews centred on this material, for example:

"Please tell us about this advertisement campaign", followed by a set of questions such as: "Was it an old or new client?", "What does the advertisement intend to convey?", "Who was involved?" and "How did you arrive at the actual solution?"

We also raised questions regarding relationships with their clients, e.g. Whether the client played any role in the creation of advertisements, and if so, how? A total of 12 interviews were conducted. Each interview lasted from one-and-a-half till two hours. All interviews were tape-recorded, transcribed and content analysed. The interviews and additional time spent in the advertising agencies also allowed for observations, informal interviewing and discussions.

Findings

This section reports the findings from our empirical investigation.

Visual symbols

An interesting observation made during our research, was the emphasis placed on visual symbols. As stated by one of the art directors: "My job is to be the visual spokesman". This as such is interesting, because the visual aspect is paid rather limited attention in marketing and marketing communication, as taught in business schools, even though "the power of the visual" has been noted by academics (cf. Wells et al 1992, pp. 407-8). This is important, due to the fact that much communication is nonverbal, and that visual symbols, in various forms, attract attention, evoke mental images and feelings, and thus exert influence upon the person experiencing these emotions.

Creative emphasis

Great variations in emphasis on creativity versus analyses were observed among the art directors studied. The extreme emphasis on creativity can be characterized by the following process:

"Start with the "creative idea" and then, "Dramatize" the message, focus on attention and surprise".

The opposite, analytical approach observed, can be described in the following way:

"Start with an analysis of customers and competitors, identify target groups; and develop the approach in a systematic way."

These variations co vary with agency-philosophy, organization and dominant person(s) within the agency. Our findings also show that internal creative norms exist within the agencies, also identified by Kover et al (1997).

Art directors' ideas and opinions about creativity were also found to vary considerably. They varied from:

- Very strong beliefs concerning the need for freedom, conceiving creativity as an introverted process that is difficult, if not impossible, to steer via the use of structured techniques to enhance creativity.

to:

- conceived as a constrained process, guided –,or driven, by analyses and facts. An art director, who is also the top manager in a medium-sized, but well-performing agency, put it this way:

"Within the given facts and the core business value and idea, my creative people have to perform."

Beliefs about the art director role

Art directors' opinions about their role and position were also found to vary considerably. At the one extreme, the "creative hero", with unlimited belief in his own importance for the outcome of the advertising was observed. An example of this can be illustrated by the following quote: "My customer could never have achieved this (increase in sales) without me".

The other extreme observed was the belief that the traditional art director is more or less obsolete. This view is reflected in the following quote: "The role of the traditional art director; i.e. the personwho makes illustrations and so on is out," and is believed to be replaced by persons with a broader focus on business.

Agency and clients

Contacts and relationships between agency and clients also showed great variations. At the one extreme we observed discrete, limited numbers of meetings between agency and client with the focus on advertisement. In such cases we also observed the use of traditional "briefing", discussed in advertising textbooks. At the other extreme we found close cooperation and continuous interactions between agency and client with real focus on learning and understanding the client, her business and problems. In such cases, the traditional briefing played a modest role, or no role at all, as reflected in the following quote:

"We don't have the traditional briefing anymore. We interact and discuss with the client - and we arrive at a mutual understanding."

Situations like this were only observed for clients staffed with highly competent persons handling the contact with the agency.

Kjell Grønhaug

Ideas about research and customers

We observed great variations in opinions of, and beliefs in, research. They varied from seeing research and analyses as extremely important and useful, to the complete opposite, i.e. finding it to be unnecessary and of no use. One art director claimed that: "People are never honest, so therefore it is pointless to ask them". This quote reflects not only distrust in people, but also a rather naive and biased view of what research is, and the role high-quality research may play in advertising.

In our study, we also observed traces of outdated views of customers, as being passive and more or less defenceless, and old maxims such as "concentrate, dominate and repeat". On the other hand, we also found beliefs about customers, portraying them as being active, with individual needs and preferences, as reflected in the modern literature on consumer behaviour.

Concluding remarks

Our findings demonstrate that art directors harbour thoughts and private theories about clients, customers and how advertising works.

Their theories and thinking vary greatly based on more or less relevant foundations seemingly influenced by factors such as education, training, work environments, focus and attention. The basis for their ideas and thinking partly reflects old advertising maxims, but in some cases are also found to be in line with modern thinking and ideas.

There is no doubt that more research is needed to uncover art directors thinking and doing. For example, a larger number of subjects should be included to allow a more extensive systematic analysis of the impact of factors such as educational background and agency philosophy on their thinking. Other approaches, e.g. the use of verbal protocols, should also be included to more systematically examine the relationships between thinking, doing and outcomes.

11

Program Context Effects on Commercial Processing

MARJOLEIN MOORMAN, PETER C. NEIJENS,
& EDITH G. SMIT

Program Context Effects on Recall and Attention towards Television Commercials

Traditionally, quantitative factors, such as information about size and composition of the audience of a television program, serve as the basic currency in negotiations between buyers and sellers of TV ad time. Recent developments, however, such as the growing amount of channels and programs, the declining audience sizes, and the increasing costs of commercial airtime, have revived interest among TV advertisers and their agencies for qualitative program factors. Qualitative program factors are those characteristics that influence the likelihood that a commercial is being seen and absorbed (Lynch & Stipp, 1999).

Qualitative program factors, which both academics and practitioners widely agree are among the most important predictors of advertising processing, are psychological responses induced by the program (Moorman, Neijens, & Smit, in press). Program-induced psychological responses are the individual and subjective mental reactions that people experience when watching television, such as involvement with a documentary or feelings of joy or sadness caused by a soap series. Although it is a widespread belief that the effectiveness of a commercial is affected by the way viewers mentally react toward the program, there is not much empirical evidence to substantiate this view. Little research is done under natural viewing conditions, i.e. outside artificial laboratories and with a representative sample of television viewers.

In this paper, we will present the results of secondary analyses on data from a large telephone survey assessing TV viewers' responses to programs and commercials embedded within and surrounding these programs. First, we have analyzed whether advertising processing is influenced by psychological responses induced by the program. Second, we have examined whether these effects were different for various placement positions. Whether, in other words, commercial breaks that interrupt a program are influenced in a different way to breaks between two programs and whether the effects vary depending on different positions of the commercial within the break. Before we discuss the results of these secondary analyses, we will elaborate on previous research and theoretical perspectives with regard to these relationships.

Psychological Responses and Advertising Processing

The general belief that psychological program responses influence advertising impact is founded on the basic assumption that the mental reactions toward program material do not immediately cease to exist when the program is suddenly interrupted by a commercial break. In other words, responses such as involvement, joy, and sadness induced by the program are still experienced by the audience when confronted with the commercials. These spilled-over reactions, in turn, influence how the commercials are received and processed. Program context influences are considered to be limited to processing effects, such as attention, recall and attitude toward the ad (A_{ad}), because these effects emerge after a single exposure, unlike advertising effects such as attitude toward the brand (A_b), purchase intention and actual buying, which require multiple exposures (e.g. Franzen, 1994; Wright-Isak, Faber, & Horner 1997).

Two aspects of psychological responses are deemed important with regard to the effect on advertising processing: valence and intensity of the response (Moorman et al., in press). Valence refers to the evaluative predisposition of the response (positive or negative). In other words, is the program appreciated or not, is it liked or disliked?

Previous research is quite equivocal in showing that the valence of the program response affects A_{ad} by influencing it in the same direction (Aylesworth & MacKenzie, 1998; Goldberg & Gorn, 1987; Moorman et al., in press; Murry, Lastovicka, & Sing, 1992). Thus, a commercial message is evaluated more positively when inserted in a program that is evaluated more positively and vice versa.

Intensity refers to the relative strength of the response, indicated by, for example, the amount of attention paid to the program or the level of involvement reported. Intensity of the program-induced response has been found to have its principal influence on memory for advertising. Past research has yielded conflicting results with regard to the direction of these effects, however. Some studies have mentioned an enhancing effect of intensity on ad recall, while others reported a diminishing effect.

Many explanations have been brought forward by several researchers (Norris & Colman, 1993: Schumann & Thorson, 1991) to account for the contradicting findings for the relationship between intensity and ad recall, including differences in the operational definitions of the psychological responses, the stimulus material used and the composition of the subject sample (e.g. student sample versus general population sample). The most important explanatory factor, however, seems to be the research setting. Negative effects on recall have predominantly been found in artificial experimental settings where exposure is forced (e.g., Bryant & Comisky, 1978; Gunter, Furnham, & Beeson, 1997; Kennedy, 1971; Norris & Colman, 1993; Soldow & Principe, 1981), while positive effects are mostly the outcome of studies conducted in settings that are more true to real-life and without forced exposure. (Lloyd and Clancy, 1991), for example, found that intensity enhanced recall in an experiment where 470 female participants were free to get involved with other tasks besides television viewing, such as drinking, eating and reading. More recently, (Moorman et al., 2001) reported, based on a field study held during the European soccer championship 2000, that viewers were more likely to watch and remember the commercials embedded within a highly involving match, compared to a less involving match.

The results of recent studies on program context effect, such as the study of (Lloyd and Clancy, 1991) and (Moorman et al., 2001), have provided interesting insight into program effects in a real-life situation.

Marjolein Moorman • Peter C. Neijens • Edith G. Smit

However, these studies harbor some shortcomings with regard to the generalization of their results. The study of (Lloyd and Clancy, 1991) was conducted for four different programs with only female respondents, while (Moorman et al., 2001) conducted their study during a special event, for which advertisers create special commercials. Therefore, the question remains if the positive findings of these studies can be transferred to regular TV programming, regular TV ads and a regular public. The present study is aimed at answering this question by means of secondary analyses on data from a representative telephone survey that assessed TV viewers' responses to various programs and commercials. Because these data were collected in a non-artificial situation, where commercial exposure is free, we expect to find positive effects of intensity and valence of the psychological responses on commercial processing, in line with earlier real-life studies.

Mediation of Variations in Commercial Placement

Next to the general effects of intensity and valence of psychological responses on advertising processing of the commercials at an aggregated level, we have looked at whether these effects could possibly be mediated by commercial position. Several authors have suggested that the influence of program context on advertising processing is affected by the position of the commercial within the break and by the position of the break in relation to the program. (Mattes and Cantor, 1982), for example, found that the enhancing effect of residual arousal from prior programming on enjoyment and perceived effectiveness of the commercial was strongest for commercials shown 2.30 to 4.00 minutes after the arousing program segments. This effect was attributed to the theory of excitation transfer, which holds that residual excitation intensifies subsequent emotional feelings, but only when it is not perceived as attributable to its actual source. Three stages are distinguished. During the first phase, individuals are aroused by the program and aware of the source of the arousal. During the second stage arousal is still present, but the individual is no longer aware that the programming has caused this. During the third phase the arousal is gone. Enhancing effects due to the transfer of program arousal to subsequent commercials are thus strongest during the second stage.

Next to the position of the commercial within the break, some researchers have mentioned that the position of the break in relation to the program is of importance for the effect of program context on commercial processing (e.g., Krugman, 1983). It is argued that the intensity of program responses diminishes when the program ends, and therefore commercials shown in the block that follows a program are less affected by these program responses than commercials inserted in a block that interrupts the program.

On the basis of these findings for different commercial positions, we expected that 'spill over' effects of the intensity and valence of program responses on commercial responses would be influenced by the position of the break and the position of the commercial within the break.

Method

To study program context effects on commercial processing, we conducted secondary analyses on data from a large survey study commissioned by a media agency in cooperation with one of the largest advertising companies worldwide. The database contained the results of 1,879 computer assisted telephone interviews (CATI) concerning responses to 15.089 commercials (8 commercials per respondent on average) inserted in and proceeding 214 different programs.

The fieldwork was carried out by a large market research company. Interviews were conducted from 6 p.m. till 11 p.m. in the period April 14th - May 12th 1999. The interviews concerned the last commercial block that the respondent saw and the program(s)[1] watched before and after this commercial block in the last two hours. The first aim of the interview was to correctly identify which commercial block was watched last. To facilitate this process, the program and commercial schedules of the eight national channels (NL1, NL2, NL3, RTL4,

---

1. Respondents were questioned about one program, whether the commercial block interrupted the program. If the commercial block was aired between programs, respondents were interviewed about both the preceding and the subsequent programs.

Marjolein Moorman • Peter C. Neijens • Edith G. Smit

RTL5, SBS6, Veronica, Net5) were entered into the computers each day, together with descriptions of most of the commercials inserted within the various blocks[2]. The following procedure was followed to correctly identify the last commercial block the respondent watched. First, the interviewer asked which was the last program the respondent watched. When this program was located in the schedule in the computer, the interviewer asked whether the last commercial block seen, followed, proceeded or interrupted this program and whether this commercial block was aired on the same channel as the television program.

When the correct commercial block was identified, the interview continued with questions about the commercials within the commercial block, the programs seen around the commercial block, and characteristics of the respondent.

Respondents

Random digit dialing yielded 33,989 existing telephone numbers, of which 13,833 led to actual contact. Of this group 1,879 respondents met the required selection criteria for the initial study and agreed to cooperate. The initial selection criteria were:

- Respondent watched television in the past two hours.
- Respondent saw (part of) at least one commercial block.
- Respondent was between 18 and 65 of age.

For the purpose of our secondary analyses, we removed an additional group of 402 respondents based on two extra selection criteria. First, we removed respondents who had indicated that they had not seen a program before the commercials, because we only wanted to analyze pro-active effects (effects of responses to the program preceding the commercials). Second, we removed respondents who had viewed the commercial block on a different channel than the program, because irregularities in the data showed that this often led to confusion about

---

2. Commercial descriptions were made on the same day as the interviews to provide as much information as possible. This resulted in descriptions of 13.511 commercials in total. Commercials without description were left out of the secondary analyses presented in this study.

the correct block on the interviewers' side, and consequently interview errors.

The average age of the remaining 1477 respondents was 40 (SD = 1.28). The sample consisted of 550 (37%) male and 927 (63%) female respondents who indicated they watched television 6.4 days a week and 3.4 hours a day on average. The majority of these respondents (57%) viewed a commercial block that interrupted the program.

Measures

Several measures of commercial processing were taken. The respondents were asked which share of the commercial block they viewed, the amount of attention paid to the commercial block and which commercials within the commercial block the respondent could mention ad-lib (free recall). Then, descriptions of the commercials that were not recalled ad-lib were read to the respondents and they were asked whether they remembered having seen this commercial in the commercial block (aided recall) and could mention the brand name (proven recall). If the commercial was recalled correctly, either with or without cues, respondents indicated their appreciation of the ad with a report grade from 1 to 10. These commercial measures (i.e. block share exposure, attention, free recall, aided recall, proven recall and appreciation) were the dependent variables of the study.

The interview was also aimed at measuring some aspects of the way respondents watched the surrounding program(s). Two of these measures were relevant for the aim of this study. First, measuring the attention paid to the program with a four-point scale, which we used as an indicator for the level of intensity of the psychological responses. Second, measuring the appreciation of the program with a report grade from 1 to 10, which we used as an indicator for the valence of the psychological responses.

Results

General linear model (GLM) analyses were conducted for each commercial processing measure separately. The ratings for the commercial block as a whole (part of block seen and attention paid to commercial block) were analyzed at the level of the respondent (N =

1477), with attention paid to the program and block position serving as independent factors. The three commercial recall measures (free recall, aided recall, and proven recall) were analyzed at the level of the commercial (N = 11005). In these analyses, commercial position in the

Table 11:1 GLM Results for Several Predictors of Commercial Processing

Dependent variable	df	Type III sum of squares	Mean square	F
Part of block seen				
Attention paid to program (A)	3	67.19	22.40	15.12***
Block position within program (B)	1	2.81	2.81	1.90
A * B	3	1.69	0.56	.38
Attention paid to block				
Attention paid to program (A)	3	7.92	2.64	6.06***
Commercial position within block (C)	1	0.00	0.00	0.01
A * B	3	0.80	0.27	0.61
Free recall				
Attention paid to program (A)	3	0.23	0.07	1.79
Block position within program (B)	1	0.14	0.14	3.16
Commercial position within block (C)	2	0.03	0.02	0.39
A * B	3	0.66	0.09	1.98
A * C	6	0.11	0.02	0.44
B * C	2	0.12	0.06	1.38
A * B *C	6	0.38	0.06	1.48
Aided recall				
Attention paid to program (A)	3	23.84	7.95	32.85***
Block position within program (B)	1	0.85	0.85	3.47
Commercial position within block (C)	2	1.31	0.66	2.68
A * B	3	2.73	0.91	3.73*
A * C	6	1.60	0.27	1.09
B * C	2	0.35	0.17	0.71
A * B *C	6	2.81	0.47	1.92
Proven recall				
Attention paid to program (A)	3	8.73	2.91	15.28***
Block position within program (B)	1	0.21	0.21	1.13
Commercial position within block (C)	2	1.01	0.51	2.66
A * B	3	0.76	0.25	1.33
A * C	6	1.49	0.25	1.30
B * C	2	0.05	0.03	0.14
A * B *C	6	1.03	0.17	0.90
A_{ad}				
Appreciation of program (Ap)	4	126.18	31.55	11.01***
Block position within program (B)	1	2.46	2.46	0.86
Commercial position within block (C)	2	3.76	1.88	0.66
Ap * B	4	30.24	7.56	2.64*
Ap * C	8	14.26	1.78	0.62
B * C	2	0.76	0.38	0.13
Ap * B *C	8	42.69	5.34	1.86

*p < .05. *** p < .001.

block was added as an independent variable next to program attention and block position. Based on the time frames presented in (Mattes and Cantor, 1982), we divided the block into three different positions: 0 to 2.30 minutes after the program, 2.30 minutes to 4.00 minutes after the program and more than 4.00 minutes after the program.

Given that each commercial's length was about 30 seconds, the first part of the break included the first to fifth commercial, the second part was comprised of the sixth to eighth commercial, and the third position contained the ninth to last commercial.

The A_{ad} measure was also analyzed at the commercial level, with program appreciation, block position and commercial position serving as independent factors. For these analyses, we recoded the report grades for the program in five new categories, because the low scores (lower than 6) and the highest score (10) were seldom assigned.

The GLM analyses for both the dependent variables concerning the block as a whole as well as the recall measures for the individual commercials yielded significant main effects of attention paid to the program for four out of five variables (see Table 11:1). Post hoc tests (with Tukey b) showed, in line with the intensity hypothesis, that the mean ratings increase as the program attention rating increases (see Table 11:2). The only measure on which attention paid tothe program did not have a significant effect was free recall. However, the failure to obtain a significant effect on this measure seems to be due to a very low recall percentage.

Table 11:2 Means and Post Hoc Results (Tukey b) for Effects of Attention paid to Program across Five Commercial Processing Variables

	Attention paid to program			
	1	2	3	4
Part of commercial block seen (1-4)	1.44[a]	1.68[a,b]	1.98[b]	2.23[b]
Attention paid to commercial block (1-4)	1.41[a]	1.51[a,b]	1.61[b]	1.69[b]
Free recall (%)	2[a]	4[a]	4[a]	5[a]
Aided recall (%)	38[a, b]	34[a]	44[b,c]	50[b, c]
Proven recall (%)	21[a,b]	20[a]	26[a, b]	28[b]

Means with different subscripts differ significantly horizontally at p<.05.

The main effect of program appreciation on A_{ad} was also found to be significant (see Table 11:1). Results showed that, in line with the valence hypothesis, higher program appreciation generated better A_{ad} scores (see Table 11:3).

Marjolein Moorman • Peter C. Neijens • Edith G. Smit

Table 11:3 Means and Post Hoc Results (Tukey b) for Effects of Report Grade of the Program on Attitude toward the ad

	Report grade program				
	<=5	6	7	8	>=9
Attitude toward the ad (1-10)	5.53[a]	5.90[b]	6.16[b, c]	6.31[c]	6.47[c]

Means with different subscripts differ significantly horizontally at p<.05.

Position in the block was not found to have either a main effect or an interaction effect on the dependent variables, meaning that commercials were not better attended, recalled or appreciated dependent on the position within the block.

Table 11:4 Means and Post Hoc Results (Tukey b) for Effects of Attention paid to Program on Aided Recall Split by Position of the Break

Aided recall (%)				
	Attention paid to program			
	1	2	3	4
Block within program	36[a]	37[a]	45[b]	52[c]
Block outside program	40[a]	30[b]	44[a]	47[a]

Means with different subscripts differ significantly horizontally at p<.05.

Table 11:5 Means and Post Hoc Results (Tukey b) for Effects of Report Grade of the Program on Attitude toward the ad

Attitude toward the program (1-10)					
	Report grade program				
	<6	6	7	8	>8
Block within program	5.74[a]	5.67[a, b]	6.04[b]	6.40[c]	6.45[c]
Block outside program	5.84[a]	5.89[a]	6.23[a, b]	6.17[a, b]	6.44[b]

Means with different subscripts differ significantly horizontally at p<.05.

Finally, the GLM analyses showed that position of the break did not have a main effect. However, small but significant interaction effects were found between attention paid to the program and position of the commercial block on aided recall, as well as appreciation of the program and position of the commercial block on A_{ad}. Subsequent post hoc tests (with tukey b) showed that aided recall and commercial appreciation scores increased significantly when inserted in an interrupted block compared to a non-interrupted break (see Table 11:4 and Table 11:5).

Discussion

The present results are in line with previous field studies investigating effects of program-induced psychological responses on commercial processing. It is shown that the amount of attention paid to the program has an enhancing effect on attention paid to subsequent commercials and various measures of recall of these commercials. Furthermore, it is shown that A_{ad} is partly a function of viewers' appreciation of the program. Appreciation carries over to the commercials, influencing it in the same direction.

The effects of intensity and valence on recall and A_{ad} were found to be mediated by position of the break. Similar to the study of (Krugman, 1983), effects were stronger for commercial breaks interrupting the program than for commercial breaks at the end of the program. These results suggest that carry-over effects from program to commercials are more prominent when viewers are still 'in' the program. A probable explanation for this is that viewers experience a higher level of arousal when the plot of the program is not yet known, and thus arousal levels are higher for program-interrupting breaks than for breaks between programs. (Kennedy, 1971) has termed this shift in level of arousal 'closure'. We cannot directly contribute present findings to closure, however, because program measures have only been taken for the program as a whole and not at the moment of the interruption.

With regard to variations in commercial placement within the break, we did not find a mediating effect. Because we wanted to rule out the possibility that this lack of significance was perhaps due to an inadequate construction of the commercial break into three parts based on the findings of (Mattes and Cantor, 1982), we also compared scores between individual positions within the break (i.e. the first, third, fifth, seventh and ninth position). The results of these additional analyses did not show a significant trend for commercial position either.

The present study contributes to the present knowledge about context effects, because results are based on a variety of programs and a large representative sample, whereas previous real-life studies (e.g. Moorman et al., 2001) have not been representative due to limited sample size, sample composition or program material. The present results could have important implications for media planning. They would suggest that the best strategy for media planners is to select programs that do not only generate the desired audience size and composition, but are also appreciated and widely followed. By anchoring measures of appreciation and attention into media planning models, a 'more systematic and sophisticated fashion' (Lloyd and Clancy, 1991) of media planning may emerge, based not only on reach and cost, but also on effects.

In conclusion, we realize that program responses explain only a small portion of the way commercials are received and processed by the audience. Many other factors, such as characteristics of the audience and the commercial, influence commercial effectiveness and may moderate the effect of program responses. The extent to which program responses enhance or hinder commercial processing might be dependent on type of product advertised, congruence between the product type and the environment, age of the target group, gender et cetera. The present results are based on analyses on an aggregated commercial and audience level only. Subsequent context studies should also investigate effects for specific commercials, products, and target groups.

12

Sports advertising: a review of perimeter advertising effectiveness

BJÖRN WALLISER

Sports advertising: a review of perimeter advertising effectiveness

While advertising expenditures have decreased over the last twenty years as compared to other communication instruments, investments in sponsorship have been steadily rising over the same period. Both phenomena are not independent. It is not that companies want to communicate less ; rather they desire to communicate differently, i.e. more effectively (and more efficiently, although the question of efficiency is rarely addressed with precision). To many, sponsorship appears as one interesting way to increase communication effectiveness. Perimeter advertising – defined largely for the purpose of this study as commercial stimuli displayed at the site of an event (Deimel, 1993) - can be considered the furthest reaching communication instrument for sponsors. During the last soccer World Cup, for example, any person being part of the cumulated audience of 37 billion spectators was exposed to the perimeter boards of 19 sponsors. If directly asked about the importance of communication instruments used for the exploitation of sponsorship opportunities, perimeter boards rank only fifth - behind media coverage, event title, entertainment of guests, and exposure to attendance (Crowley, 1991). However, opportunities for title sponsorship are limited and the direct audience of an event is usually very small compared to the indirect (media) audience. When companies quote media coverage as the most important communication vehicle, for many of them this is synonymous with pictures of perimeter boards being seen in print or on television.

Perimeter advertising presents two major advantages compared to classic advertising. Unlike the latter, it is linked to real events and not based on fiction. Thus, perimeter advertisers are typically perceived as more credible by the audience. Second, perimeter advertising is more likely than advertising to break through the media clutter. A spectator at a sports event can barely escape the commercial messages, which are linked to it. The only choice he/she has is to attend or not to attend the event. If the first option is chosen, the target is automatically exposed to the commercial stimuli of the sponsors. The question of the impact of this forced exposure remains, however, to be answered. This is precisely the motivation of this study.

Perimeter advertising has been frequently investigated in the sponsorship literature. Although several articles have looked at perimeter advertising in a more encompassing way (e.g. Walliser, 1994), to our best knowledge no up-to-date review of the effectiveness of this form of communication exists. The primary objective of this chapter is to review perimeter advertising effectiveness in terms of awareness and image. Before addressing these effects, some conceptual lines between sponsorship and advertising will be drawn and the methodology of this review will be explained. The chapter ends with sections devoted to the discussion of the results as well as managerial implications and limitations.

The overlap between sponsorship and advertising

Advertising and sponsorship are increasingly considered complementary elements of an integrated communication strategy. They partly share the same objectives, i.e. awareness and image, but deliver their messages in different ways. Advertising messages generally are more direct, explicit and can be more easily controlled. Sponsorship, on the other hand, can overcome certain communication barriers and has practically unlimited target selection possibilities (Erdogan and Kitchen, 1998). Nevertheless, the line between sponsorship and advertising is not always easy to draw.

A first overlap between advertising and sponsorship exists with regard to broadcast sponsorship. It presents at the same time elements of advertising, such as buying airtime from a television or radio station, but it is also a form of association, albeit indirect, to an event or activity. Broadcast sponsorship is increasingly used by sponsors to achieve a stronger impact on their targets, but it is also popular among « ambushers ». By associating themselves with the broadcast of an event, the latter are perceived as sponsors by large parts of the general public without ever paying a sponsor fee.

Furthermore, sponsorship and advertising largely coincide when sponsors use billboards or similar supports. It has been shown that outdoor advertising and perimeter advertising are similar with regard to communication objectives, physical supports used, conditions of exposure, and information content. At the same time, both forms of communication differ with regard to location, target selection, dominant concepts and appeals, as well as credibility (Walliser, 1997a). Table 12:1 summarizes the similarities and differences between both forms of communication.

Outdoor and perimeter advertising are both characterized by dual-task situations, where the target's primary attention is not allocated to the advertising message. Neither outdoor nor perimeter advertising can transmit large amounts of information to their targets. Typically, perimeter board messages are limited to the name of a brand or a company. In some cases, a logo or other kind of pictorial element, as well as a short slogan can be added. More recently, telephone numbers or references of websites are found on some perimeter boards. Outdoor campaigns contain an average number of 9.8 words and 2.89 concepts per campaign. More than two thirds of all appeals are emotional, and dominant concepts are pictorial. Almost 60% of the billboards have illustrations (Bhargava et al., 1994).

Credibility is maybe the most important distinction between both concepts. Perimeter board messages are unseparately linked to real events. Unlike outdoor advertising, where products are presented in a fictitious setting chosen by the advertiser, the values, images and outcome of a sponsored event cannot be modified by the sponsor. This adds extra credibility to perimeter advertising, which other forms of impersonal advertising do not have. Besides, this feature places the

Björn Walliser

discussion of perimeter effectiveness clearly more in the context of sponsorship than advertising.

Table 12:1 Comparison of outdoor advertising and perimeter advertising. Source: Adapted from Walliser, 1997a, p. 23.

Comparison Criteria	Outdoor Advertising	Perimeter Advertising
Similarities		
Communication objectives	Awareness, image, sales	Awareness, image, sales
Physical supports	Wooden, metallic, fibre-glass, etc. boards; neon lights	Wooden, metallic, fibre-glass, etc. boards, large dummy products
Conditions of exposure	Target person is primarily concentrating on another task (i.e. driving a car)	Target person is primarily concentrating on another task (i.e. watching a sports event)
Information content	Small information content (about 10 words on average, less than three concepts per campaign	Very small information content (mostly less than five words, short slogans)
Differences		
Communication integration	Integrated in advertising strategy (media mix)	Integrated in sponsorship strategy
Location	Along public routes, on bus shelters, public transportation, houses, etc.	Site of (sports, cultural, social) events
Target selection	Limited	Practically unlimited
Dominant concepts	Pictorial	Textual
Appeal	Emotional (humour and intrigue frequently used) plus rational (text)	Emotional (based on the event) and rational (text)
Credibility	Low	Low to medium

Methodology: Identification of relevant articles and analysis

Partly building on existing reviews about sponsorship (e.g. Fuchs, 1994; Cornwell and Maignan, 1998), 15 leading marketing journals were hand-searched for the period 1985-2000 for articles reporting an empirical or conceptual investigation of perimeter advertising. The ancestry approach led us to articles published in more than 10 other journals. International marketing conferences (European Marketing Academy, American Advertising Association, etc.) and professional meetings (e.g. ESOMAR) were other valuable sources of information. Contributions published in English, German or French (all languages understood by the researcher) are included. Results of studies conducted by professional research institutes (SRI, Sample Institut and Institut Française de Démoscopie) known to the authors were only included to the extent that they have been published in one of the aforementioned sources (e.g. Abel and Long, 1996). Studies in which perimeter boards were only one stimulus among many others to evaluate overall sponsorship effectiveness (e.g. Couty, 1994) are only included in this review if the partial impact of the boards has been perceived as significant (e.g. Merbold, 1989). From the work of (Quester and Farrelly, 1998), for example, results concerning awareness levels of sponsors present on the race track (perimeter advertising) are included, while effects of naming rights are not. Doctoral dissertations have not been evaluated. In this way, 35 studies presenting at least some results relating to perimeter advertising effectiveness were identified and are the basis of the subsequent analysis. While three of these studies concern cultural events, all the others investigate the use of perimeter boards at sports events.

The studies found take into account such a wide array of dependent variables that a meta-analytical approach did not seem appropriate. Instead, they will be analysed in a primarily qualitative way that distinguishes two broad categories of dependent variables: awareness and image effects.

Awareness of perimeter board advertising

The large majority of studies measuring perimeter board effectiveness have chosen awareness as the independent variable. Three broad approaches can be distinguished: measuring to what extent the public takes notice of sponsors on perimeter boards, identifying factors influencing perimeter board recall/association, and analysing the internal processes related to recall taking place in the spectator's mind.

Especially among the early studies examining perimeter board effectiveness, many studies focus either on the general awareness of sponsors in the public's mind (Renner and Tischler, 1977) or on awareness levels of sponsors associated with specific events and activities (Abel and Long, 1996; Easton and Mackie, 1998; Müller,

Björn Walliser

1983; Schumann, 1987; Studiengruppe Naether, 1974; Troll, 1983a, etc.). The results of these studies are inconsistent. Generally speaking, sponsors appearing on perimeter boards see an increase in public awareness of them as compared to non-sponsors (Otker and Hayes, 1988). The degree and duration of this effect is, however, variable. In some extreme cases, sponsor recall is (judged) very low (e.g. Troll, 1983a) or insignificant (Mayer and Christner, 1991). To illustrate, Table 12:2 provides an overview of memorization scores of the perimeter board advertisers of the last soccer World Cup.

Table 12:2 Recall scores of perimeter board advertisers of the 1998 soccer World Cup. Source: Walliser and Nanopulos, 2000.

Brand	« Top of mind »			Spontaneous recall			Recognition		
	1997	1999	Diff.*	1997	1999	Diff.*	1997	1999	Diff.*
First category sponsors									
Adidas	14.0	25.7	11.7	11.3	17.7	6.4	68.0	79.0	11.0
Canon	0.3	0.7	0.4	0.5	1.2	0.7	22.1	24.2	2.1
Coca Cola	30.2	28.3	- 1.9	17.5	19.8	2.3	69.1	76.8	7.7
Fujifilm	0.4	0.0	- 0.4	1.2	1.0	- 0.2	24.1	23.7	- 0.4
Gillette	0.7	0.5	- 0.2	1.5	1.1	- 0.4	25.5	21.2	- 4.3
JVC	1.5	0.5	- 1.0	1.8	0.8	- 1.0	18.2	14.7	- 3.5
McDonald's	3.1	6.3	3.2	5.1	10.1	5.0	41.3	53.0	11.7
Mastercard	0.9	1.9	1.0	2.8	3.2	0.4	33.2	31.1	- 2.1
Opel	1.3	0.8	- 0.5	2.9	2.7	- 0.2	28.6	29.8	1.2
Philips	0.1	0.6	0.5	0.8	1.4	0.4	21.1	21.2	0.1
Snickers	6.9	4.4	- 2.5	5.5	4.9	- 0.6	37.6	42.0	4.4
Average	5.4	6.3	0.9	4.6	5.8	1.2	35.3	37.9	2.5
Second category sponsors									
Crédit Agric.	9.7	4.2	- 5.5	7.1	3.4	- 3.7	38.9	30.5	- 8.4
Danone	2.6	1.5	- 1.1	3.7	2.1	- 1.6	38.7	30.5	- 8.2
EDS	0.1	0.0	- 0.1	0.3	0.3	0.0	9.7	7.7	- 2.0
France Téléc.	6.5	4.7	- 1.8	6.7	5.5	- 1.2	48.1	43.7	- 4.4
Hewlett Pack.	0.9	0.1	- 0.8	1.1	0.7	- 0.4	17.1	18.1	1.0
La Poste	5.7	4.6	- 1.1	6.2	5.9	- 0.3	40.8	40.7	- 0.1
Manpower	1.5	1.1	- 0.4	1.9	2.2	0.3	19.0	20.5	1.5
Sybase	0.0	0.3	0.3	0.1	0.1	0.0	5.0	8.2	3.2
Average	3.4	2.1	-1.3	3.4	2.5	-0.9	27.2	25.0	-2.2

Diff.* = difference between 1997 and 1999 measures.

In the example given in Table 12:2, memorization scores vary by brand, by type of sponsor (first category vs. second category), by type of control instrument (top of mind vs. spontaneous recall, recognition), and over time (« 1997 » measures are control measures taken seven months before the event; « 1999 » measures are taken nine months after the event). The shaded figures signal statistically significant differences between « before » and « after » measures.

More generally, variables influencing perimeter board memorization can be categorized into five groups (Walliser, 1994): conditions of exposure, product and message, as well as target characteristics and sponsorship integration. Tables 12:3a and 12:3b summarize studies concluding on the influence of these different variables on perimeter advertiser memorization.

Table 12:3a Exposure, product and message-related variables influencing perimeter advertiser memorization.

Factor	Variable	Author(s), year of study	Influence on memorization		
			In-crease	*De-crease*	*Non signi-ficant*
Exposure	Presenceat the site of the event	Anne, Chéron (1991)	X		
		Quester (1997)	X		
		Meir et al. (1997)	X		
		Bennett (1999)	X		
		Nötzel (1988)	X		
	Duration of appearance in films/videos	Schumann (1987)	X		
		Walliser (1997b)	X		
		Hermanns et al. (1986)	X		
		Gabrielsen, Hansen (2000)	X		
		Moore et al. (1999)	X		
		Deimel (1993)	X		
	Amount of TV viewing	Troll (1983a)	X		
		Otker, Hayes (1988)	X		
		Hackforth (1989)	X		
		Walliser (1996)	X		
		Pope, Voges (1997)	X		
		Reiter, Serr (1991)	X		
	Multiple locations of boards	Drees (1987)	X		
	Location close to human elements	Hermanns et al. (1986)	X		

Exposure	Location close to the centre of the action	Arthur et al. (1998)	X		
		Olivier, Kraak (1997)	X		
		Pope, Voges (1997)	X		
Product	Previous brand awareness	Anne, Chéron (1991)	X		
		Deimel (1993)	X		
		Walliser (1997b)	X		
		Hermanns et al. (1986)	X		
	Product/even t affinity	Drees (1987)	X		
Message	Short messages	Drees (1987)	X		
	Tall, easily readable characters	Drees (1987)	X		
	Differential design of boards	Drees (1987)	X		
		Olivier, Kraak (1997)	X		
	Rotating boards (movement)	Coley (1992)	X		
		Olivier, Kraak (1997)	X		
		Gabrielsen, Hansen (2000)	X		

There is considerable evidence that recall increases as a function of duration of exposure to perimeter boards notwithstanding whether duration of exposure is measured as duration of presence at the site of an event (e.g. Anne and Chéron, 1991), amount of television viewing (e.g. Reiter and Serr, 1991) or duration of appearance of perimeter stimuli on television (e.g. Schumann, 1987). Location is another determinant of exposure and is therefore found to affect recall levels.

Previous brand awareness of perimeter advertisers is consistently found to influence board advertiser recall positively. The same is true for message-related factors, such as message length, character size, board design, and movement (rotating boards).

Mixed evidence exists regarding the influence of target characteristics on recall. While interest in the activity sponsored and involvement with the activity/event is most often shown to increase recall, variables such as gender, age, education, practising a sport, etc. do not seem to have a systematic influence.

With regard to the integration of perimeter advertising and other communication instruments, an increase of awareness scores is observed when sponsorship is used in conjunction with broadcast sponsorship (ARD Werbung, 1993; Lardinoit, 1998 and 1999; Olivier and Kraak, 1997) or classical advertising (Eilander, 1992; Parker,

Table 12:3b: Target-related variables influencing perimeter advertiser memorization.

Factor	Variable	Author(s), year of study	Influence on memorization		
			In-crease	De-crease	Non significant
Target charac-teristics	Interest in the activity sponsored	Troll (1983a)	X		
		Anne, Chéron (1991)	X		
		Anne (1992)	X		
		Walliser (1996)	X		
		Cornwell et al. (1997)			X
		Hermanns et al. (1986)			X
		Bennett (1999)	X		
		Wright (1988)	X		
		Reiter, Serr (1991)			X
		Schumann (1987)		X	
	Age (young spectators)	Renner, Tischler (1977)	X		
		Deimel (1993)	X		
		Cornwell et al. (1997)			X
		Müller (1983)			X
		Reiter, Serr (1991)			X
		Hackforth (1989)			X
		Shanahan (1990)			X
	Gender (male)	Renner, Tischler (1977)			X
		Müller (1983)	X		
		Schumann (1987)		X	
		Pham (1992)	X		
		Anne, Chéron (1991)			X
		Cornwell et al. (1997)			X
		Hermanns et al. (1986)		X	
		Studiengruppe Naether (1974)			X
		Moore et al. (1999)			X
		Reiter, Serr (1991)			X
		Troll (1983)			X
		Deimel (1993)			X
		Hackforth (1989)		X	
		Shanahan (1990)	X		
	Arousal (emotional response)	Pham (1992)		X	
		Walliser (1996)		X	
	Pleasure (while attending)	Pham (1992)			X
	Activity/event involvement	Pham (1992)	X		
		Deimel (1993)	X		
		Cornwell et al. (1997)			X
		Lardinoit (1998)	X		
	Involvement with perimeter advertising	Deimel (1993)	X		

Target charac-teristixs	Education	Schumann (1987) Müller (1983) Renner, Tischler (1977)		X	X X
	Practice of a sport	Schumann (1987) Anne (1992) Anne, Chéron (1991)			X X X
	Knowledge of the event/activity	Pham (1992) Cornwell et al. (1997) Deimel (1993)	X		X X
Sponsor-ship inte-gration	Additional use of classic advertising	Cornwell et al. (1997)	X		
	Additional use of broadcast sponsorship	Olivier, Kraak (1997) Lardinoit (1998)	X X		
	Media coverage of the event	Hackforth (1989)			X

1991). Some go as far as to claim that stand-alone sponsorship activities – even when used for a longer period of time – are not very effective in generating additional brand awareness (Koschler and Merz, 1995). Classical advertising can help to create a link between the sponsor and the activity or event sponsored if it explains the logic of the association (Crimmins and Horn, 1996). In contrast, the link is less likely to be perceived if competitors' advertising accompanies the event. Broadcast sponsorship messages not only have an awareness effect on their own (Iordanov and Nobi, 1997) but even seem to overwhelm most, if not all, messages from event, team or other kinds of sponsors (Deutsche Städte-Reklame, 1996; Millmann, 1995). Comparing recall levels for a beer brand in three countries, Olivier and Kraak (1997) observe that the integrated use of broadcast sponsorship and perimeter advertising results in awareness levels more than six times higher than levels for brands relying on perimeter boards only. The correlation between the media coverage obtained for an event and sponsor recall has been addressed (Hackforth, 1989), so far without providing a conclusive answer.

The evolution of recall scores over time has been at the centre of studies by (Cornwell et al., 1997), (Quester, 1997), (Walliser and Nanopoulos, 2000), and (Wright, 1988), among others. They have shown that each brand has a basis recall level which rises shortly before and during an event and falls back close to its initial level a few weeks after the event. Duration and magnitude of the variation depend on the overall communication effort of the sponsor. If the time span between different sponsor appearances (events) becomes too long, cumulative effects are not observed (Quester and Farrelly, 1998).

The third group of contributions relating to sponsorship awareness adopts a consumer-behaviour perspective. (Pope, 1998) discovers that sponsorship awareness can lead to an increase of the perceived consumption value of the sponsor brands. (McDaniel, 1998) as well as (Hermanns and Drees, 1989) evaluate the influence of the perceived match or mismatch of brand attitudes on consumer response. (Troll, 1983b) observes a substantial learning effect when respondents are repeatedly interviewed about sponsorship, and (Lardinoit, 1998, 1999) puts into evidence the positive role of enduring involvement on memorization. (Johar and Pham, 1999) investigate the individual heuristics of sponsor recall. If the association between the sponsor and the event has been perfectly encoded, spectators later retrieve the sponsor name from their memory without any problem. In contrast, if encoding has been weak, sponsor identification involves a substantial degree of construction. Spectators then use market prominence and brand-event relatedness as major heuristics to infer sponsor names. This might at least partly explain why many authors note a substantial degree of erroneous perimeter advertiser recall (Nicholls et al., 1999; Wright, 1988) – also termed « incidental ambushing » (Quester, 1997) or « false consensus » (Bennett, 1999) - or confusion between perimeter advertisers and classic advertisers (Cornwell et al., 1997; Kerstettner and Gittelson, 1995). Besides, sponsorship is characterized by strong carry-over effects. Repeatedly, there are examples of former sponsors in the literature which reach their highest recall scores at moments when they are no longer associated with the event (Quester and Farrelly, 1998).

Image (and attitudinal) effects of perimeter advertising

Only very few articles evaluate image effects of perimeter advertising. There is ample evidence that sponsorship at the least can contribute to the modification of certain image dimensions (e.g. Otker and Hayes, 1988; Rajaretnam, 1994). Clearly, each sponsorship activity or area has specific image values which can be transferred to external or internal audiences. Globally, it appears as if image transfer was positively influenced by the number of common perceptions of the sponsor and the activity (Gierl and Kirchner, 1999), by the attitude of the spectators towards the association of the sponsor and the activity (Giannelloni and Valette-Florence, 1992), and by the spectators' involvement in the sponsorship process (Mayer and Christner, 1991).

Typically, spectators at an event indicate that sponsorship raises their opinion of the sponsor brands and that they are more likely to buy and/or try for a first time sponsor products (Easton and Mackie, 1998). Frequency of attendance at events and knowledge, but not gender, are significant predictors of purchase intention (Daneshvary and Schwer, 2000). However, when it comes to real behaviour, it should be noted that product use is not necessarily higher for sponsor products than for competitor products (Pope, 1998).

But, as was the case for awareness, image effects are shown to be only temporary (Merbold, 1989) and may depend on the integration of sponsorship with other communication instruments, although conflicting evidence exists (Lardinoit, 1997).

Perimeter advertising supposedly contributes to such effects since image transfer seems to be more likely for sponsors having a high visibility during the event than for others (Stipp and Schiavone, 1996; Parker, 1991). Recall and preference of sponsor brands – but also for non-sponsor brands - are correlated (Nicholls et al., 1999). However, it is impossible to evaluate the relative contribution of perimeter advertising on any possible change of image or attitude. The theoretical underpinning of image effects is discussed on several occasions in the literature (Baux, 1990; Ganassali and Didellon, 1996; Gwinner, 1997; Hoek et al., 1997; Walliser, 1993). None of the rationales offered, such as emotional conditioning, the awareness-trial-reinforment model and mere exposure effects, has so far proven its superiority in empirical research.

Media and media/vehicle effects may be another issue to follow closely when thinking about image transfer due to perimeter boards. Goodwill derived from the sponsor investment of a company varies by sponsorship category and by degree of exploitation. Goodwill effects are per se smaller for mass sports than for social causes. They also decrease with the perceived level of exploitation of an event (Meenaghan and Shipley, 1999). As the very sense of perimeter boards is to commercially exploit an event, they are probably not the best suited way of achieving goodwill effects. In reality, studies comparing static vs. rotating boards have concluded on a lower esteem for the sponsored event when the latter type of boards was used (Olivier and Kraak, 1997).

Discussion

The evaluation of sponsorship impact is without any doubt the area where sponsorship research has progressed most over the last few years. Perimeter advertising effectiveness is one issue covered by this stream of research. A considerable number of studies have investigated the impact of perimeter boards on awareness. Research has gradually shifted from descriptive studies measuring perimeter memorization to explanatory approaches analysing various intermediating variables as well as the internal processes taking place in the spectator's mind. Although results are not always consistent, several tentative conclusions can be drawn.

Awareness of perimeter advertisers undoubtedly is linked to length of exposure. The relationship between both variables is, however, not linear. High levels of awareness are achieved after relatively short periods of exposure but only remain high or rise further if the communication effort is well sustained over time. Integrated communication programmes combining perimeter advertising with either classic advertising or broadcast sponsorship seem promising in terms of achieving such results. Conversely, once a brand is well associated with an event in the public's mind, it benefits from important carry-over effects well beyond the duration of its engagement.

The quality of the message as well as the previous brand awareness of the advertiser are other factors contributing positively to awareness.

Conflicting evidence exists concerning target characteristics favouring the build-up of awareness. Spectators interested in or involved in the activity sponsored typically remember perimeter advertisers better than more « neutral » targets. Conversely, strong emotional responses of the target inhibit recall of advertisers. The predictive strength of variables such as age, gender, level of education, and knowledge of the activity is comparatively lower. The target does not retain a perimeter advertiser because he/she is educated, young or knowledgeable about the activity, but rather because he/she is interested - and thus involved - in the event. Depending on the type of activity (e.g. figure skating vs. snowboarding), specific segments of the population (female vs. male, young vs. old, etc.) show specific levels of interest. Most socio-demographic variables have a lower general predictive power with regard to awareness than the aforementioned psycho-graphic variables.

Contrary to awareness effects, the impact of perimeter boards on image – not to mention other objectives such as sales - remains difficult to estimate. First of all, the processes of image transfer in the context of sponsorship are not yet clearly known. Furthermore, the relative contribution of perimeter boards to such effects can hardly be isolated. Thus, any conclusions on the contribution of perimeter boards to image transfer remain hypothetical and should be limited to two simple statements : Perimeter advertising is one suitable instrument for building awareness; and globally, it appears as if once awareness is built, image transfer can also take place.

Most of the managerial implications from these findings are straightforward (and are developed in more detail in an excellent article by Otker, 1988). Exploitation is the key word. To start with, perimeter boards should have tall, easily readable characters, short messages and a design which differentiates them from competing boards. Exploitation should be on an appropriate scale. Too little exploitation results in competing boards overshadowing the others, and too much exploitation irritates the target, especially when advertisers are associated with other events than sport. Perimeter advertising can only be a reinforcing – not an initiating - factor to achieve communication objectives. It needs to be integrated in a coherent sponsorship strategy, which in turn should be part of a coherent communication strategy. The activity sponsored could well deliver the theme used in PR, advertising, sales promotion, direct marketing, etc. Exploitation of perimeter/sponsorship activities should be original, well planned and sustained. Awareness, and of course image even more so, is not built in the short term. If a company is not committed to sponsorship, it should not engage in such an activity.

Limitations and future research

An important effort was made to include as many studies about perimeter advertising as possible. Altogether, 35 studies relating at least partially to perimeter advertising have been identified and analysed. On this basis, future contributions cannot claim any longer – as was frequently the case in the past - that research on perimeter advertising has been sparse. Nevertheless, this review is neither exhaustive nor truly global. Writings published in English, French and German should be reasonably well covered, but the work of researchers publishing in other languages might be less visible. The majority of the contributions summarized come from highly industrialized Western countries. Asia, Africa, the Middle East, South America, Eastern Europe and emerging countries in general are, at best, marginally represented.

Many of the studies identified are only briefly summarized in Tables 12:3a and 12:3b, and are not as thoroughly discussed as they deserve. Thus, at times, this review might appear somewhat « piecemeal ». Whenever quantitative data was available, conclusions about the significance of effects were drawn at the 5% error level. But neither are all the conclusions of the studies reviewed based on quantitive data, nor confidence levels systematically indicated. Besides, exploratory studies, such as (Hermanns et al., 1988), are also included in this review.

The most serious limitation is due to the design and origin of the studies reviewed. Some of them investigate awareness and image effects of sponsorship in general and do not specifically focus on perimeter boards. Although it can be argued that perimeter boards are the most important communication vehicle for sponsors with regard to the general public, studies about sponsorship effectiveness do not allow for conclusions to be made on the relative impact of perimeter boards with regard to the effects investigated.

As sponsorship expenditures are steadily increasing all over the world, perimeter advertising will remain under scrutiny. Investments will have to be justified in a context within which it is becoming more difficult to succeed. With the proliferation of sponsorships and sponsors, public acceptance of perimeter advertising might decrease. Perimeter advertisers will find it more difficult to stand out. In the past, advertising clutter and legal constraints to advertising accelerated perimeter advertising growth. In the future, perimeter advertising clutter and legal constraints to sponsorship will become a threat to sponsorship development. Thus, continued research interest in this area will be of great importance.

13

Advertising and the Image of Politicians

National Elections in Poland, France, and Germany

WOJCIECH CWALINA & ANDRZEJ FALKOWSKI

Abstract

The chapter undertakes an analysis of the constructivist and realist approaches in research on voting behavior in national elections. The influence of the politician or party image on an affective attitude towards the candidate is stressed in the first approach. The other approach stresses the role of affect in forming such an image.

Within the constructivist approach the sequential model of the influence of political advertising on voter behavior is presented. The model was tested according to two research methodologies: a) structural equation modeling and b) multiple regression analysis on the basis of the research results in Poland (presidential election in 1995 and 2000), France (presidential election in 1995) and Germany (general election in 1994). The analysis of data allows us to precisely define the way in which the image of state officials should be created in order to efficiently appeal to affects and influence citizens' voting behavior.

The analysis of data, according to the realist approach, points to the key role of affects as a starting point for designing and creating the images of politicians.

Both approaches to voting behavior have significant implications for political marketing as well as for commercial marketing. They point to the fact that when any advertising strategy is being created, it must include the mutual „strengthening" of the image and affects. When introducing changes to brand, corporate or political image, the influence of affective attitude is the main mediator in voting or consumer behaviors.

The image

"As I sit at my desk, I know where I am. I see before me a window; beyond that some trees; beyond that the red roofs of the campus of Stanford University; beyond them the trees and roof tops which mark the town of Palo Alto: beyond them the bare golden hills of the Hamilton Range. I know, however, more than I see. Behind me, although I am not looking in that direction, I know there is a window, and beyond that the little campus of the Center for Advanced Study in the Behavioral Sciences; beyond that the Coast Range; beyond that the Pacific Ocean".

With these words K. E. Boulding begins *The image* (1956), and in the same way – by quoting Boulding's words – Miller, Galanter and Pribram (1960) begin their book *Plans and the structure of behavior*. The quoted passage stresses the assumption of the authors, according to whom the possessed knowledge imposes interpretations on the perceived reality. Boulding and Miller et al stress that *image* is man's own knowledge about the world. Man's behavior is determined by this image, which may be changed under the influence of information. Such an understanding of the notion of the „image" is illustrated by the authors' use of a metaphor, that images are best characterized as photographs of man's mind working (Miller et al., 1960).

In cognitive psychology, according to the branch of research defined as constructivism, the perceived reality is created in man's mind on the basis of sensory information. The perceived stimuli are processed in cognitive structures in such a way that they become meaningful for man. Illustrative of this point are equivocal figures showing different meanings of the same sensory stimulus in psychology handbooks. An example of such a figure is the image of an old – young woman, presented in Figure 13:1.

Figure 13:1. Old – young woman

Looking at this figure we can see a young woman. But the same picture also allows us to see an old woman. This phenomenon is undoubtedly a result of the overlapping of our knowledge of the perceived graphics of the picture. If we had not seen an old woman (as well as a young one) in the past, we would never have noticed her in the picture. Thus knowledge has a decisive influence on what we perceive.

Following this, we can put forward a hypothesis stating that it is possible to control the process of perception by manipulating our knowledge. In practice marketing specialists, who create various images of politicians, have studied this process for many years. Nowadays, this process has become so significant that it is said that modern democracy has found itself in „the age of manufactured images" as B.I. Newman put it in the title of one of his books (Newman, 1999a).

The structure of the image consists of cognitive and affective elements. The latter are particularly significant in the sphere of social cognition, to which political marketing belongs (Schwartz, 1973; Newman, 1999b). Current research points to the fact that the main factors influencing human behavior are affects. Wattenberg (1987) found that, one-third of voters know nothing about particular politicians but despite that, have strong feelings about them. There hence arises a significant question related to mutual relationships of cognitive and affective elements, the solving of which has a particular practical implication. When it comes to developing marketing strategies, is it important to establish whether the construction of the object's image influences the affective attitude towards it or whether, on the contrary, it is affects that form the image (define the set of significant attributes) of a given object.

Currently two approaches to causal relationships of cognitive and affective elements and their influence on voting behavior prevail. The first, constructivist, approach stresses the role of the politician's image on the affective in influencing the attitude toward him. The other approach, following the realist school of thought, points to the relevance of affects in forming the image itself. Thus, taking into account the following simple sequences: cognition $\rightarrow$ affect or affect $\rightarrow$ cognition, we are using either a constructivist or realist approach to perceive the social environment.

The political marketing strategy should follow the assumed and empirically tested epistemic background of voter behavior. Do voters recognize the social reality on an affective basis, or are affect a consequence of social cognition and the images of particular social phenomena have little in common with the real world? Depending on which causal-effect relationship is selected on empirical grounds, a different precise marketing strategy should be elaborated. On the other hand, one should not neglect the possibility of combining the strategies resulting from realist and constructivist approaches, as they can both be used in explaining voter behavior. Therefore the empirical test of the two approaches to voter behavior, constructivist and realist, will be presented, respectively.

Political image formation: A constructivist approach

The dominance of political advertising in political campaigns has raised the importance of determining how candidate attributes and images are formed. The ability to elicit affective connection may be central to the voters' image formation process (Cwalina, Falkowski & Kaid, 2000; Falkowski & Cwalina, 1999, 2002; Kaid & Holtz-Bacha, 1995; Sullivan, Aldrich, Borgida & Rahn, 1990). In this context, the image means creating a particular representation, which, by evoking associations, adds extra value to the object and thus contributes to its affective reception.

The existing studies conducted in many countries confirm that political advertisements influence voters' image of the candidate and may lead to a reconfiguration of the structure of image features (Cwalina & Falkowski, 2000; Falkowski & Cwalina, 1999; Holtz-Bacha & Kaid, 1995; Kaid & Chanslor, 1995).

Most frequently a candidate's image is operationalized by semantic differential or other adjective scales (Kaid, 1995; Osgood, Suci, & Tannenbaum, 1957; Patton, 1978). Some scientists use measurements of candidates' personality features (Douglas, 1972; Roberts, 1981), as well as analysis of their interpersonal communication behaviors (Harrisin, Stephen, Husson, & Fehr, 1991; Jakubowska, 1999). Despite different operationalizations of the notion of image, most scientists try to reduce the number of variables in their models by using the methodology of factor analysis.

An example of this type of research is the study of the influence of political television advertisements on politicians' image by Kaid and Holtz-Bacha (1995) and Kaid and Chanslor (1995). Kaid and Chanslor used a 12- scale semantic differential to measure candidate image before and after exposure to televised political spots, during the US presidential campaign in 1992. Factor analysis was used to determine changes in candidate images at the two points in time (before and after viewing). The result was shown to be a compacting of Bush's image and a more substantial reconfiguration of Clinton's image.

This research can definitely be of use in preparing an election campaign, as it provides information on how to control the image of a candidate. On the other hand, this research does not provide any rationale as to whether the controlled change of the image is, in fact, effective. To solve this problem the sequential model showing the influence of political advertisement has been developed.

Sequential model of the influence of political advertisements

The majority of the analyses conducted so far have focused exclusively on the changes in the candidate's image resulting from the advertisements, the attitude towards the candidate, and the voting intention (Kaid & Holtz-Bacha, 1995; Kaid & Chanslor, 1995). However, the analyses have not tried to reveal the relationship between the created image, one's affective attitude toward the candidate, and the voting intention. These aspects of the effect of political advertising, however, provide little understanding of the overall behavior of voters, if they are analyzed separately. One can only say, that viewing the spots leads to a decrease or an enhancement of the candidate's appraisal without a possibility of analyzing the consequences of this appraisal for the electoral decision. Thus, in order to find out whether the spots in fact change voters' image of the candidate in such a way that he or she is more or less likely to vote for a particular candidate or change their vote completely, it is necessary to find a causal link between the following four components (Falkowski & Cwalina, 1999):

1. Cognitive-affective elements (candidate image);
2. General feelings toward the candidate;
3. Intention for whom to vote;
4. Decision for whom to vote.

A causal relationship between these components exists, which can be represented in the model of the influence of spots on voters' behavior (see Figure 13:2). This model fits the constructivist approach to voting behavior very well.

In most of the studies on the influence of candidate image presented in advertisements, cognitive and affective elements are analyzed separately. However, the key element of the sequential model is that these elements are connected and should not be analyzed separately.

Figure 13:2. Sequential model of the influence of spots on voters'
behavior

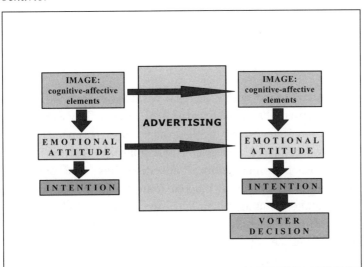

The model assumes the division of voters into electorates, with the division criterion being that of intention. For this reason, the image analysis should be performed separately for each of the electorates, because each electorate perceives their candidate differently, depending on whether they support the candidate or not. This resembles the experiments involving switch-gestalt (i.e. fields vs. ground) mentioned earlier, in which looking at the same picture, a person may see two different things.

On the basis of the sequential model, two analyses for empirical research on the image of politicians can be applied.

1. Structural equation modeling defining causal-effect relationships between cognitive elements of politician's image, affective elements and choice (voting intention). The specificity of the cause-effect relationship obtained by the structural equation methodology allows us to put forward some practical suggestions regarding the way (general strategy) electoral campaigns should be conducted.

2. Multiple regression analysis, which allows us to determine those features of a politician, which are significant to voters' decisions. Hence the analysis answers two questions: a) How do the candidates' images change in relation to one's affective attitude to those candidates when

one is influenced by advertisements? and b) How can efficient political advertising be constructed?

Structural equation constructivist model of voter behavior

Method

The research conducted during national elections in Poland, France, and Germany used the same experimental design. The experiment consisted of three stages. At the first stage, an experimental group anonymously completed a research questionnaire (pre-test). This group then watched four political advertisements. The presented advertisements were chosen at random from the advertisements that each of the candidates used in their television campaign. Subjects were exposed to two of each of the candidates' advertisements in an alternating sequence chosen at random - Lech Walesa's and Aleksander Kwasniewski's in the Polish 1995 election, Aleksander Kwasniewski's and Andrzej Olechowski's in the Polish 2000 contest, Jacques Chirac's and Lionel Jospin's in France's 1995 contest, and Helmut Kohl's and Rudolf Scharping's in Germany's 1994 election. After the subjects had watched the spots, the examiner handed out research questionnaires (post-tests). Both questionnaires included semantic differentials and tests of feelings.

The differential in each of the countries consisted of 12 identical bipolar 7-point scales, and 2 additional scales were added to the Polish version. The results of the research by semantic differential were analyzed by factor analysis and two factors were obtained for each country, describing the image of each of the candidates (Image$_1$ and Image$_2$)[1]. These were then introduced into the structural model, according to the constructivist sequential model (see Figure 13:3).

The thermometer of feelings is a standard method of measuring the general affective attitude toward the candidates (Kaid, Holtz-Bacha, 1995; Sullivan et al., 1990; Wattenberg, 1991). The task of the subjects

---

[1]   For detailed results of the factor analysis, see Cwalina, Falkowski, & Kaid (2000).

Figure 13:3. Structural equation constructivist model of voter behavior

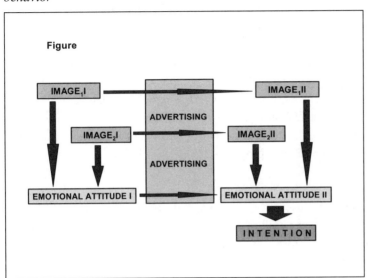

is to mark a point on the section describing the temperature of their feelings towards individual candidates on a scale from 0 to 100 degrees.

In the questionnaire used in Poland, there was also a question concerning voting intention, i.e. the intention to vote for a given candidate. On the basis of this intention, one could divide voters into electorates, which is assumed by the model. In the case of France and Germany making the division into electorates required using a different grouping procedure based on the thermometer of feelings (Cwalina, Falkowski, & Kaid, 2000).

Subjects

Poland

The first empirical research in Poland was conducted between November 10-18, 1995, in the period separating the first and second round of presidential elections (November 19). The subjects were students of sociology and political science from three universities: Lodz University, Maria Curie-Sklodowska University and the Catholic

Wojciech Cwalina • Andrzej Falkowski

University of Lublin, as well as students of CUL's College of Social Communication. Altogether, 203 subjects between the age of 18-52 (average age 20.95) participated in the examination, including 124 women (61.39% of all the participants) and 79 men (38.61%).

The second Polish research was conducted in central and southeastern parts of Poland in November 2000, a month after the Polish presidential election. The sample consisted of 325 subjects between the age of 18 and 53 (average age 21.2). The subjects were students (Lodz University, Rzeszow University and persons working or studying in postsecondary schools. 30.77% of the sample were men (n=100), and 69.23% women (n=225).

France

The empirical research was conducted on May 2 and 3, 1995, just before the second round of presidential elections (May 7). The subjects were students from the Department of Applied Languages and Communication of Université Blaise-Pascale in Clermont-Ferrand. 84 subjects participated in the experiment, including 67 women (79.76% of the subjects) and 17 men (20.24%).

Germany

The empirical research was conducted between October 6 and 14, 1994, immediately prior to national parliamentary elections. The subjects were students of four universities, two from Western Germany (Munich and Bochum) and two from Eastern Germany (Dresden and Leipzig). 200 subjects participated in the experiment – 93 women (46.5% of the subjects) and 107 men (53.5%).

Results

According to the sequential model, the image, operationalized by two factors – $Image_1$ and $Image_2$, influences the general feelings in the first sequence. In the second sequence, after viewing the advertisements, some image reconfiguration, as well as change in affect, takes place in the voters' minds. According to the constructivist approach one can assume both, the exerting of image on affect within the sequence, and exerting of image on image as well as affect on affect between the sequences. The results of the study for Poland, France, and Germany are presented, respectively.

Poland

The results of the structural equation analysis are shown in Figure 13:4 and 13:5. The partition of the sample into two electorates was based on voting intention.

It is worth comparing these research results with the results obtained during the presidential elections in 2000.

Figure 13:4. Structural equation constructivist models: Polish 1995 presidential election

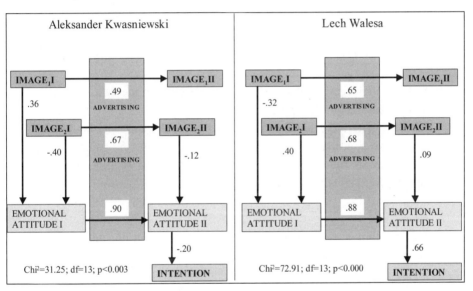

The models present specific arrangements of causal relationships obtained empirically, connecting image with affects and voting intentions for particular candidates in relation to two presidential elections. Despite some differences in the arrangements of paths, it can be said that the obtained results point to the fact that these models explain the assumed causal relationships in a similar way to each other (see the values of χ^2 for particular models).

Wojciech Cwalina • Andrzej Falkowski

Figure 13:5. Structural equation constructivist models: Polish 2000 presidential election

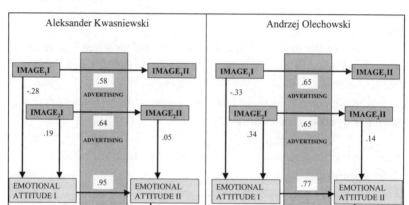

Besides, the degree of the model's „fit" is similar to the data obtained in 1995 and 2000. The mean χ^2 for particular elections is 52.08 and 52.62, respectively, and they do not differ significantly. It should be noted, however, that from the statistical point of view, the goodness of fit indices are not satisfactory for these models and suggest that the constructivist solution should be rejected.

France

The research carried out in France and Germany did not include the voting intention variable, and subjects did not indicate whom they would vote for. Thus we assumed the feeling thermometer to be a good predictor of voting intention, i.e. the voter will choose a candidate who is „warmer", who evokes more positive affects. This assumption was empirically tested on the Polish sample by discriminant analysis, which showed an excellent prediction of voting intention from affective attitude (Falkowski & Cwalina, 1999; Cwalina, Falkowski & Kaid, 2000).

Relying on this assumption it is possible to divide the subjects into two groups. On the one hand, the respondents supporting Jospin perceive him as being „warmer" than Chirac. Conversely, the people supporting Chirac perceive him as being „warmer" than Jospin. A group expressing the same temperature of feelings towards both candidates was excluded from further research at this stage. After the division of the subjects into electorates, structural equation analysis was performed for each of the two electorates. The results are presented in Figure 13:6.

Figure 13:6. Structural equation constructivist models: French 1995 presidential election

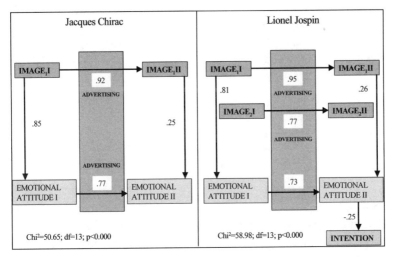

As in the Polish experiments, the statistical models obtained in France do not meet the statistical requirements of good fit (see χ^2 for particular models). Hence, the underlying constructivist assumptions were not empirically validated.

Germany

The specificity of the German research lies in the fact that it was made for parliamentary elections. However, the advertisements that were used in the experiment presented the leaders of the main parties taking part in the elections. That is exactly why it is possible to compare this these studies with the Polish and French ones. It does not, however, mean that the examined model of the influence of advertisements is applicable only in a situation where particular politicians are running for a state office. It can also be useful for the analysis of a party's image.

Wojciech Cwalina • Andrzej Falkowski

After the subjects were divided into electorates as in French experiment, a structural equation analysis was performed resulting in the flowchart presented in Figure 13:7.

Figure 13:7. Structural equation constructivist model: German 1994 parliamentary election

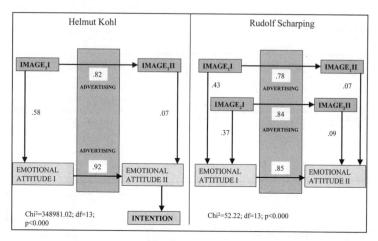

As in the Polish and French experiments, the statistical models obtained in Germany do not meet the statistical requirements of good fit (see χ^2 for particular models). Hence, the constructivist assumptions were, once again, empirically rebuffed.

However, in order to better establish the validity of these models, they should be compared with the results of the analyses for the model formulated on the basis of the realist approach, in which it is assumed that it is voters' affects that form the image of the politician. The foundations of such an approach will be presented in paragraph 3. First, however, it seems worthwhile to discuss the second way of analyzing the image of the politician, as mentioned above, through the use of multiple regression analysis (MRA). The structural equation constructivist model also employs this method of analysis (see Figure 13:3).

Multiple regression models of voter behavior

As voting intention is based on the "feelings thermometer scale", which refers to the affective component of the sequential model (see Figure 13:2), the connection between the candidate's image and the thermometer can be defined for the voters of a given electorate. This relationship can be defined through the use of multiple regression analysis (MRA) in which the feelings thermometer, as a dependent variable, is accounted for by semantic differential adjectives. The results of the study for Poland, France, and Germany are presented, respectively.

Poland

The results of the MRA are shown in Table 13:1. The partition of the sample into two electorates was based on voting intention.

An analysis of the data from Table 13:1 allows us to ascertain that in Walesa's electorate, the semantic differential accounts for the thermometer showing a similar percentage for both candidates. The average size of R^2 from the pre-test to the post-test for Kwasniewski and Walesa was 0.47 and 0.44 respectively. A different situation was evident in Kwasniewski's electorate. Here the semantic differential accounts for the thermometer variance for both candidates. The average size of R^2 from the pre-test to the post-test for Kwasniewski and Walesa was 0.56 and 0.22 respectively.

We therefore state that in Walesa's electorate the thermometer for both candidates is basically equally sensitive in relation to the image of the given candidate, defined by significant adjectives of the semantic differential. The size of multiple correlations indicates a possibility of „regulating" this thermometer by manipulating the image that is broadcast for the voters of both candidates, which is achieved through concentrating on adjectives carefully selected in the process of regression analysis. In other words, voters from Walesa's electorate are susceptible to the influence of information in relation to both candidates. Their beliefs, therefore, are not polarized.

An entirely different situation is found in Kwasniewski's electorate. In this case the thermometer is sensitive only to the local candidate, and is not sensitive to the opposing candidate. In the case of the opposing candidate, therefore, the small multiple correlation indicates an inability to „regulate" the thermometer by controlling his image.

Wojciech Cwalina • Andrzej Falkowski

Table 13:1. Adjectives accounting for the variance of the thermometer of feelings based on the MRA: 1995 Polish presidential election

Candi-dates	Condi-tions	R^2	Characte-ristics	Variance accounted for (%)	Beta
Walesa's Electorate					
Kwasni ewski	pre-test	0.47	Friendly**	5.8	.32
			Honest*	5.0	.29
			Attractive*	4.0	.23
			Believable*	3.7	-.21
			Aggressive*	3.0	.19
	post-test	0.46	Aggressive***	13.0	.50
			Believable**	8.0	-.34
			Qualified*	2.9	-.18
Walesa	pre-test	0.42	Friendly**	8.3	.32
			Honest**	6.9	.31
			Strong*	4.0	.22
	post-test	0.46	Honest***	10.9	.38
			Unsophisticated*	4.1	.21
			Believing	4.0	.25
			Christian*	3.9	,21
			Aggressive*		
Kwasniewski's Electorate					
Kwasni ewski	pre-test	0.52	Honest***	17.0	.50
			Attractive**	4.1	-.26
			Calm *	2.3	.19
	post-test	0.60	Friendly*	2.6	.26
			Serious*	2.6	.25
Walesa	pre-test	0.21	Strong*	3.7	-.23
			Open for world	2.9	-.19
			Unsophisticated	2.9	-.18
	post-test	0.23	Open for world*	4.1	-.23

* $p<0.05$; ** $p<0.01$; *** $p<0.001$

The voters from this electorate, however, react to their candidate within the range of adjectives, which are selected in the process of regression analysis, but are equally „cold" in relation to the other candidate, irrespective of the image he presents. Thus, this electorate has strongly polarized beliefs.

We are interested in the extent of the influence of watching the spots used in the experiment on voters' overall cognitive behavior and therefore the influence on the image of the candidate. In other words, it is not sufficient just to look at the differences in adjectives before and after watching the spots. The difference in variances of adjectives accounting for the thermometer variance before and after viewing the spots (R^2) must be analyzed.

Thus, it was possible to observe a minor effect of spots on cognitive behavior of both Walesa's and Kwasniewski's voters. One can say that spots did not influence the relationship between the image and the feeling (it is on the same level of intensity; about the same R^2 for the pre-test and post-test). However, they do change some elements in the image of the candidate. After viewing the spots, a reconfiguration of items in the voters' minds occurred. The set of adjectives accounting for variances in the thermometer is different after viewing the ads (see Table 13:1).

It seems clear that after watching the spots, the pictures or images of the candidates have been changed within the overall cognitive behavior, which links all the components of the model: image, feeling and intention. In other words, after watching the spots the voter is sensitive to different adjectives. We can „warm up" or „cool down" the feeling toward the candidate by manipulating selected characteristics of the candidates' images in a promotional advertising strategy.

A similar analysis was performed in the Polish presidential election in 2000, the results of which are presented in Table 13:2.

In Kwasniewski's electorate the mean values of R^2 for „our" candidate (Kwasniewski) and the opponent (Olechowski) are 0.38 and 0.52, respectively. In Olechowski's electorate, the values are 0.66 for the appraisal of Kwasniewski's image and 0.53 for Olechowski's. In the case of both electorates the percentage of the explained variance ($R^2 \times 100\%$) is smaller for „our" candidate that the „outsider".

Table 13:2. Adjectives accounting for the variance of the thermometer of feelings based on the MRA: Polish 2000 presidential election

Candidates	Conditions	R^2	Characteristics	Variance accounted for (%)	Beta
Olechowski's Electorate					
Kwasniewski	pre-test	0.62	Attractive**	18.4	-.48
			Friendly*	13.5	.59
			Honest*	13.4	.46
			Believable*	11.2	,50
	post-test	0.70	Qualified*	7.3	-.42
			Passive*	6.6	-.33
			Attractive	6.3	-.32
			Aggressive	5.4	.30
Olechowski	pre-test	0.39	Strong**	23.3	-.76
			Passive*	13.2	-,56
	post-test	0.66	Honest***	33.5	,75
			Passive**	19.9	-1.07
			Successful*	10.7	-.56
Kwasniewski's Electorate					
Kwasniewski	pre-test	0.43	Attractive***	21.5	-.50
			Aggressive**	11.8	-.40
	post-test	0.33	Attractive*	7.9	-.30
			Successful*	7.3	-.34
			Honest	6.0	.25
Olechowski	pre-test	0.55	Honest***	23.8	.52
			Successful**	13.0	-.45
			Believing	9.1	-.32
			Christian*	5.6	-.26
			Attractive*		
	post-test	0.49	Friendly**	10.2	.48
			Serious*	8.1	.36
			Open for world	4.4	-.28

* p<0.05; ** p<0.01; *** p<0.001

This may imply that the affective attitude towards „our" candidate is dependent to a lesser degree on his image and to a larger degree on other candidate's attributes (e.g. his political program, party affiliation, system of values). The „outsider" candidate is monitored more carefully, mainly in order to find his negative features or features which discredit him as a potential president. In the case of both electorates a strong polarization of convictions towards individual candidates can also be noticed.

Despite this, the percentage of the explained variance in the thermometer of feelings by differential adjectives is relatively high. This points to the possibility of controlling the affective attitude towards candidates by proper emphasis on their relevant attributes (see Table 13:2). As in the case of the Polish presidential election in 1995, a reconfiguration of politicians' images under the influence of their spots can be observed. The set of significant adjectives explaining the temperature of feelings towards a given candidate is different after the broadcast.

France

A similar MRA was conducted in the French sample. The results are presented in Table 13:3.

Among Chirac's electorate, his own advertisements positively influenced voters' feelings. The R^2 value increased from 0.67 in the pre-test to 0.75 in the post-test. Jospin's advertisements, on the other hand, weakened the relationship between his image and the affective attitude towards him - R^2 decreased from 0.67 in the pre-test to 0.43 in the post-test. It can thus be said that the advertisements caused a very strong polarization of the voting preferences among Chirac's electorate.

Among Jospin's electorate – under the influence of the advertisements – a very big increase in the R^2 value, from 0.27 to 0.65, regarding his image, occurred. It seems that the advertisements prepared by his electoral advisors hit the target of his potential supporters. In the case of Chirac, the relationship between his image and the affects toward him weakened (R^2 decreased from 0.57 in the pre-test to 0.45 in the post-test).

Table 13:3. Adjectives accounting for the variance of the thermometer of feelings based on the MRA: French 1995 presidential election

Candidates	Conditions	R^2	Characteristics	Variance accounted for (%)	Beta
Jospin's Electorate					
Jospin	pre-test	0.27	Attractive***	27.0	.52
	post-test	0.65	Believable***	21.5	.59
			Aggressive**	7.7	-.29
			Qualified*	5.7	.31
Chirac	pre-test	0.57	Believable***	28.7	.59
			Qualified*	6.4	.28
	post-test	0.45	Sincere***	45.0	.67
Chirac's Electorate					
Jospin	pre-test	0.67	Qualified***	51.7	.72
			Calm**	11.0	.34
	post-test	0.43	Qualified***	43.0	.65
Chirac	pre-test	0.67	Believable***	10.4	.42
			Aggressive*	5.4	.27
			Qualified*	5.4	.30
	post-test	0.75	Believable***	28.2	.66
			Strong*	5.5	.29

* $p<0.05$; ** $p<0.01$; *** $p<0.001$

Summing up the changes in R^2 it can be said that the effectiveness of Jospin's advertisements in his own electorate was bigger than that of Chirac's advertisements in his. Analyzing the fluctuations of R^2 for the same candidate it can be said that the same advertisement has a different influence, depending upon which electorate the voters belong to. It confirms the predictions concerning the perception of the candidate's image, which is subject to the same rules as switch-gestalt.

The adjectives explaining the variance of the thermometer of feelings towards the candidates in both electorates also changed after the viewing of the advertisements (see Table 13:3). A good example of such changes is the change of the perception of Chirac's image within his electorate. In the minds of voters, features such as "believable, aggressive and qualified" turned into "believable and strong". The ads thus led to the conversion of the aggressive and qualified attributes into one characteristic – strong. This illustrates a qualitative change in the perception of Chirac's image, i.e. its reconfiguration.

Germany

A similar MRA was conducted in the German sample. The results are presented in Table 13:4.

Among Scharping's electorate his own advertisements had little influence on the feelings of voters. The R^2 value increased slightly from 0.35 in the pre-test to 0.40 in the post-test. In the same way, Kohl's advertisements weakened the relationship between his image and the affective attitude toward him as R^2 decreased from 0.47 in the pre-test to 0.42 in the post-test.

Among Kohl's electorate, under the influence of the advertisements, the R^2 value decreased from 0.46 to 0.35, relating to his image. In the case of Scharping, the relationship between his image and the affects towards him increased significantly (R^2 increased from 0.16 in the pre-test to 0.32 in the post-test). It can therefore be inferred that the advertisements prepared by Kohl's electoral advisors were unfavorable for him and favored his opponent.

Scharping's advertisements, at least the ones used in the experiment, were thus more efficient than Kohl's and their efficiency can be observed in both electorates.

After the advertisements were screened, the reconfiguration in the perception of both of the candidates' images was also altered. The features-adjectives that were significant for the affective perception of both Kohl and Scharping changed (see Table 13:4). This also points to the qualitative changes in the perception of the politicians' image under the influence of their advertisements.

Table 13:4. Adjectives accounting for the variance of the thermometer of feelings based on the MRA: German 1994 parliamentary election

Candi-dates	Condi-tions	R^2	Characteristics	Variance accounted for (%)	Beta
Scharping's Electorate					
Kohl	pre-test	0.47	Honest***	23.8	.53
			Qualified***	5.9	.25
			Successful*	2.2	.14
	post-test	0.42	Qualified***	7.9	.31
			Honest**	4.9	.27
			Aggressive**	3.7	.23
Scharping	pre-test	0.35	Friendly***	6.4	.28
			Successful**	4.9	.25
			Qualified**	3.4	.23
			Unsophisticated*	2.0	-.15
	post-test	0.40	Honest***	27.0	.53
			Successful***	8.2	.29
Kohl's Electorate					
Kohl	pre-test	0.46	Friendly**	8.8	.35
			Successful*	6.7	.28
			Honest*	5.3	.27
	post-test	0.35	Successful**	13.3	.38
			Honest**	11.5	.35
Scharping	pre-test	0.16	Qualified**	16.0	.40
	post-test	0.32	Attractive**	19.2	-.44
			Believable*	11.1	-.34

p<0.05; ** p<0.01; *** p<0.001

Taking into account the results of research in Poland, France, and Germany, one may conclude that even slight changes in the attribute weights, or even a significant change in only one of the attribute's weights, may elicit a complete reconfiguration of the image of the candidate. The image change relies not so much on the exchange of particular attributes as on an exchange of the whole attribute configuration.

Political image formation: A realist approach

According to the realist approach to research on social cognition, we can assume the following causal-effect sequence: affect → cognition that is affective feeling toward the candidate influences his images. This approach is well justified in Zajonc's cognitive theory of affects (1980). The author, on the basis of a number of empirical studies, demonstrates that an affective reaction evoked by the perceived object appears first, and is only then followed by cognitive elements. Therefore it is quite reasonable that the affect plays an important role in forming the image of politicians.

In terms of the sequential model of voting behavior presented in Figure 13:2, the arrows connecting the image with the affective feelings should be reversed as presented in Figure 13:8.

Figure 13:8. Structural equation realist model of voter behavior

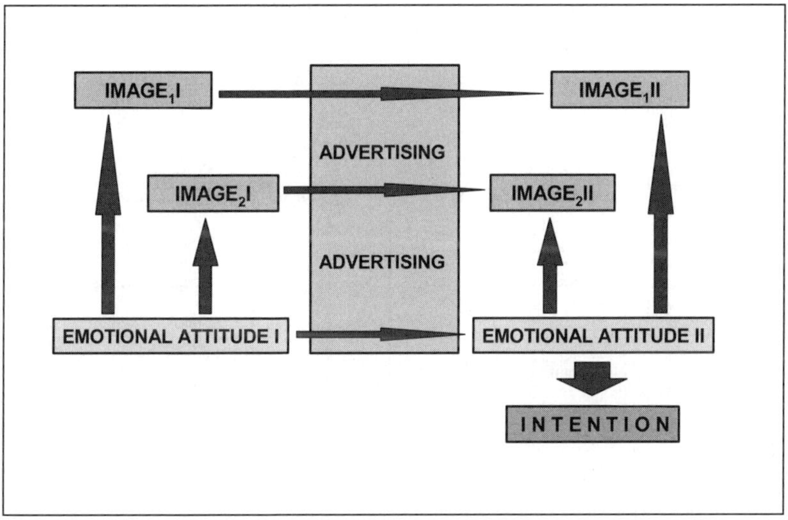

This modification to structural equation models results in the following flowcharts for each country (see Figures: 13:9, 13:10, 13:11 and 13:12).

Wojciech Cwalina • Andrzej Falkowski

Poland

*Figure 13:9. Structural equation realist models: Polish 1995
presidential election*

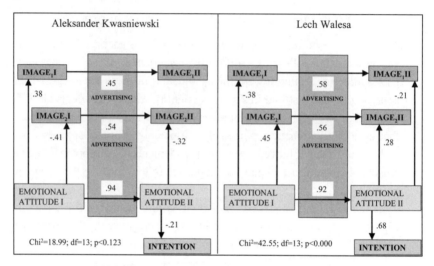

*Figure 13:10. Structural equation realist models: Polish 2000
presidential election*

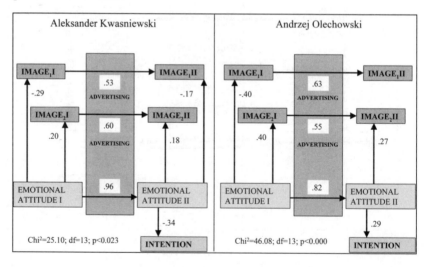

France

Figure 13:11. Structural equation realist models: French 1995 presidential election

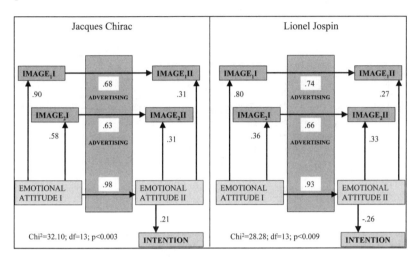

Figures 13:9 to 13:12 show empirical sets of causal relationships between affects and image with reference to particular countries and particular candidates. Despite some differences in specific paths, it can generally be stated that the results obtained here point to the higher explanatory power of the realist approach as compared to the constructivist approach (see level of significance and values of χ^2 in figures 9-12). It means that affects form a politician's image in a significant way. That is, affective attitude towards a politician is the primary reaction of voters when encountering a specific candidate. This is the sole basis upon which voters make cognitive appraisals and attribute the characteristics, of which the politician's campaign image consists. Therefore, from the marketing point of view, the key task is to evoke a positive affective attitude towards the promoted politician, and only subsequently should one suggest to voters that these affects are connected with the particular attributes of the politician.

Wojciech Cwalina • Andrzej Falkowski

Germany

Figure 13:12. Structural equation realist models: German 1994 parliamentary election

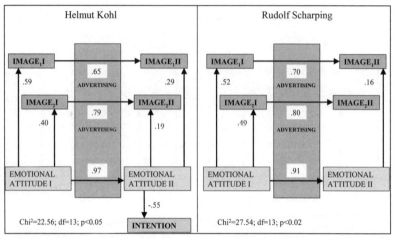

This does not mean, however, that the procedure of creating promotional-advertising strategy, based on multiple regression analysis in order to create or change an image, should be rejected. Identifying affective sensitivity to various features of a politician's image can be a useful direction in preparing advertising spots. We can observe feedback, in which image and affects reinforce one another.

Practical implications

The results of studying voting behavior in Poland, France and Germany according to the constructivist and realist approach allow us to develop a number of concrete practical suggestions connected with creating political advertising. They refer to 1) the key role of evoking a positive affective attitude towards a candidate; and 2) selecting affectively saturated adjectives/attributes, which may significantly improve the image of a candidate and increase his persuasive efficiency in forming the desired voting behavior.

What is more, the results of the research can also be extended to commercial marketing, which has the relevant task of forming images of various brands, products and services, as well as building corporate images.

230

It can therefore be said that the presented sequential model of voters' behavior according to the constructivist approach provides very precise measurements of the changes in the perception of a candidate's image or the image of a brand in general, under the influence of promotional activities. In addition, a reconfiguration of the image of voters' or consumers' attitudes toward the brands and their choosing intention is connected with it. Showing such a relationship has great pragmatic value. It demonstrates the elements upon which a brand's image is based and how reactions to such an image might be controlled. The sequential model, based on multiple regression analysis, can also turn out to be useful in pre-testing advertisements. It allows for the strengthening of a brand's persuasive power and, if necessary, modification of the brand, before its release. However, one must recognize, the already developed advertising strategy of forming the brand's image according to multiple regression influences affective attitude towards a given brand. This attitude, independent of the advertisement's contents, also forms the brand's image, as was demonstrated in the realist approach. Therefore, the influence of this affective attitude should be included in projecting the expected results from the applied advertising strategy of forming of the image of the brand.

14

New Subtle Advertising Formats: Characteristics, Causes & Consequences

ROY LANGER

Introduction

On February 4th 2000, "The Washington Post" announced in a front-page article: "Ford Offers Home PC To Every Employee". Ford had given its about 350,000 employees all over the world home computers and Internet-access for free. President and CEO of Ford Motor Company Jacques Nasser argues for this decision in the company's press release as follows: "We want to unlock the full intellectual capital of Ford Motor Company, and I can think of no better way to do that than by putting every employee online, linking them with the same sources of information that our customers have. When 'Model E' is complete, we believe it will be a powerful, competitive advantage for us" (www.ford.com).

Making this offer to all employees of the company might be interpreted as an (effective) PR-gimmick. But it is more than that, as Nasser states in "Jacques Nasser on Transformation": "To transform our company, we're requiring our employees to interact directly with consumers. We want every Ford Motor Company employee to have the sensibility of a small business owner, where knowing your customers is essential" (www.ford.com).

Obviously, Ford Motor Company has acknowledged that traditional market research and studying consumers is not any longer enough when developing and promoting products. Instead, the company now wants all employees to engage in direct interaction with consumers. In

"Jacques Nasser on Corporate Citizenship", the CEO refers to the famous slogan, "What is good for General Motors is good for America", and argues: "It was not so long ago that leading companies believed 'what was good for them was good for the world.' Business leaders made decisions without scrutiny or accountability and assumed the world would accept the consequences of those choices - be they good or bad. At Ford, we believe exactly the opposite is true. What is good for the world is good for Ford Motor Company" (www.ford.com). Remarkably, many other companies believe the same and offered their employees shortly after the Ford announcement a similar deal (e.g. Delta Air Lines, American Airlines, Intel and Bertelsmann – cf. Locke 2001:51[1]).

However, most remarkable from a historical perspective is the fact that precisely Ford Motor Company now (and again) was one of the first movers among the major companies of the world – as the company gave its name to a term (Fordism) referring to another era, namely the age of industrialism, mass production and mass consumption. That was also the era of cold war, of assembly lines in production and of standardised consumerism. It was the era when companies believed they could gain competitive advantages and growth from using a combination of force and persuasion targeted at both their workforce and customers. It also was the era when commercial messages exploded in public space through massive promotional marketing efforts based on the use of mass media. Finally, it refers to the era when Henry Ford (1863-1947) believed that "men work for only two reasons: one is for wages, and one is for fear of losing their jobs" (Thompson, 1999:405).

This chapter seeks to explore, to understand and to explain current trends in advertising as well as their reasons and rationales. Moreover, it analyses advertising professionals' reflections on this development. Finally, the chapter presents implications for advertising theory and practice as well as for the marketing ethics. The study is based on contextual historical analysis, twenty in-depth interviews with Danish marketing professionals on current trends in advertising and

---

[1] Also Locke (2001), co-author of the "Cluetrain Manifesto", refers to Ford's Model E employee computer programme in his recently published book – but uses the case for another purpose when arguing for the importance of Internet marketing and the disregard of established marketing research and planning.

commercial communication, as well as secondary data about socio-cultural developments and trends. The emergence of new advertising formats, strategies and contents and their increasing use are discussed from the perspective of advertising professionals.[2] These data are part of a recently published project on the use of product placement and other forms of new subtle marketing promotion in Denmark (Langer & Nielsen, 2002). The project was initiated by the National Consumer Agency of Denmark at the Ministry of Economic and Business Affairs in response to a political quest for further legal regulation of advertising in Denmark – as some of the new subtle advertising strategies, formats and contents challenged existing regulations and raised political and ethical debates in the Danish public.

As advertising – like any other social practice – is continuously changing and transforming, not all of these new subtle advertising strategies, formats and contents raise ethical debates. Neither are all of the new advertising strategies, formats and contents very subtle. Whether they are or not and whether they give birth to ethical debates or not depends on the particular features and contextual aspects. However, as all of them are indicators of a general transition of advertising practices, the ethical implications of this transition will be discussed from case to case.

Promotional seduction and Fordism – two sides of the same coin

> You've got to persuade everybody that all this grand industrial civilization is just as bad smell and that the real, significant life can only be lived apart from it. (Aldous Huxley: Point Counter Point 1928)

> It is by manipulating "hidden forces" that the advertising experts induce us to buy their wares - a toothpaste, a brand of cigarettes, a political candidate. (Aldous Huxley: Propaganda under a Dictatorship, 1958)

---

[2] Note the contribution of Neijens & Smit, chapter 15 in this volume, presenting audience reactions towards non-spot advertising and thus discussing a current trend in advertising from a consumer's perspective.

James Vicary, an unemployed market researcher from New Jersey, claimed in 1957 that sales increases would be possible if sales promotion messages like "Eat Popcorn" of about 1/60,000 second would be placed into movies. The myth of subliminal advertising was born, a pseudo-science of subliminal advertising research was created, and popular conceptions of promotional seduction were confirmed – though neither Vicary nor his followers (e.g. Key, 1972, 1976, 1980, 1989) were able to offer valid documentation for their claims. In fact, Vicary admitted later that he had never done the research he claimed.

Without going into details of this discourse (see e.g. Rogers, 1992/93 & 1993; Langer & Nielsen, 2002 for further discussion), it is important to understand why Vicary has been so successful in establishing this myth, why he found so many followers among professional and political experts and why this myth matched popular conceptions of how advertising works. In order to understand this, one has to look at the socio-cultural situation in highly industrialised countries between the 1920s and 1970s. Advertising critique was founded in the 1920s in the US, as advertising at that time had changed character from just providing information about products and their characteristics to being a social adviser. Schudson (1984) explains this change by pointing at the increasing gap between conditions of production and conditions of consumption for increasingly large sections of the population. This growing gap resulted in an increasing division of individuals and the products these individuals consumed. Consumers did not know any longer very much about production processes and product characteristics of the products they consumed. Urbanisation, professional differentiation and specialisation made it more and more difficult for consumers to see and evaluate products in relation to their production context (Jhally, 1989). Advertising became a social practice compensating for these deficits by moving consumers' focus from product characteristics towards functionality of products and their social meaning (cf. Bell, 1976; Marchand, 1985). This development was initiated, accompanied and facilitated by technological progress – not just in industrial production but in the media as well. Both modern journalism and modern marketing were founded during the 1920s as independent commercial practices and as research disciplines, reflecting on these practices and their social functions and relevance. While mass media advertising was initially predominantly bound to the print media, it soon also played an important role in the new electronic mass media (radio, film and TV) as well.

It was, however, first in the late 1940s that advertising experienced such tremendous growth and social importance that it could be acknowledged as one of the most noticeable and evident characteristics of modern market economy and culture. This goes together with the invention of TV ads, as the first TV ad was transmitted on NBC's New York channel in 1941 (Lewis & Bridger, 2000:149). Also the first examples of product placements in movies are reported from the 1940s (DeLorme & Reid, 1999:71). Both the political, economic and socio-cultural shadows of World War II and further technological progress (in particular TV broadcasting) might be seen as reasons for this delay. Though some authors (e.g. Nietzsche) already in the 19th century criticised growing materialism in mass society, it was first the impressive economic growth in the postwar decades that created a cultural climate, where critics could get wider social response in public opinion on their description of negative consequences of modernity. As advertising was one of the most visible and evident aspects of the ongoing modernisation process, it also became one of the major targets in this critique. Another target for critique was the role of journalism and public opinion building in mass media, for example in the famous Dewey-Lippman debate about the role of journalism for public opinion and the "pictures in our heads" created by the mass media in the early 1920s (cf. Spichal, 1999).

In order to understand the tradition of advertising critique, one must look at the socio-cultural context. This context was, especially during the 1950s and again after 1968, determined by a general climate of manipulation and conspiracy theories and Cold War paranoia. When reflecting on the ongoing modernisation process in society – particularly in politics and economy – many prominent Western intellectuals expressed their worries that modern society with its mass media, its mass production and its mass consumption would be a threat against the individual's autonomy and integrity. These worries were expressed by fictional writers such as Aldous Huxley in "Brave New World" (1931) and George Orwell in "Animal Farm" (1945), by philosophers such as Theodor Wiesengrund Adorno and Max Horckheimer in "Dialektik der Aufklärung" (1947), by sociologists such as Vance Packard in "The Hidden Persuaders" (1957), and by economists such as John Kenneth Galbraith in "The Affluent Society" (1958). In many of these works advertising appeared to be one of the most evil symbols of materialist societies, sharing major responsibilities for manipulating and seducing people to give up their individual and democratic rights, colonising the public and lacking social responsibility and values (cf. Berman, 1981; Brailsford, 1998). Galbraith claimed that advertising produces "wants that previously did not exist" (1958:150) and transforms consumers into almost defenceless victims of promotional seduction: "Given that consumer wants are created by the process by which they are satisfied, the consumer makes no choice. He is subject to the forces of advertising and emulation by which production creates its own demands." (ibid.:500)

Advertising critique rooted from its very beginnings in a general cultural climate of fear that modern industrial societies would – by force or by persuasion – streamline and brainwash individuals to accept and to participate in the ongoing modernisation process. Advertising critique became a central part of a general social and civilising critique, as advertising was one of the most central symbols of modern and industrialised societies. In line with this argument, Philips (1992:112; see also Moog, 1990; Goldman 1992) concludes: "Our own capitalist economic system directly causes the negative conditions which lead to increased materialism. Advertising, as the mouthpiece of capitalism, presents values and assumptions that colour consumers' perceptions of reality. Therefore, advertising becomes a target for social criticism. However, advertising does not create the values it presents. Capitalism is the creator, and the cause of negative social conditions underlying materialism, perhaps encouraged by basic human nature." Supported by psychoanalytical, behaviourist and Marxist theories, advertising was considered to be the dialectical contrast to substance and truth (cf. Reekie, 1981; Madsen, 1998; Boutlis, 2000).

However, advertisers and marketers also contributed themselves to this climate of opinion by claiming that modern marketing promotion in mass media could have a strong impact on buyers' behaviour. Euphoric optimism about potential effects of promotional seduction was reflected in sender-oriented models of mass communication and mass marketing (e.g. the Laswell formula, the S-O-R model, the AIDA model, the DAGMAR model or the "Hierarchy of Effects" model, cf. Langer & Nielsen, 2002:44-47). These models were not just used for analytical purposes, they also had a normative and directive character for political communication (e.g. election campaigns) and marketing planning. And they reflected a pragmatic interest of professional advertisers and marketers, as they highlighted the tremendous importance of modern advertising and marketing in modern society.

However, these models did not sufficiently recognise the active role of receivers of mediated political, commercial or other messages. As Boutlis (2000) argues, consumers do not reject materialism and advertising as such, but rather an understanding of consumers as uniform masses in the way expressed in both early communication and marketing models and practices. Only more recent research, in particular since the 1960s, has focused on how people reject the reception of messages, select reception among the many messages they are exposed to, and transform these messages in perception processes. Despite the results of this research, sender-oriented communication and marketing models show an almost amazing ability to survive in both popular and professional understanding of how mass communication works. Their simple narrative and structure often facilitates the legitimacy of arguments on advertising practice and advertising critique as well as the popular understanding of how mass communication and advertising work.

Behind the scenes of the promotional seduction game and the debate about advertising as a mouthpiece of capitalism, technological progress and changes in the modes of industrial production were decisive aspects. These changes are covered by the concept of Fordism, which is widely discussed in the research literature on industrial relations, organisational studies, management studies, business history, political economy, business ethics etc. Except for a few studies on macromarketing and postmodern marketing (e.g. Brown, 1993; Brown, 1994; Firat & Venkatesh, 1995; Gabriel & Lang, 1996; Venkatesh, 1999; Holbrook, 1999), the concept has rarely been mentioned or even applied in studies of marketing management, marketing promotion and advertising. There is, however, a certain overlap to the marketing discipline, in particular regarding the debate about global standardisation versus local adaptation, regarding the debate about how the Internet changes business (e.g. Levine, Locke, Searls & Weinberger, 2000; Locke, 2001), and - in particular - regarding the debate on "McDonaldization" (note Holbrook, 1999, for a comprehensive review), as the concept of Fordism flourished in the contextual periphery of these debates. Without echoing the dotcom hype or postmodern enthusiasm of some of these contributions predicting the death of mass marketing and "the end of business as usual" (Levine et al, 2000) and that "[C]ompanies don't give a damn about advertising..." (Locke, 2001), the following argument attempts to acknowledge and unfold the underlying argument in this literature that promotional seduction strategies and Fordism in fact are two sides of the same coin.

Fordism refers to the system of mass production and consumption established in highly developed and industrialised economies from the 1940s to the 1960s (cf. Thompson, 1999:404).[3] Ford was a popular symbol of the transformation from an agricultural and craft production to an industrial mass production and mass consumption economy. The conventional credit to Henry Ford goes for the development of the first moving assembly lines at Ford's Highland Park in Dearborn, Michigan, in 1913 (Harvey, 1990:125). More comprehensively, Fordism refers to division of labour, to increased mechanisation, standardisation and coordination of large scale production processes, to a shift to less skilled assembly-line labour performing tasks minutely specified by management, and, finally, to the use of a combination of force and persuasion in order to create a docile workforce (see also Jessop, 1991). All these aspects were designed to gain economies of scale and economies of scope. Economies of scale were achieved by standardisation and larger volumes of output, economies of scope by professional specialisation and division of labour (Taylorism). This process resulted in both increased exploitation and increased standards of living. Gabriel & Lang (1995:12) note: "The basic bargain on which consumerism flourished

---

[3]   One might – in line with the traditional argument in political economy - claim that the term Fordism exclusively refers to the period from the 1940s to the 1970s (cf. Mayhew 1997). However, as the term in the context of this chapter first of all attempts to signify a particular conceptual way of organising and understanding production, transmission and consumption of products, and messages and products in general, it might as well be used in order to signify this particular way of organising and understanding social relations.

was a more docile workforce in exchange for ever-increasing standards of living." Correspondingly, some authors (e.g. Albo, Langlille & Panitch, 1993) refer to the welfare state as the Fordist state.

However, Fordism extends beyond process engineering in production. It also refers to the social institutions of mass production – including advertising and modern marketing. Michel Aglietta (1976) underlines the complementarity between mass production, consumption and politics, when referring to the Italian Marxist Antonio Gramsci, who coined the term Fordism in "Americanism and Fordism" (1949/71). Gramsci (ibid.:280-281) recognised the political and cultural significance of Fordist production and working methods and criticised it for replacing active participation, intelligence, fantasy and initiative with automatic and mechanical stupidity. This process included a de-radicalisation of industrial trade unions and the construction of new social power relations – not just in work places and in the sphere of production - by using force and persuasion (Rupert, 1995; Rupert, 2001).

Fordism was mirrored in traditional advertising theory and practice, as well as by advertising critiques, all claiming that mediated promotional messages, due to their potential of broad exposure of consumers, can have a high potential for socio-cultural impact. Correspondingly, mass marketing promotion was closely connected with - and to a large extent based on - mass media. Sender-centred one-way communication dominated the theoretical understanding of mass marketing, and advertising strategies and formats corresponded to such an understanding. Such understanding also implicitly includes a particular perspective on consumers – consider for example the word "target group" – underestimating consumers' reflexive minds and victimising them. Critical success criteria for advertising campaigns were quantity, popularity, mass appeal and majority opinion. Correspondingly, advertising formats predominantly relied on suitability to mass media channels, and advertising contents included heavy stereotyping and a trend towards lowest common denominators in order to attract mass media audiences.

To sum up: Fordism and promotional seduction ARE two sides of the same coin. They have in common that both are rooted in the age of industrialised society, bound to the technologies and media of this era and closely interlinked with socio-cultural characteristics of the rising welfare state. As two sides of a coin – one mainly referring to production process, but closely connected to the other side, namely the consumption sphere – they share a behaviourist perspective on human action and view of human nature. They also apply the same strategies, as force and persuasive seduction are used to trigger both workforce and consumers. And they share the same ideals and guidelines for both mass production and mass marketing in the mass media, when focusing on quantity, popularity, mass appeal and majority opinion.

Current trends in advertising strategies, formats and contents

The bottom line is that markets are changing faster than marketing. Today, most company marketing strategies are obsolete! We are noticing a blurring today in the distinction between products and services, between buyers and sellers, between companies and their environments. (Philip Kotler, "Reflections on Marketing", 2001)

Things are not any longer as they used to be. Several authors – many of them practitioners or former practitioners in marketing – emphasise that the marketplace today is a consumer democracy and predict the death of mass marketing (e.g. Schultz, Tannenbaum & Lauterborn, 1994; Zyman 1999). They argue that "[t]he shift from a verbal to a visual society will continue to be a major factor in why integrated marketing communications will be so necessary for marketing organizations in the years to come." (Schultz et al :20).

Even Philip Kotler – after all, one of the main theorists of modern marketing for about three decades and whose textbooks on marketing management were guidelines for generations of future marketers throughout the past decades – acknowledges in his recent publications (Kotler, 2001; Kotler, Jain & Maesincee, 2002) that we are about to enter a new era in marketing. Most of the discipline's conventional models and methods are not working any longer due to the fragmentation of markets, the diversification of values and lifestyles and the growing disloyality of consumers, reflecting the shift from a producer-centric to a consumer-centric and technology-driven world.

As a consequence, there is an urgent quest for a renewal of marketing models and for deconstruction and redefinition of classic marketing.

Political economists claim that Fordism reached its limits by the end of the 1960s. As the growth of social productivity based on it declined markedly, Fordism transformed itself in the last decade of the twentieth century (Rupert, 2001). The socio-economic foundation of the post-war period was transcended culturally and ideologically by the end of the Cold War. Already during the 1980s, flexible production and quality production methods (e.g. TQM and JIT) became common in the sphere of industrial production. In line with this, modern workplaces demand a more equal participation and responsibility of all employees in knowledge sharing and decision-making. Both economies of scale and scope are losing importance, as computerisation and digitalisation of production and marketing processes reduce information costs. Again, this is not only a development characteristic for structural and cultural changes at work places, but of wider social and political range, leading to even somewhat optimistic predictions like: "[M]ass production's decline has been accompanied by a decline in mass consumption. Instead of standardized products designed and manufactured for the lowest common denominator, final products reflect the full array of preferences and pocketbooks" (Thompson, 1998). Flexible work practices have been elevated over the specialisation of labour, hierarchical management structures have been superseded by flat or matrix organisations, and mass production has been reputedly replaced by computer-aided customisation of the post-Fordist era (Murray, 1990).

Despite this view, some postmodern authors maintain that efficiency, predictability, quantification and control are a threat to humanity, as the debate about McDonaldization in the 1990s confirmed, e.g when Ritzer concludes in his revised update of his first McDonaldization book (1996:152): "Fordism is alive and well in the modern word, although it has been transformed into McDonaldization." Belk (1996:33) comments on this: "Similar concerns were raised by the rise of Taylorism and Fordism in the workplace earlier in the century. The difference may be that globalized hyperreality in the various forms of Coca-Cola, McDonald's, and Disney, has a much more appealing face and seems far more innocuous than the drab efficiency of the Metropolis assembly line. Rather than our being coerced into compliance, it is more like a seduction." (Belk, 1996:33).

Firat, Dholakia & Venkatesh 1995, and in particular Venkatesh 1999, postmodern marketing researchers opposed to the modernist assumption of analysis, planning, implementation and control of marketing, questioned universalising, generalising models and marketing planning procedures – thus highlighting the inherent limitations of marketing models and theories and emphasising the plurality, diversity and uniqueness of individuals versus the mass. For example, "The more politicians, industry and consumer organisations try to manage consumers, the more unmanageable they seem to be" (Gabriel & Lang, 1995:213). However, apart from putting emphasis on individuality, abolishing most of the models developed by "modern" theorists and replacing them with often rather airy calls for particularism, aesthetics, creativity, narratives and storytelling, and apart from demanding that marketing should move from being an instrumental discipline to become a reflexive socio-cultural science discipline, postmodern marketing researchers have not been able to offer much help for marketing practitioners who wanted to react on the shift from Fordism to Post-Fordism (note, however, Firat & Dholakia, 1998, for a discussion of the coexistence of standardised mass production with product, price and promotional differentiation).

Even though postmodern and dotcom writers take such a stand or point of departure and obviously do not agree on whether the so-called postmodern shift has led to the collapse of Fordism or to its transformation (note Holbrook, 1999:2-12 for a critique of McDonaldization), their argument about shifting reality and socio-cultural change is still valid. Clancy & Lloyd (1999:4-6) note an increasing resistance of consumers and audiences towards mass advertising. As a consequence, "advertising effectiveness continues its steady decline" (ibid.). A recent German study also claims that 68% of the population are not any longer aware of traditional mass media advertising and envisages that conventional advertising formats at best stagnate, whereas new subtle advertising formats, such as viral marketing and sponsoring, will experience ongoing growth. Today in Germany, already more than half of the revenues spent on advertising are designated to such formats (Werben & Verkaufen, 10.8.2001:25;

see also Lewis & Bridger, 2000). The share of the total amount of marketing promotion money spent on mass media ads declined considerably in the past decades (ibid., see also Shergill, 1993, for a similar development of expenditures in the US). This decline of conventional and traditional mass marketing happened in favour of new advertising formats, strategies and contents.

One of the most popular marketing theory responses on the development described above is the concept of "mass customisation" (also 1-1 marketing, relationship marketing or micromarketing). This approach is based on the assumption that cost-efficient mass production can be combined with customer-oriented and differentiated segmentation (Pine, 1993:44-54) as well as standardised modularisation of production. However, Holbrook (1999:63-8) reveals mass customisation's implicit paradox by arguing that the output of standardised modules are still standardised products and that operations management has taken over many functions formerly associated with marketing. In fact, Holbrook calls this approach "engineering", as "each consumer will simply tell us what he or she wants, and we will agilely build it for him or her, using modularized techniques of production that will permit us to achieve the greatest possible uniqueness and suitability of each offering at the lowest cost but at the highest possible price" (ibid.:67).

Other responses to the development described above include an increase of traditional market segmentation, resulting in very small and tiny niches (niche marketing) and the tremendous focus on branding, symbolisation and storytelling. While segmentation is nothing else than the application of traditional techniques on smaller and smaller segments, much of the storytelling and symbol communication going on is based on a sender-oriented "Who am I" narrative. Thus, these techniques are to a certain degree just old wine in new bottles, not offering solutions for the major task that advertising practitioners have to face: How to cut through the clutter, and how to pretend there is no mass production any longer?

In a study on new subtle marketing promotion in Denmark (Langer & Nielsen, 2002), three further and interconnected strategies for the renewal of advertising practice could be identified: 1) the application of new channels and formats in promotion activities and the increasing use of non-traditional channels in marketing promotion; 2) the blurring of boundaries to other public discourses and social practices; and 3) the production of new advertising contents. These strategies are applied in order to counter ad avoidance, legal regulation and information overload by creating Trojan horses, in order to gain advantage from the credibility of other public discourses and social practices, and in order to expose potential consumers, including children, to commercial messages. In the following, these three strategies will be discussed in further detail.

The application of new subtle channels and formats in marketing promotion

The application of new channels and media in promotion activities and the growing use of non-traditional channels in marketing promotion can be interpreted as a result of the general marketisation and commercialisation of society (Fairclough, 1995), as commercial communication infiltrates almost all domains of society. Such new channels and formats include viral marketing, media alliances, programming, sponsoring and event marketing, social and cause related marketing, gifts and masked spokespersons, masked art, product placement in movies and TV programmes, advertorials and infomercials and so forth. In fact, some of these formats are not so new any longer (e.g. sponsoring of television programmes), but the extent to which these channels and formats are used is today larger than ever and still growing. Other formats – such as viral marketing – are based on new digital technologies (e.g. the Internet and cell phones) or use uncommon media (e.g. art, fictional literature), channels (e.g. scent marketing) or social discourses (e.g. education) when communicating commercial messages.

Apart from the spread of advertising messages in various channels and the invention of new advertising formats due to technological development, a remarkable increase of commercial messages based on the growing use of various lobbying, sales and direct marketing and PR-techniques – sometimes combined with the application of sponsoring, gift-giving and even conventional advertising formats – can be observed. Though direct marketing, PR and – to a certain degree – sponsoring are distinguished from advertising in theories on marketing promotion, and though there exist agencies specialised in each of these marketing promotion techniques in practice, the boundaries between PR, sponsoring and advertising are not at all that clear in reality. PR agencies apply techniques conventionally situated in advertising and vice versa. The same goes for agencies specialised in sponsorship, direct marketing or even corporate identity and image. Thus, the theoretical distinction between these different forms of marketing promotion cannot – at least not any longer – be relied on when analysing the practice of marketing promotion and the communication of commercial messages (note also section 6.1).

As many of the new media, channels and formats in advertising apparently make it more difficult for consumers to identify the commercial purpose of the message and/or the identity of the commercial sender, these advertising formats were labelled in the Scandinavian countries (Danish: "skjult reklame"; Swedish: "dold reklam") and in the German-speaking countries ("Schleichwerbung"). However, there exists no metonym in the English language referring to all these channels and formats in advertising. Even though the term "non-spot advertising" has a quite clear reference to "the compensated inclusion of branded products or brand identifiers, through audio and/or visual means, with mass media programming" (Kahhr, Frith & Callison, 2001; note also the contribution of Neejens and Smit in this volume), also this term appears to be rather too narrow when trying to establish a metonymic reference to all the new advertising channels and formats applied in commercial advertising. But neither the metonyms in the German or Scandinavian languages are able to offer a clear definition in regard to the choice of media, channels and formats in advertising – as some of these media, channels and formats try to blur the identity of the commercial sender and/or the commercial purpose of a message, while others sometimes do it and others never. However, the question of how to define these new subtle advertising formats is closely related to the purpose of such definition, namely to summarise all advertising that attempts to blur the identity of the sender as a commercial agent and/or the commercial purpose of the message. This trend gives birth to new debates about advertising ethics (cf. Nebenzahl & Jaffe, 1998) and is interrelated to the second strategy for the renewal of advertising that can be suggested, the blurring of boundaries to other public discourses and social practices.

The blurring of boundaries to other public discourses and social practices

Advertising is increasingly blurring traditional boundaries towards journalism, art, sport and education. The purpose of this blurring of boundaries is to gain spill-over effects from the credibility of these discourses. Such blurring of once solid boundaries was already in 1994 noted by Brown, when "the advent of advertorials, informercials, interactive shopping channels, EDI-linked buyer-supplier relationships, scrambled merchandising, shopping centres-cum-theme parks and bookshops-cum-restaurants" (Brown, 1994:39) Today, there is almost no advertising-free space left. Commercial messages are displayed in schoolbooks, in fictional literature, at sport events, in movies, in comedies, even in news programmes. Promotion of products and companies can be found in editorial articles in newspapers and magazines, in public health information and in higher education, where professors and university departments have the title of their commercial sponsors. There is no doubt that advertisers seek to find alternatives in order to avoid information overload and ad rejections in conventional advertising discourse.

However, the blurring of boundaries to formerly advertising-free discourses and practices is not just a one-way lane expressing parasitic infiltration of social practices and discourses by advertising. In fact, much of this blurring is initiated from these formerly advertising-free discourses and practices in order to gain economic revenues, allowing their further existence and development. Commercial sponsors are actively invited, as their support is needed in order to reach the goals for IT implementation in primary schools formulated by political decision-makers without giving sufficient financial support to the acquisition of IT equipment. Many sports and art events would not exist without similar support from commercial sponsors. Also media channels – be they newspapers, TV channels or movie production – increasingly need commercial sponsors in order to meet the expectations of their audiences. Often, gaining commercial support – and displaying commercial messages in return for it – is even an existentialist issue. Moreover, public campaigns (e.g. health campaigns) and information (e.g. about educational issues) as well as

NGOs draw heavily on marketing discourse by integrating advertising language and formats into their communication.

Thus, the blurring of formerly clearly separated discourses is a general trend, which all social agents and institutions involved contribute to. However, as this blurring of boundaries often makes it more difficult to distinguish between public information and commercial interests - between art, education etc. on the one hand and business on the other – this development gives birth to ethical concerns on behalf of consumers. Public health information and medical advice, for example, gained its traditional directive authority from its independence and from being exclusively based on scientific arguments. The blurring of boundaries to commercial discourse can result in a decline of its trustworthiness and reliability of both public institutions and professional authorities in art, journalism, education or science.

The production of new subtle advertising contents

Christensen (2001) describes in his recent book another trend, when highlighting auto-communication and self-reference as two of the main characteristics of current advertisements. Many of these advertisements refer to each other in a positioning game among different products and invite consumers to participate actively in the construction of meaning and images. By applying new creative formats, channels and media, these ads acknowledge that consumers are not just passive receivers and promise consumers entertainment and satisfaction. Christensen (ibid.:48) claims that advertisements by doing so are points of reference for other cultural products and signs and presuppose cultural knowledge from consumers. Advertisements are not just commercial products, but cultural products as well. Product references are often secondary or even absent, as their appeal is based on the invitation to accept the offer to participate in a sophisticated interpretation game (ibid.:55).

Before presenting the perspective of advertising professionals on the ongoing transition of advertising, the following matrix attempts to summarise the main characteristics of the transformation from Fordism to Post-Fordism in marketing, i.e. from promotional seduction and persuasion to new subtle advertising formats, strategies and contents:

Figure 14:1: The transition of advertising

	Fordism	Post-Fordism
Market situation	• producer/sender-centric • economic growth • materialism • industrialism • mass production & consumption • mass media as intermediaries • rationalism	• consumer/receiver-centric • market fragmentation and diversification • information overload • individualism • pluralism • marketisation of society • hyper-reality
Methods and models applied	*In production:* • standardisation • mechanisation • coordination / Taylorism *In marketing promotion/advertising:* • force & persuasion/seduction • mass marketing: S-O-R models, AIDA, 4 Ps, Hierarchy of Effects	*In production* • knowledge economy • innovation • (mass) customisation *In marketing promotion/advertising:* conventional approaches: • market segmentation (niche marketing) • storytelling/value • 1-1 marketing new subtle strategies, formats & contents: • product placement, non-spot advertising, programming, social and cause-related marketing, viral marketing, media alliances • blurred boundaries between business and all other discourses and practices (e.g. sport, art, journalism, education) • auto-communication, open-end stories, social responsibility, lack of explicit product references
Ideals and success criteria	• quantity • mass appeal • majority opinion • economy of scope and scale	• impact • entertainment • imaging • positioning
Understanding of markets based on	• behaviourism • cognitive psychology • capitalist/liberalist ideology critics: • behaviourism • psychoanalysis • marxist ideology	• social constructivism • de-constructivism • postmodernist theory • art • utalitarian pragmatics
Status of advertising	Advertising as the commercial	Advertising as a general cultural

	mouthpiece in and off mass society with its mass production, mass media and mass consumption.	and communication technique in most social domains.

The practitioners' perspective: professionals on current trends in advertising

In the following section the results of an analysis of 20 qualitative research interviews (cf. Kvale, 1996) with Danish marketing professionals (R1-20) will be presented. The purpose of this study was to investigate marketing professionals' reflections on current trends in advertising. Sixteen of the interviewees were managers in Danish advertising and PR agencies, four were employed in top-level positions in marketing in companies or were CEOs in professional organisations. All interviews were conducted by the same interviewer in autumn 2001. They were transcribed and analysed in concordance with conventional phenomenological techniques, such as key word analysis, meaning condensation and topical analysis (ibid.). The presentation of the results of this study emphasises the following topical aspects: 1) the informants' general perception of advertising, 2) the informants' reflection on the current situation of the advertising market, 3) the informants' perspective on consumers and advertising effects, 4) the informants' observation of and reflection on current trends in advertising, and 5) the informants' expectations for the future of advertising and hot spots in advertising development.

Advertising professionals' general perception of advertising

Advertisers regard, not unexpectedly, advertising as a totally legal and legitimate business like all other commercial activities. When confronted with the negative image of advertisers and marketing professionals in the general public, they argue that advertising is just another cultural expression of market society like any other business on the market. However, when it comes to the amount of advertisements they are exposed to as private persons and consumers, several of the informants expressed reservations regarding the overload of commercial messages in public space. For example:

"To be honest, I don't like commercials. Each time there are ads on TV, I just zap to another channel. And when I am going to the movies, I am usually 5-10 minutes late – I just want to see the film...I have a 'No ads, thanks' sign on my door at home." (R13)

"These interruptions on TV ... as a consumer, they irritate me." (R5)

"It would be great if there was one single place to go to, where there were no advertisements at all." (R15)

Advertising professionals are also consumers and audiences. Both the general commercial information overload and, in particular, advertising breaks in TV programmes seem to irritate advertising professionals as consumers. Nevertheless, all informants in this study put particular emphasis on the fact that their business – in their opinion – has an undeserved negative image in society. Though they admit that their business is much more exposed to public judgement and that the impact of black sheep of the family might be larger on the overall image of the profession, they underline that advertising just reflects general values in society. The frequent discussions about advertising and marketing ethics are seen as an expression of the publicity of their professions, as it is the frontline position of business towards all other stakeholders in society. Some of the informants also argue that public debates about advertising often overestimate the impact of commercial communication and underestimate the consumers' critical attitude towards advertising and their ability to reflect critically on it.

Advertising professionals' reflection on the current situation of the advertising market

When expressing personal critique of the overload of commercial communication, the informants not surprisingly emphasise that commercial communication strategies are used by non-commercial individuals and institutions. Several informants pointed out that even governmental institutions and non-governmental institutions use commercial and advertising techniques in order to sell products or messages:

"Any kind of public exposure is a kind of advertising, whether you are a new author, a rock group presenting a new CD, a theatre staging a new play. It could also be a TV station, even the media themselves." (R15)

"Greenpeace is actually a fantastic example. They are able to create a lot of "hidden advertisements" by being there, where they know TV cameras will be on set: chaining yourself to an oil-platform, being in the way of any type of transport. They even calculate this in relation to the legal rules, so the worst they can get is a fine for public distortion or for not regarding private property. They do this and hope to get attention and to attract new members to the organisation. So, in that sense, the effective NGOs are those able to create events attractive to the media, so they can get all the attention. You can see that, even Amnesty International is doing the same thing. You go public with a message, and you have a hidden agenda – and they do it to get more members to Amnesty International." (R12)

"In reality there is no difference, right. Because our political system is also based on that some politicians and spin doctors try to get us on their bandwagon. And these attempts are highly professional, and sometimes even more than that, aswell as more well-documented than even the most perfect PR people in private companies, who just sell products instead of political attitudes." (R2)

The informants of this study confirmed a growing use of sponsoring, PR and other strategies and formats for commercial messages, whereas conventional advertising formats stagnate and even decline. One respondent explains the reasons behind this development as follows:

"The reason for why the PR industry has had that much success is simply that they have been able to tell the story about damage control, or how you can get a story launched in the media. And there we have the journalists, who are somewhat behind because they are not used to people doing it in a systematic way. That's why we have experienced that the effect of traditional TV commercials has declined, whereas the effect of editorial coverage has increased. PR agencies have played on another ground than we have. A ground where almost everything is possible. While we had to play on a ground where you find a clear cost-benefit calculation on the media market that we had no influence on…And here we have the PR industry that actually uses some of the techniques when advertising had its tremendous growth during the 1970s and 1980s. They go out and prove with case stories that they have been able to do damage control, even though there are lots of examples where they haven't been able to do it. So, they have the good cases and argue: Look at this, you have spent 10 million on building your brand. But if you get just one negative PR story, you have lost your 10 million." (R1)

However, several informants also underline that the development in Denmark has not gone so far yet as in other countries, in particular the US. But – as some of them point out – especially among younger Danes there exists a different attitude towards commercial products and messages; an attitude that is supporting the trend towards the application of new advertising formats and contents:

"Well, the real problem is in fact that young people are very much interested in what companies produce and what the culture industry produces. When I was young, we all were opponents of business – though we were obsessed by pop groups and the like. But – and we have proved it in our campaigns directed towards youngsters – it's today that easy. They are already into it, before the game even starts. So, in a way they just HAVE to get it. That's the boring thing, if you look at it from a consumer perspective. This means, in particular the youngsters are so ready to perceive the ads produced by agencies. You can see this everywhere, you can see this in those reality-TV shows, everybody wants to be a pop-star, everybody wants to be an actor in Big Brother. Everybody wants to be famous, everybody is tuned to the media and educated in this sense."(R13)

Summing up, advertising professionals confirm the theoretical observations presented in the first part of this chapter about the blurring of boundaries between commercial and other social discourses and the drivers behind this blurring. They also confirm that advertising is a cultural expression of a more general socio-cultural trend, including consumers' expectations and ways to act and re-act in relation to commercial messages in a mediarised society. Finally, practitioners also confirm the stagnation and even decline of conventional advertising and the success of alternative methods in order to spread commercial promotion.

Advertising professionals' perspective on consumers and advertising effects

Though practitioners confirm the observation of changing attitudes towards advertising and commercial messages among – especially younger – consumers, they also underline that times are over when marketing promotion expected powerful effects from the mere, simple exposure of passive audiences to commercial messages. Instead, all informants in this study support an understanding of consumers as critical, self-reflective beings not very interested in or open-minded towards advertising:

> "People are not stupid. Don't underestimate them and their intelligence." (R20)

> "I do not share this distrust of consumers' total lack of mental capabilities." (R16)

> "If you look at the market today, most of the products have the same qualities. They are very much alike each other. So, what you sell in order to differentiate is branding and positioning. "(R15)

> "Direct sales is selling products. Everything else is about showing your position, your image…it's a matter of differentiation and lifestyle." (R12)

> "If you present something new – a new product or a new form of communication - the shock effect disappears in no time. I just don't believe that an advertising campaign is able to create a sales success for a new brand overnight." (R1)

Advertisers thus express a great deal of respect for consumers. The idea of just being able to trigger and to manipulate them appears to be totally absent. Also the idea of being able to change markets by just launching a promotion campaign appears to be absent. Informants confirm that expectations towards advertising should be measured in relation to the ability to hold market shares and to retain a position on a market compared to competing or substituting products instead of "conquering" new markets and consumers.

Advertising professionals' observation of and reflection on current trends in advertising

The vast majority of informants in this study support and participate in the application of new advertising channels, formats and contents. They deny that this development creates new ethical problems in general and they do expect a further growth based on these new subtle advertising channels, formats and contents. This seems in particular valid for PR, lobbying, sponsoring and product placement. Though some of the informants seem to be concerned about their own children's exposure to commercial messages, they generally do not oppose advertising in schools and other educational institutions. Here, they rely on the professional authority and knowledge of teachers, principals and boards ensuring the protection of children and youngsters. However, some practitioners also express professional and ethical reservations towards the increased use of some of the new subtle advertising formats, in particular towards the use of advertorials / infomercials, lobbying and masked spokespersons:

"I agree, I am really concerned about the blurring of boundaries between editorial articles and commercial messages." (R20)

"But company portraits in infomercials – I can simply not understand that this is legal." (R17)

"To be honest, I think the mixture of editorial content and commercial messages is a sad thing. And in one or other way I get irritated when I read my newspaper and read just beside the article something about the company XXX printed in exactly the same type…I feel a little bit cheated. I have the expectation that at least some kind of objectivity is the point of departure in journalism…"(R1)

"Lobbying is, I would like to say, I feel it's problematic. We are in the same situation: when I am reading an article that in fact is something else, if one can buy a researcher etc., then…" (R5)

However, there is a clear tendency that the informants put the blame for these kind of disliked formats for commercial communication on those individuals in the media, in research and in the entertainment business, who are cooperating with the companies applying these methods. In fact, some of the informants seem to think that for companies "anything goes", whereas there are stricter rules for journalists, teachers, researchers and celebrities, who are considered to be gatekeepers. However, all informants accept special rules with regard to advertising targeted at children.

Advertising professionals' future expectations and hot spots in advertising development

Due to the fact that even practitioners seem to be hesitant, reserved and even worried when reflecting about the ethical dimension of new subtle advertising formats and contents – at least some of the informants in regard to some of the developments in current advertising practice –, they express a quest for self-regulating codes of conduct reflecting the social responsibility of commercial communication. They all agree on that there is no need for legal regulation. Opposing further legal regulations, advertising professionals agree on and repeatedly mention several arguments, namely that:

1) Regulations should not delimit and hinder a legal and creative industry,
2) Increased regulation would just support those companies trying to attack these rules and finding new ways to bypass these regulations,

3) Ethical problems are not the regular practice in the business and ethical black sheep should not determine the practice for all other agencies,

4) Further regulations would be difficult to administrate and thus decrease the legal security of commercial communicators,

5) Existing regulation is sufficient and should instead of new regulation be more consistently applied,

6) National regulation would not change advertising practice as the internationalisation of business would just transfer the problem and, as a result, take the opportunity from Danish marketers to compete with non-Danish competitors,

7) Further regulation would not change advertising practice, but it would surely have an – even existential - impact on a number of other industries (e.g. different media, sports, arts and entertainment) by removing their economic foundation for production, and finally,

8) Alternative methods, such as codes of conduct, self-regulation and negotiation among stakeholders would be more well-equipped to guarantee that advertising would be in concordance with the ethical expectations of consumers and other stakeholders.

An informant mainly working in the PR industry argues in an ironical-realistic way:

"Well, I really think that further restrictions for advertising would be fine. Of course, I don't – but this would be good business for a company like ours – and bad for those specialised in advertising. The more prohibitions there are, the more work we will have to do. The more you cut off the core-advertising business, the more you support the development of new hybrids we are participating in to create. If you want to pour sauce into a pot to the top and you then pour the sauce into a smaller pot, what do you do with the rest of your sauce? It doesn't just disappear, does it? So, companies will no matter what always communicate their commercial messages – and then they just choose other channels and strategies. So, new restrictions would just encourage the development of new communication formats – it's just that easy." (R14)

When asked to point out hot spots and future developments in advertising, informants predict a further growth of new subtle advertising formats and contents, in particular closely connected with the digitalisation and convergence of media channels. Furthermore, the informants mention storytelling and reputation management based on the communication of values and symbols – thus confirming previous theoretical observations of current advertising trends – as hot spots for advertising business in the near future. Finally, informants also emphasise the integration of advertising in an integrated commercial communication strategy for companies (Integrated Marketing Communication) as one of the hot spots for future development:

> "The most obvious thing happening is the integration of different communication disciplines: advertising, PR, direct marketing, multimedia marketing etc. will be coded altogether in the same direction. So, the buzz is at the moment in all branches of communication branding, to create a brand out of a company. You shall brand your company, you shall brand your products – that's what branding is about and that's, on the bottom line, PR thinking. That's why we, like all others in the PR business, shake our heads, as we have advocated this for at least 15 years." (R15)

After having presented in this section the reflections of practitioners on the current and ongoing development of commercial communication in general and advertising in particular, the following section will discuss the theoretical, practical and ethical implications based on the shift from producer and sender-centred marketing to consumer-centred new subtle advertising formats, strategies and contents.

Discussion

The ongoing shift from sender-centred promotional seduction to consumer-centred new subtle advertising technologies reflecting the shift from Fordism to Post-Fordism and from industrial capitalism to late modernity has a number of implications for both advertising theory and practice and gives birth to new ethical debates about the role of advertising in society. These implications will be sketched out in the following and thus indicate a new agenda for advertising practice and research.

Implications for advertising theory

The first and most salient theoretical question raised by the development described above regards the very definition of what advertising is about. One of the most conventional and often quoted definitions of advertising stems from Kotler (2000:578, see also Lancaster & Massingham 2001:241): "Advertising is any paid form of nonpersonal presentation and promotion of ideas, goods or services by an identified sponsor." Other researchers withhold an even more traditional definition of advertising, in which the mass media are defined as the communication channel of advertising (e.g. Jobber, 2001:353; Pickton & Broderick, 2001:456). But as – due to media convergence and digitalisation – traditional distinctions between non-personal one-way mass media and personal interactive communication become obsolete, advertising cannot any longer be defined as being bound to the application of non-personal mass media in commercial communication. As Kotler's definition indicates, neither does it make very much sense to distinguish between sponsoring and advertising, as sponsoring is just a particular format of advertising. This becomes obvious when looking at the practices of non-spot advertising on TV, where the different forms of product placement in fact are often also labelled as program sponsoring. Even traditional boundaries towards PR techniques are not so clear any longer. Though agencies are still specialised in certain formats and strategies of commercial communication, PR agencies often apply strategies and formats from ad agencies and vice versa. Moreover, an up-to-date definition of advertising should reflect that advertising is not any longer just a practice of commercial companies, but also a common mode of expression for political parties, NGOs, public institutions, and so forth. Finally, the notion of an identified sponsor raises the question who is to decide whether the sponsor of a presentation and promotion of ideas, goods or services can be identified. Infomercials and advertorials, for example, often intend to blur the identity of the sponsor; nevertheless, they are rather well-established formats of marketing promotion, sometimes executed by ad agencies, sometimes by PR practitioners.

In sum, conventional – and too narrow – definitions of advertising do not work any longer, as they do not reflect the ongoing transition in advertising and other forms of marketing promotion. Clear-cut distinctions between advertising, PR, branding, reputation management, sponsoring etc. are difficult to make. Thus the concept of integrated marketing communications (Clow & Baack, 2001) appears to be helpful in the attempt to define current trends, as it summarises the various formats and strategies applied. However, much work still has to be done in order to integrate the different points of departure in theoretical attempts and concepts, as intimated by Stuart & Kerr (1999) in their question: "Marketing communication and corporate identity: are they really integrated?"

Holistic communication ideals and the focus and images as well as practitioners' expectations towards the effects of communication (positioning) do not just call for conceptual and terminological work. They also have consequences in regard to the expectations towards advertising effects. Conventional expectations towards strong advertising effects should be replaced by more moderate expectations. Even the often quoted bonmot, "We know that half of the advertising messages work, we just do not know which half of it", expresses a rather (too) optimistic position. Ehrenberg's weak theory of advertising (1974) might be a more realistic point of departure. According to this theory, advertising is able to increase knowledge among consumers and stimulate them to test products. But it is not able to change people's attitudes or to persuade or manipulate consumers, as consumers are usually not very interested in advertising. Instead of being escapist and non-reflexive, consumers are rather apathetic and intelligent. Due to selective perception, consumers choose messages that fit their already established attitudes and experiences. Thus, advertising cannot just change resistant opinions and attitudes; they are rather reactive, defensive and much better off when protecting existing market shares and brand positions. Davis (2000) launched a similar approach when discussing the potential effects of PR. Based on empirical studies on the development of PR in Great Britain in the past two decades, he argues that PR does not have considerable impact on broader public opinion. Instead, PR messages are mainly designed to prevent competitors from influencing the news agenda for business-related issues. Moreover, PR messages are mainly consumed by other business elites – not by consumers.

Implications for advertising practice

As stated above, the main problem for advertisers is to find answers to the questions: How to cut through the clutter of information overload and at the same time pretend that there is no mass production any longer. We are witnessing that advertisers apply new advertising formats, strategies and contents to do so. However, many advertising practitioners clearly stick to old-fashioned and outdated concepts and models predicting linear communication effects – partly because advertising and marketing theories have not yet succeeded in providing practitioners with new reflexive guidelines and often still work on refinements of conventional approaches (e.g. segmentation strategies). On the other hand, recent research on global tribes and cultural diversification might be useful when applied in market analysis. As a consequence, trend spotters with detailed inside knowledge about tribes and sub-cultures identifying and mapping values, psychographics, roles, communities and cultural fads might become more important than traditional desk analysis and surveying. However, also ad agencies need a more professional planning section that brings market knowledge into the agency.

Like advertising theorists, also advertising practitioners face a challenge in regard to the convergence and integration of the various forms of marketing communication. Except for very few large companies, the market of corporate and marketing communications is divided into various specialised agencies due to the conventional differentiation of the communication field into sub-disciplines and various formats. The challenge is here to preserve the specialised and professional in-depth knowledge about particular methods, channels, strategies and formats in marketing communication, while at the same time to create a ground for holistic thinking. This includes for advertising agencies an increased knowledge about organisational culture and communication, PR and the processes of strategic media planning and market knowledge. The latter goes as well for PR agencies, whereas CI agencies often could gain further knowledge about the implementation of concrete communication plans from advertising and PR practice.

It remains to be seen whether and how the concept of integrated marketing communication will be implemented in organisational terms. Several models are possible – starting from increased coordination and partnerships between different specialised agencies and reaching to IMC agencies offering a wide range or even the total spectrum of sub-disciplines, formats and channels. Also, it is possible that the responsibility for the integration task for marketing communication remains in the hands of the customers of specialised agencies.

Implications for advertising ethics

New subtle advertising strategies, formats and contents include attempts to hide the identity of a commercial sponsor/sender and/or the commercial purpose of a message communicated. Sometimes the format itself makes it more difficult for consumers to stick to learned avoidance reactions towards commercial advertising. Other times advertisers blur the identity and/or commercial character of a message on purpose in order to cut through the clutter. Clearly, such attempts to create "Trojan horses" give birth to ethical debates. Also the blurring of boundaries between commercial messages and journalism, education, public information, arts etc. are controversial and are often creating a quest for further legal restrictions against advertising in order to protect consumers and in order to keep professional standards and legitimacy in social discourses and practices that formerly have been regarded as purely non-commercial.

The following matrix on advertising ethics, adapted from Nebenzahl and Jaffe (1998), maps the field of new subtle advertising formats with regard to whether ads intend to blur the identity of a commercial sponsor/sender and/or the commercial purpose of a message communicated. Using Nebenzahl and Jaffe's terminology, ads blurring the identity of a commercial sponsor/sender of a message are characterised as highly disguised messages, and ads blurring the commercial purpose of a promotional message are characterised as highly obtrusive messages. Disguise is "the degree of source concealment, i.e. the extent to which the sponsor is identified and/or is able to cloud the fact that the message is a paid advertisement" (ibid.:809). Obtrusiveness is "the degree to which the message is secondary to more salient communication, such as sport contests or a scene in a movie" (ibid.).

Figure 14:2: Advertising Ethics Matrix

video news releases	"anonymous" press releases, informercials, rumours, viral campaigns based on word-of-mouth-expectations, advertorials, masked spokespersons, gifts, lobbying (behind closed doors), implicit product placements etc.
HIGH DISGUISE & LOW OBTRUSIVENESS	HIGH DISGUISE & HIGH OBTRUSIVENESS
traditional/conventional mass advertising formats, e.g. print ads, TV commercials, etc., direct mails, identified press releases, on-screen-logo etc.	Billboards in sport arenas, event sponsoring in art, sport, music, media alliances, product placement of a clearly identified sponsor, social marketing, cause-related marketing etc.
LOW DISGUISE & LOW OBTRUSIVENESS	LOW DISGUISE & HIGH OBTRUSIVENESS

When evaluating the ethics in advertising, of course ads characterised by low disguise and low obtrusiveness clearly are the most ethical, and ads showing a high disguise and high obtrusiveness are the least ethical. In between these two poles are ads blurring the commercial identity of the sender/sponsor or the commercial purpose of a message by claiming some sort of philanthropic interest.

The Advertising Ethics Matrix should, however, be used with caution when applied in ethical evaluations of particular campaigns or ads. As for many models and matrixes, the epistemological and ontological background or roots of the matrix have to be considered. In epistemological terms, the matrix only intends to provide an overview for understanding advertising ethics – nothing else. In other words, it is not designed in order to decide whether a certain advertising format and strategy is ethical or unethical in general. In ontological terms, it only offers a simplified view on advertising ethics, thus not being able to offer a fair basis for evaluation of particular ads and campaigns.

However, the matrix can still be and is used for evaluation purposes. If so, such evaluation reflects a normative and de-ontological point of departure of the evaluator, when evaluating advertising ethics. With such a point of departure, it is rather the concrete action than its results and consequences that are an object for evaluation. Referring back to the roots of the era of the Age of Enlightenment, for example Kant's categorical imperative and the idealist philosophy of Hegel, such an evaluation envisages normative ideals and values about communication (Kreikebaum, 1996:127). With such a point of departure, conflicts between moral and market communication are almost pre-formulated (e.g. Habermas, 1962). Not surprisingly, the normative perspective of this approach is often used by advertising critics demanding further legal restriction and regulation of advertising practice. However, with this point of departure it is decisive who is formulating the universal norms and rules that the particular actions are related to.

The opposing point of departure to the de-ontological approach is the utalitarian approach. This point of departure is more pragmatic, as it focuses on the results and consequences of actions – in this case, particular advertising campaigns and their specific formats, channels, media and contents. With this point of departure, it is more important to investigate whether a particular action is doing some harm to somebody. Thus, with this point of departure it is much more interesting to investigate the effects of and attitudes towards a particular advertising campaign and its underlying format, strategy and content. From such a point of departure, advertising theory and research about the potential or real effects of advertising as well as consumer attitudes towards advertising (formats, strategies, contents) as well as consumers' perceptions of particular advertisements and advertising campaigns are decisive when evaluating advertising ethics. Taking such a point of departure, ads blurring the commercial identity of the sender/sponsor or the commercial purpose of a message are NOT a priori unethical. Applied to the rise of new subtle advertising formats, strategies and contents, it is important to know that consumers' attitudes towards advertising are complex, multi-dimensional and ambiguous (O'Donohoe, 1995). Moreover, that many research studies confirm that consumers in general are active, reflexive and critical perceivers of advertisements (e.g. Calfee & Ringold, 1994; Obermiller & Spangenberg, 2000), and that many consumers rather prefer some of the new subtle advertising formats (e.g. sponsoring and product placement) than traditional and conventional mass advertisements (e.g. Parker 1991; Secunda & Nebenzahl, 1993; DeLorme & Reid, 1999; Jespersen & Møller Jensen, 1999; see also Neeiens & Smit in this volume). However, the number of studies on effects and of consumer perceptions of new subtle advertising formats, strategies and contents is still limited. Thus, further studies on these topics would be of great importance when arguing from a utilitarian perspective against further general legal regulation of advertising.

Despite the debate about advertising from a de-ontological and a utilitarian perspective respectively, there is sufficient evidence that both advertising practitioners, political decision-makers and professional organisations are aware of ethical problems related to the current development. This goes in particular for children's advertising, where the majority of research has offered sufficient evidence that children up to a certain age should not be exposed to ads', as they are not aware of the commercial purpose of ads. Moreover, the ongoing blurring of boundaries between advertising and journalism or advertising and public information (e.g. about politics or health affairs) puts professional ethics on the agenda for the involved agents. Journalists, scientists, teachers etc. will have to decide how far the incorporation of commercial factors into their own production could go without questioning their trustworthiness, authority and even social legitimacy in terms of professional independence. And commercial communicators, of course, will have to formulate their ethical position by expressing how far they are willing to go in order to sell their messages. In regard to legal regulation of advertising, however, decisions remain ultimately a political task.

15

Audience Reactions towards Non-Spot Advertising:

Influence of Viewer and Program Characteristics

PETER C. NEIJENS & EDITH G. SMIT

Summary

In this chapter, three questions are posed: (1) what is the extent and the character of non-spot advertising on Dutch television? (2) How does the audience react to non-spot advertising? (3) Which viewer and program characteristics play a role in these reactions? The research comprises a literature review, an analysis of the content of television programs and a survey among a random sample (n=1450) of the Dutch population.

The research shows that non-spot advertising frequently appears on Dutch (commercial) television and is evaluated positively by the public. The information and amusement qualities of the non-spot advertising are important for a positive evaluation. For viewers there should be something to be gained. Irritating elements such as overdone or implausible approaches are dangers to a positive evaluation. Women, young people and the lower educated watch more non-spot advertising programs than men, the elderly and those with a higher education. Non-spot advertising is appreciated the most in lifestyle programs; it is least popular in soaps and police series. These differences are due to differences in (perceived) informative, amusing and irritating elements in non-spot advertising in these programs.

Introduction

All over the world, new forms of commercial communication are being developed. One of the forms is non-spot advertising: sponsoring of television programs with the aim to make the message of the sponsor better known via the programs. Companies see this as a way to promote their brands. Governments use it to bring government policy to the attention of citizens. The mixture of editorial and commercial can also be found in other types of media, has many forms and will become more important.

Communication science research on non-spot advertising is rare. In the research that we have carried out, three questions were posed: (1) What is the extent and character of non-spot advertising? (2) How does the public react to non-spot advertising? (3) Which program and audience characteristics play a role in these reactions? The study comprises a literature review, a content analysis of television programs and a survey under a random sample (n=1450) of the Dutch population. The study aims to provide scientific insight into the attitude and behavior of media audiences and the factors that are involved therein. This insight is not only relevant in forming scientific theory, but also in practice, i.e. for media operators, program makers and advertisers.

Different forms of non-spot advertising

Sponsoring of television programs is not a new phenomenon. Shortly after the beginnings of commercial television in the United States – in the 1940's – the names of television programs were connected to sponsors, for example titles such as *Voice of Firestone* and *Texaco Hall of Fame*. There was a form of *product placement* even in those days: in the program *I love Lucy*, Lucille Ball smoked cigarettes made by Philip Morris. The same Lucille also appeared in a commercial for this brand (Sandler & Secunda 1993).

Sponsoring takes many forms, e.g.: title sponsoring; bill boarding ('This program is presented to you by ....'); item sponsoring, where the commercial message of the advertiser is handled as part of the editorial content of a program; in-script sponsoring, where the product of the advertiser is worked into the script; and product placement (or brand placement), where the product of the advertiser is brought into the picture during the program (Sijtsma 1996; Ruijgrok 2000).

Non-spot advertising can be described as 'the compensated inclusion of branded products or brand identifiers, through audio and/or visual means, with mass media programming' (Kahhr 1998, 33; Kahhr, Frith & Callison 2001). Attention to brands in programs does of course not always have to be commercially inspired. We only speak of non-spot advertising when it involves overt, commercial attention to brands in programs.

Non-spot advertising is also known under the name program sponsoring because attention to the message is obtained through sponsorship of the television program in question.

Background for the growth in non-spot advertising

The media supply has risen explosively in recent years. Presently, the media are *everywhere, always* and *abundantly* available (Van Cuilenburg, Neijens & Scholten, Eds. 1999). Because consumption has not grown at anywhere near the same rate as the growth in supply, it stands to reason that the number of viewers of a television program – the audience of the program – has decreased significantly. This means that the same production costs must be earned back from fewer viewers. The television stations are therefore forced to look for new sources of income. In this way, the decrease in the number of viewers has led to a growth in non-spot advertising.

The growth in the number of television programs also has consequences for the advertiser and spokesperson who want to reach the public. This has become more difficult. Advertisers and spokespeople are therefore looking for alternatives. Non-spot advertising is potentially a successful alternative, because the advertising is interwoven in an attractive context.

Public reactions to non-spot advertising: findings from the literature

Research on non-spot advertising is limited. Research into public reactions is dominant; primarily research into acceptance and appreciation of this new form of advertising and research into sponsor recognition, by means of 'aided or unaided same-day and day-after recall' (Karrh 1998, 36). Research into effects on attitudes and behavior with regard to the brand has hardly ever been carried out. We summarize the findings of the research below.

Attention, judgment and effects

The evaluation of non-spot advertising that emerges from different research projects is reasonably positive: the phenomenon is accepted and appreciated by many viewers. From the studies, it seems that non-spot advertising also contributes to sponsor recognition. Based on multi-year IPSOS-RSL research, wherein every week a panel of 400 adults is interviewed, Millman (2000), for example, argues that sponsoring has a positive effect on recognition of the sponsor.

In The Netherlands, IP has studied a large number of television programs. A database with 164 cases has been compiled to date (IP 2001). The most important effect measured is the recognition of the sponsor of the program. On average, 7% of the viewers can name the sponsor spontaneously and, in addition, 33% recognize the sponsor's name when this is presented to them ('aided recall'). IP also carries out (on a modest scale) research into recognition of the products and services that are shown in a program. The reported recognition percentages vary between 5 and 25%.

Research by The Media Partnership (TMP 1992) under a cross section of the population, who were shown a tape with sponsor fragments and television spots (forced exposure), measured the unaided (and aided) recollection of the sponsors of different types of non-spot advertising. These were (aided recollection between parentheses): 31% (54%) for bill boarding, 17% (45%) for in-script sponsoring, and 14% (51%) for product placement. In addition, there are large differences between the different cases. TMP concluded that the recollection of non-spot advertising is lower than the recollection of spots: 62% for in-script sponsoring, 45% for bill boarding and 33% for product placement. (These percentages are compared to those for the level of recollection of the spot.)

Only one study concluded that non-spot advertising had an effect on purchase intention, but the empirical basis for this finding is not very strong because of the laboratory setting with forced exposure and students as respondents. No effects on attitudes towards placed brands have been found. Karrh has summarized the results as follows: "Overall, then, empirical studies have found consistent, but mild effects on audience memory from brand placement. In addition, some studies report effects on purchase intention while none have found significant impact on audience attitudes toward placed brands or the programs themselves" (Karrh 1998, 42).

Research into the mixture of editorial and commercial content of magazines can teach us something about non-spot advertising. 'Advertorials' are a well-known mixture and can be described as "blocks of paid-for, commercial messages, featuring any object or objects (such as products, services, organizations, individuals, ideas, issues, etc.) that simulates the editorial content, and/or context in which it appears" (Ju-Pak, Kim & Cameron 1996). From research by Cameron, Ju-Pak & Kim (1996), it appears that approximately one third of the advertorials are not explicitly labeled as such and this is not in accordance with the guidelines of the ASME (American Society of Magazine Editors). In approximately two thirds of the studied cases, the font of the advertorial is practically the same as that used for the editorial text. Also, the label 'advertorial' is often small and/or only presented halfway through the advertorial. All these factors contribute to disguising the distinctions between advertorials and editorial content.

Experiments by Cameron & Curtin (1995) have shown that editorial messages are valued more highly and are remembered better than commercial messages. This finding is in contrast with the findings of TMP with respect to TV (see above). In addition, it seems that the label 'advertorial' is often not noticed and, if it is, it is often quickly forgotten, while people do remember the content of the advertorial. Forgetting who sent a message is in agreement with the so-called 'sleeper effect'. According to this theory, with the passage of time people forget episodic information (a title), but remember semantic information (the message) (Cameron & Curtin 1995). A possible sleeper effect is counteracted if information about the sender ('advertorial') is given at the beginning of the message. If the reader notices from the beginning that an item is an advertorial, it is consumed as such and remembered. The question is whether this process is also valid for non-spot programs.

Influence of broadcast(er) factors

A study by Brinkhoff, ter Woort, Sikkema, van de Leur & Rood (1996) of 500 respondents (a cross-section of the Dutch population) identified a number of factors that influence the evaluation of non-spot advertising. The first factor was the *nature of the medium*: 70% of the respondents believed that the nature of the medium determines whether non-spot advertising is acceptable: in objective programs, no non-spot advertising is accepted. The second factor was the *nature of the product*: the most acceptable is non-spot advertising for food (82% agreement) and government messages (49%). Less acceptable is non-spot advertising for medicines (42%), tobacco products (31%) and political parties (28%). The *nature of the placement* is also important: a too transparent, amateurish approach arouses irritation in the viewer, in the same way as *too much*. Finally, non-spot advertising should have something to offer the viewer; in other words it should be informative and/or amusing.

From research (an experiment with students) by Brennan, Dubas & Babin (1999), it seems that prominent product placements (ppl) in films generate more brand recognition than non-prominent ppl's. We talk about a prominent ppl when, for example, the product is consumed or named by one of the leading actors. Research by Weaver & Oliver (2000) with 83 US communication science students as subjects confirmed this finding for the Seinfeld series. In a study by Ruijgrok (2000), it appeared that the viewer pays more attention if a brand is clearly recognizable. A conspicuous placement on the other hand also led to more irritation. In the research of Weaver and Oliver, it was observed that the attitude towards the brand is positively influenced by prominent ppl's, but only by the viewers who judged the program positively.

From the overview by Karrh (1998), it appeared that 25% of the viewers remembered a non-spot brand if the brand was only a part of the setting of a scene. If an actor used the brand, the recall rose to 40-60%, and if the actor named the brand the recall was highest: 50-75%.

The length of the placement influences the recall of the brand name positively; though a placement of longer than 10 seconds has no extra effect (Brennan et al. 1999). The study by IP (1999) showed that with prolonged sponsoring (5–8 years), recognition of the sponsors is high

(85%) and stable. The recognition of sponsors who sponsor for shorter periods (2–5 years) is lower (about 40%), but growing.

The effects of non-spot advertising differ per form. IP (2001) concluded that bill boarding has a strong effect on brand recognition. In-script sponsoring also had, in addition to an effect on brand recognition, effects on knowledge about products.

Influence of audience factors

On the basis of the studies of IP (2001), we can conclude that the youth, those interested in the program and viewers who regularly see installments, are more positive towards non-spot advertising. They also have a better idea of who the program sponsors are and have more knowledge of the sponsored message, and are possibly also more influenced by the advertising in the program.

Psychological processes in non-spot advertising

Why does non-spot advertising influence recognition and possibly also the appreciation of brands? What underlying psychological processes play a role? We must make a distinction here between 'attention' and 'elaboration'. With regard to attention: the exposure to brand information by non-spot advertising is more or less guaranteed because viewers do not have (simple) possibilities to switch to another channel as with blocks of advertisements. In addition, theories and research into the influence of context on the attention for advertising indicate that the involvement that a context (program, magazine) elicits can be carried over to the advertising blocks (Moorman, Neijens & Smit 2002) and thus possibly also to the advertising in the program itself.

With regards to the elaboration of non-spot advertising, we can assume that due to the lack of a sender who undoubtedly wishes to influence the viewer, the message is received less critically. In other words, it can be assumed that the viewer thinks of fewer counter arguments with non-spot advertising. In addition, for a theory about the elaboration of non-spot advertising, we can call upon social learning theory (Bandura 1977) that posits: 'most of what individuals learn comes through either conscious imitation of or unconscious identification with social role models'. On the basis of brand use by a television personality, "viewers can validate their interpretations of the character, their purchasing behavior, and their own identity" (DeLorme, Reid & Zimmer 1994: 14). Finally, theories and research into the influence of context on the elaboration of advertising indicate that the positive feelings that a context (program, magazine) elicits can be carried over to the advertising blocks (Moorman, Neijens & Smit 2001) and thus possibly also to the advertising in the program itself.

Research design

Research into the extent of non-spot advertising: content analysis

A content analysis was carried out in order to gain more insight into the extent of non-spot advertising on Dutch television. Because the legal requirements for the commercial and public stations are different, examples from both were included in our study. We chose RTL 4 and Netherlands 2. All programs that were broadcast in week 42 of 2000 (the week of Monday 16 October through Sunday 22 October), were coded on the appearance of non-spot advertising. The coding was restricted to Dutch programs that were broadcast between 8.00 and 24.00 hours. The observational unit is the trajectory: the unbroken period of time in which a sponsored element was shown. The form of sponsoring (title sponsoring, item sponsoring, etc.), the brand and product, the time it began and the time it ended was coded for each trajectory. The characteristics of the television program (genre, etc.) were also coded.

Audience research

Three types of reactions to non-spot advertising were investigated: attention, 'beliefs' and appreciation. We decided to do a survey using a structured questionnaire. Six programs were included in the study: a soap Goede Tijden, Slechte Tijden (GTST), a police series (Baantjer), a magazine (Koffietijd!), two life-style programs (Eigen Huis & Tuin and TV Woonmagazine) and a cooking program (Koken met Sterren). The respondents were asked to evaluate the non-spot advertising in each of the different programs. Next to these evaluations, questions were posed with respect to non-spot advertising in general.

The different concepts were measured by propositions which respondents were asked to comment on using a 5-point scale (completely disagree ... completely agree). 'Attention' was measured by means of the proposition: I notice the products in [name of program]. Opinions about non-spot advertising in the programs (informative, amusing and irritating) were taken from Smit (1999) (see Table 15:3). The overall evaluation is measured by means of the proposition: In general, are you in favor of or against the naming or showing of products in [name of program]. The viewers were also asked: Do you think that you are influenced? Do you find non-spot advertising plausible?

The following personal characteristics were included in the study: gender, age, education and viewing behavior.

The questionnaire was filled in by 1450 respondents from the Centerdata panel of the University of Brabant. The members of the panel form a representative sample of the Dutch population and were given a home computer to answer questions on a weekly basis.

The nature and extent of non-spot advertising

Non-spot advertising is widespread on Dutch television. In total, 385 trajectories (program components) with non-spot advertising were found. These trajectories cover more than 5 hours of television. That means that in one week more than 5 hours of sponsored program components (non-spot advertising) were broadcast. The most was on RTL 4: 4.75 hours; on Netherlands 2, it was much less: a little more than 20 minutes.

In order to put these figures into perspective, it is useful to make a comparison with the time given to advertisements in regular advertising spots. In the week in question, 14 hours of advertising blocks were broadcast on RTL 4. This means that non-spot advertising on RTL 4 takes up over 25% of all advertising minutes. On Netherlands 2, the share of the advertising time for non-spot advertising was 5%.

The non-spot trajectories are spread across the days of the week fairly evenly, with the exception of Sunday (with a share of 4%). Two types of non-spot advertising are dominant: product placement (57% share in the non-spot broadcast time) and item sponsoring (33%). The share of each of the other types, such as bill boarding, in-script and prize sponsoring, amounts to about 2%. Almost all non-spot advertising occurs in two genres: lifestyle programs (65%) and soaps (22%).

Audience reactions

Recognition

Almost all Dutch people say that they are familiar with one or another form of non-spot advertising: 94% are aware of bill boarding or title sponsoring ('this program is brought to you by...') and 73% said they are familiar with product (brand) placement (see Table 15:1). In this study, we asked to what extent the viewers noticed the special attention to brands and products in six non-spot programs. On average, 55% of the viewers answered affirmatively. This percentage is somewhat disappointing, especially as the confidence in the ability to notice non-spot advertising is large: more than three quarters of the Dutch claim to know when there is advertising for products in a program. The bad performance of the viewers can perhaps be attributed to the fact that only 23% say they pay attention to the program credits (where the sponsoring must be mentioned).

Evaluations

Only 16% of the viewers had a negative evaluation of non-spot advertising in the programs mentioned (see Table 15:2). Most of the viewers (54%) were neutral and 31% were positive. The evaluation of non-spot advertising is more positive than the evaluation of ordinary advertising. In this study, 42% of the viewers evaluated advertising negatively and only 18% evaluated it positively (41% were neutral). When they were asked to choose between conventional advertising and non-spot advertising in the non-spot programs that were included in the study, most of the subjects chose the alternative form of advertising. This does not mean that most viewers will always have a preference for non-spot advertising. When asked to choose between ordinary advertising and non-spot advertising in general (thus also in news programs, etc.), most people chose conventional advertising.

Peter C. Neijens • Edith G. Smit

Table 15:1 Familiarity with non-spot advertising

	% Viewers
Familiar with title sponsoring	94%
Familiar with product placement	73%
Notices non-spot advertising in the mentioned n.s.- programs (average)	55%
Claims to know when advertising is present	76%
Pays attention to program credits to identify the sponsors if s/he does not yet know	23%

N= 1450 respondents; *N= 1170 evaluations[1].

An important question for the media operators is whether non-spot advertising impacts the credibility of programs negatively. According to this study, only 17% of the Dutch hold this opinion. It also appears that 91% of the Dutch consider non-spot advertising acceptable. The Dutch apparently consider that they have enough media sophistication to deal with non-spot advertising.

Specific opinions on non-spot advertising: beliefs

Research by Smit (1999) into attitude and behavior with regard to advertising shows that three 'beliefs' are very important for the total evaluation of advertising, namely the evaluation of the amount of information, amusement and irritation in the advertising. Her measurement instrument for these three beliefs includes seven propositions. In this research, these seven propositions were adapted and used to measure the beliefs about non-spot advertising in the different programs.

---

1. The 1450 respondents in our research were asked, for each non-spot program, how many installments they had seen. For each respondent, two programs (if possible) were chosen randomly from the group of programs of which the respondent saw three or more installments. Specific questions about non-spot advertising were related to these two programs. In this way, we obtained 1170 non-spot evaluations (respondents * programs).

Table 15:2 A comparison between evaluations and preferences with respect to conventional advertising and non-spot advertising

	% viewers with this opinion
Total evaluation non-spot advertising *	
Positive	31%
Neutral	54%
Negative	16%
Total evaluation conventional advertising	
Positive	18%
Neutral	41%
Negative	42%
Preference (in the programs included in the study) *	
Conventional advertising	28%
None	27%
Non-spot advertising	45%
Preference (in general)	
Conventional advertising	49%
None	28%
Non-spot advertising	23%

N= 1450 respondents; *N= 1170 evaluations.

Table 15:3 shows the (average) beliefs with respect to non-spot advertising in the programs included in the study. Non-spot advertising was considered informative by approximately one third of the viewers. These viewers said that non-spot advertising gave them new ideas and useful information. Approximately one quarter of the viewers consider programs with non-spot advertising fun to watch. An equally large group considers non-spot advertising to be implausible and experiences too much of it.

Table 15:3 Opinions (beliefs) about non-spot advertising

	% viewers with this opinion
Informative	
Gives useful information about special offers	28
Gives new ideas about products	39
Gives useful information about specific products	33
Amusing	
Is amusing	22
Is funny	24
Irritating	
Too many products are shown	21
Implausible	18

N= 1170 evaluations.

Factor analysis shows that the seven propositions can be summarized in three factors in the manner assumed (see Table 15:4). The factor structure corresponds with that of Smit (1999). The scalability of the factors is satisfactory: all Cronbach's alphas are larger than 0.65.

On the basis of these analyses, it was decided to calculate scores for the three belief dimensions that were distinguished (the average of the scores for the items). As with non-spot advertising, these beliefs appear to be important for the total evaluation of non-spot advertising (see Table 15:5). In other words, those viewers who consider non-spot advertising to be more amusing and informative and less irritating value it more highly.

In order to put the evaluations of non-spot advertising into perspective, we compared them with evaluations of advertising in other types of media. These results are taken from Smit (1999). Her research showed that the evaluation of advertising in print media (newspapers and magazines) was much more positive than the evaluation of advertising on radio and television. In Table 15:6, it can be seen that non-spot advertising, in comparison with television advertising, is considered to be far less irritating, somewhat more informative and more amusing.

Table 15:4 Results for the factor analysis of belief items

	F1	F2	F3
Belief: Amusing			
- Amusing	.93		
- Fun	.63		
Belief: Informative			
- Useful information about special offers		.85	
- New ideas about products		.87	
- Useful information about specific products		.88	
Belief: Irritating			
- Too many products shown			.83
- Implausible			.83
Explained variance	20%	37%	22%
Cronbach's alpha	.68	.88	.67

Only factor weightings larger than or equal to 0.40 are included in the table. N=1170 evaluations.

The irritation caused by non-spot advertising is, together with the advertising in newspapers, the lowest of the media types. The amusement quality of non-spot advertising was evaluated the highest. With respect to information quality and the overall evaluation, non-spot advertising scored in between print media and broadcasting media.

Attention and influence

This research into non-spot advertising was not designed to study its effect. However, the viewers of the non-spot programs were asked if they paid attention to the products and brands and whether they (thought that they) were influenced.

Table 15:5 Correlation between beliefs and total evaluation of non-spot advertising

	Correlation coefficient	Path coefficient (Beta)
Irritating	-.59	-.36
Informative	.55	.27
Amusing	.56	26

Explained variance: 51%. N=1170 evaluations.

Table 15:6 Comparison of beliefs about different types of advertising

	Newspaper	Magazine	Radio	Television	NSA
Irritating	2.7	2.9	3.2	3.7	2.7
Informative	3.1	3.0	2.4	2.4	2.7
Amusing	2.6	2.6	2.4	2.5	2.8
Overall evaluation	3.6	3.4	2.8	2.4	3.1

Source (non NSA-data): Smit (1999). Scale (1) very negative ….. (5) very positive

Only 21% of the viewers said that they paid attention to the products in the programs. However, 62% thought they were influenced. A higher percentage (69%) thought it possible that they were unconsciously influenced. In agreement with the 'third person effect', most people thought that the effect on others was even higher: 96% of the Dutch think that others are influenced by non-spot advertising.

Effects of program characteristics

To what extent does the genre wherein non-spot advertising is included influence the evaluation? The beliefs regarding advertising in different types of programs are summarized in Table 15:8 together with the overall evaluation (average scores on a 5-point scale).

Non-spot advertising in the two lifestyle programs ('TV Woonmagazine' and 'Eigen Huis & Tuin') was appreciated the most. Least popular was non-spot advertising in the soap and police series. The magazine 'Koffietijd!' and the cooking program 'Koken met Sterren' scored in-between.

Table 15 7 Attention and influence

	% viewers
Attention to products (*)	21%
Think that they are influenced	62%
Think that they are unconsciously influenced	69%
Think that others are influenced	96%

N= 1450 respondents; *N= 1170 evaluations.

The differences between the programs can be explained by the various forms of non-spot advertising. The viewers considered non-spot advertising in, for example, the lifestyle programs to be much more informative and amusing than the non-spot advertising in GTST and Baantjer. In the table, we see that programs with informative, amusing and non-irritating (plausible) non-spot advertising are valued more positively.

Table 15:8 Evaluation of non-spot advertising in the various programs

	GTST	EH&T	Koffietijd!	TV Woon	Koken*	Baantjer
Irritating (1-5)*	2.7 a	2.9 b	2.8 ab	3.1 bc	3.1 bd	2.2 e
Informative (1-5)*	2.5 a	2.8 b	2.8 c	2.9 bcd	2.7 ce	2.7 a
Amusing (1-5)*	1.9 a	3.2 b	2.8 ab	3.1 bc	2.9 ab	2.1 ab
Overall evaluation (1-5)*	1.9 a	2.3 b	2.1 ab	2.4 bc	2.0 a	1.9 a

*Significant differences (Anova, row wise): *irritating*: $F(5,976)=25.8$, $p< .01$; *informative*: $F(5,976)=93.6$, $p< .01$; *amusing*: $F(5,847)=3.9$, $p< .01$; *overall*: $F(5,976)=14.9$, $p< .01$; a-e: average scores with different letters differ significantly (Post-hoc tests, Tukey).

Audience characteristics

In Table 15:9, the relationship is shown between the audience characteristics and the evaluation of non-spot advertising. It appears that women, the youth and those with a lower education see more non-spot advertising programs than men, the elderly and those with a higher education.

It also appears that those who have a higher education are more irritated by non-spot advertising and find it less amusing and less informative. Their overall evaluation is thus also more negative than that of those with lower education. Gender and age have no relation to the evaluation of non-spot advertising.

People who see more non-spot programs consider non-spot advertising to be less irritating, more amusing and more informative and have a more positive overall evaluation. They also said that they paid more attention to the products shown.

Table 15:9 The relationship between audience characteristics, exposure to and the evaluation of non-spot advertising

	Exposure	Irritation	Amusing	Informative	Overall evaluation	Attention
Gender	.19	ns	ns	ns	ns	ns
Age	-.28	ns	ns	.06	ns	ns
Education	-.09	.10	-.11	-.07	-.12	ns
Exposure	n/a	-.11	.09	.11	.09	.09

N=1170 evaluations; ns=not significant (p>.05).

Conclusions

Non-spot advertising is now a regular feature of Dutch (commercial) television and is evaluated reasonably positively by the public. The information and amusement value of what is offered is important for a positive evaluation. There should be some definite advantage for viewers. Irritating elements such as overdone or implausible approaches are danger to a positive evaluation. Women, the youth and less educated people see more non-spot advertising programs than men, the elderly and the more educated. Non-spot advertising in lifestyle programs is appreciated the most; non-spot advertising in soaps and police series is the least popular. These differences are due to differences in (perceived) informative, amusing and irritating elements in non-spot advertising in these programs.

Advertisers and others who wish to influence an audience will gather from this research that there is an attractive extra possibility of influencing the public because the new forms of advertising are accepted by it. Media operators can conclude that as the boundaries become blurred an extra source of income is available. There are, however, dangers. Media operators and advertisers must beware of excessive use of non-spot advertising as this can quickly lead to irritation. The fact that non-spot advertising is considered to lower the credibility of programs is a dilemma for media operators. This opinion is presently held by a limited number of viewers. In order to guarantee the credibility of non-spot programs and audience belief in the editorial integrity, media operators should (continue to) approach the form and type of non-spot advertising with reserve and caution, and the choice of the programs in which it appears.

A large number of questions with regard to non-spot advertising have not yet been answered. As we can see from the literature survey, so far there has been little research directed at the effects of non-spot advertising on knowledge, attitude and behavior with respect to the placed brands. Also, the effects of the different forms of non-spot advertising have hardly been characterized. The mixture of advertising and editorial content in other medium types (magazines, free local newspapers, radio, www) has seldom been investigated. These gaps present an interesting agenda for communication science research.

16

Conceptualising Television Advertising:

From 'content' to genre, from USP to ISP

LARS PYNT ANDERSEN

Television and cinema commercials are the great beasts of the marketing epiphany. Expensive, prestigious and fascinating in their very complexity, they are very difficult to grasp or compare. But how do they compare? What kind of experience do they offer?

The most reasonable answer is probably that certain knowledge about the *general* effects of *specific* parameters in these complex communications is unlikely. Nonetheless, many attempts have been made at comparing a volume of TV ads across a selection of form and content dimensions with some kind of effect measurement, thus trying to come up with the 'golden rules of advertising' or maybe just a few rules of thumb. The general trend in the attempts within marketing science has often been to adopt a perspective which one might label 'atomistic': The researcher isolates advertising form and content into tiny 'fragments' or 'slices', sometimes ignoring even the internal structure of the ads.

One of the most well-known and impressive attempts in this exercise is the work of (Steward and Furse, 1986), who analysed no less than 1,059 commercials with a range of 90 (initially 293) variables and compared them with a range of effect measurements. Their primary finding was an empirical foundation for Rosser Reeves' (and others') strong advocacy for a brand-differentiating message, thus justifying *Unique Selling Propositions.*

Another study is (Timmermann's, 1993) research on 213 cinema commercials. The variables in this study ranged from the level of spot (single/split/campaign) to 'close-ups', 'day of showing' and even 'protagonists kissing'. A total of 173 executional and environmental variables were used. One of Timmermann's most significant findings was that the use of split spots positively correlated with higher recall (aided and unaided).

The research mentioned above is somewhat 'omnivorous', in that it tries to take an impressive range of executional and other factors into account in a quantitative quest for the significant 'atoms' of advertising. Research projects that single out a few factors are much more common and often experimental in their design. However, the problem of largely ignoring the internal and external contexts remains.

From an intuitive as well as interpretive perspective, it is very unlikely that simple, isolated elements of content or form should make a significant and general contribution to the communicational effects of an ad. Although one might expect basic arousal from 'beach babes in bikinis', what the consumer actually does with this is very uncertain (Mick and Buhl, 1992). Studies within these behaviouristic frameworks seem only to have established that very little can be learned from this approach. This does not mean that conditional effects do not happen or that simple neurological processes may not be important, but rather that human experiences are much more complicated than the accompanying simplistic frameworks seem to allow.

Genre

The concept of 'genre' is one way of trying not to 'atomise' the stimulus, and it probably comes closer to the way human cognition deals with experiences of ads, movies and maybe even the world. Everything is experienced in extremely complicated contexts-in-contexts that make up a set of expectations as to 'what appears on television in programme breaks' and 'this is the exact moment the pack-shot is to be flashed before our eyes'. The complex set of expectations involved in consumption of cultural products is very often conceptualised as 'genre' in the humanistic sciences.[1] Admittedly, this is a concept that carries many definitions, that bears witness to a long history and widespread use (Berge and Ledin, 2001).

What is 'genre' then? It could be defined as: a shared expectation of a set of elements of form and content - which may be more or less explicitly agreed upon as 'defining features'.

Thus, most modern-day humans quickly identify movies depicting vengeful men wearing silly hats in dusty environments as *a western*. Genres work intuitively, as consumers of media products try to group or describe experiences. They do not, of course, use the word 'genre' or try to look things up in a book of genre theory. When a group of friends debate whether to go and see 'an action movie' and someone says "oh no, not a science fiction one!", everybody knows with reasonable precision what kind of experiences and texts s/he is referring to. Intuitively, it is known that the genres 'action movies' and 'science fiction' overlap, although not all action movies are science fiction, or vice versa. But television advertising is not a cultural artefact about which a discourse of choice or elaborate criticism is a practice (such as amateur art criticism). There are probably many reasons as to why this is so: at present television advertising is not interactive[2] and, historically, advertising is associated with low culture. In a not too distant future, however, TV spots may become more interactive, and if one subscribes to the views of post-modernity, there is no low/high culture anymore.

In Denmark, in recent years, it seems that a few television campaigns have managed to become a common conversational topic (e.g spots with 'Polle', a fictional character in advertising for Sonofon, a Danish telecom company). A common popular discourse on ads is still not as qualified or structured as discourse on movies or popular

---

1. 'Genre' is also a generally used term. A search on 'genre' in google.com gives you 6,150,000 hits.
2. An important feature of television advertising is the impossibility of positive choice; one cannot 'look up', switch on and watch a specific ad, or, unlike print, billboards and posters, stop or go back to experience it (for a period of time). Some television ads are available on the Internet, where some advertisers offer low-resolution playback of their own TV ads on their Internet sites. The site of AdCritic.com was formerly a site open to all consumers for rating and discussing TV ads (music in ads, etc.). Following dot-com-implosion, this has now changed into a professional and commercial members-only site.

music, as tacit knowledge on advertising probably takes time to develop into a common language of informal discourse, facilitated by genre concepts.[3] Such concepts could be 'borrowed' from other fields, such as feature movies, or developed from tentative genre concepts, or what could be called *ad hoc genre concepts*.

Ad hoc genre concepts

In a pilot study, focus groups with advertising professionals show that the discourse on television advertising relied heavily on *ad hoc* genre concepts as means of quickly communicating and classifying the complex experience of the television ads presented to them (Andersen, 2001). See Table 16:1 for examples from these sessions.

Table 16:1

Concepts used to describe TV spots	
*Lifestyle	*Testimonial
*Demonstration	Product spot
Gimmick spot	'Spell-it-out' spot
Image spot	"Winter landscape"
Animated storyboard	Concept spot
Tactical spot	Disney
Simple signs spot	Mini-musical
Pity spot (Pity appeal)	*Spokesperson
Expert spot	Propaganda spot
Jingle spot	Intro-spot (as to the Olympic Games)
Music video	Sponsor ID
*Slice-of-life	1980's retro spot
Engineer spot	Symbolic spot
'Squash' spot	Humour
*Conventional genre-related concepts	
Note: Translation of the above by the author of this chapter. Some of the ingenuity and descriptiveness has been lost in this translation.	

---

3. Structured scientific discourse on advertising also takes a great deal of time to establish, irrelevant of any one attempt to stipulate a framework for the discourse (such as the feeble attempt before the eyes of the reader).

Lars Pynt Andersen

In Table 16:1, some conventional genre concepts, such as 'music video', 'testimonial' and 'lifestyle', appear, though most are ad hoc expressions produced in the context of the group session. Often, a descriptive label is turned into an ad hoc genre by adding 'spot' to it; 'engineer spot', for example. In the example of 'Squash spot', the long-running campaign for an orange soda (Squash) is used as a prototypical example and turned into a genre concept. Most of these ad hoc genre concepts are probably not going to survive outside the particular group session, as this type of discourse is unsystematic. However, it does show how discourse on TV spots works in a pragmatic context.

The marketing literature on genre elements (thematic or executional elements) and ad genres only contains a few genres that are commonly accepted ('testimonial' is one example). The term 'genre' is not always used, but is often comparable with terms such as 'executional style' (Laskey et al., 1995) 'main message strategy' (Laskey et al., 1989) or 'scripts' (Rossiter and Percy, 1996). No system of relating the genres has been agreed upon, though the simple distinction between 'informational' and 'transformational' strategies is often used.

When making a systematic genre description, a set of genre dimensions is a way of systematically comparing genres. These 'dimensions' should, of course, be significant in order to be able to discriminate the sample, and in the present case it is theory driven (rather than an empirically 'grounded' approach).

The five dimensions, shown in Table 16:2, were chosen.

Meta-genres

The meta-genre is the uppermost domain that the genre belongs to. There are three meta-genres: Didactic/Narrative/Lyric. This division into three major genres can be found in literature on media and marketing (Liisberg, 2001) and can also be traced back to antiquity, although with some differences (the concepts of lyric/ballad/epic (Stern and Gallagher, 1991)).

Table 16:2

Dimension	Short description
Meta-genre	'Top layer' of genres, a group of genres that is in itself a sort of broad genre.
Sender construct (mode of address)	Category of persona or implied author. At an abstract level similar to the 'tone of voice' or 'the way spoken to'.
Communication objectives	Typical objectives that function well within this genre.
Expressions	Typical expressions of form, content or theme.
Sub-genres	A sub-class of a genre within a genre.

Sender construct (mode of address)

The meta-genre connects to a typical implicit sender construct that could also be viewed as a 'mode of address', depending on the perspective used (sender/receiver). This is a very important aspect of the type of experience the genre may be to a consumer.

Communication objectives

This is not the actual communication objectives of any single spot (as any advertiser could theoretically claim any objective – no matter how preposterous or unrealistic), but typical objectives that function well within the genre.

Expressions

Could be anything from 'jump-cut editing' to 'price' or a theme or situation. A genre is rarely recognised or identified by one element, but through co-occurrence of several elements. It is very rare to find one expression that is confined to one genre exclusively, but all genres have typical expressions (otherwise they could not establish a genre identity).

Sub-genres

Often, a successful idea spawns a series of similar attempts. Large well-established genres tend to 'sprout' new sub-genres within the 'old' format, but still within a sub-category of similar expressions. A classic example is the celebrity testimonial.

Pro's and con's of genre as concept

What should we do with the idea of genre? For a traditional quantitative hardliner, it may sound too 'soft' for any scientific use. In the arts and humanities, the idea of *genre* is quite well known and used, although in many different ways (as with any popular concept) (Berge and Ledin, 2001). If put in simplistic terms, one might list the advantages with the disadvantages:

Pro's	Con's:
•Flexible	•Loosely defined
•Does not dichotomise form/content	•Difficult to quantify
•Includes 'intuitive' thinking	

The genre matrix

When using the above dimensions in a matrix, it is possible to relate some of the better-known genres in a matrix (see Fig. 16:1). The version presented is simplified and contains the most well-established, but does not claim to contain all contemporary genres (as the chosen level of detail is for the purpose of an overview). For example, in the meta-genre of 'Narrative', 'comedy' could be listed beside 'drama' or as a sub-genre of drama (Stern, 1996) (possible sub-genres are not listed in this matrix).

Figure 16:1

Traditional Genre Matrix
(Simplified)

Meta-genre	Didactic				Narra-tive	Lyric
Sender construct (role)	Authority				Enter-tainer	Seducer
Genre	Testimonial	Expert	Demon-stration	Promo-tions	Drama	Lifestyle montage
Communication obj.	Attributes	Attri-butes	Attributes (usp)	Sale/Trial	Sympathy branding	Symbolic branding
Expressions	Recommendations Eye contact Voice-over	Expert Eye contact Voice-over	Product in use Voice-over	Price Voice-over	Plot Fictional realism	Montage Time manip. Music

What kind of validity can be claimed for this matrix? It is a conceptual model that is constructed on the basis of literature, a sample of Danish TV ads and two expert focus groups.[4] The genres seen in this matrix should be observable in most samples of TV advertising (see (Andersen, 2001) for a more detailed description of the genres).

The matrix should not be seen as any sort of fixed system to be validated. The idea is first and foremost to suggest that genres should be presented as matrixes with relations to meta-genres, other genres and typical expressions (of which Fig. 16:1 is just one simplified example).

The matrix does not say anything about the quantities of ads in the different genres. However, it seems to be the case that there are more didactic genres. One explanation could be that there are more ads in this segment and according to (Liisberg, 2001), didactic ads made up about 50% of all ads shown on Danish television in 2000. (Stigel,

---

4. The groups included both creative managers and a marketing manager.

2001) actually found more than 50% of the Danish ads to be 'factual'[5] in 1989, but within his classification system the share diminishes through the 1990's to 38% in 1997.

Another explanation could be that these genres are simply more successfully conceptualised by the marketing professionals (because they fit the predominantly rationalistic 'persuasion paradigm' of marketing?[6]), and therefore they are more easily recognised and discriminated as separate genres.

Experiences of genres

The meta-genres can be understood as focusing on one predominant mode of appeal. In rhetorical concepts: logos/docere, ethos/delectare or pathos/movere[7] (see Fig. 16:2), the mode of appeal connects to sender ('mode of address') as if it were two sides of a coin.

Figure 16:2

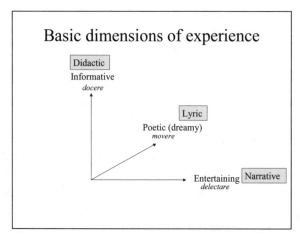

One of the big questions is how consumers experience the genres. It is hypothesized that the genres, at least to some degree, are connected to

---

5. 'Factual formats' is quite comparable to, though not exactly the same as, 'didactic genres'.
6. Not only post-modernists now feel the need to criticise this 'rational persuasion paradigm', see also the work of Robert Heath (Heath, 2001).
7. This is all very basic rhetorical theory, as found from Aristotle to Cicero.

the experienced, in the sense that genres are descriptive of the consumer experiences.

A very limited pilot study of this possible link was carried out using a convenience sample of 30 university students (not in marketing or advertising). Eight Danish television ads were chosen as examples belonging to the three meta-genres (see appendix A for the featured advertisers and products). Some were reasonably clear-cut, and some contained elements of different genres. The respondents were asked to describe the ads along five dimensions, of which three were simply the basic dimensions from rhetorical theory as shown in Fig.3. The last two were liking (good-bad) and fascinating (a measure also of 'newness', 'freshness').

In Fig. 16:3, the dimensions of the experience of six ads are summarised (two ads for every meta-genre).

Figure 16:3

Experience of ad

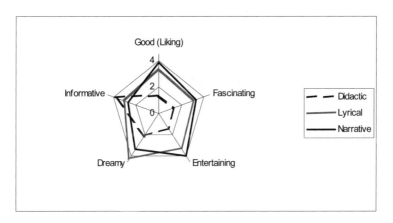

It seems that in this simple experiment, there are significant differences between the experience of didactic ads and narrative/lyrical ads.

One interesting signal in the data is the 'narrow' experience of the didactic ads. An informative experience is not negative as such, but the very low liking could be connected with a lacking sense of relevance of the information offered in the spots for body shampoo (Lab. Garnier) and a roller brush (Kärcher).

In this case, it seems to be hard to differentiate between the experience of lyrical and narrative ads, though the lyrical are experienced as slightly more 'dreamy' and the narrative as slightly more 'entertaining' (as theory predicts). This could be explained by the fact that in the ad sample, the lyrical ads were not completely without a narrative element, nor were the narrative ads without a lyrical element. As explained earlier, genres are seldom 'pure' or clear-cut, but it would be possible to find recent ads that are more clear-cut than the ones used here. Also, the questions used could be better validated through a qualitative method to ensure that they actually describe the experience dimensions of the ads as desired.

One might join (Percy & Rossiter, 1996) in asking why it should matter that the experiences of didactic *ads* are 'narrow' or not liked. But does it matter whether the experience of the *sender* is negative? In the simple experiment, the respondents were also asked to evaluate the sender along five dimensions: one general, 'sympathetic', as well as four that were more specific (see Fig. 16:4).

Figure 16:4

Experience of sender

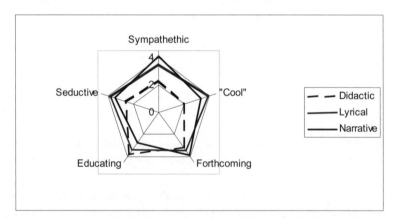

As can be seen in Fig. 16:4, there is a clear connection between a relatively more negative experience of the sender in didactic ads and the narrative scoring highest on the general dimension of 'sympathetic'; just as anticipated lyric scores highest on seductive and cool, and narrative dominates forthcoming and sympathetic.

If we compare experience of ad with experience of sender, it seems that the experience of sender is *less* differentiated (lyric/narrative vs. didactic) than the experience of the ad. This is probably due to some inertia in the pre-exposure knowledge of the senders and brands involved in the experiment (of which were used relatively well-known brands). The possible consequence of 'negative experiences of sender' needs to be researched further.

With the small sample in this simple experiment, it must be said that the difference in this data between lyric and narrative is not statistically significant, whereas the difference between lyric/narrative and didactic is.

Thus, the conclusions of the experiment are that didactic ads are not liked and can probably influence the experience of sender in a negative way. Furthermore, genre and experience do seem to connect, as well as experience of ad and sender.

Genre evolution?

The development of Danish commercial television is quite unique, in the sense that there was no TV advertising before 1988. This means that many of the first TV ads were adaptations from international versions or from cinema. It makes the study of Danish TV ads a case study in the development of television advertising, as the advertising 'evolution' found elsewhere could be hypothesised to be somewhat compressed into the 15 years that followed the introduction of commercial television ('TV2' in 1988 to present). This could be important not only from a genre perspective, but also in broader terms: the attitudes and adherence to TV advertising in general; the argument being that Danish television audiences were more 'naïve' in the first years, and could also possibly have developed a 'backlash effect' of 'ad-boredom' or disillusion after the first years when Danish commercial television expanded rapidly with more channels ('TV3', 'TvDanmark', etc.).

Not that this need be a Danish phenomenon; the sense of disenchantment seems to be relevant in many Western society markets

(Ritzer, 1999). We do not have an 'index of attitudes toward genres' but it would be extremely interesting for commercial as well as scientific use.[8] It would be very helpful for assessing the risks and benefits in using the genres, such as wear-out of genres or campaigns. It could also be interesting to see if attitudes towards didactic advertising, for example, change in correspondence with other trends in sociological perspectives.

In marketing and advertising, it is often assumed that good advertising balances between the conservatism of the generally accepted norms and forms and the need to be 'fresh' in order to gain attention and 'enchant' consumption. So if advertising has an inherent need for renewal, do the genres develop accordingly? Are there many 'new genres' that are not recorded in the literature and in the matrix above?

One problem in trying to capture the 'state-of-the-art' or 'new' genres is that until a 'shared expectation' has been reasonably established and recognised one cannot really talk of a new genre, even though the artefacts may be there (recognised in retrospect). Thus, it often seems as though advertising (or art) critique is a perspective that is necessarily a retrospective. To the researcher, it will probably seem as if there are no big fresh genres, but only a mesh of narrow sub-sub-sub-genres or genre hybrids (a problem often seen in discourse on, for example, popular culture and music).

The genres in the matrix (Fig.16:1) date back to the beginning of television. It may not be possible to 'get the complete picture' as of the present, but surely advertising has changed with recognisable genres or features since the 1980's (maybe even comparable to earlier times in markets with earlier commercial television).

A general comparison of TV spots from October 1988 and October 1998 gives a clear impression of an innocence lost[9]. The characteristics may be stated in broad terms and simple opposites:

---

8. It is probably difficult to have an index with too many genres for a small country like Denmark. There have simply not been produced enough TV spots as to generate statistically-sound material if classified into many genres. The problem is diminished if several countries, i.e. for Scandinavia, are combined, though this also poses new problems of reliability.
9. A systematic content analysis of the TV spots is in progress. The following comments are based on this unfinished work.

1988	1998
Self-appreciative messages	Self-ironic messages
Authoritative appeals	Ironic use of authority
Classic ad genres	Ironic use of classic genre formats

Figure 16:5

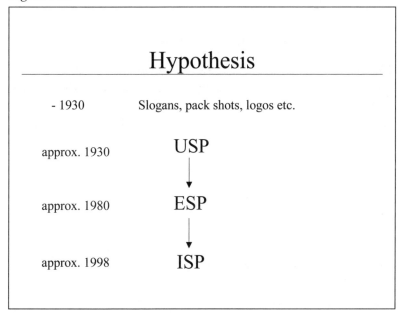

What seem to have happened in 1998 were not 'new' genres, but a different use of genres. Some developed a slightly different style, but also *ironic* use of traditional genres was used as a way of re-enchanting or re-invigorating old genres.[10] This is not just polishing the old furniture, as the meanings and experiences created by consumers are most likely going to be different and more varied. The ads of 1998 are clearly more self-referential, ironic and (one dares hardly use the term) 'post-modern'.

---

10. The first results of a classification of ads from 1988, 1998 and 2001 indicate that ironic use of genre increases radically from 1988 to 1998 and stays high in 2001.

It is very tempting to generalise on the evolution in advertising history, namely that the evolution somehow goes through a focus on USP, the ESP and 'ends' in ISP, see Fig. 16:5.[11]

Advertising does not end, so what lies beyond ISP? Advertising probably goes 'full circle'; new trends incorporating old ideas on 'mere exposure effects' now gives new credit to simple media types like billboards (Heath, 2001).

Ironic Selling Propositions

The trend in the TV spots seems to be going in a direction towards what might be labelled *Ironic Selling Propositions* (ISP). The meaning of the term stretches in two directions: a selling proposition pretending not really to be a selling proposition, and/or a selling proposition that refers to selling propositions in an ironic or sarcastic way (using genres of advertising, ad-clichés etc.). This is not the same as using humour or comedy, although combinations are possible. The concept of irony is very elusive and difficult to describe.[12] Nonetheless, most humans in real contexts with real artefacts seem to intuitively agree on the occurrence of irony. The claims of potential 'innocent victims' (persons not discovering the irony) are often exaggerated in discussions on irony (Booth, 1974).

Irony in this context is not simply a negation of literal meaning. In this chapter, the concept of irony takes its cue from Wayne C. Booth (Booth, 1974)[13]. Booth compares the initial experience of irony to that of 'cognitive dissonance'[14]; the experience of incongruent 'clues' forces the mind into a mode of irony when dissonance of the 'straight' interpretation becomes too great (unfortunately, he does not develop this idea further (Booth, 1974)). This experience of incongruity may be

---

11. This resonates in many presentations of advertising history; see for example Myers p. 24 (Myers, 1994).
12. The literature on irony is very extensive and the concept of irony is very complex and deserves a much deeper discussion than is possible within this paper. Most of the scientific papers within marketing focus on verbal irony alone, as does most of the literature within the arts and humanities. In this paper the concept may refer to the experience of all levels of the audio/visual artefacts of TV advertising.
13. Booth is relevant in a pragmatic context such as this, because he is primarily interested in the *communicational* aspects of irony.
14. The concept originally developed by Leon Festinger.

within the artefact itself or between artefact and an aspect of the context. Booth then tries to make a distinction between stable and unstable irony. Stable irony is a meaning that is initially recognised as 'unstable', something not to be taken at face value, but the meaning does stabilise once this is interpreted. It is possible to express this 'new' more stable meaning to a reasonably satisfactory degree (or rather, a finite set of possible meanings). The irony of simple negation belongs to this category, but the possibilities are much wider. Irony is unstable when it seems impossible to arrive at a new more stable interpretation of the ironic expression; the possible meanings seem infinite and the only certain thing is the need to reject the face value of the expression. These two types of irony are to be understood as belonging to a continuum, not as exclusive categories.

It is important to stress that this definition of irony puts more emphasis on a polysemic interpretation, which clears the way for a better understanding of the unstable qualities of irony, than the commonly held simple idea of irony as a negation or exaggeration of the literal meaning.

Another relevant topic in most theories on irony is the degree of *criticism* inherent in the use of irony (Booth, 1974; Sigrell, 2001; Sperber and Wilson, 1995). When this criticism or ridicule becomes very apparent and direct, one might speak of satire; though direct satire is not really present in Danish advertising (direct comparison is illegal). It is possible to perceive the ISP as criticising the institutions and conventions of advertising. In these cases, the irony is manifold: The advertising regains adherence and persuasive potential by ridiculing conventional persuasive techniques, thus apparently transcending trite impersonal commercialism of 'selling propositions'.

What sub-strategies or elements may be used in constructing Ironic Selling Propositions?

The following is an attempt at identifying sub-strategies of the ISP.

Ironic use of genre

The ironic use of genre has already been mentioned above, but deserves some elaboration. It differs somewhat from the strategies below, in that the irony is often constructed through many subtle or overt references to the genres of advertising, to *the genre format as a whole.* This is often referred to as a *pastiche* (Brown, 2001). In the early ISP of 1998, these references are quite overt and stable in their irony. In the Mobilix pre-paid mobile phone ads of 1998, for example, the clearly absurd use of problem/solution format (dog gets caught in bicycle wheel/dog gets cut in two with scissors), all presented very authoritatively by an 'airhostess' look-alike in heavy make-up. Recent ironic use of genre is more complex and subtle, using only fragments or combining genres etc. This often means a more unstable form of irony; i.e. how much is ironic, where does irony end?

Ironic nostalgia

Nostalgia is a traditional element with great ESP potential, but in ISP it is more ambiguous. The reference to things gone past is not 'straight', not to be taken literally. It can be slightly humorous in a caricature of the 1950's USP-style (as the OBH home appliances of 1998), or more difficult to place historically as styles blend. The ironic nostalgia is comparable to the 'retro' trends that were particularly in vogue in the late 1990s (Brown, 2001), but the ironic nostalgia is a wider concept compared to the more consistent and stylishly rounded 'retro'.

Ironic negative scenario

The use of negative scenarios means situations depicting 'the problem' or the absence of the product or service. Traditional marketing literature (Rossiter and Percy, 1996) often warns against a single focus on this, although it is not that uncommon as it holds creative rewards in the freedom of presentation. Admittedly, it is problematic to differentiate between general exaggeration in advertising and an exaggerated negative scenario that is ironic.[15] In the case of irony, it should be apparent that more is at stake than 'normal exaggeration'.[16] That the exaggeration is not at all to be taken seriously is too absurd, or subtle cues make the depiction of the negative scenario polysemic

---

15. One may argue that exaggeration is simply a genre feature of all advertising that is to be expected, and that negative or positive scenarios are never to be taken literally. In this sense, advertising has always been 'generically ironic'. Albeit interesting, this view seems in itself exaggerated.

16. In rhetorical theory, this 'normal exaggeration' may be referred to in the terms of 'hyperbole' or 'amplification'.

and unstable. Examples could be the young man going berserk in a croquet game with the in-laws in an ad for Danica (2001) or the violently naughty boys of the 1998 McDonald's campaign trying to bully parents into having their children's birthday celebrations at McDonald's.[17]

Ironic positive scenario

The ironic positive scenario is a natural extension of the negative scenario, and in combination they make up an ironic problem/solution. Ironic positive scenarios seem to be less frequent in isolation. Maybe the reason for this is that showing only the positive effects tends to make the cause of the scenario (the product or service) less clear, with disastrous results for the desired branding effect.

Also, in these positive scenarios, it is somewhat difficult to separate 'straight' but exaggerated visualisations of effects of products from what might be termed ironic. One good example of this is the Interflora campaign of 2001[18], where the effect of giving flowers is visually communicated by showing situations of, for example, a male couch potato who is continuously served beer by his wife or when the sports trophy gets a prime spot on the shelf (the ironic cues are underlined from the completely nonverbal executions, with tension building through the use of sound or music with strong pathos).

Ironic protagonist or antagonist

An ironic protagonist or antagonist is a spokesperson or main character who appears in a seemingly incongruous or self-contradictory way. This must transcend the conventional use of heroes or anti-heroes in problem/solution formats or the silly stock characters of comedy. Admittedly, this is again a problem of interpretation.

One such example could be the spot for Diesel Jeans from 1997 "Little Rock, 1873", which utilises references to the western genre: The 'successful' clean-cut hero (wearing Diesel jeans) gets shot in a showdown on the street by a disgusting villain. So who is the hero?

---

17. The McDonald's ad was subsequently banned because of the extreme behaviour.
18. This campaign was awarded an Arnold prize for its creativity.

In a very Danish context, the kitsch spokesperson "Harske Hubbi" (means something like "Stale Hubbi") is recommending new CD releases in a series of ads for Universal Music under the slogan "quite all right music taste"[19]. This campaign really explores the limits of the advertising world's self-referentiality: "Harske Hubbi" is actually a spin-off character from another series of TV spots from the telecom company Sonofon. This company also uses an ironic protagonist, "Polle", though this character borders on the clichés of folk-comedy ('the town fool').

The antagonist is usually 'the villain' of a drama, and in classic advertising a natural place for her/him is the negative scenario. An ironic antagonist is a somewhat oxymoronic concept, because the ironic antagonist can easily be confused with an ironic protagonist; the antagonist being 'ironic' i.e. 'not anta-' may seem to equal 'pro-'. However, following the definition of irony above (polysemic rather than just negation), the ironic antagonist becomes 'much more than antagonist'.

An interesting example is the Danish continued series of ironic docu-soap spots for Kim's snack food, in which the evil brother of the founder Kim[20] takes over the company. Kim is never seen, and the continued story is an unsuccessful search for him. Kim's evil brother Jørgen is a sleazy Elvis look-alike with an attitude. After the search for Kim has ended (unsuccessfully) Jørgen actually changes role to spokesperson for the company and is now in effect presented as an ironic protagonist. In the latest spots from Kim's, the seemingly 'normal' product-orientated spot is interrupted and it turns into a meta-spot with Jørgen arguing about the spots' creative potential with the director (played by the actual director, a well-known ad and movie director).[21]

An IKEA ad from 2001 extends the idea of an ironic antagonist all the way to an ironic sender. A fictional society, the JetSetSociety, is leading a campaign against IKEA's 'Democratic Design'. It is a kind

---

19. The full connotations of this slogan cannot really be translated from the Danish dialect of Fyn.
20. 'Kim' is a male name in Denmark.
21. The irony does not end here: Jørgen also pops up in ads for Tuborg beer as a salesperson for Tuborg. In the first spots he refers to his 'old job', claiming "he knows what the customers want".

of 'civil rights movement of the rich', in which spokesperson Benedicte de Reinsing protests against 'cheap designer furniture'. "Designer furniture is a prerogative of the rich" is the claim. This is anti-positioning: IKEA equals modern distaste for the conservative claims of class and 'outdated' quality ideals. IKEA in these spots makes a virtue out of *not having* these ideals; instead they have cheap 'Democratic Design'. In the 2002 IKEA fan club campaign, the focus changes to another ironic society: the IKEA fan club. These ironic protagonists *live* IKEA; they treat IKEA as a religion complete with pilgrimage to Älmhult.[22] In these spots, the instability of the irony is increased radically, also becoming more self-ironic.

Ironic didactics

The use of a mode of address that is ironically didactic is an ISP sub-strategy often combined with others. Ironic didactics uses elements of authority appeal, such as old educational films, and may have nostalgic traits of 'old military educational' aesthetics. The long-running campaigns for Diesel has the continuous label "How To...Guides To Successful Living", an ironic didactic framing of their lifestyle dictates.[23]

Possible advantages of ISP

No doubt the creative potentials of ISP is important when explaining why creatives choose these strategies. All professions have an introvert undercurrent: the need to be admired and respected by peers. Often journalists write for journalists (not readers) (Kock, 2002) and advertising people sometimes showcase themselves rather than the products they were paid to promote, and in the process relate more to advertising than to 'real life' (Christensen, 2001).

However, there are possible advantages of ISP when applied successfully. One of the most important is the potential for adding essential facets to the Brand Identity of the advertiser, an ethos of more

---

22. The place of the first IKEA store.
23. All the Guides To Successful Living can currently be seen at the web page: www.diesel.com.

than competence, of goodwill towards the consumer. On the experience of ironic communication, Booth comments:

"The shrewd sceptic that we all learn to become as we meet life's con-men is delighted to find, behind the presented words, a fellow sceptic, demolishing illusions; and *then* - marvel of marvels - that sceptic turns out to be a great dreamer, a man of passion who can multiply implications and proclaim mysteries: here is a soul-mate indeed." (Booth 1974, p. 178)

Booth's point is that one of the most important aspects of irony is the capacity of building relations between audience and author, brand and consumer, and building a community of shared understanding.

The advantages and risks of ISP could be summed up as follows:

WHY?
- Fuses otherwise difficult/conflicting communicational goals
- Builds sympathy
- Invites better processing
- Potential WOM/Viral effect
- Creative potential

WHY NOT?
- Polysemic means less control
- Central processing may be essential
- If you fail, you may fail miserably

Research perspectives

Genre analysis is a field with much more pragmatic potential than is currently recognised. If genre concepts were better described and agreed upon, it would make buying and evaluating advertising less mysterious. When advertisers think or rethink their positioning strategies, it would be a powerful tool to be able to track their own as well as competitors' advertising through a genre index of regions, markets or product categories.

More research is needed to gain a qualitatively as well as quantitatively better insight into the spectrum of consumer experiences that ad genres are related to. In light of the recent cognitive communication models, such as the P/E/M model (Hall, 2002) or Heath's focus on implicit memory (Heath, 2001), knowledge on the genre experience is critical, as these theories consequently leave little or no effects to persuasive *messages*.

Unfortunately, it seems much discourse on irony and post-modern marketing gets stuck knee-deep in French philosophy and does not embark upon an empirical investigation of consumer experiences. ISP is just one facet of post-modern marketing, although this chapter is trying to claim that ISP is a pragmatic way of looking at post-modern marketing.

In order to know the potentials of ISP, more research into the consumer experience of ISP is needed. Much is written and said on the apocalypse of post-modern times, but is the occasional use of ISP really the end of communication, or just a corrective option for the re-enchanting of advertising and consumption, a strategy for gaining adherence in contexts of high ad pressure and low confidence? It may very well be that in 2002 the ISP has already been overly exploited during the 1990s by creatives gone autopoesis and ad buyers trying to be hip. It may also be that ISP could be established as a durable possibility for certain situations, high in constraints.

17

The Role of Lifestyle and Personality in Explaining the Attitude toward Ads and the Purchase Intentions

SANDRA DIEHL & RALF TERLUTTER

Abstract

The authors analyze the question how recipients of advertising can be segmented in a way that renders efficient communication. Advertising models often neglect individual predispositions, which influence the effects of advertising. The suitability of the variables *lifestyle* and *personality* to predict the consumers' attitude toward the ad (Aad) and their purchase intentions is examined. Personality is analyzed on the basis of the NEO-FFI (five-factor structure). Three different product-specific lifestyles (clothing lifestyle, living lifestyle and cultural lifestyle) are examined on the basis of three 2nd order dimensions of lifestyle. Hierarchical cluster analyses are conducted, which extracted personality groups and lifestyle groups. Using ANOVA, these groups are analyzed to discover whether there are differences in their attitudes toward four different ads and their purchase intentions.

The results show that personality on its own cannot explain and predict the attitudes toward the ads and the purchase intentions. The product-specific lifestyles are suitable for explaining and predicting differences in the evaluation of those ads that correspond to the specific product category.

Introduction

A great deal of research deals with the effects of advertising and there are many models which try to explain the effects of advertising.

Communication is often tailored to market segments built on varying variables. Though there has been a shift from demographics to more specific concepts such as behavior-based concepts and considerable research during the last decades, it is still not clear which of the individual characteristics are especially suitable for segmentation. As media costs have continued to accelerate at a high rate, advertising managers are becoming increasingly concerned about the efficiency of their market segmentation. One important question to answer is „How can the recipients be segmented in a way that renders efficient communication?" In this chapter, a comparison is made of the suitability of the variables *lifestyle* and *personality* for predicting consumers' attitudes toward the ad (Aad) and their purchase intentions for the advertised product or service. Concerning personality, the Five-Factor Model of personality (FFM) by (Costa and McCrae, 1992b) is applied. Concerning lifestyle, three different product-specific lifestyles (living lifestyle, clothing lifestyle and cultural lifestyle) are applied, each of which is measured on the basis of three 2nd order dimensions following (Richter, 1994) and (Lüdtke, 1995).

Research on the effects of advertising

It is impossible to integrate all factors influencing the effects of advertising in advertising models. However, it is important to analyze whether or not general advertising models do comprise the important factors or whether it is necessary to add additional relevant components.

In a meta analysis (*Vakratsas* and *Ambler,* 1999) reviewed more than 250 journal articles and books, and classified the existing advertising models in six categories summarizing the empirical findings of each category. *Vakratsas* and *Ambler* classify the models in *Market Response Models, Cognitive Information Models, Pure Affect Models, Persuasive Hierarchy Models, Low-Involvement Hierarchy Models, Integrative Models* and *Hierarchy-Free Models* (for an overview of advertising models, see also *Meyers-Levy* and *Malaviya,* 1999; *Ambler,* 2000; *Mayer* and *Illmann,* 2000, pp. 406ff.).

The class of hierarchical models is one of the most important categories of advertising models. Examples are the AIDA Model (Attention, Interest, Desire and Action, attributed to *Lewis,* 1898) or

Sandra Diehl • Ralf Terlutter

the DAGMAR Model (*Colley*, 1961), which are also called linear or sequential models, respectively. The advertising model shown as an example in Figure 17:1 is an often-cited advertising model in the German research community developed by *Kroeber-Riel* (*Kroeber-Riel* and *Weinberg*, 1999, p. 588). In principle, this model belongs to the class of Hierarchy Models, but the strictly linear sequence characteristic for this class is abandoned, admitting interactions between the different steps. (*Petty* and *Cacioppo's*, 1986) Elaboration Likelihood Model (ELM) can be characterized in a similar way.

Figure 17:1 Advertising effects path model from Kroeber-Riel
(Kroeber-Riel and Weinberg, 1999, p. 588)

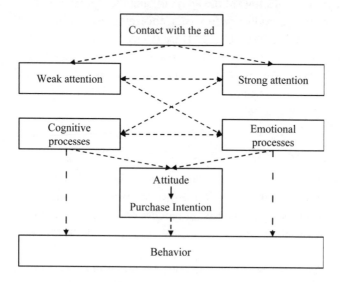

Most of the models mentioned above share the SOR paradigm as a common basis. This implies that the models consider mediating factors between the advertising stimulus and the reactions to the ad. The selection of the factors taken into consideration often seems arbitrary and depends on the theoretical position of the author (*Mayer* and *Illmann*, 2000, pp. 424-425). Furthermore, the above-mentioned models have in common that they mostly neglect individual differences between the recipients. The path model of advertising effects shown in Figure 17:1 starts with the contact of the consumer with the advertisement and analyzes the mediating variables as cognitive or emotional processes, which determine the attitude toward the ad and the behavioral intentions.

It can be assumed that within these paths a number of individual predispositions (personality, lifestyle, mood etc.) exist, influencing the mediating variables and thus the effects of the advertisement. These individual predispositions are not sufficiently taken into consideration by most of the advertising models. Despite much research in the area covering the effects of advertising, there is still no advertising model that meets all the requirements. The aim of this study is to gain more insight into the influence of individual predispositions on the effects of advertising.

Individual differences

We differentiate between short-term and long-term individual predispositions.

Predispositions of recipients with a rather short-term validity

These predispositions have only temporary effects on the evaluation of advertisements and change rather quickly.

- *Present mood*: The present mood of a person is a temporary varying state. The mood can by influenced by:
    a) Factors which are *independent of the advertising medium,* e.g. personal experiences, emotional state (for a literature overview regarding the mood as factor influencing advertising effects, see *Silberer*, 1999),
    b) Factors, which are *dependent on the advertising medium*: A study from (*Aylesworth* and *MacKenzie,* 1998) has shown that the program context in which the stimulus ads were embedded influences the effects of the advertisement. This is due to the fact that the television program has impacts on the mood of the recipients. The program-induced mood influences the processing of and the attitudes toward the advertisements. The effects of advertisements depend upon the contents in which the advertisements are embedded (e.g.

a sad or funny film) (for a literature overview, see *Hirschman* and *Stern*, 1999, pp. 4ff.).

- *Situational factors* (environment in which the advertising is consumed, e.g. reading a magazine in a noisy environment or in peace at home, number of persons around, time pressure, situational involvement).

These short-term predispositions influence the mediating variables in an advertising model. They are rather difficult to predict for a marketer and therefore difficult to plan. In the present study, they are not further elaborated.

Predispositions of recipients with a rather long-term validity

These predispositions characterize individuals for a longer period of time and are more stable. Due to their long-term validity and their stability, they are of major importance for market segmentation (*Freter*, 1983). In the following, we focus on the differences in the effects of advertisements due to relatively stable individual differences.

From consumer behavior (see *Solomon*, 2002; *Blackwell* et al., 2001; *Schiffman* and *Kanuk*, 1997; *Kroeber-Riel* and *Weinberg*, 1999), we know that *personality* and *lifestyle* are long-term variables with an important influence on different aspects of consumer behavior. Both variables and their importance for the research on the effects of advertising will be analyzed in detail.

Further long-term predispositions which might also influence the effects of advertisements are discussed below.

- *Cultural differences* might account for differences in the effects of advertising. Cultural differences have to be taken into consideration in international advertising campaigns. (*Aaker* and *Maheswaran*, 1997) were able to show that the Elaboration Likelihood Model (*Petty* and *Cacioppo*, 1986) was robust across cultures, which differed in the dimension individualism vs. collectivism of Hofstede (e.g. *Hofstede* 1997). Nevertheless, there have been significant differences in the perceived relevance of the information conveyed by advertising in the different cultures, accounting for differences in advertising effects in individualistic and collectivistic cultures.

Cultures differing in the dimension masculinity vs. femininity of Hofstede (e.g. *Hofstede*, 1997) significantly vary in the depictions of relationships for male and female characters in television advertisements (significantly higher in feminine countries) (*Milner* and *Collins*, 2000).

- According to (*Rice* and *Bennett*, 1998), the *consumer's prior psychological relationships with brands* have to be taken into account when formulating communication strategies and when measuring the effects of advertising. Users of a brand are more likely to note and like the brand's advertising than non-users. Non-consumers of a brand can be differentiated between those who are close to switching to the brand and those who are not prone to switching. The two groups of non-consumers significantly differ in their response to advertising.

- Socialization - especially the type of family communication patterns - influences adolescents' attitudes toward advertising (cf. *Mangleburg* and *Bristol*, 1998; *Rose* et al., 1998). *Mangleburg* and *Bristol* differentiate between socio-oriented vs. concept-oriented family communication. Socio-oriented communication fosters control and deference to authority and the generating and maintaining of harmonic relationships in the family. Socio-oriented parents control and restrict their children's purchasing behavior. Concept-oriented communication encourages children to develop an independent evaluation of an issue. In the context of consumption, concept-oriented parents encourage children to develop independent preferences and evaluations (see also *Rose* et al., 1998). Adolescents' skepticism toward advertising (for measuring skepticism toward advertising, see also *Obermiller* and *Spangenberg*, 1998) is significantly intensified by a concept-oriented family communication. The study by (*Rose* et al., 1998) supports these findings, as the authors found that mothers with high concept-orientation have the most negative attitudes toward advertising.

These variables will not be further elaborated, as the focus is on the variables *lifestyle* and *personality*.

Sandra Diehl • Ralf Terlutter

Personality and advertising

Personality refers to stable characteristics within the individual accounting for consistent patterns of behavior. Aspects of personality may be observable or unobservable, and conscious or unconscious (*Ewen*, 1998, p. 2). An important approach to personality is *trait theory,* which aims at identifying the stable characteristics (personality traits) of individuals. In trait theory, there are approaches in which one specific and *isolated trait* is analyzed, whereas other approaches aim at analyzing personality in its *entirety.*

The research on one isolated personality trait analyzed *extroversion/introversion* (*Jung,* 1921/1967), *innovativeness* (*Price* and *Ridgway,* 1983), *self-monitoring* (*Snyder,* 1974, 1979), *self-consciousness* (*Duval* and *Wicklund,* 1972; *Fenigstein* et al., 1975; *Fenigstein,* 1979), *need for cognition* (*Venkatraman* et al., 1990; *Haugtvedt* et al., 1992), etc. In advertising research, (*Barr* and *Kellaris,* 2000) empirically show that individuals differ in their *susceptibility to advertising.* Individuals with low susceptibility process advertising with a lower elaboration than individuals with high susceptibility. (*Moore* and *Homer,* 2000) investigated the influence of differences in *temperaments* on advertising responses. They show that individuals with high affect intensity respond with significantly stronger levels of emotion when exposed to an affectively charged advertising appeal, but did not when exposed to a non-emotional appeal. (*Smit* and *Neijens,* 2000) showed that groups of consumers with high *affinity* for advertising pay more attention to advertisements and commercials.

The research on personality and similar constructs exemplarily presented takes only a small number of individual differences into account. Advertising research that considers personality in its entirety is lacking. The question is raised whether or not the approaches to personality research that attempt to analyze personality as an entirety are suitable for explaining differences in the evaluation of advertising. The approach to trait theory which tries to analyze personality in its entirety presupposes that personality has an underlying core of fundamental personality traits which can be identified. The idea is that all individuals share the same personality traits and that individual differences are due to differences in the identified traits.

(*Cattell* et al., 1970) identify 16 personality traits in a person. According to (*Eysenck*, 1970, 1990), there are three basic and broad personality traits (introversion-extraversion, neuroticism, psychoticism).

In recent research, numerous researchers assume a five-trait structure of personality (for an overview, see *Digman*, 1990; *Wiggins* and *Pincus*, 1992; *Wiggins*, 1996; *De Raad*, 2000; for criticism, see *Eysenck*, 1992). Within this five-factor tradition, there are two directions of research: (1) the lexical approach to the five-factor structure (e.g. *Norman*, 1963; *Tupes* and *Christal*, 1992); and (2) the approach by (*Costa* and *McCrae*, e.g. 1985; 1992b).

The lexical approach to the five-factor structure is often referred to as the „Big Five". It contains the dimensions Extraversion, Agreeableness, Conscientiousness, Emotional Stability and Culture (following the work of *Norman*, 1963). Other researchers have found similar solutions. (*Goldberg*, 1992), for example, identified the dimensions Surgency, Agreeableness, Conscientiousness, Emotional Stability and Intellect. (*Tupes* and *Christal*, 1992) identified the dimensions Surgency, Agreeableness, Dependability, Emotional Stability and Culture.

The approach by *Costa* and *McCrae* is often referred to as the Five-Factor Model (FFM). The FFM contains the dimensions *Neuroticism, Extraversion, Agreeableness, Conscientiousness* and *Openness to Experience*. The measurement tool for the FFM is the NEO-PI-R or its shorter version, the NEO-FFI (*Costa* and *McCrae*, 1992b).

Despite the different histories of the „Big Five" and the FFM, there are many correspondences in the trait structure, but also some deviations. Both approaches are based on five dimensions and these are quite similar with regard to the content. Most discussions were caused by the factor which (*Costa* and *McCrae*, 1992a; 1992b) called "Openness" resp. "Openness to Experience". This factor was called "Culture" by (*Tupes* and *Christal*, 1992) and (*Norman*, 1963), "Intellect" by (*Goldberg*, 1992), and "Imagination" by (*Saucier*, 1994). The five personality traits are a classification that allows for a description of individuals by dimensions important to the personality of a person. It is assumed that the five personality traits are to be found in each individual.

Until today, it has not been possible to decide which of the different approaches is the „true" one. The NEO-PI-R resp. the NEO-FFI, however, is the most frequently used personality questionnaire to assess a five-factor structure of personality traits (*De Raad*, 2000, p. 80). Therefore, the empirical study on personality in this research is based on the NEO-FFI as well.

The five personality traits of the FFM by (*Costa* and *McCrae*, 1992b) can be briefly described as follows:

- *Neuroticism*: Persons with high scores on this factor are characterized by anxiety, angry hostility, depression, self-consciousness, impulsiveness, vulnerability.
- *Extraversion*: Persons with high scores on this factor are characterized by warmth, gregariousness, assertiveness, activity, excitement-seeking, positive emotions.
- *Openness to Experience*: Persons with high scores on this factor are characterized by fantasy, aesthetics, feelings, actions, ideas, values.
- *Agreeableness*: Persons with high scores on this factor are characterized by trust, straightforwardness, altruism, compliance, modesty, sensibility.
- *Conscientiousness*: Persons with high scores on this factor are characterized by competence, order, dutifulness, striving for achievement, self-discipline, deliberation.

If these five dimensions are taken as a basis for market segmentation, the question is raised whether or not the resulting personality groups differ with regard to their reactions to advertising. It is analyzed whether personality is a valuable basis for segmentation due to its universality or whether it is too broad a concept for advertising issues.

Lifestyle and advertising

Lifestyle can be defined as a mode of living, identified by how people spend their time (activities), what they consider important in their environment (interests), and what they think of themselves and the world around them (opinions) (*Wells* and *Tigert*, 1971). Often in marketing, the consumption behavior of individuals is taken into account when lifestyle is defined. According to (*Solomon*, 2002, p. 173), lifestyle is „a pattern of consumption reflecting a person's choices of how he or she spends time and money" (similar to *Kroeber-Riel* and *Weinberg*, 1999, pp. 430-431).

In many cases, a lifestyle is ascertained which is tailored to a specific research question. The foci of the analysis were the *leisure lifestyle* (*Andreasen* and *Belk*, 1980), the *lifestyle associated to drinking-driving behavior* (*Lastovicka* et al., 1987), the *lifestyle of the tight and frugal* (*Lastovicka* et al., 1999), the *culture-specific lifestyle* (*Terlutter*, 2000), the *Internet-specific lifestyle* (*Diehl*, 2002), etc. In addition, there are a number of non-academic approaches in which companies try to identify the lifestyles of their customers.

Due to the heterogeneity of lifestyle research, there was less effort – in contrast to personality research – to identify the „true" dimensions characterizing (different) lifestyles of persons. However, due to the heterogeneity of the existing approaches to lifestyle, this is an important aim. In addition, many approaches to lifestyle are very complex and contain up to 300 items (e.g. the AIO by *Wells* and *Tigert*, 1971). Such a complexity is not practicable for marketing purposes, since usually additional variables besides lifestyle have to be ascertained as well.

In this study, the authors follow an approach which tries to reduce lifestyle to its underlying dimensions. Based on the similarities of different lifestyle studies in Germany, (*Richter*, 1994) and (*Lüdtke*, 1995) reduced different lifestyle dimensions to basic dimensions which could be found in all of the studies taken into consideration. The basic dimensions were called 2nd order dimensions of lifestyle. According to (*Richter*, 1994), there are three 2nd order dimensions, which are briefly characterized as:

- *Changing vs. Preserving*: Trying to make changes, moving with the time, following trends vs. conventional, conservative attitude, following traditions;
- *Active vs. Passive*: activity, showing interest vs. passivity, adopting a policy of wait-and-see;
- *Outer-oriented vs. Inner-oriented*: directing own behavior to others, own behavior dependent on others vs. self-directed behavior, own behavior dependent on oneself.

According to (*Richter,* 1994, p. 174), the 2nd order dimensions of lifestyle permit a comprehensive and comparable description of lifestyles in society.

Through their lifestyles, consumers try to demonstrate group identities and a membership of specific lifestyle groups (*Holt,* 1997). They demonstrate specific behavior in environmental settings, for example by consuming specific products in peer groups (*Solomon,* 2002, p. 174). Consumption is therefore an important prerequisite for the demonstration of a specific lifestyle. As many products are specifically tailored to meet the lifestyles of target groups, a close relationship between the lifestyle of consumers and their consumption behavior is to be expected. For this reason, lifestyle seems to be a highly valuable variable for the explanation and prediction of consumer behavior, especially if a product-specific lifestyle is applied. Typically, lifestyle categorizations are not the same across product domains. One and the same person may have different lifestyles with regard to different products, for example with regard to clothing lifestyle, living lifestyle and sports lifestyle. As a consequence, lifestyle has to be investigated empirically for each product domain (*Antonides* and *van Raaij*, 1998, p. 376).

In this study, different product-specific lifestyles are analyzed, namely clothing lifestyle, living lifestyle and cultural lifestyle. It is further analyzed whether or not the market segments based on the product-specific lifestyles differ in their evaluation of advertisements and if market segmentation based on product-specific lifestyles is a valuable concept for advertising issues.

Method

A total of 141 students attending the University of the Saarland in Germany answered a questionnaire that included questions on personality traits and lifestyles, specifically clothing lifestyle, living lifestyle and cultural lifestyle. The respondents ranged from 19 to 34 years of age. 56% were men, 44% were women. After the respondents had answered the questionnaire, they were asked to evaluate four different print advertisements with regard to their attitude toward the ad (Aad) and their purchase intentions for the products or services advertised. Attitude toward the ad is a common concept in advertising research (*MacKenzie* and *Lutz*, 1989, and the literature cited there; *Behrens* et al., 2001, p. 114). According to (*MacKenzie* and *Lutz*, 1989) Aad is defined as „a predisposition to respond in a favorable or unfavorable manner to a particular advertising stimulus during a particular exposure occasion". Often it is criticized that behavioral intentions are neglected in the research on advertising effects (*Mayer* and *Illmann*, 2000, p. 424-425). As this is a variable of high value for marketers, the purchase intentions are taken into consideration in this study as well. The four advertisements were for furniture (Ad_1 $_{(living)}$), for clothes (Ad_2 $_{(clothing)}$), for a museum (Ad_3 $_{(culture)}$) and for a social institution (Ad_4 $_{(social)}$) (see Figure 17:2).

Figure 17:2 The four advertisements used in the empirical study

It was decided that clothing and living should be analyzed, as these parts of life are essential to most individuals. Especially clothing is seen to have a defining role in society (*O'Cass*, 2000), and therefore, we chose to analyze living lifestyle and clothing lifestyle. In the study, we integrated print advertisements for living (Ad_1 $_{(living)}$) and for clothing (Ad_2 $_{(clothing)}$). In addition to these ads for two concrete products, we included an advertisement for a service (a cultural service). A study by (*Terlutter*, 2000) has shown that a culture-specific lifestyle was an adequate predictor for behavioral intentions in the cultural area, and therefore cultural lifestyle and a print advertisement for a museum (Ad_3 $_{(culture)}$) were integrated in the study. The fourth ad we included was a print advertisement for a social institution (Ad$_4$ $_{(social)}$). We chose this advertisement for validation. In all advertisements the brand name was erased. Figure 17:3 gives an overview of the empirical study.

Figure 17:3 Overview of the empirical study

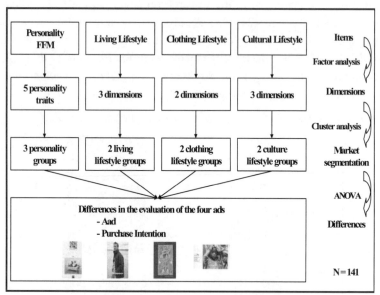

We assume that the groups based on the product-specific lifestyles are well suited to explaining differences in the evaluation of those ads corresponding with the product category.

To assess the influence of the respondent's personality and their lifestyle on the Aad and the exploratory factor analysis on purchase intentions, hierarchical cluster analyses and ANOVAs were applied.

Results

Personality

Personality was measured using items from the NEO-FFI by (*Costa* and *McCrae,* 1992b). Due to restrictions in the length of the questionnaire, it was necessary to select items from the original tool. Ten statements based on a German translation by (*Borkenau* and

Ostendorf, 1993) were selected to represent the five dimensions of personality.

The exploratory factor analysis extracted five factors with an eigen value > 1. The factors explained 76.6 % of the total variance. The five factors represent exactly the dimensions of the FFM.

Table 17:1 Factor analysis of personality

Statement	1	2	3	4	5	Interpretation of factor
Work hard	.877					*Conscientiousness*
Clear aims	.837					
Talkative		.882				*Extraversion*
Good-humored		.870				
Many self-doubts			.886			*Neuroticism*
Often discouraged			.858			
No monotony				.856		*Openness to*
Try new things				.812		*Experience*
Egoistic					-.895	*Agreeableness*
Considerate					.705	
Eigen Value	2.52	1.77	1.27	1.09	1.02	
Variance extracted (cum.)	25.2	42.9	55.6	66.5	76.6	

Principal Component Analysis, Rotation: Varimax (values below 0.3 were suppressed)

The five factors could be confirmed by a confirmatory factor analysis as well (estimation: ML, GFI .980; AGFI .956; CFI 1.000; RMR .048; RMSEA .000; df 25; p .945).

The hierarchical cluster analysis was used to segment the subjects. The Elbow criterion suggested a three-cluster solution. The three clusters differ significantly in all dimensions of personality (for details, see Table 17:2).

Cluster one (n=71) is especially characterized by conscientiousness below average and by an agreeableness that is clearly above average. This group is therefore called the *non-conscientious/agreeable personality group.* Cluster two (n=54) is characterized by conscientiousness and by openness to experiences above average and by extraversion, neuroticism and agreeableness below average. Based on the personality traits characterizing this group strongest, they are called the *conscientious/non-agreeable/open-to-experience personality group.* Cluster three is a small cluster (n=16). The personality traits of this group are extreme. The dimensions conscientiousness,

Table 17:2 Hierarchical cluster analysis of personality factors

Factor	Cluster 1 (n=71)	Cluster 2 (n=54)	Cluster 3 (n=16)	Sig.
Conscientiousness	-.491	.446	.675	.000
Extraversion	-.001	-.150	.553	.046
Neuroticism	.103	-.247	.378	.041
Openness to Experience	.009	.343	-1.548	.000
Agreeableness	.556	-.694	-.127	.000
Interpretation	*non-conscientious/ agreeable personality group*	*conscientious/ non-agreeable/ open to experiences personality group*	*conservative personality group*	

Algorithm: Ward; Distance: Squared Euclid, values characterizing the groups are t-values

extraversion and neuroticism are above average, whereas agreeableness and especially openness to experience are below average. The fact that especially the personality trait openness to experience is clearly below average leads to the denomination of this group as the *conservative personality group*.

Lifestyle

Living Lifestyle

Living lifestyle was measured using seven items that represent the three 2nd order dimensions of lifestyle as described above. The exploratory factor analysis extracted three factors with an eigen value > 1 representing the three dimensions. The factors explained 68.3 % of the total variance. The first factor summarizes the items *no fashion baubles in the flat, functional flat* and *modern flat* (reverse). These items refer to a *preserving living lifestyle*. The second factor, which was named *outer-oriented living lifestyle,* combines the items *buy furniture with friends* and *no advice with regard to furniture* (reverse). The third factor with the items *flat often coordinated* and *take a look at furniture stores* refers to the dimension of activity and was interpreted as *active living lifestyle*.

The hierarchical cluster analysis based on the factors of the living lifestyle identified two segments. Cluster one is characterized by an outer-oriented living lifestyle and by activity with regard to the style of

Table 17:3 Factor analysis of living lifestyle

Statement	1	2	3	Interpretation of factor
No fashion baubles in the flat	.826			*Preserving living lifestyle*
Functional flat	.782			
Modern flat	-.722			
Buy furniture with friends		.842		*Outer-oriented living lifestyle*
No advice with regard to furniture		-.825		
Flat often coordinated			.822	*Active living lifestyle*
Take a look at furniture stores			.804	
Eigen Value	2.09	1.50	1.19	
Variance extracted (cum.)	29.9	51.3	68.3	

Principal Component Analysis, Rotation: Varimax (values below 0.3 were suppressed)

living compared to cluster two. No significant differences could be found with regard to the preserving living lifestyle (for details, see Table 17:4). Cluster one was called the *outer-oriented, active living lifestyle group*, cluster two the *inner-oriented, passive living lifestyle group*.

Table 17:4 Hierarchical cluster analysis of living lifestyle factors

Factor	Cluster 1 (n=77)	Cluster 2 (n=64)	Sig.
Preserving living lifestyle	-.009	.114	.219
Outer-oriented living lifestyle	.272	-.328	.000
Active living lifestyle	.638	-.768	.000
Interpretation	*outer-directed, active living lifestyle group*	*inner-directed, passive living lifestyle group*	

Algorithm: Ward; Distance: Squared Euclid, values characterizing the groups are t-values

Clothing Lifestyle

Clothing lifestyle was measured by eight items which were also expected to represent the three 2nd order dimensions of lifestyle. However, the exploratory factor analysis extracted only two factors with an eigen value > 1. The two factors explained 59.7 % of the total variance. Factor one combined items that showed activity and modernism, such as *interest in fashion, moving with the times in fashion* or *take a look at fashion stores*. This factor was called active, modern (non-preserving) clothing lifestyle. The second factor represents an outer-oriented clothing lifestyle, summarizing the items

Sandra Diehl • Ralf Terlutter

interest in the fashion of other people, self-conscious with regard to fashion (reverse) and *ask for advice with regard to fashion* (for details, see Table 17:5).

Table 17:5 Factor analysis of clothing lifestyle

Statement	1	2	Interpretation of factor
Interest in fashion	.789		
No interest in fashion	-.774		*Active, modern (non-*
Moving with the times in fashion	.771		*preserving) clothing*
Take a look at fashion stores	.768		*lifestyle*
Try new clothing styles	.682		
Interest in the fashion of other people		.820	*Outer-oriented*
Self-conscious with regard to fashion		-.720	*clothing lifestyle*
Ask for advice with regard to fashion		.664	
Eigen Value	3.53	1.24	
Variance extracted (cum.)	44.2	59.7	

Principal Component Analysis, Rotation: Varimax (values below 0.3 were suppressed)

A hierarchical cluster analysis identified two clusters. Both factors contributed to characterizing the two-cluster solution. Cluster one is more active and modern and also more outer-directed with regard to clothing than cluster two. Cluster one is called the *active, modern and outer-directed clothing lifestyle group*, whereas cluster two is called the *passive, preserving and inner-oriented clothing lifestyle group*.

Table 17:6 Hierarchical cluster analysis of clothing lifestyle factors

Factor	Cluster 1 (n=94)	Cluster 2 (n=47)	Sig.
Active, modern clothing lifestyle	.496	-.993	.000
Outer-oriented clothing lifestyle	.286	-.571	.000
Interpretation	*active, modern and outer-oriented clothing lifestyle group*	*passive, preserving and inner-oriented clothing lifestyle group*	

Algorithm: Ward; Distance: Squared Euclid, values characterizing the groups are t-values

The cultural Lifestyle

With regard to cultural lifestyle, exploratory factor analysis extracted three factors that had an eigen value > 1. The factors explained 62.8 % of the total variance. Factor one summarizes the items *cultural*

322

initiative, have fun at cultural events and *frequent visits to cultural events,* showing an *active cultural lifestyle.* Factor two was named *outer-oriented educational cultural lifestyle.* This factor combines the items *importance of cultural education in society, like cultural education myself* and *classically oriented regarding culture.* Factor three integrates the items *rejection of today's music styles* and *modern culture* (reverse) and represents a *preserving cultural lifestyle.* However, it should be mentioned that the last-mentioned factor is mainly determined by the item *rejection of today's music styles.*

Table 17:7 Factor analysis of cultural lifestyle

Statement	1	2	3	Interpretation of factor
Cultural Initiative	.817			*Active cultural lifestyle*
Have fun at cultural events	.772			
Frequent visits to cultural events	.748			
Importance of cultural education in society		.779		*Outer-oriented educational cultural lifestyle*
Like cultural education myself	.347	.748		
Classically oriented regarding culture		.680	.396	
Rejection of today's music styles			.824	*Preserving cultural lifestyle*
Modern culture			-.461	
Eigen Value	2.73	1.18	1.12	
Variance extracted (cum.)	34.1	48.8	62.8	

Principal Component Analysis, Rotation: Varimax (values below 0.3 were suppressed)

Again a hierarchical cluster analysis was performed. A two-cluster solution was extracted. Cluster one (n=91) is more active and clearly more traditional with regard to cultural activities than cluster two (n=50). There were no significant differences with regard to the factor outer-oriented cultural lifestyle (for details, see Table 17:8). Cluster one was called the *active and preserving cultural lifestyle group,* cluster two the *passive and non-preserving cultural lifestyle group.*

Regarding the extracted lifestyle groups, it can be assumed that the lifestyle dimension activity is related to the dimensions non-preserving and outer-directed. This is valid for the living and clothing lifestyles. The cultural lifestyle consists of two groups: an active and preserving cultural lifestyle group, and a passive and non-preserving cultural lifestyle group. This can be explained by the fact that people who do not like cultural offers, such as classical museums and exhibitions, are more passive with regard to cultural activities and therefore probably

Sandra Diehl • Ralf Terlutter

Table 17:8 Hierarchical cluster analysis of cultural lifestyle factors

Factor	Cluster 1 (n=91)	Cluster 2 (n=50)	Sig.
Active cultural lifestyle	.131	-.238	.036
Outer-oriented educational cultural lifestyle	-.001	.003	.817
Preserving cultural lifestyle	.559	-1.018	.000
Interpretation	*active and preserving cultural lifestyle group*	*passive and non-preserving cultural lifestyle group*	

Algorithm: Ward; Distance: Squared Euclid, values characterizing the groups are t-values

do not visit cultural events, whereas the culturally active people like the classical cultural offers and are therefore more active. Preserving in the cultural area was understood as liking classical music and classical cultural offers.

In the following, it is analyzed whether personality or the product-specific lifestyles are superior for segmenting the recipients of advertising. The analyses are based on the different groups that were extracted.

Using ANOVA, the influence of the personality groups and the influence of the different product-specific lifestyle groups on the evaluation of the advertisements (on the variables Aad and purchase intention) are analyzed. It is tested whether or not the different groupings lead to differences in the evaluation of the advertisements. It is expected that the product-specific lifestyle is able to explain differences in the evaluation of the advertisement which corresponds to the relevant lifestyle.

Personality

The results for personality are shown in Table 17:9.

The results of the ANOVA for the personality groups showed that the different personality groups did not differ significantly in their attitudes toward the four ads nor in their purchase intentions. The groups based on personality do not show any influence on the evaluation of the different advertisements.

Table 17:9 ANOVA personality groups and evaluation of ads

Ad	Variable	Personality group 1	Personality group 2	Personality group 3	Sig.
Ad 1 (Living)	Aad$_1$ (Living)	3.07	3.09	3.63	.367
	Intention$_1$ (Living)	2.60	2.62	2.75	.920
Ad 2 (Clothing)	Aad$_2$ (Clothing)	3.26	3.20	3.69	.479
	Intention$_2$ (Clothing)	2.63	2.47	2.50	.835
Ad 3 (Culture)	Aad$_3$ (Culture)	2.34	2.15	2.31	.723
	Intention$_3$ (Culture)	2.13	1.81	1.75	.324
Ad 4 (Social)	Aad$_4$ (Social)	3.80	3.45	4.25	.081
	Intention$_4$ (Social)	3.50	3.09	3.67	.211

Living Lifestyle

The results for living lifestyle are shown in Table 17:10.

Table 17:10 ANOVA living lifestyle groups and evaluation of ads

Ad	Variable	Living lifestyle group 1	Living lifestyle group 2	Sig.
Ad 1 (Living)	**Aad$_1$ (Living)**	**3.41**	**2.84**	**.022**
	Intention$_1$ (Living)	**2.97**	**2.22**	**.001**
Ad 2 (Clothing)	Aad$_2$ (Clothing)	3.54	3.00	**.025**
	Intention$_2$ (Clothing)	2.58	2.52	.837
Ad 3 (Culture)	Aad$_3$ (Culture)	2.24	2.29	.840
	Intention$_3$ (Culture)	1.92	2.02	.665
Ad 4 (Social)	Aad$_4$ (Social)	3.75	3.69	.793
	Intention$_4$ (Social)	3.51	3.19	.201

The ANOVA for living lifestyle shows that living lifestyle is suitable for explaining differences in the attitude toward the ad for furniture (Aad$_1$ (living); sig. = .022) as well as in the intention to purchase the product (Intention$_1$ (living); sig. = .001).

Living lifestyle cannot be used to predict differences in the evaluation of the cultural or social ad. Concerning the clothing ad

$(\text{Aad}_2 \text{ (clothing)})$, living lifestyle shows significant differences in the attitude toward the clothing ad $(\text{Aad}_2 \text{ (clothing)}; \text{sig.} = .025)$.

Clothing Lifestyle

The results for clothing lifestyle are shown in Table 17:11.

Table 17:11 ANOVA clothing lifestyle groups and evaluation of ads

Ad	Variable	Clothing lifestyle group 1	Clothing lifestyle group 2	Sig.
Ad 1 (Living)	Aad_1 (Living)	3.48	2.48	**.000**
	Intention_1 (Living)	2.90	2.09	**.000**
Ad 2 (Clothing)	**Aad_2 (Clothing)**	**3.55**	**2.79**	**.002**
	Intention_2 (Clothing)	**2.83**	**2.15**	**.009**
Ad 3 (Culture)	Aad_3 (Culture)	2.15	2.47	.184
	Intention_3 (Culture)	1.98	1.94	.861
Ad 4 (Social)	Aad_4 (Social)	3.80	3.55	.290
	Intention_4 (Social)	3.56	2.98	**.024**

The ANOVA for clothing lifestyle shows significant differences for the clothing ad regarding the Aad_2 (clothing) (sig. = .002) and the Intention_2 (Clothing) (sig. = .009). The clothing lifestyle is also capable of predicting differences in the evaluation of the Aad_1 (Living) (sig. = .000) and the Intention_1 (Living) (sig. = .000). The clothing lifestyle also explains differences in the behavioral intentions toward the social ad $(\text{Intention}_4$ (Social); (sig. = .024)).

Like living lifestyle, the product-specific clothing lifestyle is suitable for the segmentation of recipients of advertising in the specific product category clothes. For the prediction of evaluations of the other advertisements, clothing lifestyle can only be considered partially suitable. There seems to be some relationship between living lifestyle and clothing lifestyle. However, clothing lifestyle is not suitable for explaining culture-specific behavior nor the attitude toward the social ad $(\text{Aad}_4$ (Social)).

Cultural Lifestyle

The results for cultural lifestyle are shown in Table 17:12.

Table 17:12 ANOVA culture lifestyle groups and evaluation of ads

Ad	Variable	Cultural lifestyle group 1	Cultural lifestyle group 2	Sig.
Ad 1 (Living)	$Aad_{1\ (Living)}$	3.29	2.88	.105
	$Intention_{1\ (Living)}$	2.64	2.60	.891
Ad 2 (Clothing)	$Aad_{2\ (Clothing)}$	3.33	3.21	.623
	$Intention_{2\ (Clothing)}$	2.66	2.35	.241
Ad 3 (Culture)	$Aad_{3\ (Culture)}$	**2.42**	**1.96**	**.048**
	$Intention_{3\ (Culture)}$	**2.16**	**1.60**	**.018**
Ad 4 (Social)	$Aad_{4\ (Social)}$	3.80	3.55	.331
	$Intention_{4\ (Social)}$	3.56	2.98	.976

As could be shown using ANOVA, the cultural lifestyle groups are suitable for explaining differences in the variables $Aad_{3\ (Culture)}$ (sig. = .048) and $Intention_{3\ (Culture)}$ (sig. = .018). There were neither significant differences in attitudes toward the other advertisements nor in the intentions. Consequently, the culture-specific lifestyle explains only individual differences between the recipients with regard to culture-specific intentions and the advertisement from the cultural area.

Discussion

The most important research question in this study was to assess whether the personality or the product-specific lifestyle is more suitable for segmenting recipients of advertisements. Table 17:13 shows a summary of the results.

In all of the advertisements used in this study, the groups based on personality did not show any differences in the attitudes toward the ad and in the behavioral intentions. Consequently, personality does not seem to be a suitable variable for explaining differences either in the attitudes toward the ads or in the purchase intentions. Personality based on the Five-Factor Model (FFM) is therefore not a suitable variable for segmentation in advertising.

These findings correlate with results from consumer behavior showing that there are many inconsistencies when the prediction of behavior based on personality traits is investigated. Though personality could be ascertained in quite a consistent manner (*McCrae*, 1982, p.

Table 17:13 Summary of results for personality and the product-specific lifestyles

Advertisement		Personality 3 groups	Product-specific Lifestyle		
			Living 2 groups	Clothing 2 groups	Cultural 2 groups
Ad$_1$ (living)	Aad	n.s.	.022	.000	n.s.
	Intention	n.s.	.001	.000	n.s.
Ad$_2$ (clothing)	Aad	n.s.	.025	.002	n.s.
	Intention	n.s.	n.s.	.009	n.s.
Ad$_3$ (culture)	Aad	n.s.	n.s.	n.s.	.048
	Intention	n.s.	n.s.	n.s.	.018
Ad$_4$ (social)	Aad	n.s.	n.s.	n.s.	n.s.
	Intention	n.s.	n.s.	.024	n.s.

300), the behavior that persons showed in different situations has not been highly consistent and could therefore not be predicted by personality traits (e.g. *Wright* and *Mischel*, 1987). This phenomenon is often referred to as consistency paradox (e.g. *Mischel*, 1990, pp. 128-129). The research on the person-situation debate (*Kenrick* and *Funder*, 1988) showed that personality is more suitable for predicting human behavior on a general level, but that personality is less suitable for predicting behavior in specific situations.

The product-specific lifestyle turned out to be the superior variable for the explanation of individual differences. Regarding the Aad and the purchase intentions, there were significant differences among the lifestyle groups for all of the three ads (living, clothing and culture). The product-specific lifestyle is therefore suitable for segmenting consumers for communication in the specific product area.

The results show that living lifestyle and clothing lifestyle are closely related. A Chi^2 Test confirmed that living lifestyle and clothing lifestyle are not independent (Chi^2 = 12.03; sig. = .000). Further Chi^2 Tests analyzing the relationships between the other groupings did not show any significant findings.

The measurement of the product-specific lifestyle by the three 2nd order dimensions *outer-orientation*, *preserving* and *activity* has proven its worth. Exploratory factor analyses extracted the three dimensions for living lifestyle and for cultural lifestyle. Only the analysis of clothing lifestyle extracted two factors, with the dimensions activity and modernism (non-preserving) loaded on one factor. However, all in all, the results indicate that the application of the three 2nd order dimensions of lifestyle is useful and it would appear possible for them to replace complex lifestyle analyses. This is especially the case when besides lifestyle other variables relevant to marketing have to be ascertained (e.g. evaluation of advertisements, behavioral intentions etc.).

A closer look at the characterization of the lifestyle groups shows that cluster analysis identifies groups that combine the dimensions *non-preserving/modern* and *outer-oriented.* This is valid for the living and clothing lifestyles. This may be an explanation for the fact that activity and modernism loaded on one factor in the analysis of clothing lifestyle.

Cultural lifestyle shows another structure when characterizing the groups. It consists of two groups: an active and preserving cultural lifestyle group and a passive and non-preserving cultural lifestyle group. Culture evokes the picture of a classical museum and classical music, at least in Germany. People who do not like classical cultural offers, such as museums and exhibitions, are non-preserving with regard to culture and do not visit the offered events (passivity). The culturally active individual, however, likes classical cultural offers and as a consequence is culturally active and preserving.

Further Research

Though the study has shown that the product-specific lifestyle.is more suitable for market segmentation than personality, there are still many directions for further research.

Personality was analyzed in its entirety using the Five-Factor Model (FFM) and did not show any influence on the four advertisements. These findings match with other results of research in consumer behavior. However, it might be possible that other individual personality traits not included in this study do influence the evaluation of the advertisements.

Though the study was able to show for three different products that the product-specific lifestyle is suitable for market segmentation, it is necessary to test the suitability of the product-specific lifestyle for other products (e.g. for food, home appliances, cars etc.).

Despite the fact that the three 2nd order dimensions could be extracted for the product categories living and culture, there is still need for research. The 2nd order dimensions should be transferred to other product categories.

The study showed that the individuals with high distinction on the dimensions active, outer-oriented and modern were often combined in one group. This result should be verified for additional product-specific lifestyles. Where this result can be found in other product-specific lifestyles as well, this might be a hint that there are – independent of the product – usually two fundamental target groups. One group is active, outer-oriented and modern, the other group is passive, inner-oriented and more preserving. Even if these groups can be extracted in a similar way for different product categories, there are not always the same individuals in these two groups. Consequently, it is possible that a person is active, outer-oriented and modern in their living lifestyle but passive, inner-directed and more traditional in another product-specific lifestyle.

Furthermore, it should be tested how lifestyle might be integrated in a model of advertising and how lifestyle influences other variables within the model. Due to the complexity of other variables we investigated, we were restricted to testing the influence of lifestyle on the Aad and the intention to purchase the product or service.

Additional variables that might be important to explain individual differences in the evaluation of advertising (e.g. intercultural differences) should be taken into consideration in further – international – studies.

Summary

In this study, the importance of considering individual predispositions of the recipient for the analysis of advertising effectiveness could be proven. The study compared the explanatory power of personality and three different product-specific lifestyles (living lifestyle, clothing lifestyle, cultural lifestyle) for the evaluation of four different print advertisements (furniture, clothes, a cultural institution and a social issue). Personality was not able to evoke any differences in the evaluation of the four ads (Aad and purchase intention), but the product-specific lifestyle was able to evoke differences in the evaluation of those ads that correspond to the specific product category. This could be shown for all three product categories. Therefore, the product-specific lifestyle can be considered as a suitable variable for market segmentation in advertising.

18

Television advertising and children: A global perspective

HANNE NISS

Abstract

This chapter presents the findings of a Danish study of children's TV commercials from 2002. The aims of the research were to document what types of products are being advertised to children on Danish TV and to analyse the contextual characteristics and executional techniques used to attract and retain children's attention. The findings indicate that Danish children are targeted by much the same commercial messages and forms of address as adult viewers. These findings correspond with recent trends observed in children's culture where it has been documented that the audiences for commercial messages are becoming ever younger as companies worldwide market an increasingly wide range of products to children. Through a discussion of these trends, the chapter discusses the challenges for academics and practitioners of bringing the increasing commercialisation of children's culture into our perspectives on advertising to children.

Introduction

Television provides one of the most powerful media for the transmission of commercial messages to children. (Postman, 1985) refers to television as a curriculum, "a specially constructed information system whose purpose is to influence, teach, train or cultivate the mind and character of youth". Like a curriculum, television contains information about the world we live in and acts as a vehicle of socialisation where knowledge about social roles and cultural values is acquired. According to (Reece et al., 1999), the average child in the Western part of the world spends as much or more time watching TV during a year than he or she spends in the classroom. Hence, television may be considered one of the primary influences in shaping children's values and understanding of the world.

From the advertiser's point of view, television offers unique possibilities for reaching a young audience. Children love films and television and any moving pictures with sound. They kindle their imagination and bring into play many more of their senses than do the written word or still-life pictures. Consequently, television is an extremely powerful medium for getting commercial messages across to children.

For many companies, children and young people represent important target groups - both in terms of the products they can buy with their own money and with respect to the influence they exert on their parents' consumption but also in terms of instilling future consumer patterns at an early age. As a result, ever-younger age groups are being targeted by commercial messages. The global television industry is at the centre of this commercialisation. The development of products linked to children's films and television shows ensures that there is an international marketplace for media products, and children are a key segment of this market.

Children's media culture and advertising

One of the driving forces behind the increasing commercialisation of children's media has been the rise of privatised commercial television around the world, coupled with the growth of satellite and cable TV, and the concomitant decline in public broadcasting systems. Children from a wide range of countries now have access to the Teenage Mutant Ninja Turtles, the Power Rangers, and the Pokemons via television, the internet, video games, movies and a whole range of toy products, comic books, clothing and children's furnishings. Programmes that link television characters to toy products are becoming increasingly common around the globe. The fact that television programme characters are created with an eye towards their marketing potential as toys is only part of the entire marketing strategy that has developed over the past decade. Starting from the premise that children like the familiar and recognizable, the creation of children's programming – which used to be based on children's books, fairy tales or films, such as the highly successful Disney movies – can be seen as an elaborated manifestation of providing children with something familiar. Now the simultaneous production of children's television shows and their toy-related characters is supported and reinforced through traditional product licensing, character appearances at shopping malls, cinemas and holiday events, movie appearances, and a host of new technology toys including home video games, story tapes, and home computer software. Since many of these television characters and accompanying products are marketed on a global scale, they are difficult to escape.

What is developing is something quite unique to the new electronic age: a network of interrelated narrative texts, or media products, constructed around a pop cultural figure or a group of figures. In addition to the Turtles, the Power Rangers and the Pokemons, there are such television and film characters as the Simpsons, the Smurfs, and the Moppets of the American television programme, Sesame Street. Such icons can be real people, too, such as Madonna or the Spice Girls. By intentionally marketing to even the very young children, this interrelated network of cultural products based on pop icons has contributed to a pervasive commercialisation of children's culture. Around the world, children are being trained to become part of an interconnected consumer group, who identify with, collect and play together with the same toys[1]. Even educational television programmes are utilising the same marketing strategies of developing an

---

[1] In an interesting paper on the global success of the Japanese Pokemon game, Ellen Seiter (1999) notes that these products, without intentionally setting out to do so, actually encouraged an increase in inter-ethnic group play across the US when the products were first introduced on the American market in 1999. In Southern California, where Korean, Taiwanese, and Japanese children are frequently excluded by Anglo-American kids, their understandings of the game and memorisation of the Pokemon hagiography made way for new social groupings. Thus Pokemon seems to actually bring children together who would not normally interact, in part because of its "strangeness" due to its retention of Japanese cultural characteristics, but also because of the diversity of the characters in the play which seem to appeal across gender, age, and ethnicity.

interconnected collection of various media, toy and other products to sustain and support the television programmes.

Global advertising and regulatory environment

Because of the growing impact of commercial television and advertising on children's lives, there has been recurring public concern about the social effects of advertising on children. The basic rules issued by The International Chamber of Commerce governing advertising contain special provisions concerning advertising to children. They are necessary in view of children's lack of experience and their gullibility. Within the EU, the individual member states must comply with certain minimum standards regarding broadcast advertising to children, as defined in the EU directive "Television without Frontiers" (Commission of the European Communities, 2001). However, national legislation and practices vary a great deal with respect to the restrictions imposed on advertisers. In Britain, for example, advertisements during programmes are allowed, whereas in Denmark advertising is restricted to designated time blocks between programmes.

Although Denmark was one of the last countries in Europe to introduce commercial television, the amount of broadcast advertising in Denmark has increased significantly since1988 when the first Danish commercial television channel, TV2, was launched. Since then, an increasing number of commercial TV channels, including cable and satellite TV, have become available to Danish viewers. With the number of children's TV programmes continually growing, there has been a concomitant increase in advertising targeted specifically at children. The content of these commercials, and the form in which they are presented, are important to study considering the powerful medium that advertising is.

Theories of influence

Much of the early work on children and television advertising was based on Piaget's theory of cognitive development. According to his theory, there will be age-related differences in children's ability to attend to, process and remember things (Ginsburg & Opper, 1979).

These differences stem from different ways of thinking by children of different ages. Younger children have more limited communication skills than older children, and they tend to focus on a single, perceptually salient feature of an object or event. As children get older, they decentrate their perceptions, understand concepts of class inclusion (e.g., product categories), and use various quantitative skills.

Another theory that has often been applied to studies dealing with consumer socialisation of children is social learning theory. According to this theory, children learn behaviours which are considered appropriate through observations of others, such as parents or teachers as well as through characters or role models in the media. Research on social learning theory supports the view that children learn by imitation, as children learn what behaviours and roles are expected of them by observing others' behaviour being reinforced or punished. Seeing someone being reinforced for a behaviour, such as a girl playing with a doll being reinforced for nurturing, may be interpreted as being what is appropriate for girl, thus reinforcing modelled (female) behaviour. Similarly, a male may be seen being reinforced for being aggressive on a TV commercial, which may create an association between aggression and proper male behaviour.

Literature review

Advertisements and the values they promote are often described as a reflection of culture, (Pollay, 1986). However, advertisements do not simply reflect culture, they also help construct culture. For example, boys' commercials often depict boys with vehicles and building equipment, constructing models, taking apart and re-assembling objects, and working with science and math-based toys. These types of toys may help a child to learn about manipulating movement, which develops mathematics and spatial skills. Girls' commercials, on the other hand, depict girls with dolls, housekeeping equipment and products relating to vanity, which develop nurturing skills (Miller, 1987). Such sex role information, instilled in children at an important formative stage of their socialisation, may have long lasting implications. The kinds of toys, and activities which are considered appropriate for girls and boys, respectively, are conveyed through television commercials. If children are exposed to such information during a period of gender identity formation, a stage of development in which children actively seek information about what is appropriate for their sex, there may be a tendency to hold stereotypical views about what types of roles and activities boys and girls should identify with. In a study by (Ruble, Balaban, & Cooper, 1981), children were more likely to avoid a toy if they were shown a child of the opposite sex playing with it in a TV toy commercial. (Greenfield, 1984) has concluded that children who are heavy television viewers have a more stereotypical view of sex roles than do light viewers, predict stereotypical adult jobs for themselves and give more stereotypical answers to questions about gender and gender roles.

Males and females in children's television commercials are present in dramatically different numbers (Sternglanz & Serbin, 1974). Although females make up 51% of the population, the world of television commercials is made up of 39% females (Riffe, Goldson, Saxton & Yu, 1987). When women are portrayed, they are most often talking to someone, such as a child, or something, such as a pet, in a subordinate position (Lovdal, 1989). Even greater differences appear when analysing the use of male or female spokespersons and voice-overs in commercials. In a study by O'Donnell & O'Donnell from 1978, 93% of the commercials used male voice-overs. In a similar study from1992, it was found that nearly 81% of the non-programme spots used male voices, while commercials using female voices were mostly for dolls, accessories, and stuffed animals (Hillyer, 1992). These data suggest that although the presence of females in television commercials has increased since 1978, children's television advertising remains predominantly male.

Another area of interest to be considered is differences in the creative form utilised in commercials aimed at boys and girls, respectively. In a study by (Welch et al., 1979) on the different production techniques for both boys' and girls' ads, it was found that boys' commercials had higher level of inanimate action and more variability in the form of changes to new scenes than the girls' or neutral commercials, in which both boys and girls were present. Boys' and neutral commercials had higher rates of cuts, while the girls' contained more fades and dissolves. Female characters did very little talking in the neutral commercials; however, they talked a lot in the girls' commercials. (Welch et al., 1979) suggest that females are deferent and do not speak when males are around; however, they are talkative and authoritative when males are absent. Boys' commercials also contained more noise: vocalisation, sound effects and foreground music, while girls' commercials contained more background music, conveying images of softness, gentleness and slow gradual change.

Research questions

The following study sought to expand on past research in the area of gender stereotypes and children's television and to provide new information on questions relating to the increasing commercialisation of children's culture as reflected in the range of products advertised to children on commercial TV. In addition, the study sought to examine the forms of address employed in commercials aimed at child audiences in Denmark. To the extent that children's ways of perceiving things and communicating with others differ from those of adults, do advertisers employ a simple, educational language when addressing children, or do they address children as miniature adults by using the same codes as those used in commercials aimed at adult audiences?

This led to the formulation of the following research questions:

1. What types of products are marketed to children in Danish children's TV commercials?
2. How are existing stereotypes of gender reproduced in the commercials' messages communicated to children?
3. What executional techniques and forms of address are used to capture children's attention and encourage them to retain the message?

The research included viewing current children's TV commercials, observing the types of products marketed, the executional form in which the commercial messages were communicated, and the cultural messages and stereotypes contained in them.

Methodology

Sample

The sample used consisted of 210 children's TV commercials, which were videotaped during Saturday and Sunday morning cartoons in March 2002. The networks included in the sample were TV2 (Danish) and TV3 (Scandinavian/Danish). The taping was spread over several weeks in order to avoid extensive repetition and to locate a wider variety of commercials than might have been the case if all of the taping had been done in a single week. Nevertheless, there was considerable commercial repetition.

A list was made of all the commercials recorded. All product ads and public service announcements (PSAs) were tallied, but not station promotional messages. From this list, duplicate commercials were identified and later removed from the sample. One example of each commercial was then copied onto another tape to facilitate the analysis of more detailed information. This resulted in a sample of 80 different commercials. Almost all the commercials were 30-second spots, all in colour.

Coding

A preliminary coding sheet was developed and tested on an initial sample of ten commercials. As a result of this test, some additional categories of responses to existing items were added. Since one of the aims of the study was to identify the types of products being marketed to children on Danish TV channels, data on product category was important to collect. Initially, a detailed list of product categories was produced, but for reasons of simplicity they were later condensed to match six broad categories (see the Results section below).

Because contextual features of ads (attractive models, upbeat music, quick cuts, and high activity) have been found to influence the effectiveness of ads (Goldberg, Gorn, and Gibson, 1978), data on some of these creative and executional dimensions were included as well. Emphasis was placed on objective measures of ad characteristics rather than subjective assessments of personality traits or values expressed.

Social learning theory suggests that model characteristics help to attract attention. In particular, special presenters such as celebrities or ad-created central characters influence brand recall (Rossiter & Percy, 1997). Hence the study sought to document the number of celebrities that appeared in the commercials, the gender of characters in each commercial, and finally whether the characters were animated or real.

Male voices have been found to attract attention better than female voices and are perceived as more objective (ibid: 266). Thus data were collected on the gender of voice-over presenters in the commercials as well as the number of male and female actors that appeared in the commercials.

Background music may enhance the effectiveness of commercials, and jingles may increase brand recall, especially among children (ibid: 222 and 283). Consequently, it was noted whether a jingle or background music appeared in the commercials.

Finally, it was noted how children are being addressed by advertisers, i.e. the form of language accompanying the visual messages.

Results

Table 18:1 shows the product categories observed in the commercials in numbers and as a percentage of the total number of commercials. The greatest proportion of commercials was for restaurant and food products (36.2%), followed by toys (18.8%) and technology and media products (16.2%). Finally, 11.2% (9) of the commercials were for games and sports-related products, 11.2% (9) for clothing and personal care products, and 6.2% (5) of the commercials were for holiday destinations and/or events.

There were 140 individuals included in the 80 children's TV commercials that were viewed. Of the 140, 41% (58) of the individuals were female, while 59% (82) were male. Voice-over announcers were almost exclusively male. Included in the sample were 12 commercials which contained only animated or cartoon characters. These were not considered representative of either sex (see Table 18:2).

The typical commercial featured real people or animals, with both children and adults, either male or female or of the same sex. However, animated or cartoon characters appeared, alone or with real people, in nearly half the ads (Table 18:2). Thus it appears that characters in commercials for children are deliberately selected to be appealing and recognisable to children.

Table 18:1 Types of products advertised as a percentage of total sample (N=80).

Product Category	Percentage	Number
Restaurants/food	36.2	29
Toys	18.8	15
Technology/media products	16.2	13
Sports/games	11.2	9
Clothing/personal care products	11.2	9
Holiday destinations/events	6.2	5

Background music was common, whereas jingles were less frequent. Celebrities were rarely used, except in the sports and games commercials which featured well-known sports stars such as the English football player David Beckham, and the American basketball player Michael Jordan. Finally, a large number of ads used multiple settings and quick cuts, noted earlier as attention getting.

Discussion

The results gathered from this study correspond with previous research performed in the domain of gender stereotypes and children's TV.

Prior research by Riffe et al. (1989) found that the world of television was made up of 39% females, while society is actually comprised of 51% females. The research performed in this study shows the world of children's advertising as being made up of 41% female, which - although it is slightly higher than 39% - still does not reach the actual percentage of women in society.

Table 18:2 Contextual characteristics of commercials

Characteristic	Number
Type of actor	
Real people or animals	37
Animated or cartoon characters	12
Real and cartoon characters	25
Other	6
Gender representation	
Male	82
Female	58
Total number of actors	140
Type of celebrity actor	
Real actor or athlete	7
Fictional character	5
Gender of celebrity actor	
Male	5
Female	2
Voice-over Announcer	
Male	56
Female	12
Type of Music	
Background	64
Jingle	10
Other sound effects	6

Research by Miller (1987) has shown that commercials aimed at girls most often depict females as playing with dolls, housekeeping equipment and with products associated with vanity, while boys' commercials contain vehicles, building equipment, objects that can be taken apart and reassembled, and science and math-based toys. The results of the present study correspond with past research, as nearly half of the females in the sample were found in the clothing/personal care products category, which portrayed females most often as mothers in a home-setting. In contrast, nearly one-third of the males were found in the technology/media products category or in the toys category and then typically playing with action figures or similarly male-oriented products. Overall, the roles and occupations in which the individuals were found portrayed a rather conventional image of gender identity for both sexes. Although there were a few instances of females in situations or settings that may be stereotypical of males, such as aggressive sports activities, the overall number of females who actually participated in activities which require independence and leadership was relatively low.

More than three quarters of the commercials containing background music and gradual changes of scenes were exclusively female. The form in which these commercials are depicted communicates a strong message. The stereotypes of females as being gentle, serene and inactive are all present here. The slow jingles that accompany girls playing with their dolls, and the lack of change or slow change of scenes, along with the enchantment with a doll or with making oneself beautiful, appeared very fulfilling to the females in the commercials. Males' commercials, on the other hand, showed substantially more noise, frequent change of scenes (quick cuts) and higher activity. Males were almost never portrayed indoors and when they were, they were working on computers or some ingenious science experiment. Male commercials exhibited frequent violence and/or aggression, while female commercials typically exhibited nurture, domesticity, and vanity.

The forms of address used in the television commercials examined in this study fall into three categories. Some commercials address children as simpler versions of adults. They are communicated to by means of a code that is stripped of much of the natural intonation and non-verbal characteristics of normal adult-to-adult conversations. The language used is simple and distinct enough to merit parody. The image of children that this form of address builds on is a perception of children as in need of education, as different from and somehow "less" than adults. Other commercials treat children as "kids", as a source of amusement for grown-ups watching, including the men behind the cameras. In these commercials, children are communicated to in a code that is fast, idiomatic and loaded with non-verbal and prosodic features. The inherent image seems to be that kids are streetwise and should be treated as fun. The third and largest proportion of the commercials, however, address children as miniature adults, employing much the same codes and creative techniques as those employed in commercials aimed at adult audiences. This result is not surprising in light of the types of products that are advertised on children's TV as many of these are also marketed to adult audiences. The question is whether children understand and interpret these strategies of address as relevant and meaningful in their own universe. These questions need to be researched further in the future.

Conclusion

The past 25 years have seen media industries move their targets increasingly downward, first to preadolescents, then to children in elementary school and younger. This trend is also reflected in Danish television advertising where an increasing number of commercials are directed at young children.

All this has created a remarkably commercialised children's culture. Importantly, it is not just that children are the target of advertising messages for cereals, cell phones and computer software on commercial TV, it is rather that commercialisation dominates an ever more significant part of their media and play culture. Hence, an important task for future research is to study the impact of the global media industry on children's culture and media consumption. To what extent is children's television being homogenized for the sake of the marketplace? Will the need to make programmes that appeal to a global marketplace of children reduce the likelihood of creating children's programmes that are expressive of different languages, cultures, and ethnic groups? Also questions relating to problems of cross-cultural interpretation, the implications of a global children's mass culture, and the impact of global media on children's play culture are important to address in future research.

19

A Changed Picture of Children on Television

How and Why?

CECILIA VON FEILITZEN

This chapter presents a few findings of a comparative systematic content analysis of the whole television output in Sweden in the early 80s when we had only two national public service channels without advertising (SVT1 and SVT2), and in the mid-90s when we also had commercial television channels (with advertising). The television output of the mid-90s in the study is represented by four channels – the two national traditional public service channels and the two most widespread new commercial channels. One of the commercial channels (TV4) is a terrestrial public service-channel reaching the whole population, whereas the other is the most watched satellite channel (TV3, also Swedish-speaking) reaching about 60% of the population.

The aim of the research project[1] is to analyse how children are constructed on television – or, more precisely, to analyse the *repeated patterns* of the constructions of children compared to those of youths and adults – in order to find out if there are any signs of change over time.

---

[1] Cecilia von Feilitzen (in progress) *Children on Television.* Department of Journalism, Media and Communication, Stockholm University, Sweden.

Main questions

The basic questions to be answered by the two content analyses are, in brief:

- How *often* are children represented on television as a whole – compared to other age groups (youths, adults, the elderly)?

  Different kinds of representation are analysed, such as if the TV persons "exist" as *pictures*, as *sounds* (if their voices are heard), and/or as *referred to or talked about*. Thus, representations of TV persons also include, for example, adults talking about children and vice versa. Other kinds of representation studied include the persons' *significance* in the programme, and/or if they are portrayed by means of *photographic techniques* or as *animated figures*.

- *How* are children constructed?

  The aspects considered here include the TV persons' *demographic and socio-cultural characteristics*, their *relations* to, and *interactions* with, other persons on the screen, the *settings* in which they are portrayed, their *activities*, and their *feelings*.

Children are, pragmatically, defined as persons aged 0 to 15 years. However, the television persons were coded under smaller age groups – below 3 years of age, 3 to 6 years, 7 to 8 years, 9 to 12 years, 13 to 15 years (and different age groups among youths and adults) – which is why, for instance, 0- to 12-year-olds, preschoolers, school-aged children, etc., also can be singled out according to different aims of the analyses.

To be a person means in this context that he/she/it has a consciousness and ability to act as a subject. Not only human beings but also certain animals (above all personified animals) are television persons, as well as most imaginary figures and certain things. Persons may also be incorporeal or spiritual.

Cecilia von Feilitzen

Although the idea was to study the repeated patterns of the constructions of children (youths, adults) in all kinds of programmes (and also in transmissions between programmes, such as announcements, trailers etc), there were, naturally, also opportunities to compare the constructions between different genres (children's programming, news, fiction and so on) as well as between domestically produced programmes and programmes imported from other countries, between programmes broadcast during different periods of the day etc.

It is important to underline, however, that the sample in combination with the sampling technique (see under 'Samples and method' below) does *not* give a sufficient base for making separate analyses of children in *advertisements* as a specific genre.

Generally, the idea behind the project is to put forward hypotheses about *why* children on television are constructed in the way they are. Television output – as well as other media contents – is seen as a symbolic environment, as an increasingly important part of our culture. Persons, events and other phenomena are represented in this symbolic environment because in some respects they are considered more relevant than persons, events and phenomena not represented there. Consequently, what is represented in media contents has some kind of weight or value.

But which factors are decisive for what is relevant to represent in the symbolic environment, for what carries weight or value? These factors have to do with media institutions, such as media policy and media economy. The factors also have to do with conceptions and purposes among media professionals; with genre and narrative traditions; and with the form and technology of the media. Moreover, expectations and viewing habits among the audiences play a role, at least in the long term, as do several economic, political, social and cultural conditions in society.

In relation to a single programme, the ambition and ideas of a special television producer are, of course, a prominent reason for how the persons and events are constructed in the programme. But when, as in this project, general, repeated patterns are studied, the role of other factors becomes more conspicuous. In fact, as will be shown in the following text, findings support the hypothesis that the policy and economy of the media institution, as well as ideology in society, are important factors for explaining the repeated patterns of child constructions in television output as a whole.

Samples and method

The samples comprise one week of television transmissions in 1982 and one week in 1995, including 1,628 and 1,239 television persons of all ages, respectively. Although the two weeks are differently composed,[2] comparisons with programme statistics for the respective year show that the samples are fairly representative.

The project is an independent part of a greater interdisciplinary research programme.[3] In line with Williams's focus on the sequential nature of television transmissions, the common view within the research programme was to see the television output as periods of time, or as a more or less continuous flow of materials carrying meanings. Consequently, a time-based sample of television transmissions (days/nights instead of programmes) and a time sampling of the units of analysis (in this case, persons) were used. From the continuous time flow (day/night), points of time were randomly sampled. Persons seen, heard and/or referred to during these points of time constitute a statistically representative sample of all persons "existing" on television that day/night – *taking the length of time the different persons "exist" on television into account.* Accordingly, our persons are *'time persons'* in contrast to television persons in content and text analyses where each person get the same weight independently of how long time he/she appears in the programme ('programme persons'). Although sampled from points of time, *the time persons have been described and interpreted with the whole programme as the context.* In other words, the programmes (announcements, trailers, etc.) constitute the units of context.[4]

---

[2] The week in 1982 is a composite one, where the weekdays are spread over the whole year, while the week in 1995 is a calendar week.

[3] The research programme *Images and Ideas on Television* started at the Centre of Mass Communication Research, Stockholm University, Sweden, in the early 1980s. Different research teams focused on different aspects of the same television output.

[4] For a more detailed account of the sampling method, see:
Gunnar Andrén, Cecilia von Feilitzen, Tove Holmqvist, Kjell Nowak, Sven Ross & Hans Strand (1986) *Forskningsprogrammet Televisionens idévärld.*

Cecilia von Feilitzen

The systematic content analyses used are mainly quantitative in nature, but as might be understood from what was said above, coding involved many and complicated hermeneutic processes, which is why a great deal of qualitative aspects are integrated in the content analyses as well.

Findings interpreted in theoretical perspectives

It is clear that the constructions of children on television in Sweden in the 90s are different from those in the 80s. In the 90s, there is proportionally much more fiction, and much more imported fiction, in the television output, due to the commercial channels that did not exist in the 80s. As for the constructions of children, this has had the following main consequences, according to the research findings:

- Children on television in the 90s are more "fictionalised" than youths and adults on television. In the 90s, 70% of all children on the TV channels studied appear in adult or children's fiction, whereas the proportion of all children in fiction in the 80s was only 10%. Even youths and adults are to a greater extent portrayed in fiction in the 90s, but compared to the percentage of children, the difference is not at all that large.

This fictionalisation of children has also resulted in a lesser diversity when it comes to TV children's nationality. The TV children in the 90s are almost only Swedes, from the U.S. or have no nationality at all – the nationality is levelled out, is not possible to decide.

Not only has the representation of children in the symbolic environment become more Americanised, ethnically less diverse or unclear, it has also changed heavily in the sense that the TV children's relations to and interactions with other people, as well as the settings in which the children are portrayed, have become more intimate and private. Society outside home has disappeared. In the 80s, children on Swedish television were portrayed both in the home, at pre-school or

Metod [The Research Programme 'Ideas and Images on Television': Method]. Centrum för masskommunikationsforskning, Stockholms universitet, MASS 10. Cecilia von Feilitzen, Hans Strand, Kjell Nowak & Gunnar Andrén (1989) "To Be or Not to Be in the TV World. Ontological and Methodological Aspects of Content Analysis", *European Journal of Communication,* Vol. 4: 1, pp. 11-32.

school, and in different cultural environments, that is in (Habermas's, 1962) words, both in the private, social and cultural spheres. Furthermore, in the 80s children's relations and feelings were mostly of a comfortable character and children were mainly interacting with other children on the screen, and, secondly, with their parents.

In the 90s, children are mostly portrayed only in the home environment, in the private sphere, and they are more often interacting with adults – not so much with their parents, but with adult friends and acquaintances. In addition, the TV children of the 90s more often express feelings, especially uncomfortable feelings, than TV children in the 80s, and they get into conflict more often, especially with adults.

Of course, problems and conflicts are necessary for the dramatic narrative. Other research shows, however, that conflicts in television drama, not least in U.S. television drama, of which Sweden imports a great deal, have increased over time (von Feilitzen, 1997). Why is that?

One explanation could be that the programmes indirectly reflect the circumstance that adults, young people and children in modern Western society have more roles to play than previously. Their role in society is not as given as before. If this explanation is correct, then their greater independence and uncertainty might increase the likelihood of tensions and conflicts in everyday life.

Another related interpretation is that children in the media, when they are represented, nowadays are more precocious and "adult-like", take more initiatives by themselves, more often protest against adults and, therefore, more often get into conflicts with adults. Such tendencies have been traced in American films and American sitcoms on television (von Feilitzen, 1997).

A third reason for the increased conflicts in fiction and drama, however, can be the increasing competition between the swelling numbers of TV channels. With the aim of keeping their market shares, authors and producers may include more conflicts, as well as violence, in the programmes, believing this to be of interest to the audience.

Cecilia von Feilitzen

The policy and economy of the media institution

Thus, there are striking differences between the constructions of children on television in Sweden in the 90s and the 80s. These differences are to a high degree dependent on the changing media landscape – the introduction and spread of new commercial channels with a different economy and policy than the economy and policy of the two national public service channels without advertising. Important to stress, however, is that the changed constructions of children are visible not only on the two commercial channels studied but also on the two traditional national public service channels. Even on these two channels, children are more often represented in fiction in the 90s (about 40% of all TV children) – not as often as on the two commercial channels (where almost all children are found in fiction) but more often than in the 80s (10%). This change in the two traditional channels may thus be a consequence of increased channel competition.

There are also other findings of the study that can be seen in this political economy perspective.

In the 80s, children were heavily underrepresented on television relative to their proportion of the population in society. Children aged 0-15 years made up 10% of all persons on television (compared to 20% of the population in Sweden). The younger the television children were the more they were underrepresented.

Although three quarters of all TV children in the 80s were portrayed in adult programming and one quarter in children's programming, children were well represented in children's programming but, compared to youths and adults, heavily underrepresented in adult programming (since there are many more adult programmes, composing 90% of the whole television output).

In the 90s, it seems that the proportion of children on television is even smaller than in the 80s. During the week studied, children aged 0-15 made up 7% of all persons on television (relative to 20% of the population in Sweden). Still, three quarters of the TV children were found in adult programmes and one quarter in children's programmes but, as a total, the proportion of children was smaller.

Thus this reduced total proportion of children can also be regarded as a consequence of media policy and media economy. Television nowadays appears to find children less relevant, give them a lower weight and value, not as an audience, but as persons worth representing, as persons important to listen to in the decision processes in society.

The ideology in society

Another approach than the political economy perspective, namely a general cultural ideological perspective, seems also fruitful to adopt in order to interpret the findings. The reason is that there are not only *different* constructions of children in the 90s compared to the 80s but also *stable*, recurrent structures in the symbolic environment. The most remarkable structure or repeated pattern over time is that children both in the 80s and in the 90s are heavily underrepresented. The same is true of the elderly and women, whereas men of productive ages are heavily over-represented.

The fact that certain population groups are underrepresented in media contents – something which is also valid for ethnic minority groups, persons holding low-income jobs etc. – and that other groups are over-represented – men, middle and upper classes, the majority population – is a result found in many content analyses all over the world. A widespread interpretation is that the underrepresented groups, which also often are portrayed in prejudiced and stereotyped manners, are regarded as groups of lower status and value in society in general, which means that culture, of which media make up an increasingly greater part, in this way reflects the power hierarchy of society and the cultural weight and value attributed to these groups.

Research indicates that, apart from children's programmes, children's books etc., children are underrepresented generally in all media output. There is only one exception – and that is in advertising, where children are relatively common (von Feilitzen & Andrén, 1984; Sebstrup, ????). This could thus reflect the fact that children in today's Western society, although naturally of great value to their parents, are not regarded important for *society* until they become grown-ups – with one exception, which is *consumption*. There is growing awareness that children in well-to-do countries and families control considerable amounts of money, both their own pocket money and, by virtue of their influence, their parents'. And advertising and marketing directly to children are rapidly increasing in many countries. In the United States, for example, corporations spent over US$12 billion in marketing to children in 1999, almost double the amount spent in 1992. Furthermore, in 1999 U.S. children were estimated to influence purchases totalling over US$500 billion a year (Center for Media Education).

In the research material, from both the 80s and 90s, the power structure in society is represented, including adults' domination of children. A reasonable hypothesis is that the symbolic environment has an ideological function of sustaining the relations of domination in society.

An objection to this reasoning might be that it is not justified or desirable that children are represented in all types of programme on television. It could be maintained, for example, that children ought not to be depicted in certain news items, in elite sports and in violent programmes, or that children should not participate in programmes broadcast later than 9.00 p.m., often regarded a "watershed" after which television stations could allow films for adults only, coarser violence, etc.

This objection is, however, not particularly weighty. It should be kept in mind that also persons referred to and talked about are included in the study. Thus, the findings also show that adult persons on television seldom talk about children. Furthermore, the question can be asked if it is reasonable that television output is composed in such a way that it makes insufficient room for children – and for the elderly, women, people belonging to the working class, and ethnic minorities – especially in light of the fact that children, the elderly and people in low societal positions watch more television than other population groups, and that all populations groups except the very young children mostly watch adult programming.

To sum up, the symbolic environment in the 90s compared with that in the 80s seems to be characterised both by stability and change and can be interpreted both from a perspective of ideology and power relations, and from a perspective of political economy of the media. These two perspectives are not opposed to each other but indicate two important factors in an interplay that jointly shape media contents, including the constructions of children.

A wider view

The findings can be seen in an even wider power perspective as well. The policy and economy of the media are closely interwoven with policy and economy in society as a whole. The findings of the research project show that, to a high degree, the symbolic environment in the 90s is a sign of important traits of media globalisation, inter-cultural power relations in the world, and the advancement of the market at the expense of a weakened state. Media contents may, consequently, be said to reflect power dynamics and fortify power hierarchies on another level than that valid for population groups. Satellite channels and many U.S. programmes in Sweden imply that structures in the dominant centres of globalisation, that is, business conglomerates, trans-national networks etc., are supported, and that the symbolic environment in Sweden to a greater and greater extent seems to reproduce values and directions of more and more global governing forces. In other words, the symbolic environment expresses and seems to legitimate power relations on a global level to a higher degree than previously.

These tendencies depend not only on the fact that Sweden has been flooded by satellite television owned by international media moguls and media conglomerates. There has also been a conscious political deregulation of media in Sweden since the early and mid-80s. And, as mentioned, it seems that the contents of the two national public service channels without advertising have also changed due to this increased competition and deregulation, at least when it comes to the constructions of children.

20

Low Involvement Processing

How advertising works at low attention levels

ROBERT HEATH

Abstract

This chapter explains the Low Involvement Processing model and discusses in detail the role of implicit learning. The effectiveness of advertising at low attention levels is illustrated by a case history of an advertising campaign which failed to achieve high levels of awareness and recall, but which nevertheless appeared to be able to shift brand attitudes.

A summary of the Low Involvement Processing model

The traditional view of advertising is that it *persuades* consumers to choose a particular brand, and models such as AIDA (Attention - interest - decision - action) were developed on the assumption that brand communication is able to influence what is essentially a rational decision. Crucial to this line of thinking is the idea that learning about brands is directly related to the amount of attention paid, and that advertising which gets a high level of attention, and communicates a strong motivating message, is by definition the most effective.

But this neat classification frequently does not fit with real life. Campaigns that achieve high levels of awareness and communication in pre-testing often turn out to be incapable of establishing a similar level of awareness and communication when run on air. Conversely, campaigns that appear to say nothing very tangible or relevant or new about a brand are often found to be highly effective.

Take for example the UK Renault Clio launch, which is generally regarded as the most successful small car launch *ever* in the UK. Introduced at a premium price in a recession, the TV campaign has been shown to have been a significant factor in the car's success (Tansey 1999). Yet all anyone could recall of the advertising were the two rather vapid characters who starred in it - 'Papa and Nicole' - flirting with their respective lovers. The success of campaigns like this points to the existence of a different mechanism by which advertising builds brand equity, and I believe this mechanism is Low Involvement Processing.

The key elements of the Low Involvement Processing model can be summarised as follows:

1. Because brands match each other's performance so swiftly, there is an underlying expectation amongst consumers that most reputable brands will perform very similarly. This deters them from trying to 'actively' find out about brand performance, and encourages them to use instinct and intuition to make brand decisions. Such intuitive decisions are strongly influenced by emotional 'markers'.

2. A direct consequence is that consumers do not expect to learn anything of real importance about brands from advertising, and are therefore not predisposed to pay much attention to it. In this low attentive state consumers make little use of cognitive processing and rely more on automatic learning processes such as implicit learning.

3. Implicit learning feeds into implicit memory, and implicit memory cannot analyse or re-interpret anything. All it can do is store what is perceived, and any simple conceptual meanings that attach to these perceptions. So messages that require a significant degree of cognitive interpretation will not to be 'received' by implicit learning.

4. Because implicit learning is automatic, it is used *every time an ad is seen or heard*. This means that each occasion on which an ad is processed at high involvement (and its content is mainly learned actively) is outnumbered five, ten, maybe even fifty times by the

occasions on which it is processed at low involvement (and its content mainly learned implicitly).

5. The unique nature of implicit learning means this type of processing does not create strong rational messages in our mind. Rather it creates powerful associations and conceptual ideas that - over time - link to the brand. These brand associations are not only extraordinarily enduring, but they can exert a powerful influence on intuitive decision-making if they succeed in triggering emotional markers.

Implicit Learning

Much of the evidence in support of the above points has been covered in previous papers (Heath 2000, Heath 2001), but one aspect not covered so thoroughly is implicit learning.

Low Involvement Processing takes place at low attention levels. In this state we use two types of learning: One is shallow cognitive processing, which is necessary to enable us to perform some important cognitive tasks such as registering brand names. Shallow cognitive processing is an inefficient learning mechanism, capable mainly of reinforcing existing beliefs (Petty & Cacioppo 1996). But alongside it there operates another, fully automated, wholly instinctive processing system known as implicit learning

Research into implicit learning and memory is difficult. You can easily find out *if* someone has learned something in the past, because if they know it they have learned it, and if they don't know it they haven't. But how do you identify if they learned it *actively* or *passively or implicitly*, given that much of the detailed memory of the learning event itself is likely to have been erased? It is not enough simply to say that an absence of explicit recall of the learning process means that it was acquired implicitly. It is necessary to establish whether the person I question knew they were learning what they were learning at the time when the learning took place.

For this reason most of the research that has been conducted into implicit learning has been carried out under experimental conditions in which implicit learning is facilitated by distraction or instructions that impede explicit learning. This type of research has demonstrated that advertising *can* be processed implicitly, and has shown that implicit processing has a measurable effect on attitudes both towards ads and towards brands. (Perfect and Askew 1994, Shapiro et al 1997, Shapiro & Krishnan 2001, etc.)

Translating these findings into real life is less easy. It remains the case that whilst implicit or incidental learning from advertising is *accepted* by the advertising community, it is still regarded as being a secondary effect, a mechanism of questionable value when it comes to making advertising effective. In the USA, the world's largest advertising market, the vast majority of practitioners still regard explicit, attentive processing as being the primary goal of advertising, and 'persuasion' as being its ultimate purpose. As Ambler writes (Ambler 2000):

> "The assumption that advertising equals persuasion is so ingrained in the U.S.A. that a challenge elicits much the same reaction as questioning your partner's parentage."

There are two powerful reasons for challenging this situation. The first is that persuasion demands attention, and attentive processing is becoming more difficult to achieve all the time. Consumers are becoming less and less interested in learning about brands, and more and more adept at avoiding the devices and strategies employed by advertisers to get their attention.

The second is that there is no empirical evidence of a correlation between attention paid to advertising and brand choice. Furthermore, there are many examples of campaigns and executions that have worked *without* achieving any exceptional level of recall or awareness. So to allow the supremacy of persuasive attention-getting advertising to be perpetuated is to devalue all other types of advertising.

In order to challenge the power of persuasion we have to show that advertising can influence brand choice equally well *without* achieving high levels of attention and without putting forward a rational, persuasive message. This we can do in three stages.

Stage 1 is to demonstrate that ads are processed more often implicitly than explicitly. This is not hard to support. Explicit learning takes place only when attention is paid to advertising. Implicit learning, on the other hand, takes place both when attention is paid *and* when it is *not* paid. Modern TV campaigns rely on multiple exposures (opportunities to see) and it has been shown that attention paid to advertising wanes with each exposure (Krugman 1971). Even if it had not, common sense dictates that no-one pays the same high level of attention to an ad they are familiar with every time it is repeated.

Stage 2 is to show that implicit learning is more durable than explicit learning. To do this I have to prove a link between implicit learning and implicit memory, and for the purposes of this chapter I will assert this as the *definition* of implicit memory, i.e. learning without knowing you are learning. Implicit memory defined in this way has been shown in a number of studies to be substantially more durable that explicit memory (Standing 1973, Allen & Reber 1980.)

Stage 3 is a little more complicated. Having insisted on a definitive link between implicit memory and implicit learning, I have to accept that the scope of implicit learning is limited by the scope of implicit memory. And implicit memory, as I discuss in the next section, is more limited than explicit memory.

The limitations of Implicit Memory

In this section I am going to summarise the properties of implicit memory and use them to analyse two UK ad campaigns. The first is the highly successful Renault Clio campaign mentioned earlier. The second is an almost equally well-known campaign for Citroen Xsara. This latter campaign, featuring the model Claudia Schiffer, achieved exceptional levels of awareness because as she walks down the stairs and gets into the car she takes all her clothes off. It is a classic example of advertising which achieved very high levels of attention and recall.

In a series of experiments in the late 80's and early 90's (Schacter 1996, p166-191), Daniel Schacter and Endel Tulving established that implicit memory works in two ways:

First, like all memory systems, it records what is *perceived*, that is, what is seen and heard. So when the Renault Clio ad mentioned earlier featured a French father and daughter flirting in the French countryside, implicit memory would have stored those characters and linked them to the Renault Clio. And when the Citroen Xsara ad featured Claudia Schiffer taking off her clothes, implicit memory would have stored her and linked her to the Citroen Xsara.

The second way Schacter and Tulving found implicit memory works is *conceptually*.   The Renault Clio ad showed people having clandestine meetings with their lovers, so implicit memory would have stored the concept 'sexy' and linked it with the Renault Clio. Likewise, the Citroen Xsara ad showed Claudia Schiffer taking off her clothes, so implicit memory would have stored the concept 'striptease' and linked it to the Citroen Xsara.

But perhaps the most important aspect of Schacter and Tulving's work is that these two things are *all* they found implicit memory could do.   What implicit memory cannot *not* do is 'reason', i.e. work out conclusions, which need to be interpreted. Direct evidence of this is provided by the stochastic independence between implicit memory and recall / recognition of words (Berry & Dienes 1991).

I believe this limitation is explained by the fact that implicit memory is subconscious and simply cannot make use of the full range of working memory which we use when we are actively concentrating. Whether this is the case or not, what implicit memory *cannot* do is analyse and understand complex messages in advertising. So it cannot work out the underlying message of the Renault Clio ad, which is that the car is just as comfortable and well-equipped as bigger cars. Likewise, it cannot work out that Claudia Schiffer is taking her clothes off because the Xsara is so well-equipped 'it's the only thing to be seen in'. Both these messages are beyond the power of implicit memory. We know that because the evidence from research was that both these messages were unknown to the vast majority of TV viewers. Of course, in the case of the Renault Clio this didn't matter, because the concept that the car was 'sexy' (and thus those who drive it were also sexy) was more than sufficiently motivating to make its launch a huge success. In the Citroen Xsara ad it *does* matter, because unless you understand why Claudia Schiffer is taking her clothes off then all you are left with is the rather dated sexist concept of using scantily-clad models to strip in order to sell cars. How motivating this was can be judged by the reported lack of sales success of what was apparently an extremely well-equipped car.

To summarise, the above outlines the case that Implicit Learning happens *more often* than Explicit Learning, that is produces memories that are *more durable* than Explicit Learning, but that it is *more limited* in what it processes than Explicit Learning - It can record concepts and perceptions, but it cannot analyse or interpret messages. We have also shown that some ads are able to exploit the durability of implicit learning to their advantage, and some cannot.

However, the Renault Clio and Ciroen Xsara ads quoted above were both examples of ads that achieved high levels of attention and good levels of recall, certainly of the specific elements of 'Papa and 'Nicole', and Claudia Schiffer. To strengthen the argument we need to find an example of an ad which achieved *low* levels of attention and recall, and see if it succeeded in changing attitudes to the brand it was advertising.

Case study

This case study concerns a new campaign for a brand 'X'. The initial execution '1' in this campaign achieved record levels of prompted advertising awareness and shifting the brand's image across all dimensions. A subsequent execution '2' was run with a message about customer care. Execution '2', in stark contrast to execution '1' had hardly any effect on prompted ad awareness, and showed no evident sign of shifting any image statements.

Tracking research identified that the problem with execution '2' was poor branding. Despite the use of a similar creative approach the music had been changed and the brand name was revealed only right at the end of the ad. When shown a de-branded version of ad '2', although 53% recognised having seen it before, only 23% of them were able to correctly identify the brand. And amongst those who *did* recognise it hardly any were aware what the message was. But does this poor performance on branding and recall mean the ad had no effect on perceptions of the brand?

Because recognition memory is very powerful, it is safe to assume that the 53% who recognised the de-branded ad had seen it (group A), and those who did not recognise the ad had *not* seen it (group B). One way to test if the ad had affected perceptions of the brand is to look at the difference in image ratings between each group. Since image questions are asked *before* the ad is exposed, any difference between group A and group B should have been caused either by structural differences in the two samples, or by exposure to the ad. In order to minimise the structural effect the analysis was restricted to non-users of the brand. The results of this analysis are as follows.

24 out of the 30 brand image statements were significantly higher amongst group A (recognisers) than group B (non-recognisers), and two of them - *'Helpful'*, and *'A brand you would recommend to friends'* - showed *double* the score for group A compared with group B. More importantly, the dimension which most closely related to the ad's message - *'Cares about its customers'* - was 56% higher amongst group A, all these shifts being significant at 99%

In order to evaluate whether or not this ad had improved overall brand equity, favourability towards all brands in the study was asked using a 7 point semantic scale ranging from 'Very Unfavourable' to 'Very Favourable'. Table 20:1 shows the mean scores in this dimension for brand 'X'.

Table 20:1

NON-USERS	Group A (Recognisers)	Group B (Non-recognisers)
Base	382	330
Mean Favourability (7 point scale	4.59	4.01
Top two box	32%	14%

There is 0.58 point rise in mean favourability between group A and group B (significant at 99.9%). Furthermore, amongst group A 14% rated the brand in one of the top two boxes, whereas amongst group B 32% rated the brand in the top two boxes. This 18% difference is also significant at 99.9% level.

Discussion

In spite of a proven dearth of attention and recall of any message, the execution '2' still managed to achieve a positive shift in image and brand equity. This is consistent with the predictions of low involvement processing. However, in order to prove that the shifts were a direct result of exposure to ad '2' it is necessary to establish that the samples of recognisers and non-recognisers were structurally similar, and that no prior bias (such as exposure to previous advertising) might have contributed to the shifts seen. This cannot be done from the data available and for this reason work continues on this and other case histories.

21

The Nature of Central and Peripheral Advertising Information Processing

FLEMMING HANSEN & LOTTE YSSING HANSEN

Summary

Strategic, executional and budgeting decisions on advertising require a mixture of quantitative and qualitative evaluations prior to the full-scale start of the campaign. Recent development in media planning has created a demand for uniform quantitative campaign effect measures. At the same time the realisation, that different advertising in different areas works differently, has directed advertising research towards measures selected specifically for the campaign being tested. The paper describes how a new generation of advertising pre-testing is growing out of past experiences to cope with these issues.

Advertising testing has been here for almost a century. From counting coupons and other direct responses, the first generation of actual testing emerged in the thirties using advertising recall and advertising recognition measures. With television, this technique developed into "day after recall", and this is still existing in many different versions.

In the sixties and seventies advertisers became concerned with persuasion measures. Cinema tests with before/after purchase intentions, preference and attitude shift measures, and controlled market exposure test with sales registration became fashionable. Everybody tried to present the one and only effect measure that revealed all information about the ways in which advertising worked.

In later years more variable approaches to the measure of advertising effects are emerging. Modelling and the use of a multitude of measures have become prominent. Academic research on the role of attitudes towards the ad (a-ad), central and peripheral processing, emotions, story telling versus informal communication etc. has revealed new ways in which communication works. These findings have emphasised the importance of understanding how the consumer treats the advertised message.

In parallel with the theoretical advances, commercial research has introduced a multitude of measures relating to ad-liking, emotions, self repeated purchase intention shifts etc., as well as the concern with diagnostics relating to these has been growing. Also, a major improvement has been that modelling increasingly has been applied in an attempt to understand the interaction between the many different effect measures.

Low involvement information processing

Low involvement information processing (Rossiter & Percy, 2000), the impact of effect of measuring (Ambler & Burne, 1999), emotional aspects of communication effects (Hansen & Rasmussen, 2001) "instinctive responses" (de Plesis and Foster , 2000) are all central in contemporary discussions of advertising effects. These new communication effects are contrasted with views on various versions of effect hierarchical thinking (Hansen, 1987). Here, effects are studied as a sequence of awareness, knowledge, image formations, preferences, and buying attention. A conceptualisation, which focuses on the peculiarities of both of the two kinds of information processing, is suggested in (Hansen, 1997) in terms of an elaboration likelihood advertising model (ELAM), inspired by the elaboration likelihood model (ELM), suggested by (Petty & Cacioppo, 1986).

Also earlier findings have raised doubts as to whether a single string's information processing approach is always an appropriate description of the way in which people receive information (Hansen, 1984). One of these lines of research originates in perceptual psychology (Kroebler-Riel, 1984) and concerns itself with picture perception. Here it is studied how little time people need to see

indves

pictures in order to be able to recognise them. Generally it has been found that 1-2 seconds are enough, suggesting that very little exposure is needed in order to generate recognition.

Another research tradition has dealt with brain lateralization (Hansen, 1985). This theory holds that while verbal, numerical, symbolic information seems to be stored in the left side of the brain, pictorial, holistic and similar impressions involve the right side of the brain. This suggests that there may be two very different ways in which information is processed and stored. Still other research suggests that emotional response may follow the exposure that cannot be related to the information processing. (Zajonc, 1968) suggested that emotions could be generated without cognition and that they may be stored, not in the brain, but in other locations of the body.

Similarly, research has focused on feelings and emotions in relation to advertising perception. (Haley & Baldinger, 1991). Findings show that emotions prior to watching an advertisement influences recall and other ad-effect measures.

Altogether these findings suggest that people may have very different ways of perceiving information in different situations. They may store information in an emotional as well as in a pictorially recognisable way, in addition to the information processing information storage.

The ELAM Model

Several models have been proposed suggesting such different ways of information processing. Early work is reported by (Michell, 1986) and (Olson et al., 1979). Probably the most extensive and the most influential is the "Elaboration Likelihood Model (ELM) proposed by (Petty and Cacioppo, 1983; 1986). Here, a distinction between central and peripheral information processing is involved. In this model the central route processing is very similar to the traditional information processing models picture of the way in which consumers treat information. The peripheral processing, however, is different. Here information is received and stored more or less unprocessed and traces have to be found in terms of recall or recognition of the advertisement, rather than in terms of brand recall, or changes in attitude towards the brand. Eventually, if the stored advertising information is aroused in a subsequent purchasing situation, and is linked to the brand advertised, it may, at this time influence the purchasing behaviour.

Figure 21:1 Advertising Response Model: Conceptual Model based on the Elaboration Likelihood Model own adoption.

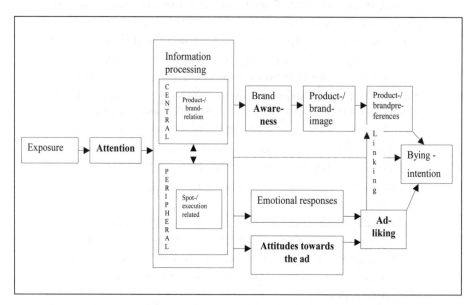

(Petty and Cacioppo, 1983) themselves say "We have outlined two basic routes to persuasion. One route is based on the thoughtful (though sometimes biased) consideration of arguments central to the issue, whereas the other is based on affective associations or simple inferences tied to peripheral cues in the persuasion context. When variables in the persuasion situation render the elaboration likelihood high, the first kind of persuasion occurs (central route). When variables in the persuasion situation render the elaboration likelihood low, the second kind of persuasion occurs (peripheral route). Importantly, there are different consequences of the two routes to persuasion. Attitude changes via the central route appear to be more persistent, resistant, and predictive of behaviour than changes induced via the peripheral route".

Petty and Cacioppo have showed the effect of some various factors influencing "Elaboration Likelihood". In their studies, they have proven that distraction, repetition, involvement, number of evaluators, need for cognition, message form, source attractiveness, source expertise, number of sources, and body position are of importance. More specifically, in advertising testing, factors one would look for would be

- Product area involvement
- Loyal versus non-loyal target group
- New versus established product
- Type of campaign: story, informational or emotional
- Type of Target Groups

Departing in such a model it is not sufficient with one overall effect measure but rather a repertoire of measures have to be applied. An overview of such measures are shown in Table 21:1.

Which ones to choose in this specific situation will depend upon the factors discussed above.

Table 21:1 . Effect measurements of centrally and peripheral processed advertisements.

Variable	Brand Level (central processing)	Ad-level (peripheral processing)
Attention	Brand Recall/ Brand Recognition	Ad Recall/ Ad Recognition
Processing	Brand Processing	Ad-Processing
Attitude	Attitude towards Brand	Attitude towards Ad (A-Ad)
Association	"Linking" to Brand	Emotions towards Ad
Persuasion	Purchase intention and self reported changes in purchase intention	Total Ad evaluation: Liking

With advertising testing tailor-made with variables like those suggested here, the quest for norm data also changes.

In the following such a semi-standardized system is presented together with some findings from its application.

Flemming Hansen • Lotte Yssing Hansen

Application of the model

In using the model in pre-testing, each test is carried out with a limited number of respondents (130-200), conducted in a Hall test facility in downtown Copenhagen. Generally, the target-group is users of the product category. Sampling is disproportionate, so that brand loyals or brand users versus others are more or less equally represented.

Interviews are conducted with the use of CAPI and the test items (the ad, the layout, the spot, the animation, the story board, etc.) are shown together with 4-6 similar items. At this time of the interview, the respondent only knows that the survey is concerned with advertising. Then recall and some brand related questions are asked after which the test item (spot, ad etc.) is shown once more. Following this the remaining questionnaire is administered.

The measurements are described in more detail in (Hansen, 1997). They cover the variables related to Figure 21:1, and listed in Table 21:1. Attention is measured as a self rated attention score. Here also brand awareness for the tested brand together with a number of dummy brands is measured.

Following the second exposure, respondents are asked to express what they liked about the ad and what they disliked about it. For each category the statements are sorted as product related (central) processing, ad related (peripheral) and combined processing. These emotional responses are measured with the use of a special advertising relevant selection of (Richins, 1997) 20 emotional consumption dimensions.

The advertisement can be more or less closely related to the brand. This is quantified through the measurement of linking. The likelihood with which the advertisement later will influence purchasing behaviour or buying intentions depends on that. Attitudes towards the ad and a total liking score are asked for also, along with buying intentions and self rated changes in buying intentions.

These measures result in a total of eleven standard scores and diagnostic data, computed for each commercial tested. These are compared with norms available partly from accumulated scores from past tests and partly with scores from other tests and published findings.

1. Advertising Recall. The extent to which advertising is recalled reflects its attention value and is based upon aided and unaided recall questions. Recall is computed so that it can be compared with experiences from other test norms. A norm score is computed by dividing the test score with the average score from other tests. This norm score is larger than one, when the tested item is better than others, and smaller than one otherwise.

2. Peripheral vs. central Processing. The extent to which one or the other of the two ways of processing information dominates is reflected in figures showing how many rely upon the one and how many rely upon the other form of processing, and the intensity with which this takes place. This measure is based on coding open-ended responses.

3. Brand Recall. Particularly in connection with new brands, products, or ideas brand recall may be an important measure of effect. The more advertising is able to generate brand awareness the better it works.

4. Attitude towards the ad (a-ad). The consumer's attitude towards the ad (a-ad) is important for the total effect. Standardised scores on eight questions reflecting four dimensions of attitudes towards the ads are measured.

5. Liking. Liking is scored on a five-point rating scale, and computed. Also a norm-based liking score is computed by dividing liking of the tested ad (commercial) with the average liking for all ads (commercials).

6. Brand Attitude. The standardised measurement for brand attitude are based upon 3 attitude questions that are averaged.

7. Brand association (linking) tells about the extent to which the story and the content of the advertisement is associated with the brand and the use of the brand. There are used 2 measurements for linking. A general score using the same scales across all tests and a specific score based upon questions related to the specific content of the campaign tested.

8. Emotions and feelings influence the way in which advertising is processed. In the test a standardised battery, measuring emotional responses to the advertisement is used (Richins, 1997).

9. Some *advertisement* can directly influence consumers' buying intentions. In such instances a buying intention measure is useful and can be compared with results from other tests.

10. Self-rated change in buying intention. In many instances buying intentions are only moderately influenced by the single advertising communication. In these instances, however, consumers are able to report the extent to which they themselves find them more or less inclined to purchase the advertised brand following the exposure. This is scaled as an average score and compared with similar data from other tests and a standardised score, dividing the score from the test with the average from all other tests is computed.

11. Finally a *summary score* reflecting the total effectiveness of the advertisement is computed. This score is based upon the three "winning" measures of the Advertising Research Corporation's "Copy Research Validity Project" (Haley and Baldinger, 1991): ad recall, liking, and persuasion (here, self reported change in buying intention). For each of these three scores a figure is computed for the tested commercial, dividing the score for the commercial with the average from all commercials. Following this a geometrical average (multiplying the three scores with each other) is computed. To the extent that each of the scores is larger than one, the tested ad is rated better than average. Similarly, to the extent that the average score is larger than the overall score for all the advertisement tested it is better than average. In interpreting these findings, it is important to remember that for some ads, liking or self rated buying intention may be the most important, for others it may be attention. This should be kept in mind when judging the total ELAM score. However, the score gives a summary measure enabling the researcher to compare the particular advertisement (commercial) tested with other advertisement commercials and with groups of advertisement commercials. And it provides a score that meaningfully can be used as an indicator of creative strength in media planning. This score is shown in Figure 21:2.

Some scores

To illustrate the sensitivity of the system and its ability to identify differences in the way in which the commercials work the range of some of the scores are shown in Table 21:2.

Figure 21:2 ELAM score computation

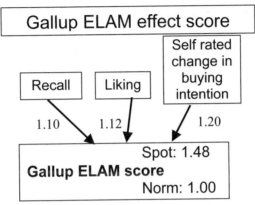

Table 21:2. High/ Low Scores on Selected Measures

	High Score	Low Score
Spot recall (%):	29%	92%
Information Processing (%):		
Distribution in Per Cent among Respondents:		
Peripheral Processing	33%	93%
Central Processing	9%	67%
Number of Elements:		
Average answer per respondent with recall	1.63	7.06
Average Product Familiarity (%):*	0.02	0.78
Average Attitude towards Brand:*	0.93	1.16
Liking (%):*	0.35	0.89
Average Linking (%):*		
It is obvious which product.......	0.70	1.4
Average Buying Intention:*	0.87	1.3
Average Self-rated Change in Buying Intentions:*	0.07	0.50

* Rated on 5 point scales from -2 to +20

Another way to evaluate the discriminative power of the test is to look upon the different measures taken in a test comparing to different versions of the same campaign. The two campaigns tested are quite similar story board versions of a 30 seconds spot for a non-alcoholic beverage.

It is sufficient to reveal that the one version (the second) is focusing on the product, its cleanliness, and relationship with nature, whereas the other version of the spot is focusing on the consumer and the usefulness of the product is satisfying the needs of the consumer. Selected figures illustrating this are presented in Table 21:3.

Table 21:3. Comparison of two different versions of storyboard for non-alcoholic beverages

	Version with Person	Version with Landscape
Sample size:	130	130
Information Processing (%):		
Distribution in Per Cent among Respondents:		
Peripheral processing	0.78	0.87*
Central processing	0.09	0.22*
Others	0.21	0.13*
Number of Elements:		
Peripheral processing	616	417*
Central processing	294	441*
Others	8	16
Number of elements total	918	874
Average answer per respondent with recall	7.06	6.72
Attitude towards Brand (average):		
The brand suits me (average)	0.68	0.65
Will recommend the brand to others (average)	-0.08	-0.24*
Likes the brand (average)	0.38	0.47
Attitude towards Spot (average):		
Reliable (average)	-0.38	0.67*
Warm (average)	0.40	0.20
Emotional (average)	-1.15	-0.10*
Entertaining (average)	0.26	-0.70*
Informative (average)	-0.52	0.10
Irritating (average)	-0.85	-1.12*
Stupid (average)	-0.57	-1.17*
Emotional Reactions (%)		
Enjoyment	0.67	0.52*
Happiness	0.14	0.22

Acceptance	0.08	0.08
Pleasure	0.22	0.23
Hope	0.12	0.29*
Inspiring	0.08	0.08
Dominating	0.01	0.01
Surprising	0.28	0.08*
Distrust	0.00	0.02
Anger	0.04	0.01
Fear	0.00	0.02
Sorrow	0.00	0.00
Linking (average):		
It is obvious which prod.....	1.42	1.66*
The commercial tells something new....	-1.35	-1.25
Buying Intention (%):		
Absolutely buy (%)	0.18	0.13
Probably buy (%)	0.45	0.59
Probably not buy (%)	0.22	0.17
Absolutely not buy (%)	0.10	0.09
Average	0.40	0.51*
Buying Willingness (%):		
Much more willing	0.02	0.13
Somewhat more willing	0.28	0.34
Same willingness	0.62	0.51
Somewhat less willing	0.07	0.02
Much less willing	0.00	0.00
Average	0.26	0.38

* significant p = 0.05

Using results from a number of tests that have been conducted, various interesting observations can be made. In Table 21:4 beta-coefficients are shown between liking, recall, and change in intention. As expected they are all positive and of moderate size. Since the number of observations based upon which they are computed are from eight to fifteen, none of them produce significant correlation coefficient, and to some extent they may also be biased by the fact, that some of the tests entering into the base came from rather special commercials. Nevertheless the observation is in line with international findings that recall, liking, and persuasions are positively related but far from perfectly, and therefore each of them contribute to the explanation of the overall effect of advertising.

Flemming Hansen • Lotte Yssing Hansen

Differences between central and peripheral information processing

In Denmark, for Gallup/TNS Sofres, advertising pre-testing has been conducted, inspired by this model since 1997. Along the way, changes in the methodology has been introduced, but still it has been possible to identify 18 tests, where basically the same measurements have been used. The measurements were listed in Table 21:1.

Table 21:4. Beta Coefficients between Recall, Liking and Self-rated Buying Intention (N = 18)

	Recall	Liking	Self-rated Buying Intention
Recall	/	0.63	0.23
Liking	–	/	0.44
Selfrated Buying Intention	–	–	/

The tests include such different product areas as apples, chewing gum, soft drinks, cosmetics, washing machines, construction material, body shampoo, and others. Tests have been conducted for print as well as television advertising, and in the case of television, tests have been conducted with the use of final productions, animations, and storyboards.

The selection of tests can hardly be said to be representative for anything general, in terms of advertising, but still the relationships established, may provide some insight into the way in which advertising works in different situations.

In the following, we shall analyse the data with a particular emphasise on differences between central and peripheral information processing.

From the test, respondents answer to the open-ended questions, regarding what they recall from the advertising, what they think it was meant to communicate, and what they particularly liked, and particularly disliked, are used to identify the extend of central peripheral processing. For each respondent, all this verbal information has been organised as a string of data, and coded across the different questions. It has been attempted to force each informational item into one of the following four categories:

- Positive product related (central) information
- Negative product related (central) information
- Positive execution /story/ related (peripheral) information
- Negative execution /story/ related (peripheral) information

Departing in the information obtained, by way of this coding, it is possible to look upon the following questions:

- The frequency with which people engage in peripheral vs. central information processing.
- Determinants of peripheral information processing.
- The effectiveness of peripheral vs. central information processing.
- Special effects of peripheral information processing.

The occurrence of peripheral and central information processing

Table 21:5 shows the frequency with which central/positive, central/negative, peripheral/positive, and peripheral/negative information processing is registered.

Table 21:5. Number of positive and negative/ central and peripheral statements.

Central positive	Central negative	Central	Peripheral positive	Peripheral negative	Peripheral
484	286	692	1579	1436	2163

It can be seen that in the selection of tests analysed here, peripheral information processing occurs three times as frequent as central information processing. It can be seen that the sum of central and peripheral information processing exceeds the number of respondents. This occurs, because some respondents may have provided central as well as peripheral information items. Similarly, it can be seen that slightly more positive than negative responses are registered, but relatively speaking, the central information processing generates more positive responses. Even though there are differences between individual ads and different types of ads, the pattern in these findings appear across all the data and it is safe to conclude, that the picture pretty well reflects the situation for primarily fast moving consumer goods advertising. There are, however, marked differences between the individual ads. One ad , tested with 153 respondents, generating the most exclusive peripheral information processing, give rise to 198 peripheral statements, and 3 central statements. For this ad, there are slightly more positive than negative indications. For a similar ad for the same brand, the same overall picture emerges, but here there are twice as many negative as positive responses. Thus, even with minor variations in ad execution, quite marked differences in evaluation occur.

The most centrally processed commercial is one for a cosmetics product. Here, 159 out of 353 responses reflect central information processing. Still, peripheral responses dominate, and with 151 respondents in the test, it also appears that the number of responses per respondent is about twice as large as that observed in the cases with high, peripheral information processing.

A similar picture emerges for a washing machine ad. Again, peripheral information processing is more frequent than central information processing, and the number of informational items, provided per respondent is 60-70 per cent larger than for the advertisements, providing highly concentrated peripheral information processing. On the whole, as shown in Table 21:6, a clear relationship emerges in terms of a growing number of elicited statements per respondent, with an increasing proportion of central statements among the responses. Thus, one may argue, that simply the number of statements, elicited from the respondents, when proper probing is conducted, reflects the degree of central vs. peripheral information processing.

Table 21:6. Connection between the average number of responses per respondent, and the proportion of central answers.

	Average number of responses per respondent Average proportion of central answers (%)
Low proportion of central processing	1,9 10,5%
High proportion of central processing	3,2 18,4%

In terms of the motivational grid of (Rossiter & Percy, 2000), providing four communicational strategies, it is possible to classify the commercials in these categories, as shown in Table 21:7. Some of the categories have relatively few advertisements ascribed to them, but still, overall comparisons between informational vs. transformational and high/low involvement advertising can be made. In all cases, peripheral information processing dominates, but least so with high involvement informational ads.

Table 21:7. Percentage of central information processing in high/low involvement and informational / transformational information processing condition.

	Informational	Transformational
High Involvement	N: 393 Central: 22,1%	N: 281 Central: 7,8%
Low Involvement	N: 609 Central: 11,6%	N: 1224 Central: 6,2%

Determinants of peripheral information processing

With peripheral information processing being dominant, as observed here, the question is, what factors generate more or less peripheral information processing.

Some factors, one may consider, are:

- The proportion of loyal consumers in the target group
- The ability of the commercial to generate attention
- Product category
- Creative quality

And as illustrated in the session before, the nature of the communication strategy, in terms of informational vs. transformational and high vs. low involvement processing, plays a role.

It is likely that more loyal consumers of a brand are found among those with the highest positive preference for the brand. In all the tests, information is available regarding the preferences for the tested brand. The scales, described earlier, are used. Grouping respondents, with the highest sum score on these scales, as more loyal than those with a lower sum score, provides two categories for further analyses.

Table 21:8. Degree of central processing among more or less loyal respondents.

	Positive preference	Negative preference
Central (N=567)	21,4%	22,5%
Peripheral (N=2018)	78,6%	77,5%

The occurrence of positive, negative, central and peripheral information processing, depending upon degree of loyalty, is shown in Table 21:8. A little, negative effect of loyalty on central and peripheral processing is found.

In 2/3 of the tests, the self-rated attention value is obtained. Again, dividing respondents across tests, into those assigning high attention value and those assigning low attention value to the commercials tested, gives two categories. Data are shown in Table 21:9:

Table 21:9. Degree of central processing among respondents with high and low attention.

	High attention	Low attention
Central (N=275)	24,4%	27,3%
Peripheral (N=761)	75,6%	72,7%

Here, it appears that attention plays a role for the occurrence of peripheral information processing. The more attention value one gets, the more likely peripheral information processing is to occur. Thus, to get attention has a price in terms of lowering the quality of the information processing.

In the data, four product categories are represented, with two or more ads each. The categories are: apples, chewing gum, cosmetics, and mineral water. The occurrence of central/ peripheral information processing in the four product categories, is shown in Table 21:10.

Important product category differences appear. Of course, these differences may reflect the executional quality of the particular ads as well. If one dares consider liking as a crude measure of creative quality, the data in Table 21:11 shows, how variations in liking positively influence the occurrence of central information processing.

Thus, all in all, peripheral information processing is more expressed among less loyal consumers, respondents considering the ads to have a limited attention value, creative quality, and the nature of the product area in question.

Table 21:10. Occurrence of central vs. peripheral information processing in four product categories.

	Apples (4) (N=510)	Chewing gum (2) (N=304)	Cosmetics (3) (N=501)	Mineral water (2) (N=256)
Central	23,4%	1,1%	22,9%	23,8%
Peripheral	76,6%	98,9%	77,1%	76,2%

Table 21:11. Degree of central information processing, depending on ad-liking

	Positive liking	Negative liking
Central (N=704)	27,8%	22,5%
Peripheral (N=2173)	72,2%	77,5%

The relative value of central vs. peripheral information processing

To understand when and how peripheral information processing occurs, may be less important, if central and peripheral information processing are equally effective and desirable. To judge whether this is so, it is possible to look at indicators of purchase intention.

In some of the tests, purchase intention has been measured directly, in others it has been measured in terms of a "self-rated change in purchase intention, following exposure" (Do you think it more or less likely, that you will purchase the brand after you have seen the commercial?)

In some tests, both measures are included. In tables 12 and 13, both intentional measures are computed for respondents with primarily peripheral, and respondents with primarily central information processing.

Here, there is little affect on the plain intention measures, whereas the self-rated changes in purchase intention makes obvious the desirability of central information processing.

In Table 21:13, the relationship between liking and the degree of central processing is illustrated.

Table 21:12. Degree of central information processing, depending on planned buying intention

	Positive planned buying intention	Negative planned buying intention
Central (N=692)	22,7%	25,3%
Peripheral (N=2163)	77,3%	74,7%

Table 21:13. degree of central information processing, depending on self-rated change in buying intention

	Positive self-rated change on buying intention	No change	Negative self-rated change on buying intention
Central (N=540)	38,0%	50,9%	11,1%
Peripheral (N=1627)	30,3%	55,1%	14,6%

Finally, linking in the test is measured by asking people two questions that have been chosen, since they can be applied, uniformly across tests. Other perceptual measures are used also, but comparisons across tests are more difficult for those. For the two general linking measures, the results shown in Table 21:14 appear. Again, the generation of more product-relevant understanding, when central information processing occurs, is evident.

All in all, from the standpoint of the advertiser, central information processing should definitely be preferred, whenever possible. Something else, however, is that the world may be so, that the advertiser frequently is forced into working primarily with peripheral information processing anyway. When this is so, it becomes important to ask what characterise the more effect-full peripheral information processing.

Table 21:14. Positive and negative linking with central and peripheral information processing

	Positive linking	Negative linking
Central (N=447)	36,7%	24,6%
Peripheral (N=1022)	63,3%	75,4%

The nature of peripheral processing

Are there any unique features of peripheral information processing? Are there things, peripheral information processing does better or differently, as compared with more central information processing?

Table 21:15. Attitudes towards the ad, when central and peripheral information processing occur.

	Central	Peripheral
Exciting	21,9% (N=1190)	18,9% (N=3668)
Credible	42,3% (N=1376)	33,4% (N=4150)
Sensitive	31,2% (N=1302)	27,2% (N=3892)
Warm	21,5% (N=1376)	21,4% (N=4150)
Entertaining	35,5% (N=1376)	32,3% (N=4150)
Informative	32,4% (N=1376)	29,4% (N=4150)
Stupid	19,3% (N=1376)	23,8% (N=4150)
Irritating	17,3% (N=1376)	24,1% (N=4150)

To answer this question, two batteries of items included in the ELAM test are analysed. First eight general questions, reflecting attitudes towards the ad, are used uniformly across the tests. Here, the percentage, arguing that the particular, evaluative statements apply to the ads, are computed, depending upon whether central or peripheral information processing has occurred. Data are shown in Table 21:15. The higher ad-liking, related to centrally processed information is confirmed, positively as well as negatively. All six positive items (the first six in the table), give higher scores for central processing, and the two negative evaluative items, "irritating" and "stupid", give higher scores for the peripheral processed advertising. Thus, the advantages of the central information processing is reconfirmed. However, still when peripheral information processing occurs, differences may be found, in the way in which advertising are evaluated. When we look upon peripheral ads only they are evaluated differently along the attitude towards the ad dimension, depending upon informational vs. transformational, high/low involvement commercials. Thus, variation in attitude towards the ad reflects different qualitative aspects of peripheral information processing, and as such be a useful effect measure, in terms of advertising testing.

Table 21:16. Emotional responses, as they relate to central and peripheral information processing.

	Central	Peripheral
Pleasure	26,4% (N=1038)	40,0% (N=3418)
Hope	28,5% (N=1038)	33,4% (N=3418)
Acceptance	22,2% (N=1038)	33,5% (N=3418)
Happiness	27,4% (N=1038)	41,2% (N=3418)
Dominate	8,7% (N=1038)	13,1% (N=3418)
Enjoyment	46,2% (N=1038)	58,0% (N=3418)
Inspiring	28,8% (N=834)	28,0% (N=3172)
Surprising	18,7% (N=834)	23,3% (N=3172)
Mistrust	7,5% (N=1038)	9,0% (N=3418)
Sorrow	6,9% (N=1038)	4,6% (N=3418)
Anger	11,6% (N=1038)	6,9% (N=3418)
Fear	3,3% (N=1038)	5,3% (N=3418)

The importance of emotional responses to advertising and the role of emotions in governing consumer choice has been discussed. In the questionnaire, people have been asked to indicate the extend to which they find, that different emotional statements apply to the ads tested. Data are shown in Table 21:16. Here, it appears that there is a remarkable tendency for the more positive, emotional responses to be generated, when peripheral information processing occur. Only for two negative items (sorrow and anger), a slightly more frequent response occurs, when central information processing takes place. On the whole, peripheral information processing generates much more emotional responses, and particularly many more positive, emotional responses.

Again here, differences can be demonstrated between different commercials, thus suggesting that emotional responses can be very useful effect measures, particularly when peripheral information processing is involved.

Concluding remarks

It has been discussed how advertising works and how its effects can be tested. Theoretical developments in consumer behaviour research and practical experiences have been moving in the same direction. An understanding is emerging that advertising works at many different levels and it works differently for different products in different situations. The need for modelling this process is obvious, and it has been shown that a "many- variable based" model is a useful instrument in studying the effects of advertising. It also has been learned that even with many different measures involved, it is possible to operate a test system, which in its basic form is standardised, although individual adoptions to particular situations naturally always must be possible.

It has also been shown that particularly recall, liking, and purchase intentions are important measures of advertising effects. These measures are related but far from perfectly. By combining them into an integrated score a measure emerges, which in a summary fashion describes important aspects of the efficiency of the particular spot or advertisement. Taken with care such summary measures are useful and they are badly needed in media planning and in other context where overall effect scores for the particular commercials, creative power are in demand. It has been discussed, that this kind of model-based multivariable testing functions very well at different levels in the creative process. In the case of commercials, tests can meaningfully be carried out with versions ranging from story board to final production.

By looking upon the differences between high and low scores it has been seen that the individual measures are highly sensitive. It has also been shown that they discriminate even between quite similar versions of the same campaign.

The data analysed here, also suggest that peripheral information processing tend to dominate, when fast moving consumer goods are involved.

To the advertiser, it would have been desirable, had this not been so, but given it is, it becomes important to ask, what influences the extend to which central information processing can be generated, along with the peripheral information processing, and how and when does peripheral information processing work more or less efficiently?

It is an observation made by many authors, that in most FMCG markets, only minute differences exist between brands, and to differentiate brands, it becomes important to focus on non-material advantages of the brands.

Frequently, when the advertiser is forced to do so, it will have to be in a manner, which implies a considerable amount of peripheral information processing. The old dilemma between attention and communication effect is at stake here also. When advertising creativity is directed towards generating more central information processing, chances are that this is done at a price of lowered attention value. The optimal blend of attention and information in the communication may at the end of the day result in ads, more appealing to peripheral information processing. Such ads may be evaluated best in terms of the emotional responses it can generate, and in terms of the attitudes towards the ads, that can be measured.

22

A Note on the Role of Advertising in Memory Creation and Memory Reconstruction of Experiences

RITA MÅRTENSON

Abstract

Experiences play a major role in modern society. While some say that we live in an experience economy, others see experiences as a major tool for product and service differentiation. This chapter shows however that there are no agreed definition of what a memorable experience is, and that much more research is needed to clarify definitions and ways to measure the concept. The discussion in this chapter is focused on positive memorable (cognitive, emotional or sensory) experiences and the role that advertising plays in the marketing of experiences.

Introduction and Background

Experiences play an important role in people's lives. Without experiences life would not be meaningful to live. Most people can easily relate to the concept of 'memorable experiences', i.e. experiences that stand out in our memory as being either exceptionally positive or exceptionally negative. A really meaningful and memorable experience feels like a gift; the memory of which we can treasure for the rest of our lives. We can talk about it, enjoy it over and over again and continuously get the warm feeling of how happy we are to have such memorable experiences. Despite its longevity, it is nevertheless a fragile property that can be influenced and gradually changed by later events including commercial activities.

Sometimes a memorable experience is based on a single event, and sometimes it is based on a sequence of events such as "my years of visits to restaurant Le Mistral" or "the smell of fresh bread every time I entered the bread store". If we search our minds, we will find a broad variety of explanations to why we remember something. Sometimes we have memorable experiences from the poorest environments such as falling or being in love and the place where much time was spent during that period. Sometimes such experiences take place in luxury environments. From a commercial perspective, however, there is one important criterion that has to be met: what companies can influence to create memorable experiences for their customers. This criterion thus excludes memorable experiences that lovers, for example, have from mismanaged restaurant visits or holiday resorts, since the memorable event has nothing or very little to do with how well the place was managed. The couple would remember the event anyway. Memorable experiences from walks on the beach are another example of events that are excluded by that criterion. However, if the walk on the beach was a memorable experience because a certain brand was included in that experience, it would have to be included in the present discussion. What is discussed in this chapter is rather what management can do to make expectations of consumption, actual consumption and memories of consumption of either products or services as memorable as possible. This means that managers must have a fair chance to create and deliver memorable experiences. People must be in the right state of mind to receive the experience, or the interaction between the event and the individual's state of mind will be less satisfying or even wasted (Pine and Gilmore 1998). Thus, sometimes managers may do everything right, but a person may be too occupied with other more dominating thoughts to get a memorable experience. That is another example of situations not discussed in the chapter. Experiences can have different valence, i.e. they can be both negative and positive. Negative experiences are not discussed in the chapter. Negative experiences play an important role for most businesses as something to avoid, since they create customer complaints and customer defections. Having acknowledged their importance, they are nevertheless omitted from further discussion due to a lack of space.

The purpose of this chapter is to discuss definitions and research on experiences to get a better sense of what an experience really is. Needless to say, this chapter is only a first step toward such an understanding. Experiences can be seen both in a societal perspective and in a commercial perspective, and both are briefly discussed. It is, for example, important to be aware of what managers can do to increase the experiential value of their products and services. Finally, memorable experiences are discussed in an advertising or marketing communications perspective, i.e. the role of advertising in particular is discussed.

Definition, Description and Research on Experiences

The concept of experience is vaguely defined in the theory (Gupta and Vajic 2000, Richardson 1999), and it is apparent that different authors have different views on the meaning of the concept. Furthermore, experience is such a broad term that it can refer to any sensation or knowledge acquisition resulting from a person's participation in daily activities (ibid.). A brief review of the field is presented as an introduction to the following discussion on what the concept is.

This chapter deals with expectations of consumption, actual consumption and memories of consumption of either products or services. Stated differently, it deals with what consumers can imagine and/or what they remember, i.e. what they encode, store and retrieve in their memories. Lately, it has been suggested that advertising, for example, can influence all those processes.

Richardson (1999) uses the concept "subjective experience" when he describes its conceptual status in psychology. One school argues that experience is private, which implies that it cannot be investigated scientifically and that, consequently, it cannot be an object of study in scientific psychology. Pine and Gilmore (1998) adhere to this school. A second group of researchers agree that we can never know anything about a subjective experience as such, but we can at least study the reports that are made about experiences. Richardson argues that one of the problems is that psychologists assume that they are using natural science procedures when, clearly, they are not. A simple solution could be that a researcher arranges to be a subject in an experiment. If that researcher reports the same or fairly similar experiences as the other participants, it would be easier to conclude that the experience actually occurred.

Experiences have been described as the "take-away impression formed by people's encounters with products, services, and businesses – a perception produced when humans consolidate sensory information" (Carbone and Haeckel 1994, p 8). Another way to describe them is as "memorable sensations" (Pine and Gilmore 1998). It occurs in the mind of an individual who has been engaged on an emotional, physical, intellectual, or even spiritual level (ibid.). There are different opinions on whether or not consumers must be active. Gupta and Vajic (2000) argue, "what distinguishes experience from both products and services is the active role that customers are given in creating their own use environment" (p. 38). In the view of Pine and Gilmore, customers can participate either actively or passively. Mathwick, Malhotra and Rigdon (2001) similarly use Holbrook's (1994) distinction between reactive (or passive) value and participative (or active) value. Reactive or passive value is derived from the consumer's comprehension of, appreciation for or response to a consumption object or experience. Active or participative value implies heightened collaboration between the consumer and the marketing entity where collaboration can take the form of cognitive, behavioural or financial investment on the part of the consumer. To them, experiential value perceptions are based upon interactions involving either direct usage or distanced appreciation of goods and services. The role of active participation versus passive participation is discussed in another perspective by Csinkszentmihlyi (2000) in the section on 'Societal view of experiences'.

The second dimension in Pine and Gilmore's model is the connection or environmental relationship that unites customers with the event or performance (absorption or immersion). Based on these two dimensions there are four different types of experience. In the *entertainment* case customers are passive and absorbed by, for example, music. In the *aesthetic* case customers are similarly passive but in combination with immersion. The *educational experience* is an active person in combination with absorption of new knowledge. The final type of experience, the *escapist experience*, is an active person in combination with immersion. Retailers have many choices in terms of these combinations. Mathwick et al also use an extrinsic-extrinsic conceptualization of experiential value. In a retail setting the extrinsic benefits are typically derived from shopping trips that are utilitarian in nature, i.e. they are often seen as errands or work. The intrinsic value is derived from the appreciation of the experience for its own sake, such as having fun shopping. Mathwick et al use the typology of experiential value proposed by Holbrook (1994) in a value landscape divided into four quadrants framed by intrinsic/extrinsic sources of value on one axis and active reactive values on the other. The four quadrants are *playfulness* (escapism, co-producer value, participant, enjoyment) when intrinsic value is combined with active value, and *aesthetics* (spectator, distanced appreciation, visual appeal, entertainment) when intrinsic value is combined with passive value. They have *Consumer Return on Investment* (CROI, efficiency and economic value) when extrinsic value is combined with active value and *service excellence* when extrinsic value is combined with passive value. What we can see is that there are similarities between Pine et al's and Malhotra et al's escapist and playfulness dimensions and between their aesthetics dimensions, but not their other quadrants.

The result of Malhotra et al's quantitative study to measure the experiential value of consumption supports Pine and Gilmore's contention that Internet shopping may be leading to a widespread commoditization of products and services with emphasis on cost reduction over brand-based differentiation. They also conclude that the scope of the scale developed for their study was restricted to the consumer context and dealt only with Holbrook's (1994) "self-oriented" dimensions of value. Holbrook also refers to the "other oriented" social dimension of value that was unexplored in their study. They argue that in both on and off-line retail service experiences, this element of value (status, ethics, esteem, and spirituality) is likely to be a significant factor in shaping the perceptions of the consumption experience.

Gupta and Vajic (2000) define experiences as a category that is different from both products and services. They also see experiences as something created by interactions between service providers and customers and that, together, they create a unique, context-specific experience (p. 35). Gupta and Vajic define an experience as the outcome of participation in a set of activities within a social context, and that it therefore needs to be conceptualized and studied in relation to the activities and social context in which it occurs (p. 34). They argue that in an experience, context stands for the physical setting, particular selection and arrangement of products, the world of objects and social actors, and the rules and procedures for social interactions with other customers and service facilitators (p. 34). To them, there are three dimensions along which experiences can be characterized and differentiated from products and services: 1) the organization's influence over the customer's use environment, 2) customer participation and 3) social interaction (p. 36). In services, they argue, customers may interact among themselves in an arbitrary way and the effect of such interactions is unpredictable. In the case of experiences, however, interactions are planned and can be an essential part of the process. An example is how Club Med has planned the interaction between its 'GOs' ('gentils organisateurs' or staff) and 'GMs' ('gentils members' or guests). An experience should be organized around a clearly defined central activity, and all other elements of the context should reinforce the central activity in a coherent manner.

A Societal View of Experiences

Csikszentmihalyi (2000) has taken a somewhat different perspective of experiences when he discusses differences between existential needs and experiential needs. Abraham Maslow's (1968, 1971) taxonomy of the lower needs (survival and safety), the midpoint needs (love and belonging) and the higher needs (esteem and self-actualization) are examples of existential needs. If consumer behaviour was driven solely by the predictable, universal needs that Maslow identified, it would also be possible to measure the value of consumer behaviour in terms of how various choices satisfy basic existential needs. As pointed out by Csikszentmihalyi, consumer choices are made for a variety of other reasons that are even less clearly understood and that may place just as great a burden on planetary resources. He calls these needs experiential needs. Whereas the Maslowian model suggests that individuals are always motivated by some discrete, specific need for survival, safety, etc, Csikszentmihalyi argues that this is not so in reality. He argues that in real life, people often find themselves in an existential vacuum where no clear need suggesting a specific goal presents itself to consciousness.

Different studies by Csikszentmihalyi and his colleagues have shown that individuals have a need to keep consciousness in an organized state, focused on some activity that requires attention. When a person feels that there is nothing to do (e.g. at home), the quality of experience tends to decline. As a result that person feels less alert, active, strong, happy, and creative and his/her self-esteem declines. Filling unstructured time with passive entertainment does not work very well, since the quality of experience while watching TV is barely more positive than that of the slough of despond that awaits the unfocused mind. Csinkszentmihalyi argues that the experiential need to keep consciousness tuned is responsible for a great deal of consumer behaviour. An example is shopping where it often does not matter what we are shopping for. Rather, the point is to shop for anything, regardless. That makes shopping a goal-directed activity thus filling the experiential vacuum that leads to depression and despair. The conclusion is that consuming is one of the ways we respond to the void that pervades consciousness when there is nothing else to do. Nevertheless, he says, a number of studies by him and his colleagues have shown that beyond a rather low threshold, material well-being does not correlate with subjective well-being. Richins and Dawson (1992) have also shown that excessive concern with financial success and material values is associated with lower levels of life satisfaction and self-esteem.

Taking a societal perspective on consumption, one could argue that there should be a direct relationship between energy consumption (e.g. in BTU[1]s) and the quality of experiences. Producing a magazine requires for example more BTUs of energy per unit of reading time than it takes to produce a book. Thus, people should get a higher quality of experience from the magazines than from reading books. Studies by Csinkszentmihalyi and colleagues show however the opposite: a slight but significant negative relationship between the average BTU load of activities and the happiness people experienced while doing them. For women there was quite a strong negative relationship, and for men no relationship at all was found between BTUs and happiness.

---

[1] One British Thermal Unit (BTU) is the heat that will raise the temperature of one pound of water by one degree Fahrenheit.

The Department of Energy in the United States has estimated that about 7% of all the energy consumed is spent on discretionary leisure activities. If the use of that energy does not make people happier it could be saved. Csinkszentmihalyi suggests that we might need a new way of thinking about consuming, one that maximizes the quality of experience while minimizing the amount of entropy produced as a result. He argues that the reason activities with low external physical energy requirements result in greater happiness is that they usually require greater inputs of *psychic* energy (stimulating conversation, reading, gardening, painting, working on crafts, writing poetry, doing mathematics). His studies have shown that people generally report being happier when they are actively involved with a challenging task, and less happy when they are passively consuming goods or entertainment.

Csinkszentmihlyi's main message is that ignoring the causes and consequences of consumer behaviour is dangerous. Furthermore, the relation between costs and benefits is usually quadratic rather than linear, meaning that up to a certain point material resources add greatly to the quality of life. Somewhere is a point of inflexion after which the relationship may no longer exist or is negative. Knowledge of that point would be beneficial to society. Consumption that involves the processing of ideas, symbols, and emotional experiences rather than the breakdown of matter should be encouraged. He mentions professions such as crafts persons, chefs, athletes, musicians, dancers, teachers, gardeners, artists, healers, and poets who create goods that increase human well being without degrading the complexity of the world. In a marketing perspective this may be interpreted as a potential for companies creating happiness without a large consumption of energy to promote themselves as good citizens. Another conclusion may be that whenever it is possible, marketing managers should try to actively involve their customers in the process. This does not mean that the more work that is done by the customer, the happier the customer is. In a customer perspective some activities may be appealing (e.g. design issues, experimentation) whereas others are not. Also, some segments on the market may be more interested in being actively involved than other segments. It is a question of providing opportunities for and encouraging them to be more active and involved.

A Commercial View of Experiences

The former British Airways chairman, Sir Colin Marshall, has noted that the "commodity mind-set" in the travel business is to think that a business is merely performing a function, such as the airline industry transporting people from point A to point B on time and at the lowest possible price (Pine and Gilmore 1998). Competition in markets with commodities, i.e. undifferentiated products and services, is different from competition in markets with strong brands. Commodity competition is price-centred and requires companies to increase economies of scale for continuous price reductions until only a few of them can survive. In a corporate perspective this is a highly undesirable situation. The problem is that in many markets a high-functional product or service quality is consequently more like an entrance ticket to the market than a guarantee of success. In addition to the functions provided, most companies need to offer something else to differentiate their offerings. One such additional benefit is to offer experiences (Pine and Gilmore 1998). In an industrial economy, companies make tangible, standardized goods that vary in terms of features offered. In a service economy companies deliver intangible customized services that vary in terms of benefits delivered. In an experience economy, companies stage memorable and personal experiences that vary in terms of the sensations offered.

The maturity of an economy also determines how much a company needs to augment its core product to be competitive. The computer manufacturer IBM makes more profits from services than from the goods they provide. Gasoline stations make more money from selling food and different consumer products than they make from selling gasoline. Similarly, it is an indication of the immaturity of the experience economy that most companies providing experiences, e.g. the Hard Rock Café, do not yet explicitly charge for the events they stage (ibid.). Pine and Gilmore's view is that an experience has been created when "a company intentionally uses services as the stage, and goods as props, to engage individual customers in a way that creates a memorable event" (p. 98). They also argue that no company sells experiences as its economic offering unless it actually charges guests an admission fee (p. 100). Gupta and Vajic (2000) have criticized this definition, by pointing out that organizations such as the Hard Rock

Café, Planet Hollywood, Rainforest Café, etc are at best providing entertainment while people eat or shop, and that they fail to create a rich and memorable experience that is enhanced with repeated interactions. They also criticize the inclusion of the pricing issue in the definition of an experience, since pricing issues are separate from what an experience is.

Pine and Gilmore suggest several ways in which memorable experiences can be designed. The experience can be themed, like the "entertainment" restaurants the Hard Rock Café, Planet Hollywood, or the Rainforest Café. Customers will immediately know what to expect when they enter such an establishment. The first crucial step in staging the experience by envisioning a well-defined theme is to help guests organize the impressions they encounter to give them a lasting memory. A theme in the store or restaurant forms the foundation for the experience, but that experience must be rendered with indelible impressions. Impressions are the "takeaways" of the experience that fulfil the theme, such as the interior design in the restaurant. Companies must introduce cues that affirm the nature of the experience to the guest, where each cue must support the theme, and none should be inconsistent with it. People use cues when they form a memorable experience in their mind. Cues can be negative, e.g. bad service, or positive, pleasant personal encounters, smells, colours, etc. One cue in the grocery store is freshly baked bread at the entrance of the store. This creates a pleasant and memorable encounter. Retailers who have an abundance of opportunities to theme experiences in the store are often said to offend this principle. Retailers talk about the shopping experience but fail to create a theme that ties the disparate merchandising presentations together in a staged experience.

Definition of Experiences in this Chapter

Experiences can be cognitive, sensory or emotional experiences or combinations thereof. The view taken in this chapter is that almost anything can be made into an experience, whether it is a product or a service. It is thus seen as a value that is added and that differentiates the brand from other brands on the market. The view taken by Gupta and Vajic (2000) that experiences are a category that is different from both products and services is not adopted. A meal can for example be a meal that is quickly forgotten. A meal can however also be a memorable experience due to the taste of the food (intensified pleasure if the cook has made a perfect blend of spicy, sour, sweet, and salty flavours). If the meal is eaten in an environment and atmosphere that are particularly pleasant, such elements would also make the whole experience more memorable. Thus, the view taken in this chapter is more similar to the French view of "savoir de vivre", i.e. you can live your life in many different ways, but if you know how to live it you will get more memorable experiences out of it. A perfect wine that is a memorable experience to drink could however be "destroyed" if served with the wrong food. Consequently, memorable experiences are created from the knowledge of the right timing and the right combination of cognitive, emotional, and sensory cues.

Memorable experiences are also related to the difference between "passive living" with mechanical registration of what happens around us, and "mindful living", i.e. having the capacity to appreciate the small things in life. Furthermore, it is related to Csikszentmihalyi's discussion of "killing time" with an unfocused mind and "actively enjoying time" with a goal-directed behaviour that can shape an action. Products can be bases for memorable experiences, although the difficulty to differentiate one brand from other brands makes it harder each year to create memorable experiences from physical products alone.

Pine and Gilmore argue that consumers can be passive and absorbed by, for example, music at a concert. In this chapter it is argued that a passive consumer will leave the concert without a memorable experience. Rather, the view adopted here is similar to the one proposed by Csikszentmihalyi, namely that greater satisfaction is received from greater inputs of psychic energy. At the theatre we can be the distant spectators, but we can also feel as if we were active participants in the events on the stage. What is required is that the experience has enough perceived intensity to become memorable, i.e. that enough psychic energy is used. Companies can assist their customers in providing more opportunities to be active.

Rita Mårtenson

Experiences in a Memory Perspective

Research of a fairly recent date has emphasized the active role consumers have in the reconstruction of their memories (Braun 1999, Gazzaniga 1998, Hoch and Deighton 1989, Shapiro and Spence 2002). In other words, consumers will interpret a message and later reconstruct it in ways that vary from one individual to another. Gazzaniga (1998, p. xiii) talks about the special device in our left brain called the interpreter, which creates the illusion that we are in charge of our actions and that the brain works according to "our" instructions, and not the other way around. The interpreter reconstructs brain events and in doing so makes telling errors of perception, memory, and judgement. He describes the process in the following way: "Reconstruction of events starts with perception and goes all the way up to human reasoning. The mind is the last to know things. After the brain computes an event, the illusory "we" (that is, the mind) becomes aware of it. The brain, particularly the left hemisphere, is built to interpret data the brain has already processed." One of his collaborators, professor Daniel Schacter at Harvard University, who worked tirelessly on the issue of false memories, has suggested a model called the Constructive Memory Framework (CFM). The CFM must solve a number of problems during both the encoding and retrieval processes. Bad solutions result in phony or false memories but, due to the information overload in modern societies, bad solutions should be the rule rather than the exception.

What is different in the new way of looking at memories is the relative role of direct product experiences as opposed to advertising information before and/or after the direct experience. Earlier research has more or less automatically assumed the superiority of direct experience where consumers can discover the objective truth of a product or service over information gained from advertising exposure (for examples, see Shapiro and Spence 2002). Recent research indicates that marketing communications can create expectations that influence the way consumers subsequently learn from their experiences (Braun 1999). A forward-framing theory where prior information from marketing communications acts as a memory schema and influences the perception of a current experience has been suggested (ibid.). Such schemas have been found to affect how consumers interpret sensory product experiences.

A review of the role of product experience versus advertising in consumer decision-making showed that it is difficult for consumers to choose the superior brand based on sensory attributes as opposed to market information (Shapiro and Spence 2002). This may explain why consumers may rely less on their direct product experiences than on other types of marketing information available. The reasons for such difficulties are:

1) The sensory attribute of each alternative must be accurately encoded. Sensory attributes are, however, inherently complex, which makes it difficult to encode them properly. An example is that non-expert wine tasters often lack the knowledge needed to evaluate relevant sensory attributes. A review of earlier research on retrieval showed that a person's memory for magnitude (e.g. intensity of light, depth of colour) decays very rapidly. Individuals do not have the necessary vocabulary to categorize the different levels of intensity of experiences, which makes rehearsal and elaboration difficult. Memory for sensory attributes often requires memory for magnitude because they tend to vary on a continuum (the sharpness of a television picture, the sound quality of a stereo). If consumers have a method to encode the experience meaningfully, their memory for sensory attributes should improve.

2) In the daily lives of consumers, brand comparisons are often done sequentially; one brand is tried first and a second brand is not tried until the next purchase of the product category, or the sound and picture of a Bang & Olufsen TV is evaluated in the B&O store and the memory of that evaluation is compared with evaluations of other brands in another store. Thus, the sensory attributes from the first trial experience must be correctly recalled from memory, which is a difficult task to accomplish for most people. For reasons to be discussed later in the chapter, memory for sensory attributes is more easily distorted than memory for market information.

3) If attribute-based brand comparisons are constructed at the time of decision making, choice processes are affected by the extent to which alternative brands can be aligned on similar dimensions. Aligned attributes (e.g. price, weight, engine size) are not only better remembered, but they also receive comparatively more weight than

nonaligned attributes. It is easier for consumers to compare products and services on attributes that are shared, i.e. are alignable. They will use alignable differences even when these attributes are considered of lesser importance than attribute information unique to one of the two alternatives (nonalignable attributes). Consumer ability to align brands on sensory attributes is however limited, given the inherent ambiguity and multidimensionality of such attributes.

The overall conclusion from this review is the apparent inability of consumers to encode meaningfully, recall accurately, and align complex sensory attributes successfully across alternatives. Furthermore, this inability has profound implications for the role these attributes have in consumers' brand choice decisions. Earlier research has however not discussed consumers' ability to evaluate sensory attributes in the long run and when brands do not play a badge role. Is it as easy to be fooled in the long run as it is when participating in an experiment? If the answer is no, we must be careful with conclusions drawn from the experiments described in this chapter.

An additional aspect to consider is intertrial time, which might hinder consumer ability to discriminate between brands along specific dimensions (Shapiro and Spence 2002). A similar example, as discussed above, is the difference between comparing two stereos in one store versus comparing two stereos from two different stores. In the first case the experience of the sound of two brands is compared. In the second case the memory of the sound of one brand is compared with either the experience of the sound of the second brand, or, if the purchase decision is delayed, the memories of the two experiences. Since most sensory attributes are highly complex and multidimensional, the experience of them will easily decay. Consumers may find that they must make decisions based on highly ambiguous information. Their ability to discriminate between the alternatives may be more like a guesswork than an evaluation of more objective differences. Experiential information is learned fast, but it is also the kind of information that is the most fragile, context-dependent, and subject to distortion (Hoch and Deighton 1989). If consumers' memories of sensory attributes are distorted, then the diagnosticity of sensory attributes in brand comparisons relative to market information such as advertising will disappear. In other words, in such situations consumers may rely more or just as much on what is said in advertising, despite the fact that they are not aware of their reliance on such easy-to-understand market information. As pointed out by Hoch and Deighton, consumers' confidence in the objectivity of their knowledge from self-generated experience with a product or service may be illusory. Source attribution comes after the reconstruction process, which may be a reason why consumers are easily biased toward believing that their own product experience is more important than advertising information.

A review of earlier research on encoding showed that advertising influenced encoding of the brand (Shapiro and Spence 2002). When consumers were exposed to positive information regarding the quality of the brand prior to the trial experience, self-assessment of the product quality assimilated to the advertising information. Exposure to advertising before the trial experience can also bias individuals to engage in search behaviour during the trial experience that confirmed the advertising information. Another finding was that when consumers were given a consumption vocabulary that differentiated visual holistic objects, it increased the consistency of preferences and their ability to articulate the basis for which preference judgements were made. Sometimes a vocabulary can have a negative effect on accuracy. Braun (1999) describes a study where people who verbalized after tasting a wine had far lower accuracy in recognizing that wine than those who did not verbalize their experiences, a phenomenon called "verbal overshadowing". It is believed that the recently generated mental representation overshadows what is learned in the perceptual experience because language cannot capture the complexity of the experience.

The new research findings show that memories do not preserve a literal representation of the world (Braun 1999). Rather, memories are constructed from fragments that are distributed across different brain regions and depend on influences operation in the present as well as the past. When people try to recall a past experience, the information is assimilated within the existing memory schema, causing them to remember only what fits their expectations. Research has also shown that information acquired after an experience can transform the memory of that experience (ibid.). Such postexperience information is most likely to distort memories when it is very similar to or brings up images which may be mistaken for the actual information experienced. Relevant, typical or consistent information is also useful. When information is consistent with assumptions it becomes incorporated into the representation and can shape future expectations. There are different ways to explain the effects of advertising on the reconstruction of memories (ibid.). The misinformation paradigm says that postexperience information will create a belief-updating process, and that recently received information may momentarily inhibit the retrieval of the information experienced. The information integration theory says that two sources of information available to consumers are balanced in an integrated impression. There are however examples from research that contradict that theory.

Advertising or any other type of marketing communications cannot influence the physical product or standardized service. Advertising can however influence the perception of both products and services. In this sense, the role of marketing can be said to be to intensify the experience by increasing consumers' awareness of attributes, make their memories vivid, etc. More details of this role are provided in the next section of the chapter. A study from psychology illustrates how this works. Richardson (1999) reports a pioneering study by White (1978) where 10 vivid, 10 moderate, and 10 weak imagers were asked to rank a set of 10 common flavours in order of preference. It is known that more-liked flavours produce more saliva than less-liked flavours and that was also measured in the experiment. Researchers used only an individual's 1st, 4th, 7th, and 10th preferences in the experiment, to ensure a sufficient degree of separation between flavours. A preweighed dental swab was placed under each participant's tongue with instructions to keep mouth, tongue, and jaws still for the next 20 seconds during which a particular flavour was to be imagined. The swab was removed after 20 seconds and weighed. The result showed that the more lifelike (vivid) the imaged stimulus, the more the physiological response (salivating) resembled the physiological response obtained to the comparable physical (actual) stimulus. The amount salivated was highest for the vivid imagers, somewhat less for the moderate imagers, and no effect was seen for the weak imagers. The weak imagers could however be trained to become vivid imagers in order to confirm the power of the presumed "active ingredient", i.e. vividness. The results presented suggest that vivid advertising can influence the perception of what is advertised, and that the power of vividness can overcome some of the dullness of everyday experiences and make ordinary products a little more special.

The Role of Advertising in Memory Creation and Memory Reconstruction

Advertising of Experiences

The creation of memorable experiences from the use of mundane products and routine services is clearly a marketing challenge. There is however very little previous research on the use of sensory cues in marketing, except for the studies on the role of music in commercials. Still, the use of sensory cues in a controlled and themed way seems to be one of the most promising ways to differentiate both product and service offerings in the future. Braun (1999) proposed that the postexperience advertising she used in her experiment exerted two levels of effect on memory: 1) immediate overshadowing, where the imagery of the advertising results in less accurate identifications and fewer negative thoughts, and 2) more enduring, as part of developing the brand schema for the new product she used in the study. Shapiro and Spence (2002) found that once the sensory attribute was more meaningfully perceived, subjects were better equipped to correctly evaluate the sound quality. They also found that clearly evaluative criteria that were nondiagnostic would not improve decision making. Another result was that when specific attributes are flagged that aid in evaluating a sensory attribute, memory for the attribute is improved. Their conclusion was that future research is needed to determine if the provision of evaluative criteria given during the trial experience strengthens the memory trace of the sensory attribute to the point where it mitigates this type of retrieval-based blending of sensory attribute and market information. Memory for both objective sensory attributes (such as taste) and affective components of an experience can become confused with posttrial advertising information, which leads to a memory for the sensory attribute blending, and hence assimilating, with advertising information. Even unfavorable experience can be reconstructed to be more favorable in retrospect. The question is whether this is an encoding phenomenon as suggested by Shapiro and Spence (2002) and/or a retrieval error as suggested by Braun (1999). Braun concluded that two types of information influence the memory reconstruction process: schemas and environmental cues. However, if advertising can influence the schemas used by consumers it can consequently influence the encoding process as well. Advertising can influence how consumers develop their own experience in that advertising can create expectations that shape the way that we perceive and remember products and services. A large advertiser can influence how consumers compare brands by emphasizing attributes that are favorable to a particular advertiser.

The reviews made in this chapter clearly illustrate how badly earlier hierarchical models on how advertising works such as the AIDA-model (Attention-Interest-Desire-Attraction) would fit the most recent findings on memory research. A good example of a model that is based on such findings is the model developed by Hall (2002), the P/E/M-model, or the Perception/Experience/Memory model (see Figure 22:1). While Hall discusses the role of advertising only, it is in this chapter assumed that any other type of persuasive influence can do the same job that advertising does. Consequently, the results discussed are not limited to the commercial world of advertising but include in addition the political world, non-profit organizations, etc, as well as other ways to influence people. The model is based on the fact that advertising plays an important role in the memory reconstruction process where consumers pull together pieces of memories of advertising with own experiences. Consumers actively interpret and reconstruct reality (advertising as well as their own experiences) in a new memory that never existed before. What does not make sense to the individual must be reinterpreted and reconstructed to something meaningful. Advertising has three roles in the P/E/M-model: *the framing of perceptions, enhancement of experience*, and *organization of memory*. The role of advertising is somewhat different in the pre-experience phase and in the post-experience phase.

In *the pre-experience exposure phase* the critical role of advertising is to *frame perceptions* and *enhance experience*. Thus, advertising should create expectations to see the brand or they may not notice it, create anticipation of how the product may taste/feel, etc and provide an implicit or explicit rationale for the anticipation it generates or, in other words, interpret the feelings advertising has created. Another important role for advertising is to enhance the experience both before and after consumers become familiar with the product.

Figure 22:1 The Three Phases and Flow of the Perception/Experience/Memory (P/E/M) Model of Advertising

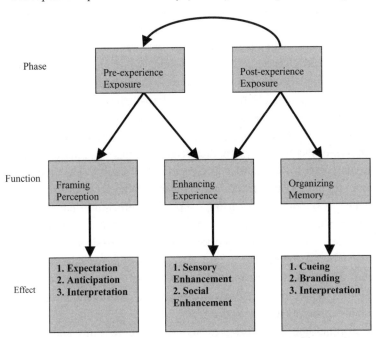

Source: Bruce F. Hall, Journal of Advertising Research, March/April 2002, p. 24 (reprinted with permission from the author)

Advertising can also establish a basis for trust in social experiences, which are the core in most service exchanges.

In *the post-experience exposure phase,* the key function of advertising is to *organize memory* but also to *enhance the perception of the experience.* Advertising provides cues for us to verbalize, see or hear the brand as well as reasons for us to believe that the experience is a good one. Braun showed that advertising can influence consumers' experiences both before and after they have encountered it. Advertising can transform "objective" sensory information both prior to and after consumers have, for example, tasted a certain juice. In Braun's experiments, advertising made students think that they had tasted a more flavourful juice by altering their memories of the tasting experience. The role of advertising is also to organize consumers' memories of all the cues available to a new memory that is in line with the objectives of the advertiser. When the respondent returns to the experience, it is framed by a new perception that corresponds to the new memory. "Objective" reality is thus a constantly shifting phenomenon that is influenced by advertising from many more different sources. Pine and Gilmore (1998) emphasized the need for theme experiences, which is a way to organize memory.

The role of advertising to enhance product or service perception is not new. William D. Wells introduced that role, the transformational role, in 1980, as one of the alternatives available to the marketer. Transformational advertising is defined as advertising that associates the experience of using (consuming/owning) the advertised brand with a unique set of psychological characteristics which would not typically be associated with the brand experience to the same degree without exposure to advertising (Puto and Hoyer 1990). It transforms the experience of owning and/or using a brand to something that is more than an ordinary brand experience. Advertising should, accordingly, in this case lead to a change in the consumer's experience with the advertised brand; otherwise it will not be effective as a persuasive medium. They see transformational advertising as being essentially affect-based rather than cognitive-based, although it can have both emotional and cognitive dimensions.

Transformational advertising must, according to Puto and Wells 1994, fulfil the following criteria:

1) It must make the experience of using the product richer, warmer, more exciting, and/or more enjoyable than that obtained solely from an objective description of the advertised brand.

2) It must connect the experience of the advertisement so closely to the experience of using the brand that consumers cannot remember the brand without recalling the experience generated by the advertisement.

The essence of transformational advertising lies in the concept of generalized emotion, which is an emotional state in which no situational cause is involved (Puto and Wells 1984). Generalized emotion tends to facilitate the selective recall of past experiences associated with the same state. The association is based on drawing similar feelings from past experiences into active memory rather than recalling the actual experience. In the commercial "Reach out and touch someone.." similar feelings generated by past (but not necessarily similar) experiences are associated with the present experience of making a long distance telephone call. Another example is to make you recall your sensory response the last time you tasted for example Gatorade, as though you were hot and thirsty when you were drinking it (Hall 2002). Braun (1999) argues that one could conceive this situation as a classic source-monitoring error where the mental representation of the taste becomes confused with the actual taste. The memory created by the advertising will feel as real as a veridical memory to respondents. The memory effects will endure over time as brand schema information, because what is perceived as own-experienced information is thought to be less resistant to decay. Generalized emotion also acts as a selective focus to create new fantasies, which will then be associated with this state and this subsequent expression. In the well-known campaign "Come to Marlboro Country" people are free to overlay their own feelings and fantasies onto the scene, and these feelings and fantasies then become permanently associated with the experience of smoking the advertised brand of cigarette. The largest advertisers are the most well-known brands on the market. In the P/E/M-model this is explained by the fact that the role of advertising is to enhance consumer experience and to organize memory. Without advertising, consumers' experience may begin to match the actual product experience. If competing brands continue to advertise, the recalled experience will fall below that of those competitors. Hall argues that consumers' recall of product quality should constantly be maintained at a higher level than the product alone can support. If not, consumers will soon abandon it. Imagery can help advertisers to add additional dimensions to the product experience.

Hall (2002) argues that since we know that advertising is operating both directly and indirectly on sensory experience and social experience, the most comprehensive and accurate measure of copy quality should be the experience itself. How has advertising altered the way we look at a particular experience? Entertaining advertising that does not do a proper job on consumers' memories of experiences is a waste of money. Advertising for intangible products and services must be tested differently. Without an actual product to sample, consumers must respond to a concept, rather than a product.

Rita Mårtenson

Summary and Suggestions for Future Research

This brief note on memorable experiences and the role that advertising has in the creation and reconstruction of memories should be seen as only a first start towards a new approach to research in the field. Much more research is needed to extend and validate the few studies available today. Examples of areas and questions for further research are:

• The role of advertising in the encoding phase for new category users as well as for new brand users. More knowledge on how to teach consumers to encode sensory attributes correctly is necessary as well as more knowledge on sequentially made decisions, the role of aligned attributes (when should alignment be avoided or created?), intertrial time and its consequences.

• Themes help consumers to organize impressions, but are there other ways that companies can use to help consumers organize their memories?

• Which cues are most helpful to affirm the nature of the experience and support the theme?

• Which factors make memory for sensory attributes veridical?

• How can advertising help consumers evaluate sensory information?

• How can imagery and language differentiate and help consumers remember experiences and at the same time distort veridical memories?

• Advertising needs to provide a language that guides consumers to imagine past experience in a way that affects postexperience choice decisions and to understand and develop their own preferences, but what characterizes such a language or vocabulary and which effect does it have?

• The role of advertising in the memory reconstruction phase. How much can advertising change in terms of consumers' sensory and affective responses to a product or service (Braun 1999)? Is it possible to reshape consumers' experiential memories (even bad ones) to become more favourable (ibid.)? Can objective sensory information such as taste be transformed in memory through exposure to postexperience advertising? Where are the limits of what advertising can accomplish for example in terms of distortion of veridical negative memories?

• Which types of message are most effective in the reconstruction process? Are they messages that are similar, relevant, typical, and/or consistent with the experience? Or, how different from the original experience can they be?

• Research by Csikszentmihalyi (2000) showed that active consumers were more satisfied. How can that knowledge be used in marketing to increase customer satisfaction?

• The studies reviewed in this chapter have not included consumers' choice in the long run. It has implicitly been assumed that advertising will continue to have as large impact as in the few experimental studies available. That conclusion needs to be confirmed. Maybe it is more difficult to influence consumers in the long run than it is to influence one single decision in an experimental setting.

• How long time does the advertising influence the recollection of experiences?

References

Aaker, D. (1996). *Building strong brands*. New York. Free Press.

Aaker, D. & Keller, K.L. (1990). Consumer evaluations of brand extensions. *Journal of Marketing,* 54(January), 27-41.

Aaker, J. (1996). Conceptualizing and measuring brand personality. *Unpublished working paper (No. 262)*, Marketing Studies Center, UCLA, US.

Aaker, J. (1997). Dimensions of brand personality. *Journal of Marketing Research,* 34(3), 347 – 356.

Aaker, J. (1999a). The malleable self: The role of self-expression in persuasion. *Journal of Marketing Research,* 36(1), 45 57.

Aaker, J. (1999b). Availability versus valence: The impact of culture-specific versus culture-invariant associations on consumer attitudes. *Unpublished working paper (No. 334)*, Marketing Studies Center, UCLA, US.

Aaker, J., Benet-Martínez, V., & Garolera, J. (2001). Consumption symbols as carriers of culture: A study of Japanese and Spanish brand personality constructs. *Journal of Personality & Social Psychology,* 81(3), 492-508.

Aaker, David A. (1991). *"Managing Brand Equity: Capitalizing on the Value of a Brand Name."* The Free Press.

Aaker, David A. (1996). *Building Strong Brands*, Free Press.

Aaker, David A. & Joachimsthaler, Erich (2000). *Brand Leadership*, Free Press.

Aaker, David A., Kumer V., & Day, George S. (2001). *Market Research*, Wiley.

Aaker, J. L.; Maheswaran, D. (1997). The Effects of Cultural Orientation on Persuasion, in: *Journal of Consumer Research*, Vol. 24, December, pp. 315-328.

Abel, Sarah and Amanda Long (1996). Event sponsorship: does it work ?, *Admap*, 31, 11, issue 368, 18-21.

AC Nielsen (2002). Advertising expenditures in Germany 2001, www.acnielsen.de.

AC Nielsen NetRating, (2001). Netscope, March

Aglietta, Michel (1979). *A Theory of Capitalist Regulation: The US Experience.* London: New Left Books.

Ahluwalia, R., & Gürhan-Canli, Z. (2000). The effects of extensions on the family brand name: An accessibility-diagnosticity perspective. *Journal of Consumer Research,* 27(December), 371-381.

Allen, R. & Reber, A.S. (1980). Very long term memory for tacit knowledge. *Cognition,* 8, 175-185, cited in Berry & Dienes (1991).

Ambler, T. (2001). Persuasion, Pride and Prejudice: How Ads Work, in: *International Journal of Advertising*, Vol. 19, pp. 299-315.

Ambler, T. (2000). Persuasion, pride, and prejudice: how ads work, *International Journal of Advertising* Vol. 19, No. 3.

Alba, J. & Hutchinson, J.W. (1987). Dimensions of Consumer Expertise, *Journal of Consumer Research*, 13, 411-454.

Albo, Gregory; Langille, David & Panitch, Leo (eds.) (1993). *A Different Kind of State?* Toronto: Oxford University Press.

Alt, M. & Griggs, S. (1988). Can a brand be cheeky? *Marketing Intelligence & Planning,* 4, 9-16.

References

Andersen, K. and T.Clevenger, Jr. (1963). "A Summary of Experimental Research in Ethos". *Speech Monographs* 30, 59-78.

Andersen, Lars P. (2001). Reklamefilmens indholdsdimensioner: Mod en bedre genreforståelse. *Working Paper 21*, Copenhagen Business School.

Andreasen, A.R.; Belk, R.W. (1980). Predictors of Attendance at the Performing Arts, in: *Journal of Consumer Research*, Vol. 7, pp. 112-120.

Antonides, G.; van Raaij, W.F. (1998). *Consumer Behaviour – A European Perspective*, Chichester.

Antonides, G./van der Sar, N. (1990). Individual Expectations, Risk Perception, and Preferences in Relation to Investment Decision Making, *Journal of Economic Psychology*, 11, 227-245.

ARD Werbung (1993). Sponsoring in der ARD, Media Marketing Info, n° 1, in *Sportsponsoring. Wirkungsforschung – Status und Pespektiven*, Hans-Jürgen Meier, Arnold Hermanns, Anton Glogger and Urban K. Wissmeier (eds.), Hamburg: Ufa Film- und Fernseh-GmbH, 61-64.

Arnold, Stewart (2001). *Advertising Development in the Baltic States// Marketing Strategies for Central and Eastern Europe.* – England.: Ashgate Publishing Limited, pp. 155-175.

Arthur, Dave, Garry Dolan and Michael Cole (1998). The Benefits of Sponsorship Success: An Analysis of the Relationship Between Television Exposure and the Position of the Motorcycle Rider, *The Cyber-Journal of Sport Marketing (online)*, 2, 2, available at www.cjsm.com.Vol2/arthur22.html.

Augoustinos, Martha and Walker, Ian (1995). *Social Cogniton.* Sage Publications Ltd.

Aylesworth, A. B., & S. B. MacKenzie (1999). Context is key: the effect of program-induced mood on thoughts about the ad. *Journal of Advertising, 27* (2), 17-31.

Aylesworth, A. B., MacKenzie, S. B. (1998). Context is Key: The Effect of Program-Induced Mood on Thoughts about the Ad, in: *Journal of Advertising*, Vol. 27, No. 2, pp. 17-31.

Bagozzi, R. (1986). "Principles of Marketing", *Chicago Science Research Associates Inc.*

Baltic Media Book - Baltic Media Facts Ltd, 1998,1999, 2000, 2001

Bandura, A (1977). *Social learning theory.* Eglewood Cliffs, NJ: Prentice-Hall.

Barich, H., & Kotler, P. (1991) A framework for marketing image management. *Sloan Management Review,* 32(2), 94-104.

Barr, T. F.; Kellaris, J. J. (2000). Susceptibility to Advertising: An Individual Difference with Implications for the Processing of Persuasive Messages, in: *Advances in Consumer Research*, Vol. 27, pp. 230-234.

Barthel, D. (1988). *Putting on appearances: Gender and advertising.* Philidelphia: Temple University.

Bath, S., Kelley, G.E., & O'Donnell, K.A.(1998). An investigation of consumer reactions to the use of different brand names. *Journal of Product and Brand Management,* 7 (1), 41-50.

Batra, R., Lehman, D.R. & Singh, D. (1993). The brand personality component of brand goodwill: Some antecedents and consequences. In: D.A. Aaker & A.L. Biel (Eds.), *Brand equity and advertising: Advertising's role in building strong brands.* Hillsdale, NJ: Lawrence Erlbaum Ass.

References

Batra, R., Myers, J.G. & Aaker, D.A. (1996). *Advertising Management.* Upper Saddle River, NJ: Prentice Hall.

Bauer, H., Mäder, R. & Keller, T. (2001). *An investigation of the brand personality scale: Assessment of validity and implications with regard to brand policy in European culture domains.* http://marketing.byu.edu/ams/bauer-mader-keller.htm

Baux, Philippe (1991). Modèles de persuasion et parrainage sportif, *Revue Française du Marketing,* n° 131, 51-67.

Behrens, G.; Esch, F.-R. et al.(2001). *Gabler Lexikon Werbung,* [Gabler Advertising Lexicon], Wiesbaden.

Belk, Russel W. (1996). "Hyperreality and Globalization", *Journal of International Consumer Marketing,* Vol.8/3;4, pp. 23-37.

Bell, Daniel (1976). *The Cultural Contradictions of Capitalism.* New York: Basic Books.

Bengtsson, Anders (2002). Consumers and Mixed-Brands. *"On the Polysemy of Brand Meaning",* Lund Business Press.

Bennett, Roger (1999). Sport sponsorship, spectator recall and false consensus, *European Journal of Marketing,* 33, 3/4, 291-313.

Berens, G. & Van Riel, C.B.M. (2001). *Does corporate brand value affect product evaluations?* Paper presented at the 5th International conference on Corporate Reputation, Identity and Competitiveness, Paris, France.

Berg, M. van den (2001). *Merkpersoonlijkheid: Concept, strategische toepassing enonderzoek (publication # 18).* Amsterdam, the Netherlands: SWOCC.

Berge, Emilie van den (2002). *Merkpersoonlijkheid langs de meetlat (publication #21).* Amsterdam, the Netherlands: SWOCC.

Berge, Kjell L. and Per Ledin (2001). Perspektiv på genre. *Rhetorica Scandinavica*, pp. 4-16.

Berger, P. & T. Luckman (1966). *"The Social Construction of Reality"*, Garden City, N.Y.

Berlo, D. K., J..B. Lemert, and R. J. Mertz. (1969). "Dimensions of Evaluating the Acceptability of Message Sources". *Public Opinion Quarterly* 33, 563-76.

Berman, Ronald (1981). *Advertising and Social Change.* Beverly Hills (CA): Sage.

Berry, Dianne & Dienes, Zoltan, (1991). The relationship between implicit memory and implicit learning, *British Journal of Psychology,* Vol. 82, Issue 3.

Bhargava, M., N. Donthu, and R. Caron (1994). Improving the Effectiveness of Outdoor Advertising: Lessons from a Study of 282 Campaigns, *Journal of Advertising Research*, 34, 2, 46-55.

Blackwell, R. D.; Miniard, P.W.; Engel, J.F. (2001). *Consumer Behavior*, 9th ed., Fort Worth.

Blattberg, Robert C. og Deighton, John (1991). "Interactive Marketing: Exploiting the Age of Addressability". *Sloan Management Review.* Fall.

Blom, C., & Cramer, K. (2002). *Merkstrategieën: Portfoliomanagement in de financiële dienstverlening* [Brand strategies: Portfolio management in the financial services]. Amsterdam: SWOCC, University of Amsterdam.

Booth, Wayne C.; *A Rhetoric Of Irony.* Chicago: University of Chicago Press, 1974.

Borch, Anita (1999). "Forbruk på Internet, mars 1999. En landsomfattende undersøkelse". *SIFO Arbeidsnotat* 2:99. Norway.

References

Borkenau, P.; Ostendorf, F. (1993). *NEO-Fünf-Faktoren Inventar (NEO-FFI)* nach Costa und McCrae – Handanweisung, Fragebogen und Schablone [NEO-Five-Factor-Inventory (NEO-FFI) by Costa and McCrae], Göttingen.

Boulding, K.E. (1956). *The image*. Ann Arbor, MI: University of Michigan Press.

Boutlis, Paulie (2000). "A theory of postmodern advertising", *International Journal of Advertising Research,* Vol. 19/1, pp. 3-23.

Bowers, John Waite & Phillips, William A. (1967). *"A note on the Generality of Source-Credibility scales,"* Speech Monographs, 34 (2), 185-86.

Brailsford, Ian (1998). 'Madison Avenue puts on its best hair shirt': US advertising and its social critics", *International Journal of Advertising Research*, Vol. 17/3, pp. 365-381.

Braun, Katryn A. (1999). "Postexperience Advertising Effects on Consumer Memory", *Journal of Consumer Research*, 25, 4, pp 319-332.

Brennan, Ian, Khalid M. Dubas & Laurie A. Babin (1999). 'The influence of product-placement type & exposure time on product-placement recognition', *International Journal of Advertising* 18(3): 323-337.

Breslow, N.E. and Day, N.E. (1980). *Statistical Methods in Cancer Research*, Vol. 1: The analysis of case-control studies. International Agency for Research on Cancer. Lyon.

Brinkhoff, Hein, Kees ter Woort, Paul Sikkema, Joris van de Leur & Tijl Rood (1996). *'Grenzen aan vervagende grenzen'* ['Limits to blurred boundaries'], Blad/dossier, no. 11. Amsterdam: VNU.

Britt, S.H. (1971). Psychological principles of the corporate imagery mix. *Business Horizons, 14*(June), 55-59.

Broadbent, Simon and Smith, Alan (1999). Use of the 2-by-2 table in Advertising Effectiveness. *Marketing and Research Today*. May 1999.

Broadbent, Simon, (1979). 'One way TV advertisements work', *Journal of the Market Research Society*, Vol. 21, No. 3, 139-166.

Broadbent, Simon, Spittler, Jayne Z., Lynch, Kate, (1997). 'Building Better TV Schedules: New Light from the Single Source', *Journal of Advertising Research*, Vol. 37, Iss. 4.

Broadbent, Simon, (1999). *When to Advertise*. Admap Publications. United Kingdom.

Brokken, F.B. (1978). *The language of personality*. Meppel, the Netherlands: Krips.

Brown, Stephen (2001). *Marketing - The Retro Revolution*. London: Sage.

Brown, Stephen (1993). "Postmodern Marketing?", *European Journal of Marketing*, Vol. 27/4, pp.19-34.

Brown, Stephen (1994). "Marketing as Multiplex: Screening Postmodernism", *European Journal of Marketing*, Vol. 28 (8/9), pp. 27-51.

Brown, T.J. (1998). Corporate associations in marketing: Antecedents and consequences. *Corporate Reputation Review,* 1(3), 215-233.

Brown, T.J., & Dacin, P.A. (1997). The company and the product: Corporate associations and consumer product responses. *Journal of Marketing,* 61(1), 68-84.

Bryant, J., & Comisky, P. W. (1978). The effect of positioning a message within differentially cognitively involving portions of a television segment on recall of the message. *Human Communication Research,* 5 (1), 63-75.

References

Brucks, M (1985). "The Effects on Product Class knowledge of information search Behaviour", *Journal of Consumer Behaviour*, Vol. 6, (March).

Bundesverband Deutscher Investmentgesellschaften (BVI) (2001). *Investment 2001 – Daten, Fakten, Entwicklungen*, Frankfurt/Main.

Burne, T. & T. Ambler, (1999). *The Impact of Affect on Memory of Advertising*, Journal of Advertising Research, March, pp.25-34

Campbell, David and Ron Hulme (2001). "The winner-takes-all economy", *The McKinsey Quarterly*, No. 1, pp. 82-93.

Calfee, John E. & Ringold, Debra J (1994). "The Seventy Percent Majority: Enduring Consumer Beliefs About Advertising", *Journal of Public Policy and Marketing*, Vol. 13 (Fall), pp. 222-238.

Cameron, Glen T. & Patricia A. Curtin (1995). 'Tracing sources of information pollution: a survey and experimental test of print media's labeling policy for feature advertising', *Journalism and Mass Communication Quarterly* 72(1): 178-189.

Cameron, Glen T., Kuen-Hee Ju-Pak, Bong-Hyun Kim (1996). 'Advertorials in magazines: current use and compliance with industry guidelines', *Journalism and Mass Communication Quarterly* 73(3). 722-733.

Camp, L. (1995). Latest thinking on optimization of brand use in financial services marketing. *The Journal of Brand Management, 3*(6), 344-351.

Caprara, G.V., Barbaranelli, C. & Guido, G. (2001). Brand personality: How to make the metaphor fit?, *Journal of Economic Psychology, 22*, 377-395.

Carbone, L. P. and S. H. Haeckel (1994). "Engineering customer experience", *Marketing Management*, No. 3, pp. 8-19.

Carlson, R.O. (1963). The nature of corporate images. In J.W. Riley, Jr. (ed.), *The Corporation and Its Publics* (pp.24-47). New York: John Wiley & Sons, Inc.

Cattell, R.B.; Eber, H.W.; Tatsuoka, M.M. (1970). *Handbook for the Sixteen Personality Factor Questionnaire*, Champaign, IL.

Center for Media Education, U.S.A: http://www.cme.org (November 2000).

Chapman, G. & Johnson, E. (1999). Anchoring, Activation, and the Construction of Values, *Organizational Behavior and Human Decision Processes*, 79, 115-153.

Chapman, G. & Johnson, E. (1994). The Limits of Anchoring, *Journal of Behavioral Decision Making*, 7, 223-242.

Chapman's & C.R. Schwenck, (1991). "Self-serving Attribution, Managerial Cognition and company Performance", *Strategic Management Journal*, Vol. 12, No3.

Christensen, Lars T. (2001). *Reklame i selvsving.* Copenhagen: Samfundslitteratur.

Christopher, Martin, Payne, Adrian og Ballantyne (1991). *Relationship Marketing.* Butterworth & Heinemann.

Chuch, T.A. & Burke, P.J. (1994). Exploratory and Confirmatory Tests of the Big Five and Tellegen's Three and Four-Dimensional Models. *Journal of Personality and Social Psychology, 66(1)*, 93-114.

Clancy, Kevin J. & Lloyd, David W. (1999). *Uncover the hidden power of television programming.* Thousand Oaks: Sage.

Clow, Kenneth E. & Baack, Donald (2001). *Integrated Advertising, Promotion & Marketing Communications.* Upper Saddle River (N.J.): Prentice Hall.

References

Clutterbuck, Clark, Armistead. (1993). *"Inspired Customer Service, Strategies for Service Quality"*, Kogan Page

Cohen, J. (1988). *Statistical Power Analysis for the Behavioral Sciences*, Hillsdale.

Coley, M.L. (1992). Ad-time - its uses and benefits, in *Sponsorship Europe '92 Conference Proceedings* (simultaneously: *ESOMAR Seminar on Sponsorship)*, Monaco, 2-4 December, Expoconsult (ed.), Maarssen (The Netherlands), 77-82.

Collett, Peter, (1986) 'Video-recording the viewers in their Natural Habitat', *ESOMAR Seminar on New Developments in Media Research*, Helsinki (Finland) 9th-12th April.

Colley, R. H. (1961). Defining advertising goals for measured advertising results, Association of National Advertisers, New York

Condry, J., Bence, P. & Scheibe, C. (1988). "Non-program content of children's television", *Journal of Broadcasting and Electronic Media*, 32(3), 255-270.

Corbett, Edward P.J. 1990 (1965). *"Classical Rhetoric for the Modern Student"*. Oxford University Press

Cornwell, T. Bettina and Isabelle Maignan (1998). An International Review of Sponsorship Research, *Journal of Advertising*, 27, 1, 1-21.

Cornwell, T. Bettina, Isabelle Maignan and Richard Irwin (1997). Long-term Recall of Sponsorship Sources. An Empirical Investigation of Stadium and Sport Cafe Audiences, *Asia-Australia Marketing Journal*, 5, 1, 45-57.

Costa, P.T.; McCrae, R.R. (1985). *The NEO Personality Inventory Manual*, Odessa, FL.

Costa, P.T.; McCrae, R.R. (1992a). Four Ways Five Factors are Basic, in: *Personality and Individual Differences*, 13, pp. 653-665.

Costa, P.T.; McCrae, R.R. (1992b). *Revised NEO Personality Inventory (NEO-PI-R) and NEO Five-Factor Inventory (NEO-FFI) Professional Manual*, Odessa, FL.

Couty, Frédéric (1994). L'évaluation de la notoriété du sponsoring sportif, *Revue Française du Marketing*, n° 150, 75-82.

Craig, R. (1990). "Men's men and women's women: How TV commercials portray gender to different audiences", in: *Issues and Effects of Mass Communication: Contemporary Voices*, Robert E. Kemper (ed.). San Diego: CA: Capstone Publishers, 1992: 89-99).

Cramer, K. (2000). *Brand strategies: Portfolio management in the service industries*. Amsterdam: SWOCC/ASCoR, University of Amsterdam.

Cramer, K. (May, 2001). *Brand portfolio management in the service industries: A case study of the Dutch temping market*. Working paper presented at the 2001 Conference of the American Marketing Associations Services Marketing Special Interest Group (SERVSIG), Sydney, Australia.

Crimmins, James and Martin Horn (1996). Sponsorship: From Management Ego Trip to Marketing Success, *Journal of Advertising Research*, 36, 4, 11-21.

Cronkhite, G., and J..Liska. 1976. "*A Critique of Factor Analytic Approaches to the Study of Credibility*". Communication Monographs 43, 91-107.

Crowley, Martin G. (1991). Prioritizing the Sponsorship Audience, *European Journal of Marketing*, 25, 11, 11-21.

Csikszentmihalyi, Mihaly (2000). "The Costs and Benefits of Consuming", *Journal of Consumer Research*, September, Vol. 27, pp. 267-272.

References

Cuilenburg, Jan J. van, Peter C. Neijens & Otto Scholten (eds.) (1999). *Media in overvloed* [Media in abundance]. Amsterdam: Amsterdam University Press

Cwalina, W., Falkowski, A. (1999). Decision processes in perception in the political preferences research: A Comparative analysis of Poland, France and Germany. *Journal for Mental Changes*, 5(2), 27-50.

Cwalina, W., Falkowski, A. (2000). Psychological mechanisms of political persuasion: The influence of political advertising on voting behavior. *Polish Psychological Bulletin*, 31(3), 203-222.

Cwalina, W., Falkowski, A., Kaid, L.L. (2000). Role of advertising in forming the image of politicians: Comparative analysis of Poland, France, and Germany. *Media Psychology*, 2(2), 119-146.

Daneshvary, Rennae and R. Keith Schwer (2000). The association endorsement and consumers' intention to purchase, *Journal of Consumer Marketing*, 17, 3, 203-213.

Darian, Jean C. "In-Home Shopping: Are There Consumer Segments? *Journal of Retailing* 63, 3 (1987). 163-86

Davis, Aeron; "Public Relations, business news and the reproduction of corporate elite power", *Journalism*, Vol.1/3, pp. 282-304, 2000.

Davis, Joel J. (1997). *Advertising Research: Theory and Practice.* Prentice - Hall, Inc.

Day, A. (1997). Branding: New entrants to financial services highlight. *The Banker,* 47, 30-32.

De Bondt, W. (1998). A Portrait of the Individual Investor, *European Economic Review*, 42, 831-844.

De Bondt, W. & Thaler, R. (1993). Does the Stock Market Overreact?, in: *Thaler, R.* (Edts.). *Advances in Behavioral Finance*, New York, 249-264.

De Chernatony, Leslie. 2001. *"From Brand Vision to Brand Evaluation. Strategically Building and Sustaining Brands"*. Butterworth Heinemann.

De Chernatony, Leslie de & Segal-Horn, Susan. 2001: "Building on Services" Characteristics to Develop Successful Services Brands. *Journal of Marketing Management*, 17.

De Chernatony, L., & Dall'Olmo Riley, F. (1999). Experts' views about defining services brands and the principles of services branding. *Journal of Business Research,* 46(2), 181-192.

De Raad, B. (2000). *The Big Five Personality Factors: The Psycholexical Approach to Personality*, Göttingen.

De Ruyter, K., & Wetzels, M. (2000). The role of corporate image and extension similarity in service brand extensions. *Journal of Economic Psychology,* 21, 639-659.

Diehl, S. (2002). *Erlebnisorientiertes Internet-Marketing*, [Emotion Based Internet Marketing], Wiesbaden.

Digman, J.M. (1990). Personality Structure: Emergence of the Five-Factor Model, in: *Annual Review of Psychology*, 41, pp. 417-440.

Duval, S.; Wicklund, R.A. (1972). A Theory of Objective Self Awareness, New York.

Deimel, Klaus (1993). Erinnerungswirkung der Sportwerbung, *Marketing - Zeitschrift für Forschung und Praxis,* 15, 1, 5-14.

References

Dellebeke, Marcel & Jan J.C. Kabel, eds. (2000) Omroep & Commercie 1999. *Adviezen, beschikkingen, uitspraken, beleidslijnen, wet- en regelgeving* [Broadcasting & Commerce]. Amsterdam: Cramwinckel.

DeLorme, D.E., L.N. Reid & M.R. Zimmer (1994). Brands in films: young moviegoers' experiences and interpretations. Paper presented to the 1994 conference of the American Academy of Advertising.

DeLorme, Denise E. & Reid, Leonard N. (1999). "Moviegoers' experiences and interpretations of brands in films revisited", *Journal of Advertising*, Vol. 28/2, pp.71-95.

Den Engelsen, B., & Hurts, F. (2001). A Virgin is an exception. *Tijdschrift voor Marketing*, February, 68-70.

Digman, J.M. (1990). Personality structure: Emergence of the five-factor model. *Annual Review of Psychology*, 41, 417-440.

Doney, Patricia M. and Cannon, Joseph P. (1997). "An Examination of the Nature of Trust in Buyer-Seller Relationships", *Journal of Marketing*, Vol. 61 (April), 35-51

Douglas, J. (1972). The verbal image: Student perceptions of political figures. *Speech Monographs*, 39, 1-15.

Douglas, S.P., Craig, C.S., & Nijssen, E.J. (2001). Integrating branding strategy across markets: Building international brand architecture. *Journal of International Marketing*, 9(2), 97-114.

Drees, Norbert (1987). Werbung an Rennstrecken. Präsenz und Erinnerungswirkung ausgewählter Werbeträger bei Fernsehübertragungen, *Werbeforschung & Praxis*, 32, 1, 9-12.

Du Plessis, E. & C. Foster (2000). Like the ad. Like the brands? Chicken or egg?, *Admap*, Dec. pp. 35-38

Dwyer, Robert F., Schurr, Paul H. and Oh, Sejo (1987). "Developing Buyer-Seller Relationships," *Journal of Marketing*, Vol. 51 (april), 11-27

Easton, Simon and Penny Mackie (1998). When football came home: A case history of the sponsorship activity at EURO 96, *International Journal of Advertising*, 17, 1, 99-114.

Ehrenberg Andrew; "Repetitive advertising and the consumer", *Journal of Advertising Research*, Vol. 14, pp. 25-34, 1974.

Eilander, Goos (1992). Improving the media performance by using sponsorship on top of other media, in *Sponsorship Europe '92 Conference Proceedings* (simultaneously: *ESOMAR Seminar on Sponsorship)*, Monaco, 2-4 December, Expoconsult (ed.), Maarssen (The Netherlands), 260-270.

Erdogan, B. Zafer and Philipp J. Kitchen (1998). Managerial mindsets and the symbiotic relationship between sponsorship and advertising, *Marketing Intelligence & Planning*, 16, 6, 369-374.

Evans, F.B. (1963). "Selling as a Dyadic Relationship - A New Approach". *American Behavioral Scientist.* Vol. 6, May.

Evensky, H. (1997). Risk is a Four-Letter Word, *Journal of Financial Planning*, 10, 5, 74-82.

Ewen, R.B. (1998). *Personality: A Topical Approach – Theories, Research, Major Controversies, and Emerging Findings*, Mahwah, NJ.

Eysenck, H.J. (1970). *The Structure of Human Personality*, 3rd ed., London.

Eysenck, H.J. (1990). Biological Dimensions of Personality, in: Pervin, L.S. (ed.). *Handbook of Personality Theory and Research*, New York, pp.129-145.

References

Eysenck, H.J. (1992). Four Ways Five Factors are not Basic, in: *Personality and Individual Differences*, 13, pp. 667-673.

Fairclough, Norman; *Critical Discourse Analysis: the critical study of language*. London: Longman, 1995.

Falkowski, A., Cwalina, W. (1999). Methodology of constructing effective political advertising: An empirical study of the Polish presidential election in 1995. In B.I. Newman (ed.), *Handbook of political marketing*, (283-304). Thousand Oaks, CA: Sage.

Falkowski, A., Cwalina, W. (2002). Structural models of voter behavior in the 2000 Polish presidential election. *Journal of Political Marketing*, 1(2/3), 137-158.

Farrelly, G. & Reichenstein, W. (1984). Risk Perceptions of Institutional Investors, *Journal of Portfolio Management*, 10, 2, 5-12.

Fenigstein, A. (1979). Self-Consciousness, Self-Attention, and Social Interaction, in: *Journal of Personality and Social Psychology*, Vol. 37, No. 1, pp. 75-86.

Fenigstein, A.; Scheier, M.A.; Buss, A.H. (1975). Public and Private Self-Consciousness: Assessment and Theory, in: Maher, B.A. (ed.): *Journal of Consulting and Clinical Psychology*, Vol. 43, No. 4, pp. 522-527.

Finucane, M., Alhakami, A., Slovic, P. & Johnson, S. (2000). The Affect Heuristic in Judgments of Risks and Benefits, *Journal of Behavioral Decision Making*, 13, 1-17.

Firat, A. Fuat, Dholakia, Nikhilesh & Venkatesh, Alladi; "Marketing in a postmodern world", *European Journal of Marketing*, Vol. 29/1, pp. 40-56, 1995.

Firat, A. Fuat & Venkatesh, Alladi (1995). "Liberatory postmodernism and the reenchantment of consumption", *Journal of Consumer Research,* 22 (December), pp. 239-267.

Firat, A. Fuat & Dholakia, Nikhilesh (1998). *Consuming People.* London/New York: Routledge.

Fisher, K. & Statman, M. (2000). Cognitive Biases in Market Forecasts, *Journal of Portfolio Management*, , S. 72-81.

Fiske, J. (1987). *Television Culture.* New York: Methuen.

Floor, J.M.G. & Van Raaij, W.F. (1998). *Marketing communicatie strategie.* Groningen, the Netherlands: Wolters-Noordhoff.

Fournier, S. (1998). Consumers and their brands: Developing relationship theory in consumer research. *Journal of Consumer Research*, 24, 343-373.

Franzen, G. & Berg, M. van den (2001). *Strategisch Management van merken.* Deventer, the Netherlands: Kluwer.

Franzen, Giep & Bouwman, Margot. (2001). *"The Mental World of Brands. Mind, memory and brand success."* WARC.

Franzen, M.P. (2000). *Merkextensies: Effectief combineren van merken en producten* [Brand extensions: Effectively combining brands and products]. In M.P. Franzen (ed.), *Combineren van merken en producten* (pp. 9-72). Deventer, The Netherlands: Samsom.

Franzen, M.P., & Van den Berg, M. (2002). *Strategisch management van merken* [Strategic brand management]. Deventer: Kluwer.

Franzen, G. (1994). *Advertising effectiveness: Findings from empirical research.* Oxfordshire, United Kingdom: NTC.

Frédéric, A. (1992). La mesure de l'efficacité du sponsoring, *Revue Française du Marketing*, 138, 1992/3, 123-136.

References

Frédéric, A. and Emmanuel J. Chéron (1991). Mesure de l'efficacité du sponsoring: une analyse des effets intermédiaires sur l'audience directe de l'événement, in *Proceedings of the 6th Congress of the French Marketing Association (AFM)*, 10-11 May, 121-148, La Baule: Association Française de Marketing.

Freter, H. (1983). *Marktsegmentierung*, [Market Segmentation], Kohlhammer, Stuttgart.

Fuchs, Stéphan (1994). La recherche en marketing sur le thème du sponsoring, du mécénat et du parrainage en France depuis 1984. Contribution à la présentation du bilan et des perspectives du champ disciplinaire, *Revue Française du Marketing*, n° 150, 55-70.

Gabriel, Yiannis & Lang, Tim (1995). *The unmanageable consumer: Contemporary consumption and its fragmentation.* Thousand Oaks, CA: Sage.

Geis, F. L., Brown, V., Jennings, J., & Porter, N. (1984). "TV commercials as achievement scripts for women", *Sex Roles: A Journal of Research,* 10(7/8), 513-525.

Gabrielsen, Gorm and Flemming Hansen (2000). Quantifying effects of banner advertising, *Advertising Research Group, Copenhagen Business School, Research paper n° 4*, August 3.

Galbraith, John Kenneth; *The Affluent Society.* New York: Houghton Mifflin, 1958.

Ganassali, Stéphane and Laurence Didellon (1996). Le transfert comme principe central du parrainage, *Recherche et Applications en Marketing*, 11, 1, 37-48.

Galotti, M (1994). "*Cognitive Psychology in and out of the laboratory*", Pacific Grove, CA.Brooks/Cole Publication Company.

Ganzach, Y. (2000). Judging Risk and Return of Financial Assets, *Organizational Behavior and Human Decision Processes*, 83, 353-370.

Garver, Eugene. 1994: *"Aristotle's Rhetoric. An art of Character"*. The University of Chicago Press.

Gazzaniga, Michael S. (1998). *The Mind's Past*. Berkeley, CA: University of California Press.

Geist, R. (1999). The Emotions of Risk, in: *Lifson, L. & Geist, R.* (Edts.): The Psychology of Investing, New York et al., 11-28.

Giannelloni, Jean-Luc and Pierre Valette-Florence (1992). La mesure de l'efficacité de le communication par l'événement: une approche structurelle, in *Proceedings of the 7th congress of the French Marketing Association (AFM)*, May, 252-276: Association Française de Marketing.

Gierl, Heribert and Andrea Kirchner (1999). Emotionale Bindung und Imagetransfer durch Sportsponsoring, *transfer, Werbeforschung & Praxis*, 44, 3, 32-35.

Ginsburg, H. & Opper. S (1979). *Piaget's Theory of Intellectual Development*, 2d ed., Englewood Cliffs, NJ: Prentice Hall.

Goldberg, L.R. (1990). An alternative "Description of Personality": The Big Five factor structure. *Journal of Personality and Social Psychology,* 59, 1216-1229.

Goldberg, L.R. (1992). The Development of Markers of the Big-Five Structure, in: *Psychological Assessment*, 4, pp. 26-42.

Goldberg, M. E., & Gorn G. J. (1987). Happy and sad TV program: How they affect reactions to commercials. *Journal of Consumer Research,* 14 (3), 387-403.

References

Goldberg, M.E., Gorn, G.J., & Gibson, W. (1978). "TV messages for snack and breakfast foods: Do they influence children's preferences?", *Journal of Consumer Research*, 5 (September), 73-81.

Goldman, Robert; *Reading Ads Socially*. New York: Routledge, 1992.

Goldsmith, Ronald E., Lafferty, Barbara A., Newell, Stephen J. 2000. *"The Influence of Corporate Credibility on Consumer Attitudes and Purchase Intent"*. Corporate Reputation Review 3. 2000. 304-318.

Gramsci, Antonio (1949/71). "Americanism and Fordism", In Hoare, Quintin & Smith, Geoffrey Nowell (eds.) (1971): *Selections from the Prison Notebooks*. New York: International Publishers.

Greenfield, P. M. (1984). *Mind and media: The effects of television, video games, and computers*. Cambridge, MA: Harvard University Press.

Gronroos, C. (1984). A service quality model and its marketing implications. *European Journal of Marketing, 18*(4), 36-44.

Grønholdt, Lars, (1990). 'Reklamens effekt – modeller og deres praktiske anvendelse', in *Medievalg i Danmark,* Civiløkonomens forlag 1.udgave, 1.oplag.

Gummesson , Evert (1995). *Relationsmarknadsføring: Från 4P till 30R*. Liber-Hermods. Malmø.

Gunter, B., Furnham, A., & Beeson C. (1997). Recall of television advertisements as a function of program evaluation. *Journal of Psychology*, 121 (5), 541-553.

Gupta, Sudheer and Mirjana Vajic (2000). "The Contextual and Dialectical Nature of Experiences", in eds. James A. Fitzsimmons and Mona J. Fitzsimmons, *"New Service Development. Creating Memorable Experiences"*, pp. 33-51, Thousand Oaks, CA: Sage Publications, Inc.

Gwinner, Kevin (1997). A model of image creation and image transfer in event sponsorship, *International Marketing Review*, 14, 3, 145-158.

Habermas, Jürgen (1962). *Strukturwandel der Öffentlichkeit. Untersuchungen zu einer Kategorie der bürgerlichen Gesellschaft.* Neuwied & Berlin, Luchterhand Verlag.

Hackforth, Josef (1989). Zwischen Bandenwerbung und Bandenwirkung. Erste Ergebnisse einer Studie zur EURO 88, in *Sport- und Kultursponsoring*, Arnold Hermanns (ed.), München: Vahlen, 100-111.

Haley, R.J. and A.L. Baldinger (1991). The ARF Copy Research Validity Project, *Journal of Advertising Research*, Vol. 31, No.2

Haley, R.J. et al. (1994). The Missing Measures of Copy Testing, *Journal of Advertising Research*, Vol. 34, 3, May/June

Hall, Bruce F. (2002). "A New Model for Measuring Advertising Effectiveness", *Journal of Advertising Research*, March-April, pp. 23-31.

Hankinson, G. & Cowking, P. (1995). What do you really mean by a brand? *Journal of Brand Management, 3*(1), 43-50.

Hansen, F. (1985). *Studies of Communication Effects - Methodological and Theoretical Papers on Left/Right Lateralization,* Civiløkonomernes Forlag, Copenhagen.

Hansen, F. (1987). Towards an Alternative Theory of the Advertising Communication Process, *International Journal of Research in Marketing*, Vol. 1, No. 1.

Hansen, F. (1997). Quantifying Creative Contributions: Advertising Pretesting's new generation, *proceedings from ESOMAR's 50th Congress*, Edingburgh.

References

Hansen, F. & A. Rasmussen (2001). *Emotional Responses to Advertising Sponsoring and Design*

Hansen, Flemming & Kock, Christian (2001). "Evaluation of Public Spokes Persons". *Research Paper. Forum for Advertising Research*. Copenhagen Business School.

Hansen, Lotte Yssing and Hansen, Flemming (2001). Advertising and promotion effectiveness – learnings from a five-year study. *Research paper no. 18, 2001*. Advertising Research Group. Department of Marketing. Copenhagen Business School.

Hansen, Flemming, Nilsson, Ole Stenvinkel, Olsen, Jørgen Kai, (1999). 'Testing the Significance of STAS scores for Brands', *Marketing and Research Today*, Vol. 28, No. 4, 152-158.

Hansen, Lotte Yssing, (2000). 'A comparison of two advertising effect models', *Research Paper no. 5.*, Forum for Advertising Research, Copenhagen Business School.

Hardy, K.G. (1970). Whatever happened to image? *The Business Quarterly,* 35(Winter), 70-76.

Harris, F., & De Chernatony, L. (2001). Corporate branding and corporate brand performance. *European Journal of Marketing,* 35(3/4), 441-456.

Harrison, T.M., Stephen, T.D., Husson, W., Fehr, B.J. (1991). Images versus issues in the 1984 presidential election: Differences between men and women. *Human Communication Research*, 18(2), 209-227.

Harvey, David (1990). *The conditions of postmodernity.* Oxford: Basil Blackwell.

Haugtvedt, C.; Petty, R.E.; Cacioppo, J.T. (1992). Need for Cognition and Advertising: Understanding the Role of Personality Variables in Consumer Behavior, in: *Journal of Consumer Psychology*, 1, pp. 239-260.

Heath, Robert (2001). *The Hidden Power of Advertising, How low involvement processing influences the way we choose brands.* Henley-on-Thames: Admap.

Heath, R.G. (2000). Low Involvement Processing - A New Model of Brands and Advertising. *International Journal of Advertising,* Vol. 19 No. 3 297-298.

Heath, R.G. (2001). *The Hidden Power of Advertising,* Admap Monograph No. 7, World Advertising Research Centre, Henley-on-Thames, Great Britain.

Hermanns, Arnold, Norbert Drees and Edgar Wangen (1986). Zur Wahrnehmung von Werbebotschaften auf Rennfahrzeugen. Ein Beitrag zur Wirkungsforschung in der Sportwerbung, *Marketing - Zeitschrift für Forschung und Praxis,* 8, 2, 123-129.

Hillyer, K. O. (1992). *Seeing through the glitz: Commercial literacy for students* (Report No. IR-016-410). Pittsburgh, PA: International. Visual Literacy Association. (ERIC Document Reproduction Service No. ED 363 291).

Hilton, D. (2001). The Psychology of Financial Decision-Making: Applications to Trading, Dealing, and Investment Analysis, *Journal of Psychology and Financial Markets,* 2, 1, 37-53.

Hirschman, E. C. and B. B. Stern (1999). The Roles of Emotion in Consumer Research, in: *Advances in Consumer Research,* Vol. 26, pp. 4-11.

Hoch, Stephen J. and John Deighton (1989). "Managing What Consumers Learn from Experience", *Journal of Marketing,* 53, 2, pp 1-20.

Hoek, Janet, Philip Gendall, Michelle Jeffcoat and David Orsman (1997). Sponsorship and advertising: a comparison of their effects, *Journal of Marketing Communications,* 3, 1, 21-32.

References

Holbrook, Morris B. (1994). "The Nature of Customer Value: An Axiology of Services in the Consumption Experience", pp. 21-71 in *Service Quality: New Directions in Theory and Practice*, Roland T. Rust and Hichard L. Oliver, (Eds), Newbury Park, CA: Sage.

Holbrook, Morris B. (1999). "Higher than the bottom line: Reflections on some recent macromarketing literature", *Journal of Macromarketing*, Vol. 19/1, pp.48-74.

Hofstede, G. (1997). *Lokales Denken, globales Handeln: Kulturen, Zusammenarbeit und Management*, [Local thinking, global acting: cultures, cooperations and management], Beck, München.

Holtgrave D. & Weber, E. (1993). Dimensions of Risk Perception for Financial and Health Risks, *Risk Analysis*, 13, 5, 553-558.

Hoogeweegen, J.W.A.M. (2000, April 6). *Parent behind the brand strategy*. Paper presented at the Corporate versus brand strategy conference, Hoofddorp, The Netherlands.

Holt, D. B. (1997). Post-Structuralist Lifestyle Analysis: Conceptualizing the Social Patterning of Consumption in Postmodernity, in: *Journal of Consumer Research*, Vol. 23, March, pp. 326-350.

Holtz-Bacha, C., Kaid, L.L. (1995). Television Spots in German National Elections: Content and Effects. In L.L. Kaid, C. Holtz-Bacha (eds.), *Political Advertising in Western Democracies. Parties and Candidates on Television* (61-88). Thousand Oaks, CA: Sage.

Holyvak, K.J. & B.A. Spellman, "Thinking ", *Annual Review of Psychology*, Vol. 44.

Huff, A.S. (ed), "*Mapping Strategic Thought*", New York, Johnson Wiley and Sons.

Hulbert, M. (1999). The Misuse of Past-Performance Data, in: *Lifson, L. & Geist, R.* (Edts.) (1999): The Psychology of Investing, New York et al., 147-157.

Hutton, James G. (1996). "Integrated Marketing Communication and the Evolution of Marketing Thought." *Journal of Business Research* . 37, 155-162.
Ind, Nicholas, (1997). *"The Corporate Brand"*, Macmillan.

Interbrand Group (1992). *World's Greatest Brands: An International review* New York: John Wiley.

Iordanov, Paul and Daniel Nobi (1989). Impact et approche qualitative de la communication sponsoring, in: *La télévision en 1989 : audiences, publicité et recherche*, IREP (ed.), Paris, 243-258.

IP (1999). *'Wat doet sponsoring voor ...? Resultaten sponsoring effect meter'* ['What does sponsoring for...? Results sponsoring effect measurer'], Amsterdam: IP.

IP (2001). *'Wat doet sponsoring voor ...? Resultaten sponsoring effect meter'* ['What does sponsoring for...? Results sponsoring effect measurer'], Amsterdam: IP.

Jakubowska, U. (1999). Approval for politicians and political ideas: Who supports whom and why? *Journal for Mental Changes*, 5(2), 65-85.

Jespersen, Marie & Møller Jensen, Pia (1999). *Nonspot-advertising – i teori og praksis.* Unpublished thesis. Handelshøjskolen i København.

Jessop, Bob (1991). "Thatcherism and flexibility: The white heat of a post-Fordist revolution", In Jessop, Bob; Kastendiek, H; Nielsen, K. & Pedersen, O.: *The Politics of Flexibility.* Aldershot: Edward Elgar.

References

Jhally, Sut (1989). "Advertising as Religion: The Dialectic of Technology and Magic", In *Angus, I. & Jhally, Sut* (eds.). Cultural Politics and Contemporary America. New York: Routledge, pp. 217-229.

Jobber, David (2001). *Principles and Practice of Marketing.* London: McGraw-Hill.

Johar, Gita Venkataramani and Michel T. Pham (1999). Relatedness, Prominence, and Constructive Sponsor Identification, *Journal of Marketing Research*, 36, 3, 299-312.

Johnson & P.A. Laird, (1983). *"Mental Models"*, Cambridge, Cambridge University Press.

Jones, John Philip, (1995a). *When Ads Work. New proof that advertising triggers sales.* Lexington Books, New York, USA.

Jones, John Philip, (1995b). 'Single-Source Research Begins to Fulfill its Promise', *Journal of Advertising Research*, Vol. 35, No. 3, 9-16.

Joyce, E. & Biddle, G. (1981). Anchoring and Adjustment in Probabilistic Inferences in Auditing, *Journal of Accounting Research*, 19, 120-145.

Jung, C.G. (1921/1967). Psychological Types, in: *Collected Works of C.G. Jung*, Vol. 6, New York.

Ju-Pak, K.H., B.H. Kim & G.T. Cameron, (1996). *Advertorial advertising: definitions and notable characteristics.* Unpublished manuscript, California State University, Fullerton.

Kahhr, James A., Frith, Katherine T. & Callison, Coy (2001). "Audience attitudes towards brand (product) placement: Singapore and the United States", *International Journal of Advertising*, Vol. 20 (1), pp. 3-24.

Karrh, James A. (1998). 'Brand placement: a review', *Journal of Current Issues and Research in Advertising,* 20(2): 31-49.

Karrh, James A., Katherine T. Frith & Coy Callison (2001). 'Audience attitudes towards brand (product) placement: Singapore and the United States', *International Journal of Advertising,* 20(1): 3-24.

Kahneman, D. & Riepe, M. (1998). Aspects of Investor Psychology, *Journal of Portfolio Management*, 24, 52-65.

Kahneman, D. & Tversky, A. (1996). On the Reality of Cognitive Illusions, Psychological Review, 103, 582-591.

Kahneman, D. & Tversky, A. (1973). On the Psychology of Prediction, *Psychological Review*, 80, 237-251.

Kahneman, D. & Tversky, A. (1972). Subjective Probability: A Judgment of Represenativeness, *Cognitive Psychology*, 3, 430-454.

Kaid, L.L. (1995). Measuring candidate images with semantic differentials. In K.L. Hacker (ed.), *Candidate images in presidential election*, (131-134). Westport, Conn.: Praeger.

Kaid, L.L., Chanslor, M. (1995). Changing candidate images: The effects of political advertising. In K.L. Hacker (ed.), *Candidate images in presidential election*,(83-97). Westport, Conn.: Praeger.

Kaid, L.L., Holtz-Bacha, C. (eds.) (1995). *Political advertising in Western democracies: Parties and candidates on television.* Thousand Oaks, CA: Sage.

Kalnapilis Annual Report (1997, 1998, 1999, 2000, 2001)

Kapferer, J.N. (1996). *Strategic Brand Management: Creating and Sustaining Brand Equity Long Term.* London: Kogan Page.

Kapferer, J. (1992). *Strategic brand management: New approaches to creating and evaluating brand equity.* London: Kogan Page.

References

Kapferer, J.N. (1996). *Strategisch merkmanagement: over het eigen vermogen van merken* [Strategic brand management]. Schoonhoven, The Netherlands: Academic Service.

Keller, Kevin Lane. (2003). *"Strategic Brand Management. Building, Measuring, and Managing Brand Equity"*. International Edition. Prentice Hall

Keller, K.L. (1993). Conceptualizing, measuring and managing costumer-based brand equity. *Journal of Marketing,* 57(January), 1-22.

Keller, K.L. (1998). *Strategic brand management: Building, measuring and managing brand equity.* New Jersey: Prentice-Hall.

Keller, K.L. & Aaker, D.A. (1992). The effects of sequential introduction of brand extensions. *Journal of Marketing Research,* 24 (February), 35-50.

Kennedy, J. R. (1971). How program environment affects TV commercials. *Journal of Advertising Research,* 11 (1), 33-38.

Kenrick, D.T.; Funder, D.C. (1988). Profiting from Controversy: Lessons from the Person-Situation Debate, in: *American Psychologist,* 43, pp. 23-34.

Kerstetter, Deborah and Richard Gitelson (1995). Attendee Perceptions of Sponsorship Contributions to a Regional Art Festival, *Festival Management & Event Tourism,* 2, 203-209

Key, Wilson B. (1972). *Subliminal seduction: Ad media's manipulation of a not-so-innocent America.* New York: Signet.

Key, Wilson B. (1976). *Media sexploitation.* New York: Signet.

Key, Wilson B. (1980). *The clam-plate orgy and other techniques for manipulating your behavior.* New York: Signet.

Key, Wilson B. (1989). *The age of manipulation: the con in confidence, the sin in sincere.* New York: Holt.

Kock, Christian (2002). *Forstå verden, politisk journalistik for fremtiden.* Copenhagen: Samfundslitteratur.

Kok, R.A. (1997). Merkenkeuzes bij Akzo Nobel [Brand choices at Akzo Nobel]. *Tijdschrift voor Strategische Bedrijfscommunicatie,* 3(1), 94-101.

Kotler, P., & Armstrong, G. (1993). *Marketing: An Introduction* (3rd. ed.). Englewood Cliffs: Prentice Hall.

Kotler, P. (2000). *Marketing Management.* The Millennium Edition. Upple Saddle River (N.J.): Prentice Hall.

Kotler, Philip (2001). "Reflections on Marketing", In Iacobucci, Dawn (ed.). *Kellog on Marketing.* New York: John Wiley & Sons, pp. pp.xiii-xvi.

Kotler, Philip; Jain, Dipak C. & Maesincee, Suvit (2002). *Marketing Moves.* Boston: Harvard Business School Press.

Kover, A.J, James, W.L. & Sonner, R.S. (1997). "To whom do Advertising Creatives write? An inferential answer." *Journal of Advertising Research*, January/February, 41-53.

Kover, A.J. (1995). "Copywriters' Implicit Theories of Communication: An Exploration." *Journal of Consumer Research,* Vol. 21,March.

Kreikebaum, Hartmut (1996). *Grundlagen der Unternehmensethik.* Stuttgart: Schäffer-Poeschel.

Kroeber-Riel, W.; Weinberg, P. (1999). *Konsumentenverhalten* [Consumer Behavior], 7. ed., Munich.

Kroeber-Riel, W. (1984). *Konsument Verhalten*, Vahlen, Munchen.

References

Krugman, H. E. (1983). Television program interest and commercial interruption. *Journal of Advertising Research,* 21 (1), 21-23.

Krugman, H (1971). Brain wave measurements of media involvement. *Journal of Advertising Research,* February, 3-9

Kunøe Gorm (1989). *Dialogmarkedsføring. Modeller i anvendt markedsføring.* ScanForum Forlag a.s. Oslo.

Kunøe, Gorm (1998). "On the ability of ad agencies to assist in developing one-to-one marketing: measuring "the core of dialogue", *European Journal of Marketing,* Vol. 32 No.11/12, MCB University Press.

Kunøe, Gorm and Svarød, Øystein (1998, 2001). *Direkte markedsføring - introduksjon, analyse, planlegging, effektmåling og kontroll.* Forlag ScanForum AS, Oslo.

Kvale, Steinar (1996). *InterViews. An Introduction to Qualitative Research Interviewing.* London: Sage.

Lancaster, Geoff & Massingham, Lester (2001). *Marketing Management.* London: McGraw-Hill.

Lafortet, S., & Saunders, J. (1999). Managing brand portfolios: Why leaders do what they do. *Journal of Advertising Research,* 39(1), 1-23.

Langer, Roy & Nielsen, Anne-Dorte Bruun (2002). *Skjult reklame – en undersøgelse af erfaringerne med denne reklameform, udviklingstendenser og reguleringsmuligheder.* København: Forbrugerstyrelsen.

Lardinoit Thierry (1997). Réaction attitudinale des téléspectateurs aux campagnes de parrainage : étude de l'incidence de la conjonction des parrainages terrain et T.V., in *Proceedings of the 13th congress of the French Marketing Association (AFM),* May, 668-697, Toulouse: Association Française de Marketing.

Lardinoit Thierry (1998). Effet modérateur de l'implication durable sur l'efficacité mémorielle de la conjonction des parrainages terrain et T.V., in *Proceedings of the 14th congress of the French Marketing Association (AFM)*, May, 261-276, Bordeaux: Association Française de Marketing.

Lardinoit Thierry (1999). Interaction des parrainages terrain et TV: impact sur deux niveaux de mémorisation, in *Proceedings of the 15th congress of the French Marketing Association (AFM)*, 19-21 May, Strasbourg: Association Française de Marketing, 585-602.

Larson, C. U. (1983). *"Persuasion: Perception & Responsibility"*. Wadsworth.

Laskey, Henry A., Ellen Day, & Melvin R. Crask (1989). Typology of Main Message Strategies for Television Commercials. *Journal of Advertising,* 18.

Laskey, Henry A., Richard J. Fox, and Melvin R. Crask (1995). The Relationship Between Advertising Message Strategy and Television Commercial Effectiveness. *Journal of Advertising Research*, March/April.

Lastovicka, J.L.; Bettencourt, L.A.; Hughner, R.S.; Kuntze, R.J. (1999). Lifestyle of the Tight and Frugal: Theory and Measurement, in: *Journal of Consumer Research*, 26, pp. 85-98.

Lastovicka, J.L.; Murry, J.P.; Joachimsthaler, E.A.; Bhalla, G.; Scheurich, J. (1987). A Lifestyle Typology to Model Young Male Drinking and Driving, in: *Journal of Consumer Research*, 14, pp. 257-263.

Levine, Rick; Locke, Christopher, Searls, Doc & Weinberger, David (2000). *The Cluetrain Manifesto*. Cambridge: Perseus Publishing.

Lewis, David & Bridger, Darren (2000). *The Soul of the New Consumer.* London: Nicholas Brealey.

References

Lewis, St. E. (1898). cited in Jacobi, H. (1963). *Werbepsychologie*, [Psychology of Advertising], Gabler, Wiesbaden, pp.54-55.

Liisberg, Kasper B. (2001). *Unpublished, classified Master's thesis.* University of Copenhagen.

Lippa, R.A. (1994). *An introduction to social psychology, 2nd edition.* Belmont, California: Brooks/Cole Publishing Company.

Lithuanian Association of Brewers Information Service

Lithuanian Trade & Investment Review 2000

Little, John D. C., (1979). 'Aggregate Advertising Models: The State of the Art', *Operations Research*, Vol. 27, No. 4.

Lloyd, D. W. & Clancy, K. W. (1991). CPMs versus CPMIs: Implications for media planning. *Journal of Advertising Research, 31* (4), 34-44.

Locke, Christopher (2001). *Gonzo Marketing – Winning through worst practices.* Cambridge: Perseus Publishing.

Lodish, Leonard M., (1997). 'Point of View: J. P. Jones and M. H. Blair on Measuring Advertising Effects – Another Point of View', *Journal of Advertising Research*, Vol. 37, Iss. 5.

Lodish, Leonard M., (1998). 'STAS and BehaviorScan – It's Just Not That Simple', *Journal of Advertising Research*, Vol. 38, Iss. 2.

Loken, B., & Roedder John, D. (1993). Diluting brand beliefs: When do brand extensions have a negative impact? *Journal of Marketing, 57*(July), 71-84.

Lovdal, L. T. (1989). "Sex role messages in television commercials", *Sex Roles: A Journal of Research*, 21(11/12), 715-724.

Lüdtke, H. (1995). *Vier Dimensionen von Lebensstilen. Zur Anwendung der Cluster- und Korrespondenzanalyse* [Four Dimensions of Lifestyle: The Application of Cluster Analysis and Correspondence Analysis], in: Angewandte Sozialforschung [Applied Social Research], 19, 1, pp. 77-92.

Lynch, K., & Stipp, H. (1999). Examination of qualitative viewing factors for optimal advertising strategies. *Journal of Advertising Research,* 39 (3), 7-18.

Maathuis, O.J.M. (1999). *Corporate Branding: The Value of the Corporate Brand to Customers and Managers.* Lochem: Lochemdruk.

Maathuis, O.J.M., & Van Riel, C.B.M. (1996). De toegevoegde waarde van het ondernemingsmerk [The added value of the corporate brand]. *Tijdschrift voor Strategische Bedrijfscommunicatie, 2*(2), 70-86.

MacGregor, D., Slovic, P., Dreman, D. & Berry, M. (2000). Imagery, Affect, and Financial Judgment, *Journal of Psychology and Financial Markets*, 1, 104-110.

MacGregor, D. et al. (1999). Perception of Financial Risk: A Survey Study of Advisors and Planners*, Journal of Financial Planning*, 12, 8, 68-86.

MacInnis, D., Moorman, C. & Jaworski, B. (1991). Enhancing and Measuring Consumers' Motivation, Opportunity, and Ability to Process Brand Information from Ads, *Journal of Marketing*, 55, October, 32-53.

MacKenzie, S.B.; Lutz, R. J. (1989). An empirical examination of the stuctural antecedents of attitude toward the ad in an advertising pretesting context, in: *Journal of Marketing*, Vol. 53, No. 2, pp. 48-65.

Madsen, Børge O. (1998). *Det var bare reklame.* København: Dansk Markedsføringsforbund.

References

Malhotra, N.K. (1981). A scale to measure self-concepts, person concepts and product concepts. *Journal of Marketing Research,* 18, November, 456-464.

Malhotra, Naresh (1999). *Marketing Research: An Applied Orientation.* Third Edition

Mangleburg, T. F.; Bristol, T. (1998). Socialization and Adolescent's Skepticism toward Advertising, in: *Journal of Advertising*, Vol. 27, No. 3, pp. 11-21.

Marchand, R. (1985). *Advertising and the American Dream: Making Way for Modernity, 1920-1940.* University of California Press.

Markeds og Media Instituttet of Norway (2001). Rapport over hinder for elektronisk handel. http://www.mmi.no/fast/s8/n_fakta/hinder.htm

Markowitz, H.M. (1952). Portfolio Selection, *Journal of Finance*, 7, 77-91.

Maslow, Abraham (1968). *"Toward a Psychology of Being"*, New York: Van Nostrand.

Maslow, Abraham (1971). *"The Farther Reaches of Human Nature"*, New York: Viking.

Mathwick, Charla, Naresh Malhotra and Edward Rigdon (2001). "Experiential value: conceptualization, measurement and application in the catalog and Internet shopping environment", *Journal of Retailing*, 77, pp. 39-56.

Mattes, J. and Cantor J. (1982). Enhancing responses to television advertisements via the transfer of residual arousal from prior programming. *Journal of Broadcasting, 26* (4), 553-566.

Mayer, Hans and Bernd Christner (1991). Der Hitchcock-Effekt im Sponsoring. Eine psychologische Untersuchung zur Wirkung des Kultursponsorings, *Jahrbuch der Absatz- und Verbrauchsforschung*, 4, 347-360.

Mayer, H.; Illmann, T. (2000). *Markt- und Werbepsychologie*, [Market and Advertising Psychology], 3. Aufl., Stuttgart.

Mayhew, Susan (1997). "Fordism", In *A Dictionary of Geography*. Oxford: Oxford University Press.

McCrae, R.R. & John, O.P. (1992). An introduction to the five-factor model and its applications. *Journal of Personality, 60,* 175-215.

McCrae, R.R. & Costa, P.T. Jr. (1989). The structure of interpersonal traits: Wiggins's circumplex and five-factor model. *Journal of Personality and Social Psychology, 56*(4), 586-595.

McCrae, R.R. (1982). Consensual Validation of Personality Traits: Evidence form Self-Reports and Ratings, in: *Journal of Personality and Social Psychology*, 43, pp. 293-303.

McCroskey, J. C. 1966. *"Scales for the Measurement of Ethos"*. *Speech Monographs* 33, 65-72.

McCroskey, J. C., and T.J. Young (1981). "Ethos and Credibility: The Construct and Its Measurement After Three Decades". *The Central States Speech Journal* 32, 24-34.

McDaniel, Stephen R. (1998). An investigation of match-up effects in sport sponsorship advertising, *Psychology & Marketing*, 16, 2, 163-184.

McDonald, Colin, (1997). From "Frequency" to "Continuity" – Is it a new dawn. *Journal of Advertising Research,* Vol. 37(4). 1997.

McDonald, Colin, (1996). 'How frequently should you advertise?', *Admap*, July/August, 22-25.

References

McKechnie, S. (1997). Consumer Buying Behavior in Financial Services: An Overview, in: Meidan, A./Lewis, B./Moutinho, L. (Edts.): *Financial Services Marketing*, London, p. 64-77.

McKechnie, S. & Leather, *P.* (1998). Likeability as a Measure of Advertising Effectiveness: The Case of Financial Services, in: *Journal of Marketing Communications*, Vol. 4, p. 63-85.

McKenna, Regis (1992). *Relationship Marketing.* Random House UK Ltd.

McKenney, James (1995). *Waves of Change.* Harvard Business School Press.

Meenaghan, Tony and David Shipley (1999). Media effect in commercial sponsorship, *European Journal of Marketing*, 33, 3/4, 328-347.

Meidan, A. (1996). *Marketing Financial Services*, Houndmills/London.

Meir, Rudi, David Arthur, J. Tobin and Claire Massingham (1997). Professional Rugby League in Australia: A Case Study in Sponsor Awareness, *The Cyber-Journal of Sport Marketing (online)*, 1, 3, available at www.cjsm.com.Vol1/Meir.html.

Merbold, Claus (1989). Sportsponsoring aus der Sicht eines Investitionsgüterherstellers, in *Sport- und Kultursponsoring*, Arnold Hermanns (ed.), München: Vahlen, 122-132.

Meyers-Levy, J.; Malaviya, P. (1999). Consumers' Processing of Persuasive Advertisements: An Integrative Framework of Persuasion Theories, in: *Journal of Marketing*, Vol. 63, Special Issue, pp. 45-60.

Mick, David G. and Claus, A. Buhl (1992). Meaning-based Model of Advertising Experiences. *Journal of Consumer Research*, 19.

Milberg, S.J., Whan Park, C., & McCarthy, M.S. (1997). Managing negative feedback effects associated with brand extensions: The impact of alternative branding strategies. *Journal of Consumer Psychology, 6*(2), 199-140.

Miller, C. L. (1987). "Qualitative differences among gender-stereotyped toys: Implications for cognitive and social development in girls and boys", *Sex Roles: A Journal of Research*, 16, 473-488.

Miller, G.A., Galanter, E., Probram, K.H. (1960). *Plans and the structure of behavior*. London: Holt, Rinehart and Winston.

Millmann, Ivor (1995). Broadcast sponsorship – the viewers' views – what does it do for sponsors?, *Proceedings of the ESOMAR seminar on Advertising, Sponsorship and Promotion*, Madrid, March, 125-145.

Millman, Ivor (2000). 'Broadcast sponsorship works', *Admap,* 37: 13-16.

Milner, L. M.; Collins, J. M. (2000). Sex-Role Portrayals and the Gender of Nations, in: *Journal of Advertising*, Vol. 29, No. 1, pp. 67-79.

Mischel, W. (1990). Personality Dispositions Revisited and Revised: A View after Three Decades, in: Pervin, A. (ed.): *Handbook of Personality: Theory and Research*, New York, pp. 111-134.

Mitchell, A. (1986). The Effect of Verbal and Visual Components of Advertisements on Brand Attitudes and Attitude toward the Advertisement, *Journal of Consumer Research*, Vol. 13, No. 1.

Moog, Carol (1990). *"Are they selling her lips?": Advertising and Identity.* New York: William Morrow.

Moore, D. & Kurtzberg, T. (1999). Positive Illusions and Forecasting Errors in Mutual Fund Investment Decisions, *Organizational Behavior and Human Decision Processes*, 79, 2, 95-114.

References

Moore, D. J.; Homer, P. M. (2000). Dimensions of Temperament: Affect Intensity and Consumer Lifestyles, in: *Journal of Consumer Psychology*, Vol. 9, No. 3, pp. 231-242.

Moore, Jesse N., Gregory M. Pickett and Stephen J. Grove (1999). The impact of a video screen and rotational-signage systems on satisfaction and advertising recognition, *Journal of Services Marketing*, 13, 6, 453-468.

Moorman, M., Neijens, P. C., & Smit, E.G. (in press). The effects of magazine-induced psychological responses and thematic congruence on ad memory and attitude toward the ad in a real-life setting. *Journal of Advertising*.

Moorman, M, Neijens, P. & Smit, E. G. (2001, May). EURO2000: A study on the influence of program-involvement on commercial selection and processing in a real life setting. *Paper presented at the 51st Annual Conference of the International Communication Association (ICA)*, Washington D.C., USA.

Moorman, Marjolein, Peter C. Neijens & Edith G. Smit (forthcoming 2002) 'Planning the impact: The effect of editorial context on processing women's magazine ads', *Journal of Advertising, forthcoming*.

Moorman, Marjolein, Peter C. Neijens & Edith G. Smit (2001). '*The effect of program-involvement on commercial exposure and recall in a real-life setting*', Amsterdam: The Amsterdam School of Communications Research.

Morgan, Robert M. og Hunt, Shelby D. (1994). "The Commitment-Trust Theory of Relationship Marketing." *Journal of Marketing,* July.

Moseley, Susan and Parfitt, John (1987). Measuring advertising effects from single-source data: the first year of the AdLab panel. *Admap.* June 1987.

Murphy, Jamie (1999). *"Surfers and searchers: An examination of web-site visitor' clicking behavior"*. Cornell Hotel and Restaurant Administration Quarterly.

Murphy, J. (1987). *Branding: A key marketing tool.* Basingstoke: Macmillan.

Murry, J. P. Jr., Lastovicka J. L, & Singh S. N. (1992). Feeling and liking responses to television programs: An examination of two explanations for media context effects. *Journal of Consumer Research,* 18 (3), 441-451.

Murray, Robin (1990). "Fordism and Post-Fordism", In Hall, Stuart & Jacques, Martin (eds.): *New Times The Changing Face of Politics in the 1990s.* London: Verso, pp. 38-53.

Mussweiler, T. & Strack, F. (2001). The Semantics of Anchoring, *Organizational Behavior and Human Decision Processes*, 86, 2, 234-255.

Mussweiler, T. & Strack, F. (2000). Numeric Judgments under Uncertainty: The Role of Knowledge in Anchoring, *Journal of Experimental Social Psychology*, 36, 495-518.

Müller, Frank (1983). Banden- und Sportwerbung. Eine Untersuchung zur Wirkung von Bandenwerbung und zur Einstellung gegenüber Werbung im Sport, *Interview und Analyse*, 10, 4/5, 152-156.

Myers, Greg (1994). Some Advertising History, in *Words In Ads* Edward Arnold, London.

Nash, Edward L. (1986). *Direct Marketing. Strategy, Planning, Execution.* Second Edition.

Nebenzahl, Israel D. & Jaffe, Eugene D. (1998). "Ethical Dimensions of Advertising Executions", *Journal of Business Ethics*, Vol.17/7, pp. 805-815.

References

Nebenzahl, Israel D. & Eugene Secunda (1993). 'Consumers' attitudes toward product placement in movies', *International Journal of Advertising* 12(1): 1-11.

Negroponto, N. (1995). *Being Digital.* Knopf. New York.

Neijens, Peter C. (2001). *Verleidingskunsten. Op het raakvlak van voorlichting, commercie en vrije publiciteit* [The art of temptation. At the edge of information providing, commerce and free publicity]. Amsterdam: Vossius Pers, University of Amsterdam.

Neijens, Peter C. & Edith G. Smit (2000). *'Onderzoek naar bereikskwaliteit'* ['Research into the quality of circulation'] in A.K. den Boon & P.C. Neijens (eds.) Media & Reclame. Mediaplanning en bereiksonderzoek [Media & Advertising. Media planning and Circulation research]. Groningen: Wolters-Noordhoff.

Neter, John, Wasserman, William, Kutner, Michael H., (1989). *Applied Linear Regression Models*, pp. 578-626. Irwin USA.

Newell, Stephen J. & Goldsmith, Ronald E. (2001). *"The development of a scale to measure perceived corporate credibility". Journal of Business Research*, 235-247.

Newman, B.I. (1999a). *The mass marketing of politics: Democracy in an age of manufactured images*. Thousand Oaks, CA: Sage.

Newman, B.I. (ed.) (1999b). *Handbook of political marketing.* Thousand Oaks, CA: Sage.

Nicholls, J.A.F., Sydney Roslow and Sandipa Dublish (1999). Brand recall and brand preference at sponsored golf and tennis tournaments, *European Journal of Marketing*, 33, 3/4, 365-386.

Nielsen, Jakob (2000). *Designing Web Usability.* New Riders.

Nordmoe, Eric D. and Jain, Dipak C. (2000). Drawing inferences from logit models for panel data. *Applied Stochastic Models in Business and Industry,* Vol. 16.

Norman, W.T. (1963). Toward an Adequate Taxonomy of Personality Attributes: Replicated Factor Structure in Peer Nomination Personality Ratings, in: *Journal of Abnormal and Social Psychology*, 66, pp. 574-583.

Norris, C. E., & Colman, A. M. (1993). Context effects on memory for television advertisements. *Social Behavior and Personality,* 21 (4), 279-286.

Northcraft, G. & Neale, M. (1987). Opportunity Costs and the Framing of Resource Allocation Decisions, *Organizational Behavior and Human Decision Processes*, 37, 28-38.

Nunnally, J.C. (1987). *Psychometric Theory.* New York: Mc-Graw-Hill, Inc.

Nötzel, Rötger (1988). Zur Werbewirkung von Sportwerbung als regionales Medium, *planung & analyse*, 3, 122-127.

Obermiller, C.; Spangenberg, E. R. (1998). Development of a Scale to Measure Consumer Skepticism Toward Advertising, in: *Journal of Consumer Psychology*, Vol. 7, No. 2, pp. 159-186.

Obermiller, Carl & Spangenberg, Eric R. (2000). "On the origin and distinctiveness of scepticism toward advertising", *Marketing Letters*, Vol. 11/4, pp. 311-322.

O'Donohoe, Stephanie (1995). "Attitudes to advertising: a review of British and American research", *International Journal of Advertising*, Vol. 14/3, pp. 245-261.

Olins, W. (1989). *Corporate identity: Making business strategy visible through design.* London: Design Council.

References

Olivier, Alexander J. and Erik M. Kraak (1997). Sponsorship Effectiveness. What Is Driving Consumer Response ?, in *Proceedings of the 210th ESOMAR Seminar, New Ways for Integrated Communications*, Paris, April 16-18, European Society for Market Research (ed.), Amsterdam, 25 p.

Olson, J. C. & A. Muderrisoglu (1979). The Stability of Responses Obtained by Free Elicitation: Implications for Measuring Attribute Salience and memory Structure, *Advances in Consumer Research*, Vol. 6, ed. William Wilkie, Ann Arbor, MI: Association for Consumer Research, 269-275.

Olsen, R. (1997). Investment Risk: The Expert's Perspective, in: *Financial Analysts Journal*, 53, 62-66.

Olsen, R. & Cox, C. (2001). The Influence of Gender on the Perception and Response to Investment Risk, *Journal of Psychology and Financial Markets*, 2, 29-36.

Otker, Ton (1988). Exploitation: The key to sponsorship success, *European Research*, 16, 2, 77-86.

Osgood, C.E., Suci, G.J., Tannenbaum, P.H. (1957). *The measurement of meaning*. Urbana, IL: University of Illinois Press.

Otker, Ton and Peter Hayes (1988). Evaluation de l'efficacité du sponsoring. Expériences de la Coupe du Monde de Football 1986, *Revue Française du Marketing*, 118, 13-40.

Oxford English Dictionary (1990). Oxford: Clarendon Press.

Packard, Vance (1957). *The Hidden Persuaders*. New York: D.K. McKay.

Parker, Ken (1991). Sponsorship: The Research Contribution, *European Journal of Marketing*, 25, 11, 22-30.

Quester, Pascale G. (1997). Awareness as a measure of sponsorship effectiveness: the Adelaide Formula One Grand Prix and evidence of incidental ambush effects, *Journal of Marketing Communications*, 3, 1, 1-20.

Quester, Pascale G. and Francis Farrelly (1998). Brand association and memory decay effects of sponsorship: the case of the Australian Formula One Grand Prix, *Journal of Product and Brand Management*, 7, 6, 539-556.

Parker, Ken (1991). "Sponsorship: the research contribution", *European Journal of Marketing*, Vol. 25, pp. 22-30, 1991.

Patterson, M. (1999). Re-appraising the concept of brand image. *Journal of Brand Management,* 6(6), 409-426.

Patton, G.W.R. (1978). Effects of party affiliation of student voters on the image of presidential candidates. *Psychological Reports*, 43, 343-347.

Pepper, Don and Rogers, Martha (1993). *One-to-One Communications*. Doubleday.

Percy, L., J.R. Rossiter, and R. Elliott (2001). *Strategic Advertising Management* Oxford: Oxford University Press.

Perfect, T.J. & Askew, C. (1994). Print Adverts: Not Remembered but Memorable, *Applied Cognitive Psychology*, Vol. 8, 693-704

Petty, R.E., J.T. Cacioppo, David Schumann (1983). Central and Peripheral Routes to Advertising Effectiveness: The Moderating Role of Involvement, *Journal of Consumer Research*, Vol. 10, September.

Petty, R.E., J.T. Cacioppo and David Schumann (1986). Central and Peripherical Routes to Advertising Effectiveness: The moderating Role of Involvement, *Journal of Consumer Research*, Vol. 10.

References

Petty, R. E.; Cacioppo, J. T. (1986). *Communication and Persuasion, Central and Peripheral Routes to Attitude Change*, New York.

Petty, R.E. & Cacioppo, J.T. (1996). *Attitudes and Persuasion: Classic and contemporary approaches.* Westview Press, Boulder, Colorado.

Pham, M. Tuan (1992). Effects of Involvement, Arousal, and Pleasure on the Recognition of Sponsorship Stimuli, in *Advances in Consumer Research*, eds J.F. Sherry and B. Sternthal, 19, 85-93, Provo, UT: Association of Consumer Research.

Philips, William (1992) "A century of modern advertising: from fin de siécle to nervous nineties", *Admap*, July.

Pickton, David & Broderick, Amanda (2001). *Integrated Marketing Communications.* Harlow: Financial Times/Prentice Hall.

Pine Joseph B. (1993). *Mass Cutomization*. Harvard Business School Press.

Pine, Joseph II B. (1993). *Mass customisation: The new frontier in business competition.* Boston: Harvard Business School Press.

Pine, Joseph B., II and James H. Gilmore (1998). "Welcome to the experience economy", *Harvard Business Review*, July-August, pp. 97-105.

Pollay, R. W. (1986). "The distorted mirror: Reflections on the unintended consequences of advertising", *Journal of Marketing*, 50, 18-36.

Pope, Nigel (1998). Consumption values, sponsorship awareness, brand and product use, *Journal of Product & Brand Management*, 7, 2, 124-136.

Pope, Nigel K. Ll. and Kevin E. Voges (1997). An Exploration of Sponsorship Awareness by Product Message Location in Televised Sporting Events, *The Cyber-Journal of Sport Marketing (online)*, 2, 1, available at www.cjsm.com.Vol1/pope&voges.html.

Postman, N. (1985). *Amusing ourselves to death.* New York: Viking Penguin.

Price, L.L.; Ridgeway, N. (1983). Development of a Scale to Measure Innovativeness, in: Bagozzi, R.P.; Tybout, A.M. (eds.): *Advances in Consumer Research*, No. 10, pp.679-684.

Puto, Christopher P. and Robert W. Hoyer (1990). "Transformational Advertising: Current State of the Art", in eds. Stuart J. Agres, Julie A. Edell, and Tony M. Dubitsky, *Emotions in Advertising*, New York: Quorum Books.

Puto, Christopher P. and Willliam D. Wells (1984). "Informational and Transformational Advertising: The differential effects of time", *Advances in Consumer Research*, Vol. 11, pp. 638-643.

Raghubir, P. & Das, S. (1999). A Case for Theory-Driven Experimental Enquiry, *Financial Analysts Journal*, 55, 56-79.

Ragutis Annual Report (1997, 1998, 1999, 2000, 2001)

Rajaretnam, J. (1994). The long term effects of sponsorship on corporate and product image – findings of a unique experiment, *Marketing and Research Today*, 22, 1, 62-74.

Reece, B., Rifon, N.J., & Rodriguez, K. (1999). "Selling food to children," in, Macklin, K. & Carlson, L. (eds.), *Advertising to Children. Concepts and controversies*, Thousand Oaks, CA.: Sage, 1999, 189-208.

Reekie, W.D. (1981). *The Economics of Advertising*. London: Macmillan.

References

Reiter, Gerhard and Thomas Serr (1991). Sportwerbung an der Bande. Wirkungsmessung anläßlich der Fußball-Weltmeisterschaft 1990 in Italien, *Planung und Analyse*, 4, 143-146.

Renner, J. and Stefan Tischler (1977). Sportfans gegen Bandenwerber 6:4, *absatzwirtschaft*, 20, 2, February, 34-36.

Restall, C. & Gordon, W. (1994). Merken: Inzicht in de emotionele binding. *Tijdschrift voor Marketing,* 28, 72-79.

Reynolds and J.C. Olson (eds.). *Understanding Consumer Decision Making* Mahwah, NJ: Lawrence Erlbaum Associates, pp 183-214.

Rice, B.; Bennett, R. (1998). The Relationship between Brand Usage and Advertising Tracking Measurements: International Findings, in: *Journal of Advertising Research*, Mai/Juni, 1998, pp. 58-66.

Richardson, Alan (1999). "Subjective Experience: Its Conceptual Status, Method of Investigation, and Psychological Significance", *The Journal of Psychology*, Vol. 133, No. 5, pp. 469-485.

Richins, Marsha L. and Scott Dawson (1992). "A Consumer Values Orientation for Materialism and Its Measurement: Scale Development and Validation", *Journal of Consumer Research*, December, Vol. 19, pp. 303-316.

Richins, M.L. (1997). Measuring Emotions in Consumption Experience, *Journal of Consumer Research*, vol. 24, Sept., pp. 127-143.

Richter, R. (1994). *Stilwandel und Stilkonflikte* [Style Change and Style Conflicts], in: Mörth, I.; Fröhlich, G. (eds.): Das symbolische Kapital der Lebensstile [The Symbolic Capital of Lifestyles], Frankfurt/M., pp. 167-180.

Riffe, D., Goldson, H., Saxton, K., & Yu, Y. (1989). "Females and minorities in TV ads in 1987 Saturday children's programs", *Journalism Quarterly*, 66(1), 129-136.

Ritzer, George (1999). *Enchanting a disenchanted world - revolutionizing the means of consumption-*. Thousand Oaks, California: Pine Forge Press.

Ritzer, George (1993). *The McDonaldization of Society.* Thousand Oaks, CA: Sage.

Ritzer, George (1996). *The McDonaldization of Society.* rev. ed. Thousand Oaks, CA: Pine Forge Press.

Roberts, C.L. (1981). From primary to presidency: A panel study of images and issues in the 1976 election. *Western Journal of Speech Communication*, 45, 60-70.

Roberts, Mary Lou og Berger, Paul D. (1989). *Direct Marketing Management*. Prentice Hall Englewood Cliffs.

Roch (1978). "Principles of Categorization", in E. Roch and B.B. Loyds (eds.) *Cognition and Categorization Hillsdale*, New Jersey, Erlbaum.

Roedder John, D., Loken, B., & Joiner, C. (1998). The negative impact of extensions: Can flagship products be diluted? *Journal of Marketing,* 62(January), 19-32.

Roehm, Harper A. and Haugtvedt, Curtis P. (1999). "Understanding Interactivity of Cyperspace Advertising", in Schuman, David W. and Thorson, Ester. *Advertising on the World Wide Web.* Lawrance Erlbaum Associates, Inc.

Rogers, Stuart (1992/93). "How a publicity blitz created the myth of subliminal advertising", *Public Relations Quarterly*, Vol. 37/4, pp.12-20.

Rogers, Stuart (1993). "Subliminal messages: Out of sight, not out of mind", *Psychology Today*, Vol.26/1, p. 19.

References

Rose, G. M.; Bush, V. D. et al. (1998). The Influence of Family Communication Patterns on Parental Reaction toward Advertising: A Cross-National Examination, in: *Journal of Advertising*, Vol. 27, No. 4, pp. 71-85.

Rossiter, John R. and Larry Percy (1996). *Advertising Communications & Promotion Management.* Singapore: McGraw-Hill.

Rossiter, J. & H. Percy, (1997). *Advertising Communications & Promotion Management,* New York, McGraw-Hill Company.

Rossiter, J. & L. Percy (2000). *Advertising and Promotion Management,* McGraw Hill.

Rossiter, J.R. and L. Percy (2001). "The a-b-e Model of Benefit Focus in Advertising" in *T.J.*

Rossiter, J.R., L. Percy, and R.J. Donovan (1991). "A Better Advertising Planning Grid," *Journal of Advertising Research* 31, 5: pp 11-21.

Ruble, D. N., Balaban, T., & Cooper, J. (1981). "Gender constancy and the effects of sex-typed televised toy commercials", *Child Development,* 52, 667-673.

Ruijgrok, Mariëlle (2000). *'Product placement in 'Goede Tijden, Slechte Tijden': to do or not to do?',* MA-Thesis, Amsterdam: Communicatiewetenschap (UvA).

Rupert, Mark (1995). *Producing Hegemony: The Politics of Mass Production and American Global Power.* Cambridge: Cambridge University Press.

Rupert, Mark; "The crisis of Fordism", In Jones, R.B. Jarry (ed.) (2001). *Routledge Encyclopedia of International Political Economy.* New York/London: Routledge, 2001.

Sandler, Dennis M. & Eugene Secunda (1993). 'Point of view: blurred boundaries-Where does editorial end and advertising begin?' *Journal of Advertising Research* 33(3): 73-81.

Sanford, A.J (1987). *"The mind of Man: Models of Human Understanding"*, Brighton, Harvester Press.

Saucier, G. (1994). Trapnell Versus the Lexical Factor: More Ado About Nothing?, in: *European Journal of Personality*, 8, pp. 291-298.

Saunders, J. & Guoqun, F. (1996). Dual Branding: How Corporate Names Add Value. *Marketing Intelligence & Planning, 14* (7), 29-34.

Schacter, D.L. (1996). S*earching for Memory,* Perseus Books Group, USA.

Schiffman, L.G.; Kanuk, L.L. (1997). *Consumer Behavior*, 6. ed., Upper Saddle River, New Jersey.

Schudson, Michael (1984). *Advertising, the Uneasy Persuasion: It's Dubious Impact on American Society.* New York: Basic Books.

Schultz, Don E.; Tannenbaum, Stanley I. & Lauterborn, F. (1994). *The New Marketing Paradigm: Integrated Marketing Communications.* Lincolnwood: NTC Business Books.

Schultz, Don E. (1993). "Can Relationships Save Marketing?" *Business Strategy*. May.

Schultz Don E., Tannenbaum, Stanley I., Lauterborn, Robert F. (1993). *Integrated Marketing Communication.* NTC Business Books.

Schultz, Majken et al. (2000). *"The Expressive Organization".* Oxford University Press.

Schumann, D. W., & Thorson E. (1990). The influence of viewing context on commercial effectiveness: A selection processing model. *Current Issues and Research in Advertising, 12* (1), 1-24.

References

Schumann, Frank (1987). Und am Rand steigt der Bekanntheitsgrad. Die Wirkung der Bandenwerbung bei zwei ausgesuchten Spielen der Fußball Europameisterschaft 1984, in *Sportmedien und Mediensport: Wirkungen - Nutzung - Inhalte der Sportberichterstattung*, Joseph Hackforth, ed., 57-79, Berlin: Vistas.

Schwartz, T. (1973). *The responsive chord*. Garden City, NY: Anchor Press.

Secunda, Eugene & Nebenzahl, Israel D. (1993). „Consumers' attitudes towards product placement in movies", *International Journal of Advertising*, Vol. 12/1, pp. 115-133.

Seiter, E. (1999). "Gotta Catch 'em all- Pokemon": Problems in the study of children's global multi-media." Paper presented at the conference *Research in Childhood, Sociology, Culture and History*, October 1999, Denmark.

Sebstrup, Preben (unpublished data). *Reklamen som socialisationsfaktor* [Advertising as a Socializing Factor]. Aarhus School of Business Administration, Institute of Marketing.

Sigrell, Anders (2001). *Att övertyga mellan raderna, en retorisk studie om underförståddheter i modern politisk argumentation*. Rhetor, Åstorp.

Sijtsma, Paul & Jeroen Bakker (2000). '*Televisie*' ['Television'], in A.K. den Boon & P.C. Neijens (eds.) Media & Reclame. Mediaplanning en bereiksonderzoek [Media & Advertising. Media planning and Circulation research]. Groningen: Wolters-Noordhoff.

Silberer, G. (1999). *Die Stimmung als Werbewirkungsfaktor* [Mood as a factor influencing advertising effectiveness], in: Marketing ZFP, No. 2, pp. 131-148.

Shanahan, Patrick (1990). Using sponsorship to communicate to teenagers: « Be Your Best » *A case study, ESOMAR*, 83-103.

Shapiro, Stewart and Mark T. Spence (2002). "Factors Affecting Encoding, Retrieval, and Alignment of Sensory Attributes in a Memory-Based Brand Choice Task", *Journal of Consumer Research*, Vol. 28, March, pp. 603-617.

Shapiro, S., MacInnis, D.J., & Heckler, S.E. (1997). The effects of Incidental Ad Exposure on the Formation of Consideration Sets. *Journal of Consumer Research,* Vol. 24, June 94-104

Shapiro, S. & Krishnan, H.S. (2001). Memory-based measures for assessing advertising effects: a comparison of explicit and implicit memory effects. *Journal of Advertising,* Vol 30, issue 3

Sharpe, W. F. (1994). The Sharpe Ratio, in: *Journal of Portfolio Management*, 21, 49-58.

Shaw, Robert & Merlin Stone (1988). *Database Marketing*. Gower.

Shefrin, H. (2000). *Beyond Greed and Fear: Understanding Behavioral Finance and the Psychology of Investing*, Boston.

Sheinin, D.A. (1998). Sub-brand evaluation and use versus brand extension. *The Journal of Brand Management*, 6 (2), 113-122.

Shergill, S. (1993). "The Changing US Media and Marketing Environment: Implications for Media Advertising Expenditures in the 1990's", *International Journal of Advertising*, Vol.12, pp. 95-115.

Sheth, Jagdish N. (1976). "Buyer-Seller Interaction: A Conceptual Framework." *Advance in Consumer Research*. Vol 3,b.

Sirri, E. & Tufano, P. (1993). Competition and Change in the Mutual Fund Industry, in: Hayes, S. (Edt.): *Financial Services – Perspectives and Challenges*, Boston, p. 181-214.

Slovic, P. (2001). Rational Actors or Rational Fools: Implications of the Affect Heuristic for Behavioral Economics, *Research Paper for the Nobel Symposium on Behavioral and Experimental Economics*.

References

Smit, Edith G. (1999). *"Mass media advertising: information or wallpaper?"*, Amsterdam: Het Spinhuis.

Smit, E. G.; Neijens, P. C. (2000). Segmentation Based on Affinity for Advertising, in: *Journal of Advertising Research*, July/August, 2000, pp. 35-43.

Snyder, M. (1974). Self-Monitoring of Expressive Behavior, in: *Journal of Personality and Social Psychology*, Vol. 30, No. 4, pp. 526-537.

Snyder, M. (1979). Self-Monitoring Processes, in: Berkowitz, L. (ed.): *Advances in Experimental Social Psychology*, Vol. 12, New York, pp. 85-128.

Soldow, G. F. and Principe V. (1981). Response to commercials as a function of program context. *Journal of Advertising Research,* 21(2), 59-65.

Solomon, M.R. (2002). *Consumer Behavior*, 5. ed., Upper Saddle River, New Jersey.

Sperber, Dan and Deirdre Wilson (1995); *Relevance, Communication & Cognition.* Oxford: Blackwell.

Spichal, Slavko (1999). *Public Opinion: developments and controversies in the Twentieth Century.* Oxford: Rowman & Littlefield.

Spremann, K. (2000). *Portfoliomanagement*, München/Wien.

Standing, L. (1973). Learning 10,000 pictures. *Quarterly Journal of Experimental Psychology: Leearning, Memory, and Cognition,* 19, 582-602, cited in Schacter 1996.

Stephan, E. (1999). Die Rolle von Urteilsheuristiken bei Finanzentscheidungen, in: Fischer, L./Kutsch, T./Stephan, E. (Edts.): *Finanzpsychologie*, München/Wien, 101-134.

Stern, Barbera B. (1996). Advertising comedy in electronic drama, The construct, theory and taxonomy. *European Journal of Marketing*, 30.

Stern, Barbera B. and Katherine Gallagher (1991). Advertising Form, Content, and Values: Lyric, Ballad, and Epic, in J. H. Leigh and C. R. Martin (eds.), *Current Issues and Research in Advertising*. Michigan: University of Michigan.

Sternglanz, S. H., & Serbin, L. (1974). „Sex-role stereotyping in children's television programs", *Developmental Psychology*, 10, 710-715.

Stipp, Horst and Nicholas P. Schiavone (1996). Modeling the Impact of Olympic Sponsorship on Corporate Image, *Journal of Advertising Research*, 36, 4, p. 22-28.

Stone, Bob (1988). *Successful Direct Marketing Methods*. NTC Business Books.

Stuart, Helen & Kerr, Gayle (1999). "Marketing Communication and corporate identity: are they really integrated?" *Journal of Marketing Communication* , Vol. 5 (4), pp.169-179.

Studiengruppe Naether (1974). Untersuchungsreihe über Sportwerbung, in: Beratungsgruppe Tischler (ed.), *Sportwerbung – Wirkungen und Werbewert*, 8th edition, p. 92-101.

Sullivan, J.L., Aldrich, J.H., Borgida, E., Rahn, W. (1990). Candidate appraisal and human nature: Man and superman in the 1984 election. *Political Psychology*, 11(3), 459-484.

Svyturys Annual Report (1997, 1998, 1999, 2000, 2001)

Tansey, R. (1999). How Clio advertising helped regenerate the Renault marque. In *Advertising Works 10*. Edited by Nick Kendall. NTC Publications, Henley-on-Thames, UK.

References

Terlutter, R. (2000). *Lebensstilorientiertes Kulturmarketing*, [Lifestyle-oriented Marketing for Cultural Institutions], Gabler, Wiesbaden.

The Media Partnership (1992). *'Televisie-sponsoring onderzoek'* ['Research into TV sponsoring']. Amsterdam: TMP.

The World Beer Report (2000, 2001)

Thompson, Fred (1998). Fordism, Post-Fordism and the flexible system of production. *Unpublished paper* downloaded on http://www.willamette.edu/~fthompso/

Thompson, Fred (1999). "Fordism and Post-Fordism", In Phillip Anthony O' Hara (ed.): *Encyclopedia of Political Economy.* London: Routledge, pp. 404-407.

Thomson, Kevin, Chernatony, Leslie de, Arganbright, Lorrie, Khan, Sajid. (1999). "The Buy-in Benchmark: "How Staff Understanding and Commitment Impact Brand and Business Performance". *Journal of Marketing Management* 15, 819-835.

Timmerman, T. (2001). *Researching Brand Images: The nature and activation of brand representations in memory.* Amsterdam, the Netherlands: SWOCC.

Tobin, J. (1958). Liquidity Preferences as Behavior Towards Risk, in: *Review of Economic Studies*, 25, 2, 65-68.

Triplett, T. (1994). Brand personality must be managed or will assume a life of its own. *Marketing News,* 28, 10.

Troll, Kurt F. (1983a). Wirkung von Bandenwerbung - Bericht über ein Pilotprojekt, *Jahrbuch der Absatz- und Verbraucherforschung*, 29, 201-220.

Tupes, E.C.; Christal, R.C. (1992). Recurrent Personality Factors Based on Trait Ratings, in: *Journal of Personality*, 60, pp. 225-252.

Tuppen, C. J. S. (1974). "Dimensions of Communicator Credibility: An Oblique Solution," *Speech Monographs* 41, 253-60.

Tversky, A. & Kahneman, D. (1974). Judgment under Uncertainity: Heuristics and Biases, *Science*, 185, 1124-1131.

Unger, R. K. (1979). *Female and male.* New York: Harper & Row.

Upshaw, L.B. (1995). *Building Brand Identity: A strategy for success in a hostile marketplace.* New York: John Wiley & Sons.

Utenos alus Annual Report (1997, 1998, 1999, 2000, 2001)

Vakratsas, D. & Ambler, T. (1999). How Advertising Works: What do we really Know?, *Journal of Marketing*, Vol. 63, No. 1, p. 26-43.

Van den Poel, D. and Leunis J. (1999). "Consumer Acceptance of the Internet as a Channel of Distribution." *Journal of Business Research.* (45).

Van Riel, C.B.M. (1994). *Balanceren tussen variëteit en uniformiteit in het corporate communication beleid* [Balancing between variety and uniformity of corporate communication management]. Houten: Bohn Stafleu Van Loghum.

Van Riel, C.B.M. (1995). *Principles of Corporate Communication.* London: Prentice Hall.

Van Riel, C.B.M. & Berens, G. (2001). Balancing Corporate Branding Policies in Multibusiness Companies. In P.J. Kitchen & D.E. Schultz (eds.), *Raising the Corporate Umbrella: Corporate Communications in the Twenty-First Century.* Hampshire: Macmillan.

Venkatesh, Alladi (1999). "Postmodernism perspectives for macromarketing: An inquiry into the global information and sign economy", *Journal of Macromarketing* Vol. 19, No.2, pp. 153-169, 1999.

References

Venkatraman, M.P.; Marlino, D.; Kardes, F.R.; Sklar, K.B. (1990). The Interactive Effects of Message Appeal and Individual Differences on Information Processing and Persuasion, in: *Psychology and Marketing*, 7, pp. 85-96.

von Feilitzen, Cecilia (1997). "Representing Families", Module Ten: Unit 60. MA in Mass Communications. University of Leicester, *Centre for Mass Communication Research*, pp. 473-520.

von Feilitzen, Cecilia & Gunnar Andrén (1984). *Barns och ungdomars ställning i kulturen* [The Cultural Position of Children and Young People]. Invited paper presented at the conference "Lyt til børn [Listen to Children]" November 23-25, 1984, Helsingør, Denmark, arranged by The Nordic Work Group for Children and Culture, The Secretariat for Nordic Cultural Collaboration, Nordic Council of Ministers.

Walliser, Björn (1994). Les déterminants de la mémorisation des sponsors, *Revue Française du Marketing*, 150, 1994/95, 83-95.

Walliser, Björn (1996). Le rôle de l'intensité des émotions éprouvées par le téléspectateur dans la mémorisation des parrains, *Recherche et Applications en Marketing*, 11, 1, 6-19.

Walliser, Björn (1997a). A Comparison of the Effectiveness of Perimeter and Outdoor Advertising. What Sponsorship can Learn from Outdoor Advertising, *Asia-Australia Marketing Journal*, 5, 1, 21-31.

Walliser, Björn (1997b). Über den Zusammenhang zwischen Markenbekanntheit und Wiedererkennung bei der Bandenwerbung, *Marketing - Zeitschrift für Forschung und Praxis*, 19, 1, 43-52.

Walliser, Björn and Phillipe Nanopoulos (2000). Qui a gagné la coupe du monde 1998 ? Déterminants et importance de l'association durable des sponsors à l'événement, in *Proceedings of the 16th congress of the French Marketing Association (AFM),* May, Montréal: Association Française de Marketing, 723-734.

Wansink, B. (1989). The impact of source reputation on inferences about unadvertised attributes. *Advances in Consumer Research, 16,* 399-405.

Wattenberg, M.P. (1987). The hollow realignment: Partisan change in a candidate-centered era. *Public Opinion Quarterly,* 51, 58-74.

Wattenberg, M.P. (1991). *The rise of candidate-centered politics: Presidential elections of the 1980s.* Cambridge, MA: Harvard University Press.

Werben & Verkaufen (2001). Neue Werbe-Holdning für Markenträume. *Werben & Verkaufen,* Vol. 32, p. 25, 2001.

Weaver, Dana T. & Mary B. Oliver (2000). 'Television programs and advertising: measuring the effectiveness of product placement within Seinfeld', *Paper presented at the Mass Communication Division, 50 Annual Conference of the International Communication Association.* Acapulco.

Welch, R. L., Huston-Stein, A., Wright, J. C., & Plehal, R. (1979). "Subtle sex-role cues in children's commercials", *Journal of Communication,* 29, 202-209.

Wells, W., J. Burnett & S. Moriarity, (1992). *"Advertising principles and Practise"*, New Jersey, Prentice-Hall, Englewood Cliffs (2nd ed).

Wells, W.D.; Tigert, D.J. (1971). Activities, Interests and Opinions, in: *Journal of Advertising Research,* 11, 4, pp. 27-35.

Wiggins, J.S. (ed. 1996). *The Five-Factor Model of Personality,* New York.

Wiggins, J.S.; Pincus, A.L. (1992). Personality: Structure and Assessment, in: *Annual Review of Psychology,* 43, pp. 473-504.

Willimas, Raymond (1974). *Television. Technology and Cultural Form.* Glasgow, Collins/Fontana.

References

Wilson, T., Houston, C., Etling, K. and Brecke, N. (1996). A New Look at Anchoring Effects: Basic Anchoring and its Antecedents, *Journal of Experimental Psychology*, 125, 387-402.

Whitehead, J. L..Jr. (1968). "Factors of Source Credibility". *Quarterly Journal of Speech* 54, 59-63.

Wright, J.C.; Mischel, W. (1987). A Conditional Approach to Dispositional Constructs: The Local Predictability of Social Behavior, in: *Journal of Personality and Social Psychology*, 53, pp. 1159-1177.

Wright, Ray (2000). Advertising. Financial Times/ Prentice - Hall, Inc.

Wright, Roger (1988). Measuring awareness of British football sponsorship, *European Research*, 16, 2, 104-108.

Wright-Isak, C., Faber R. J., & and Horner L. R. (1997). Comprehensive measurement of advertising effectiveness: Notes from the marketplace. In   W.D. Wells (ed.) *Measuring advertising effectiveness*. Mahwah, NJ: Lawrence Erlbaum, 3-13.

Wärneryd, K. E. (1999). *"The Psychology of Saving – A Study in Economic Psychology"*, Cheltenham/Northampton 1999.

Yoon, E., Guffey, H.J., & Kijewski, V. (1993). The Effects of Information and Company Reputation on Intentions to Buy a Business Service. *Journal of Business Research, 27*, 215-228.

Young, M. & O'Neill, B. (1992). Mind over Money: The Emotional Aspects of Financial Decision Making, *Journal of Financial Planning*, 5, 1, 32-38.

Zajonc, R.B. (1980). Feeling and thinking: Preferences need not inferences. *American Psychologist*, 35, 151-175.

Zajonc, R.B. (1968). Attitudinal Effects of Mere Exposure, *Journal of Personality and Social Psychology*, Vol. 9, No. 2, Part 2, June, (Monograph Supplement).

Zyman, Sergio (1999). *The end of marketing as we know it.* London: HarperCollins.

Homepages used in chapter 6:
   http://reports.huginonline.com/hugin/753004.pdf,
   http://verslas.banga.lt/lt.php
   http://www.alutis.lt/alutis.php?tema=naujienos&id=current&page=news
   http://www.cms.lt/rinka.htm
   http://www.gubernija.lt
   http://www.hartwall.fi
   http://www.iaa.lt/index.html
   http://www.kalnapilis.lt/1/index.html
   http://www.lukrecija.lt/strategijaf.html
   http://www.ragutis.lt/NEW/
   http://www.rinkodara.lt
   http://www.sic.lt/naujienos/view/20010320prekzenkl_tyrimas.htm
   http://www.svyturys.lt
   http://www.utenosalus.lt
   http://www.drinks-net.com/Beer/beermain.htm
   http://www.mediafacts.com

About the Authors

Lars Pynt Andersen is Ph.D. student at the Center for Marketing Communication, Department of Marketing, Copenhagen Business School, Denmark.

Emilie van den Berge is Research Associate at SWOCC, the Foundation for Scientific Research on Commercial Communication, Amsterdam, The Netherlands. The foundation is affiliated with and located at the University of Amsterdam, and financed by about 90 organizations in the field of advertising and media (research).

Kristina Birch is Master of Science in Business Administration and Management science and Ph.D. Candidate at the Statistics group, Copenhagen Business School, Denmark.

Kim Cramer is Ph.D. candidate and Research Associate at The Amsterdam School of Communications Research *ASCoR*, University of Amsterdam, The Netherlands.

Wojciech Cwalina is Assistant Professor at the Department of Marketing Psychology, Warsaw School Of Social Psychology, Poland.

Sandra Diehl is Habilitand/Assistant Professor at the Institute for Consumer and Behavioral Research, Saarland University, Saarbrücken, Germany.

Andrzej Falkowski is Professor and Director of the Department of Marketing Psychology, Warsaw School Of Social Psychology, Poland.

Cecilia von Feilitzen is Senior Researcher and lecturer at Södertörns högskola (University College). She is also Scientific Co-ordinator for The UNESCO International Clearinghouse on Children, Youth and Media, Nordicom, Göteborg University.

Giep Franzen is Adjunct Professor at the University of Amsterdam, The Netherlands, and member of the board of directors of SWOCC, the Foundation for Scientific Research on Commercial

Communication. The foundation is affiliated with and located at the University of Amsterdam, and financed by about 90 organizations in the field of advertising and media (research).

Kjell Grønhaug is Professor at the Norwegian School of Economics and Business Administration, Bergen, Norway.

Lars Grønholdt is Professor at the Center for Marketing Communication, Department of Marketing, Copenhagen Business School, Denmark.

Flemming Hansen is ekon.dr. and Professor at the Center for Marketing Communication, Department of Marketing, Copenhagen Business School, Denmark.

Lotte Yssing Hansen is Research Assistant at the Center for Marketing Communication, Department of Marketing, Copenhagen Business School, Denmark.

Robert Heath is managing director of The Value Creation Company, a consultancy which advises marketers and advertising agencies on how to make brand communication more effective. He is also completing a doctorate at Bath University School of Management.

Jenny Jordan is Research Assistant at the Department of Marketing at the University of Frankfurt/Main, Germany.

Klaus Peter Kaas is Professor at the Department of Marketing at the University of Frankfurt/Main, Germany.

Gorm Kunøe is Assistant Professor with The Norwegian School of Management, Oslo, Norway.

Roy Langer is Professor of Communication at the Department of Communication, Journalism and Computer Science, Roskilde University, Roskilde, Denmark

About the Authors

Marjolein Moorman is Ph.D. Candidate in the Amsterdam School of Communications Research, ASCoR, and Assistant Professor at the Department of Communication of the University of Amsterdam, the Netherlands.

Rita Mårtenson is Professor at the Department of Marketing, University of Gothenburg, Sweden.

Peter C. Neijens is Director of The Amsterdam School of Communications Research, ASCoR, and Full Professor of commercial communication at the University of Amsterdam, The Netherlands.

Hanne Niss is Associate Professor at the Department of English, Copenhagen Business School, Denmark.

Larry Percy is a consultant in marketing and communications, and also has appointments as visiting Professor at the University of Oxford Said Business School, Copenhagen Business School, Stockholm School of Economics, and the Stockholm University Graduate School of Communication.

Pernille Schnoor is Ph.D. Student at the Center for Marketing Communication at the Department of Marketing, Copenhagen Business School, Denmark.

Laimona Sliburyte is Associate Professor at the Department of Marketing, Faculty of Economics and Management, Kaunas University of Technology, Kaunas, Lithuania.

Edith G. Smit is Senior Associate Professor at the University of Amsterdam, The Netherlands, and Director of SWOCC, the Foundation for Scientific Research on Commercial Communication. The foundation is affiliated with and located at the University of Amsterdam, and financed by about 90 organizations in the field of advertising and media (research).

Ralf Terlutter is Habilitand/Assistant Professor at the Institute for Consumer and Behavioral Research, Saarland University, Saarbrücken, Germany.

Regina Virvilaite is Associate Professor at the Department of Marketing, Faculty of Economics and Management, Kaunas University of Technology, Kaunas, Lithuania.

Björn Walliser is Professor of Marketing at the Research Group in Financial Economy and Management (GREFIGE) at the University of Nancy 2, France.